Caroline Perry Sinnickson. Photograph taken in Germany.

An Enchanted Journey

The letters of the Philadelphian wife

of a

British Officer of the Indian Cavalry

Alan Jones

The Pentland Press
Edinburgh – Cambridge – Durham – USA

First published in 1994 by
The Pentland Press Ltd
1 Hutton Close
South Church
Bishop Auckland
Durham

British Library
Cataloguing-in-Publication Data

A catalogue record for this book
is available from the British Library

ISBN 1-85821-181-6

Typeset by Carnegie Publishing, 18 Maynard St., Preston
Printed and bound by Antony Rowe Ltd., Chippenham

Contents

Author's Preface

At a dinner party in Philadelphia I learned, after five minutes of conversation, that a fellow guest was niece to a lady of Philadelphia who, in 1908, married a British officer of the Indian Army, the 18th (Prince of Wales' Own) Tiwana Lancers. During World War II I served in this same regiment, by then entitled the 19th King George V's Own Lancers. I was asked if I would like to look at a box of papers 'which have been in storage in our cellar for years, unlooked at'. This book is the result.

The box contained the unsorted letters of Caroline Perry Sinnickson, known to all as 'Lina', born 27 August 1870, written to members of her family resident in Philadelphia: her parents, Charles and Emma Sinnickson, at 230 Rittenhouse Square, and her Aunt Fanny Rosengarten and her Uncle Joseph George Rosengarten at 1704 Walnut Street.

It is from one of these letters written to Aunt Fanny from the Hyde Park Hotel, London, in August 1917 that the book's title comes. Life is disrupted by air-raids, coal is in short supply, food is rationed, her husband has just departed to travel alone via Petrograd, through a revolution in progress, to an attachment to the Russian Army of the Caucasus. Lina is lonely and anxious. 'Perhaps,' she wrote, 'it is because I have lived for years as though I pursued an enchanted journey with him.'

In addition, the box contained scrap books, press cuttings, dinner menus, seating plans, photographs, diaries, dance programmes complete with pencils, public announcements, Christmas cards, and even samples of the wall-papers she used when decorating Wildflower Hall, one of the houses they occupied when living in Simla.

Caroline Perry Sinnickson was a letter writer from childhood. She wrote to her parents when they were travelling; to her father when, in her twenties and thirties, she and her elder sister Betty accompanied their mother on long European tours and, after her marriage at the age of thirty-eight, to her family in Philadelphia. Approximately one thousand letters have been preserved. None of the many she received have remained except three from her husband written during one of the many occasions when his official duties separated them. Presumably their life-style inhibited the accumulation and preservation of paper. Memorabilia she wanted to keep: Royal Commands, invitation cards, photographs, press cuttings, were sent to Philadelphia 'to be put in my box'.

She wrote as if she were talking, her sentences and phrases strung together with dashes and liberally sprinkled with exclamation marks and underlinings. Often when she thought she was too near the end of a letter for it to be worth starting another piece of her four-paged, linen note-paper she would write sideways across her own writing, as reproduced at the end-papers of this book. Not infrequently she found that she had more to say than she had first thought, so that the cross-writing continued back through the letter for several pages. Her letters are a running commentary, purely for her family's interest, on the public affairs of her time, international, British, and American. With forthrightness, and sometimes audacity, she evaluates Kings, Presidents and Crown Princes, high officials of the British and Indian Governments, her husband's brother officers. She gives an almost day by day account of personal reactions in India to the outbreak of World War I and perhaps a unique account of the life of an American in London in the last eighteen months of the war, including the parade along Piccadilly of the first contingent of United States forces and the celebration of American Independence Day on 4 July 1918. And regularly and throughout there flows her love and admiration for her husband, Offley Bohun Shore, and evidence of his for her.

The letters have been transcribed largely as written except for the omission, without so indicating, of passages of no general interest, or of repetitions, inevitable since weekly letters were regularly sent to four members of the same family.

Spelling, punctuation and syntax have been left unaltered except when necessary for clarification or in instances which it might be supposed the writer herself would have corrected had she paused to read what she had written.

The differences between British and American spellings need a comment, in particular the case of those words which currently the British end in 'our' and the Americans in 'or', as colour/color, harbour/harbor. It will be found that sometimes the writer used one of these endings and sometimes the other. Her British husband, some of whose letters are included, more frequently used the 'or' form. Another case is the word which currently the British spell 'manoeuvre' and Americans 'maneuver'; this appears in the letters as 'manoevre'.

Recognisable variations in the spelling of place names occur and variations in the transliteration of Indian words are to be expected: Webster's Third International Dictionary has *khidmatgar, khidmutgar, khitmatgar, khitmutgar* for the servant who serves at table.

A glossary of foreign words, biographical notes on all the identifiable persons appearing in the letters, and short lists of viceroys and commanders-in-chief will be found at the end of the book.

Acknowledgements

To Sheila Newman and Patricia Wood who live outside Philadelphia I am indebted for giving me access to a large accumulation of family photographs and to the letters of their aunt, Caroline Perry Sinnickson, the letter-writer of this book. They, and other members of the family, particularly Charles Sinnickson in London and the late Andrew Sinnickson in Richmond, Virginia shared generously their recollections of 'Aunt Lina'. I came to feel that I had known her personally.

In writing Appendix C on the British Mission to the Russian Army of the Caucasus and on the service of Lina's husband, Offley Bohun Shore, with that Mission, I was greatly assisted by conversations with Mrs. Dorothy Burr Thompson of Hightstown, New Jersey, one of the two young daughters who accompanied the Shores to the July 4th American Independence Day celebrations in London in 1918. Mrs. Thompson loaned me the 1918 diary of her sister Pamela, who reports many of Offley Shore's own accounts of his service with that Mission. I am grateful also to Mr. David Smurthwaite of the National War Museum, London, for his assistance in searching for material on this subject.

In 1987 I attended the inaugural meeting of the Offley Family Society at Great Offley, Hertfordshire and have corresponded frequently with its President, Mr. Jack Russell Richards. To the Society's archivist, Mrs. Jane Evans, who descends from Hannah Maria Offley, sister of Offley Shore's great-great-grandmother Urith Offley who married Samuel Shore, I am grateful for her information and advice concerning the Offley family ancestry. To Mr. Kenneth Woollard of London who descends from John Shore, brother of the same Samuel Shore, I am indebted for information which enabled me to write Appendix A clarifying Lina's confusion of the two Shore families.

While researching Offley Shore's boyhood, I was given a comprehensive account of the early days of the school he attended, the Sheffield Collegiate School, later to become the King Edward VII Grammar School, by Mrs. Susan Hulse, Senior Library Assistant at the Sheffield City Library.

To Carolyn and the late Robert Ferguson of Santa Barbara, California, I am indebted for local topographical information about the land which the Shores bought in the hope that one day they would build their retirement home there.

Finally, my most grateful thanks to my wife Emily, for her encouragement, criticism and advice and for assistance in proofing the manuscript.

1993   Alan Jones
                                                           Haverford
                                                         Pennsylvania

House of Lords

Foreword

by the Rt Hon The Lord Weatherill PC DL

I served in the same regiment of the Indian Army, the 19th King George V's Own Lancers, as did Brigadier Offley Bohun Shore, the husband of the letter-writer of this book. He died in 1922 in Scotland.

Through his wife's letters, and the few of his own which have been preserved, the reader learns of his career as a staff officer in charge of Training for India, his appointment as Chief of Staff to Sir Percy Lake in command of the Anglo-Indian force in Mesopotamia against the Turkish attempt to expand eastwards, and his attachment to the Russian Army of the Caucasus.

Lina Shore's letters, written with clock-like regularity back home to her family in Philadelphia begin with her marriage and departure from Philadelphia in 1908 and continue until Offley Shore's death. From Canada, India and England she records and comments upon great events and public figures but also on the details of a soldier's life: the contents of the bags ready packed for instant departure; the social obligations of dancing with stout ladies at vice-regal Lodge; the poignancy of bidding farewell to men on the Simla Parade Ground who may never return from the trenches in France. Later, from Santa Barbara, California, the letters with good humour and courage sketch in the insoluble problems of buying land on a retired officer's pension and of realizing the dream to settle there.

More than half of the letters come from India, where Offley Shore's service totalled seven years. It is well that these letters were selected, edited and commented upon by someone who knows something of that country through study and military service there.

Alan Jones' explanatory material is minimal. With an historian's care he explains but does not embroider on Lina's rather dashing prose and declines to speculate on some rather strange circumstances to which she refers.

These perceptive letters, begun almost a century ago, humanize happenings in a world at peace and later at war.

Bernard Leathquee

Introduction

Caroline's mother, Emma Sophia Rosengarten, born in 1847, was the youngest daughter of George David Rosengarten, who arrived in Philadelphia from the Electorate of Hesse Cassel in 1819 at the age of eighteen, and Elizabeth Bennet who came with her parents from Hamburg in the same year, aged ten. The Rosengarten family had been bankers to the Landgrafs of Hesse Cassel; their business had been ruined by the Napoleonic Wars and the related European disturbances. George David came with letters of introduction from European bankers to the leading merchants of Philadelphia, Baltimore and New York. Within a few years he established a pharmaceutical business which in due course developed into the firm of Powers, Weightman, Rosengarten Co. which in its turn was, in 1927, absorbed into Merck and Co. Inc.

Caroline's father, Charles Perry Sinnickson, born 1844, was descended on his father's side from Scandinavian immigrants who settled in Salem, New Jersey, about 1640 and acquired, developed and retained wide farming interests. At the age of twenty-four he joined the business established by his father in mining and distributing Pennsylvanian anthracite. From this he retired in 1882.

Caroline's other two correspondents, her Aunt Fanny and her Uncle Joe, were the fourth and fifth children of George and Elizabeth Rosengarten, and with them she had a very close family relationship, in which would later be included her husband: Offley Bohun Stovin Fairless Shore.

To Aunt Fanny, described in one newspaper story as the Fairy God-Mother of the Sinnickson daughters, Caroline would write regularly, without reservation, on the most intimate of subjects. Uncle Joe was a lawyer, scholar, author and linguist with a wide acquaintanceship throughout Britain, France and Germany. He was a trustee

1

George David and Elizabeth Bennet Rosengarten,
Lina's maternal grandparents.

of the University of Pennsylvania, and sat on the Boards or was President of several learned societies and civic institutions.

Caroline, known to her family as Lina, was the eldest of five surviving children, being followed by Elizabeth (Betty), Charles, George and Fanny. She was educated at the still flourishing Agnes Irwin School, from which she graduated in 1889. It is believed that her education was continued in Europe, but no details have been found.

The public life of the Sinnicksons and the Rosengartens is well documented by press cuttings preserved in a scrap book by sister Betty.

The first entry, dated 1890, reads:

Mrs. Charles P. Sinnickson, a handsome and wealthy lady, is having a large and magnificent mansion built opposite Rittenhouse Square where she expects to extend a princely hospitality to her many friends upon its early occupation.

followed by:

There was a great crowd at the Sinnicksons—a number of people, I'll venture, impelled chiefly by a latent curiosity to see the inside of the new house. It is a remarkably pretty house and Miss Lina Sinnickson's room, which was open for inspection, is a delight-fully fragile and dainty picture.

In 1895 it is recorded that at a diplomatic reception at the White House, for whom is not apparent, among the 'striking toilettes', taking precedence over 'those present', were the 'Misses Sinnickson of Philadelphia'.

Also in that year 'Mrs. Charles Sinnickson's tea on Tuesday was pleasantly varied with music. Miss Margaret Elliot sang several times . . . the daughter of the hostess, Miss Lina Sinnickson, also sang.'

Other cuttings record the annual summer migrations from Phila-delphia to Newport, Rhode Island, or Narragansett Pier.

A good many of the Rosengarten family of Philadelphia have been at Newport this summer, but the best known there and the most distinguished socially, for the simple reason that he has not missed a season in many years showing himself on horseback of a morning on Bellevue Avenue, is Gen. J. G. Rosengarten. General

Caroline Perry Sinnickson – 'Lina''
1870–1957.

Rosengarten gave a dinner party there the other night at which
the Misses Sinnickson, of Philadelphia, were the bright particular
stars. In the old days the Rosengartens were Israelites—which I
suppose they will be to the end of the chapter—but the Protestant
Episcopal Church now claims them as its own.

or:

Mr. and Mrs. Charles P. Sinnickson and the Misses Sinnickson expect to pass the coming summer in New England, instead of making their usual trip abroad for the season.

or:

Whatever may be said of the early part of the season at Newport, it is the testimony of all who are returning thence . . . that more is going on there every day than man or womankind can do justice to in twenty-four hours . . . Mr. and Mrs. Charles Sinnickson and Miss Sinnickson have been visiting Mrs. Sinnickson's relatives, the J. G. Rosengartens, at the fashionable resort, and have, of course been right in the midst of the social fray. The Sinnicksons who reside when in Philadelphia on West Rittenhouse Square, are heard very little of in Society during the winter, but each summer the Misses Sinnickson are pronounced belles at Newport. The family is, I believe, a very wealthy one, Mrs. Sinnickson having a good sized fortune in her own right. By the way, Miss Sinnickson who is an artist of a greater ability than the clever amateur type, has spent much of the summer sketching in the Berkshire hills.

Undated comes a reference to proper attire for bathing:

Bathing is, as of yore, the chief attraction at the Pier. Everybody repairs to the beach at noon, and a majority of the visitors take religiously their daily dip. Sherry's large bathing pavilion, which was the most fashionable meeting-place last summer, has been rather deserted this year by the smarter element for the more primitive bathing-houses of the older hotels. The tendency in the last two or three summers at Narragansett, since it gained an unenviable notoriety through certain sensational bathing costumes, has been to sober apparel on the part of bathers. The smart women of Narragansett now goes to her ocean bath most quietly clad in a suit of dark blue serge, plain black stockings and an oil cap often surmounted by a small picture hat for the beach. The fashion now is to comport oneself very demurely and abstain from skylarking in the water. The prettiest and most observed of the bathers at the Pier this summer are . . . Miss Sinnickson of Philadelphia, and . . .

In 1900 and 1901 there are a number of cuttings relating to foreign travel, as:

> The proposed trip to Europe of Mrs. Charles P. Sinnickson and the Misses Sinnickson threatens to rob the city of several of the fairest of its hostesses, and many are the hopes that the contemplated residence in Germany for three years may not materialize.

On 5 December 1907 appeared the following announcement:

Mr. and Mrs. Charles P. Sinnickson
announce the marriage of their daughter
Caroline,
to
Lt. Colonel Offley Bohun S. F. Shore,
18th (P.W.O.) Tiwana Lancers, Indian Army,
on Wednesday, January 29th
1908,
St. James Church,
Philadelphia

Three of Offley Bohun Stovin Fairless Shore's names indicate his ancestry. The first two descend from the marriage in 1732 of Joseph Offley of Norton Hall, in the county of Derbyshire, near Sheffield, to Mary Bohun of Beccles in the county of Suffolk. Their daughter, Urith, in 1759 married Samuel Shore of Meersbrook, also near Sheffield.

Norton Hall came into the possession of the Offley family in 1699 and it is clear from Lina's letters that she for long thought it was still in the possession of the descendants of Urith Offley and Samuel Shore when her husband was born. In fact it had been put up for sale nineteen years earlier, in 1844, to meet the losses suffered by his grandfather, Offley Shore, as a result of the bankruptcy, before the development of the concept of Limited Liability, of the family bank, the Old Sheffield Bank.

Offley's father, Offley Bohun Shore, aged five when the family left Norton Hall, married in 1861 Anna Maria Leishman of Edinburgh. Offley was born in 1863 in the parish of St. Martin's, Stamford, Lincolnshire. His birth certificate gives his father's occupation as 'M.D.'. Two sisters, Florence and Urith, were born in 1865 and 1867.

Captain Offley Bohun Stovin Fairless Shore,
18th (Prince of Wales' Own) Tiwana Lancers.

Little is known of Offley's early life. The only source of information is a vast scrapbook and diary begun by his father in 1877, taken over by Offley in 1900 and ending with the latter's marriage. It records almost exclusively Offley's military career. Information concerning other members of the family comes from the steady

Joseph Offley (1702–50) and his wife Mary (1702–40) née Bohun;
their brother-in-law Edmund Bohun and their three children, Hannah Maria,
Urith and Edmund. Urith married Samuel Shore (1738–1828).
Joseph and Mary Offley were Offley Shore's great-great-great grandparents, and
Urith his great-great-grandmother.

stream of affectionate letters from son to father with occasional ones
from the daughters. It is from this source that come the quotations
which follow.

After schooling at the Sheffield Collegiate School, Offley won
admission to the Royal Military Academy, Sandhurst, from which
he passed out in 1882. For his period of service with a British regiment, an attachment required of all officers joining the Indian Army,
he was posted to the Prince of Wales' Own (West Yorkshire) Regiment. Later in the year this Regiment was sent to India.

It is clear that some time prior to mid 1882 his father had suffered
some financial disaster. It is also clear that the family was dispersed.
A letter of May 1882 records that his mother and grandmother were
in London and had moved from the Kensington Road to the Richmond Road, 'the former rooms having been let over their heads'.

Norton Hall, near Sheffield.
The birthplace of Offley's father, Offley Bohun Shore.

In September of the same year the three children addressed letters to their father in Iceland.

Offley wrote, after separate visits to Urith and Florence:

> . . . Urith seemed to think that if obliged to 'go out' she would take to music more readily than anything else . . . Florence quite likes the Children's Hospital idea and is going to write Florence Nightingale . . . I fear it's a poor concern she is going for, as regards pay, and will tax her growing strength . . . I said nothing at all about the possibility of the success of this Borax rendering them free of

Offley Bohun Shore, Offley's father.
Iceland, 1882.

the necessary to work for themselves . . . What a difference in quarters you and I are experiencing, but by this time let us hope your hut is erected and the stores away under cover from the beastly snow: I hate cold and shudder at the thought of your experiences . . . I forward the best papers (illustrated) I could find of the last few weeks, but am quite at a loss for books for you.

Florence wrote:

I only knew yesterday that you had gone back to Iceland . . . I hope that you will be well rewarded for your long journey and almost banishment from home. I trust that you will be able to find a good estate which may bring you good return.

Urith wrote:

I hope you are getting on successfully at Iceland . . . Aunt and Uncle are still very kind.

No further references have been found to Iceland or to Borax.

In July 1883 Offley wrote:

. . . am so grieved to hear you are in such a devil of a fix . . . would like to know what you intend doing in case the worst should come to the worst.

and in January 1886:

I am so sorry to hear of your financial worries dear Father and sincerely trust you will not be obliged to leave your club [the Reform—Ed.]: which will indeed be a blow to you . . . I hear Florrie has been offered a place at £40 a year: is it true?

and in June of the same year:

So awfully distressed to hear of your financial hole: it is most annoying and distressing. Especially to me, who can't assist you and can't even float my beastly self yet.

and, nine years later, in 1895:

Have just made arrangements to practically pay off everything in India and in a month's time may reasonably hope to begin paying off some debts at home. You may be sure the first time I can, I shall send a fiver to [your bank] for you.

The only reference found to the cause of the father's financial situation is in a letter Offley wrote to Lina's Uncle Joe in 1910 (20 March) where Offley asked him if he could obtain any information concerning a gold mining project in which he had been invited to invest. 'Not that I have any spare capital to waste,' he wrote, 'and my father's experience as a coal owner being prominently before one's eyes I have a very definite horror of speculation pure and simple.'

In 1885 Offley was gazetted to the regiment of his choice, the 18th Bengal Cavalry, in 1906 to be re-titled the 18th (Prince of Wales' Own) Tiwana Lancers when George, Prince of Wales, was appointed Colonel-in-Chief. He already had some fluency in French and German and during the next seven years he acquired varying degrees of fluency in Hindi, Punjabi, Persian and Russian, spending nine months in Russia in 1888. In the following

Offley Bohun Stovin Fairless Shore.
Above: 18th Bengal Lancers, c.1890.
Below: 18th Bengal Lancers, Russia, 1888.

year he took third place on the Staff College entrance list and in 1892, third place on the pass list with special commendation in Russian, French and Persian.

He had early shown considerable facility with the sketch book and by 1881 his sketches of military subjects were appearing in the *Illustrated London News* and the *Sporting and Dramatic*. His military training had included topographical sketching, in those days an important military function, and two surviving sketch books illustrate the campaigns of the Malakand Field Force and the Tirah Expeditionary Force in 1897. (See page 113. Also reproduced are examples of his illustrations to Lina's letters.)

In September 1898 he arrived in England on leave. Medical examinations revealed indications of tuberculosis and in June 1899 he went for treatment at Davos in Switzerland. By the end of the year his doctors reported him as so much better that 'he might risk South Africa if it is absolutely necessary'. He disembarked in Cape Town and remained in South Africa until the end of the Boer War in June 1902. In 1901 he was awarded the D.S.O. His letters make frequent references to coughs and fevers.

After three months leave in England, during which he received further medical treatment, he returned to India, but in 1906 a 'bronchial affecting of the trachea' was diagnosed and he was sent to a sanatorium at Nordrach-on-Dee in Scotland. Here doctors declared him unfit for service in India for at least three years, but recommended South Africa or Canada. Lord Kitchener offered him a two-year secondment to an Imperial Military Mission, advising the Canadian Government on the organisation and strengthening of its army. He sailed for New York on 15 December 1906.

The cable reporting his safe arrival was sent to Miss Rachel J. Jardine, of Dryfeholm, Lockerbie, Dumfries-shire. Rachel Jardine, sometimes referred to as 'R.J.J.', appears frequently throughout these letters as a family friend. She wrote to Urith in 1901 with news concerning Offley in South Africa. He visited her when home in 1902. He cabled her of his arrival on sick leave in 1906 and visited her during that period. She will be found involved frequently with the important occasions in the lives of Offley and Lina.

It is known that Offley was carrying letters of introduction to the Sinnickson family from mutual friends in England and his diary records that on Christmas Day he was in Philadelphia at the Bellevue

Stratford Hotel. There is no reference in his diary to his having called on the family on his first arrival in the States, but it can be deduced from Lina's letters later that he did so. For Lina it was a memorable occasion. Writing to Aunt Fanny a letter of condolence on the death of Uncle Joe in 1921 she recalled that he had once bought a dress for her: 'such a fateful dress: it was the one I was wearing when I first met Offley.' On 31 December he arrived in Ottawa.

He was next in Philadelphia in May of 1907 and his diary records:

'Shopping with Lina S. who tried on gowns.'
'Mr. and Mrs. S., Lina S. and self dining.'
'Park with L.S. in afternoon' where he was astonished to see 'two women riding astride'.
'Taken to Philadelphia Club/Zoological Gardens by Mr. Charles Sinnickson.'
'Academy of Fine Arts with L.S.'
'Gave L.S. new cap badge, 2 Prince of Wales Feathers, and 1 new button.'

Some of these items still embellish a silver cigarette box in the possession of Lina's family in Philadelphia.

On 17 May he proposed to her, Lina recorded in a letter written a year later, 'but I did not give him a final answer until I saw him again in December.'

Two days after his return to Ottawa appears the diary entry: 'Long letter from L.S. explaining position.' Thereafter the diary frequently, and at some periods daily, records, 'Letter from L.S.' or alternatively, 'No letter from L.S.' or, 'Wrote all evening to L.S.' In August there is the following sequence:

15 August   'Sent slip [sic] instead of letter to L.S.'

16 August   'Wire from L.S. "Did you expect to find me sitting here by wire?", mysterious.'

17 August   'Wrote L.S. long letter remarking upon the extraordinary telegram.'

19 August   '3 charming letters from L.S. dated 15/16/17.'

These entries are interspersed with records of his medication programme, with notes on his work with the Canadian militia, on preparing proposals for a Colonial Conference in April, on preparations for war—the British Dreadnought programme and the American warship programme, the establishment of naval bases, the British at Rosyth and the American at Pearl Harbour, and the writing of mobilisation tables.

On 2 December he arrived back in Philadelphia where he was met by Lina at the station, 'such a surprise', booked a room at the Bellevue Stratford Hotel, walked over to 230 Rittenhouse Square, where several people came to tea and where, during the next few hours, Betty, Fanny, 'Mother' and 'Mr. S.' all came in and he 'arranged with Lina to see Father tomorrow'. The diary entry for the following day reads: 'Saw Mr. Chas. Sinnickson about 4 p.m. and had long talk—most civil: asked for time to consider: I mentioned 29 January as most suitable date—talked to Mrs. Sinnickson.' Thereafter he shopped with Lina, lunched and dined with various members of the family, went to the opera, to the oculist and dentist. On 13 December appears the entry: 'the only annoying thing is Papashka's continued delay in saying "yes".' However the very next day 'Mr. Sinnickson gives his consent and Linoshka spends the day telling everyone she can think of! Great relief to her.' Three days later the diary records: 'L.S. only gets £300 p.a. just now and a house worth £5000 and on January 6 Mr. S. is going to settle £800 p.a. upon her until she comes into her fortune.' Never during the course of the letters do the 'house' or the 'fortune' materialise.

Though Mr. Sinnickson took eleven days to say 'yes', the Press believed that:

> Miss Sinnickson's engagement did not come as a great surprise to her friends, who have been expecting the announcement ever since the handsome English officer came to this city. It was love at first sight between the big, handsome soldier and the petite and pretty Philadelphian.

Indeed it later became clear that neither to Mr. Sinnickson did the engagement come as a great surprise. In her early letters to him from India, Lina identified more than one of Offley's superior officers as being among those to whom, despite his daughter's age of thirty-seven and the potential bridegroom's of forty-five, he had written for testimonials as to Offley's suitability.

It is also clear that Lina and Offley were taking Mr. Sinnickson's approval for granted. During the period of waiting they inspected the church where they hoped to be married. Offley bought the ring which, he noted later, was valued by two people at very much its purchase price, and wrote to his mother, his father and his Aunt Caroline Stovin, to Rachel Jardine to order the wedding cake to be made and sent over by R. Bollard and Sons of Chester, 'noted builders of wedding cakes' and to Col. James, British Military Attaché at Washington, who would be his best man.

One newspaper commented on the engagement announcement with the following:

It must delight Mrs. Charles Sinnickson's soul that she is actually marrying off one of her trio of daughters and that it is the eldest who is making the first matrimonial break on the female side of the family. Two more beautiful girls than Caroline and Betty Sinnickson I do not remember in Philadelphia. They were graceful as nymphs and had eyes like sloes, and the rich dark coloring that reflected their semitic ancestry. I shall never forget how they burst upon the Bryn Mawr Horse Show, one radiant September day ten or more years ago, fresh from a summer in England, resplendent in foreign finery and an accent that out-Britished the British. Since then time has robbed them of their slender figures, but not their fascinating manner nor their sparkling conversation, and as they have plenty of money which Grandpa Rosengarten made selling quinine to the United States Army during the Civil War, such slight drawbacks as increasing avoirdupois does not in the least detract from their popularity.

Another columnist commented:

Grandpa Rosengarten would turn over in his grave with a sigh of joy to think that the first of his trio of lovely grand-daughters has won so gallant a gentleman.

For the wedding the church 'was taxed to the utmost to accommodate the throngs of "society folk".'

The bride's gown was of white satin with rare old French lace, a gift from her mother, and she wore diamond ornaments given by her father. The bridegroom and best man were in uniform, giving, said one reporter, a 'touch of oriental splendour that made the familiar ceremony of the church seem more like a foreign function

than an American marriage rite.' The head-dresses of the brides-
maids, Lina's two sisters, took the form of Prince of Wales feathers.

The ceremony was followed by a reception at the bride's home
where, according to one reporter, the bride's mother had been subjected to 'terrible mental strain': the wedding cake was late! The
ship bringing this across the Atlantic, packed in three separate boxes,
had been storm bound in the Atlantic for three days. Customs officers
were specially stationed on the wharf to clear the cake as soon as
the ship docked, but only two of the three boxes could be found.
These were quickly cleared, on payment of a 20% *ad valorem* duty,
and more men were sent into the hold to find the third. This was
found just in time for the whole cake to be properly assembled.
'Many a hopeful maiden,' concluded this reporter, 'slept last night
with a piece of it under her pillow.'

On the day after the wedding, Offley and Lina left the Bellevue
Stratford Hotel to embark on the *Amerika* for England.

The years ahead would test Lina's adaptability and her courage.
Although she would greatly enjoy the delights and pageantry of
living among the powerful and influential, particularly in Imperial
India, it was really her marriage which would bring her the deepest
satisfaction and happiness. Although there would be serious problems—lean finances, ill health and long separations—their marriage
was to be one of love, firmly rooted in mutual respect and admiration.
During the sixth year of her marriage, on hearing of a broken marriage in Philadelphia, she wrote:

> How blessed one really is in a happy marriage, it is indeed a
> Heaven on Earth. My own for instance. How wonderful it is. I
> often wonder if I am sufficiently appreciative of all Offley does
> for me—all he is and means. He wrote a little note with my
> Christmas presents and put 'For the dearest creature in the whole
> world'. And now after six years close together, closer perhaps
> because we are so alone here in India, there are no illusions shat-
> tered, and an affection constantly increasing and a confidence
> and trust made stronger every day we live.

THE LETTERS

Prior to Marriage

Lina's letters start in 1878, when she was eight years old, with two to her parents then travelling in Europe.

A dozen cover the next twenty years written to her father in Philadelphia, whenever her mother took her and her brothers and sisters to resorts such as Newport, Rhode Island, or Bar Harbor, Maine, for the summer; or travelling to Niagara Falls, the Canadian Rockies, Alaska or Yellowstone Park.

Then in 1897 Mrs. Sinnickson and her daughters with Uncle Joe and Aunt Fanny went to Europe for six months, to include the celebration of Queen Victoria's Diamond Jubilee on 22 June. Lina recorded the tour in letters to her father. The boys Charles and George to whom she refers were her brothers.

May 5, 1897   **Leamington, Warwickshire**

My dearest Father,

Another letter came from you this morning and we were delighted to get it. God bless you and help you and grant that everything may go smoothly with you in the future. I feel very deeply appreciative of the step you have taken, very especially as you have told me how you disliked such a thing as the present treatment. However it is sure to do one good from all I have heard and it will always be a comfort to you to know you have done your utmost under the circumstances to please Mother. I am so much better here than I was at Torquay and my cough has almost entirely disappeared. Warwickshire is as lovely, if not lovelier than ever and if I do not, cannot, live here I hope at least I may die here in this happy pretty countryside. This is putting it rather strongly, isn't it?

My friend Selwyn is away at the Earl of Dudley's on a visit, he
is the Colonel of his Yeomanry, but he sent us some tickets for a
concert at Warwick which was very good and where there were a
lot of smart people and he is good to us in every way possible—but
I suppose I shall scarcely see him until we get to London.

Today we drive to Stratford and each day so it is, one place or
another to drive to or picnic for luncheon.

Much to my surprise I got a letter from Mr. Savage saying Mother
had written and asked him to come and see her. Needless to say I
am exceedingly angry about it as I think I have been more honest
and considerate towards Mother in this case than most girls of my
age would even have thought it necessary, much less have been so.
I think a little more confidence and a little less meddling might,
under the circumstances, have been placed in me.

Do write soon again dear Father and with much love and a good
hug——

June 22, 1897   **London, Jubilee Day**

My dearest Father,

It is almost impossible for me to begin to tell you what a wonderful
and splendid sight the procession was today or how one is touched
by the devotion and loyalty of the English people to their Queen
who however deserves it all for she is no less than a great and noble
woman. It is something to remember all one's life and describe for
years to those who were not so fortunate as myself as to see this
great pageant. In the first place we have had Queen's weather, a
more glorious day could not have been wished for. The order and
quietness with which all passed off was wonderful, while for the
actual procession itself I have no words!!!

Aunt Fanny has posted a program of the procession to you and
you will no doubt see good accounts of it in all the American papers.
The genial Prince [of Wales] looked his best in his uniform and my
friend the Marahja of Ketri, Prince of Bahadur [*sic*] etc., etc., was
by all odds the most bejeweled and exquisite creature in the whole

thing, though to my mind nothing can surpass the Princess of Wales in her own simple loveliness.

Yesterday I went to a large fashionable Bazaar at the botanical gardens where the Princess Louise had a stall, the Duchess of Devonshire and Lady Cadogan and any number of celebrated actresses including Sarah Bernhardt and hosts more. Alice tells me Charlie thinks something of coming to England. I do hope he will let me know what he is doing and how the dear boy's cold is. I am feeling proud to hear of Georgie's honors in passing his examinations well. Thank you very much for saying you will send my allowance. I will look out for it. Write soon.

August 27, 1897

Hotel Riechelmann
Bad-Homburg

My dearest Father,

We are amusing ourselves in a very mixed company at Homburg but the life is so simple and easy going I rather like it—tho' give me little England or anywhere in Great Britain or Ireland first.

Yesterday we went to the old ruined castle of Königstein on a picnic Col. FitzGeorge[1] gave—and we were caught in several showers of rain—and obliged to give up lunching in the castle grounds and take it on the terrace of an hotel nearby. We drove out in two big char-a-bancs, the Duke of Cambridge[2] coming, in spite of the threatening clouds, in a landau with Lord and Lady Cork, and there must have been 50 of us altogether. We none of us could get up from the table until his R.H. got up and we had to sit a most jolly long time. Betty and I came home with the Col. and on our way took in Kronberg which is his cousin the Empress' lovely place—and dined last night with Sir Henry Havelock. Today has been rainy too so with the exception of lunching with Baroness Haugwitz I've spent the whole day at the Camerons.

What awful rubbish these customs are. I shall not take anything but what I already have back to America. From what I hear the country is in rather poor hands even tho' American values are going up—that could scarcely have been affected by the new government in so short a time.

The soldiers are already beginning to come on here for the maneuvers, some regiments arriving today. The Review will surely be a wonderful sight. We go to Geneva on the 5th and will then be with Mother the rest of the time. Fanny spent yesterday at Frankfurt 'blowing off' the 3 pounds you sent her a short time ago.

Good-night, write as often as you can and with much love to you and the boys.

In 1900 Mrs. Sinnickson again took her three daughters to Europe, this time to be away for fifteen months. They landed in June at Liverpool, which Lina thought was a quite splendid city particularly for its illuminations, which reminded her of Coney Island. Several weeks were spent at the Walsingham House Hotel in Piccadilly meeting a wide circle of friends, some of them Philadelphians with British husbands, visiting the Ladies' London Kennel Club Show, Hurlingham and Ranelagh and arranging for Fanny, the youngest sister, to attend the school in Eastbourne which had been chosen for her. Mrs. Sinnickson left her daughters at this time to go alone to Paris.

In the letters which Lina wrote to her father during the course of this tour there are frequent references to the state of her mother's health and to a succession of nurse-companions, each at first considered to be an improvement on her predecessor, but each, sooner or later, having to be replaced. The most concise description of Mrs. Sinnickson's condition is to be found in Col. Offley Shore's diary where, seven years later, just before his marriage to Lina, he wrote:

Lina Sinnickson evidently much worried about her mother who has been ailing with neurasthenia for 12 years—gout and 4 operations to her eyes—worst time daily—daylight to midday—when most despondent—more lively in aft. and evening.

July 29, 1900

My dearest Father,

Thank you so much for your nice letters and also for tending to the bothersome small bills I seem to have had and which I assure you I did try to pay up entirely before leaving America. Are you surprised to see we are back in Homburg? I confess I am a little at being here, but during the bad heat at Paris both B. and I did feel exhausted and Mother was determined that we should come here, especially as the reports from Switzerland were of great heat. Madame Torrigiani has left us, but I think the change is all for the best as she did not get on at all with Mother, and she seemed quite impatient and in none too good health herself. The new woman is much better in every way I should think. [She was not. Mde. Torrigiani returned. Letter of 28 Feb., 1901—Ed.] Mother seems wonderfully well, that is she can 'go' from morning to night and talk without ceasing as well, but I confess it is a great strain on us and she is often put out with us because we like to take things differently and do less talking. There was also a great difference of opinions with regard to the schools for Fanny. Mother seemed to prefer one near Paris, while both B. and I felt convinced from what we saw and heard that England and English schools were decidedly better for young American girls. Mother asked us for our opinions and was exceedingly displeased that we did not agree with her. I know I am rather boring you with all this but as Mother tells me she wrote to you that we behaved so badly—I think it only fair that you should know our side of the question.

Dr. Hoeber thinks I should do much better by not taking any waters or cure whatever here but I may take ten mud baths (and I always like them so much) and B. is given quite a strict diet and waters, etc., so we shall stop here until August 15th when on our way back to England we shall go to Holland and Denmark and see the Dutch pictures, while Mother and Fanny leave on Monday for Oberammergau, going afterwards to the Austrian Tyrol before they go to Contreville.

Before we left Paris I saw a good deal more of the Exposition and what I did see, quite thoroughly. I don't think it at all comes up to Chicago, in fact young America is a most wonderful country, and England the most blessedly peaceful and beautiful place, none of the charms of the Continent that I have seen are equal to it to live in, but then perhaps I don't know.

Homburg w.d. Höhe
August 25, 1900   **Germany**

Dearest Father,

This will be my last letter from Homburg as we leave now early on Monday morning for Dresden, and after two or three days there on to Berlin where we look forward to seeing Emma again and have visions of splendid German officers always running about us, for she has invited us especially for a great parade of 36,000 picked soldiers and officers, which comes off on the second of September. It scarcely seems possible we are so nearly at the summer's end, but then we came away so late this year.

Monday we dined at Ritters with some friends who had the very next table to the Prince of Wales. We knew all but one gentleman dining with him and three of the four ladies. B. and I gave the required 'duck' or curtsy to the royalties, which B. describes as 'a sudden pain in one's stomach appearance', and on the way out they wished us good-night. H.R.H. looks very fat, and talks extremely thickly, but he is the most simple unaffected person in the world.

September 7, 1900   **Berlin**

Dearest Father,

Emma and Carl [von Schirach] have done more than anyone could wish for or dream for us. They both seem perfectly delighted to see us and we talk over old times and are very happy together. Carl's regiment is the smartest in Berlin and that and his personality (which is greatly improved) and his name give him a splendid position. Then Mrs. Lay, now the Countess Götzen, has been giving us dinner parties and taking us to drive in the afternoon and making us come to lunch or dinner whenever we are not otherwise engaged. Her husband is delightful and Helen King is here at the Austrian Embassy. She also has a very agreeable husband and we have met simply hundreds of lovely Americans with foreign husbands, but of all, Helen is the one who has struck us as too full of it, but then the Germans in their own country and in their own homes are so nice, so unaffected, and the men such men of the world, well-mannered. I can't say quite the same for the German ladies, unless they have travelled. I find them dull, heavy and bad, awfully bad housekeepers. Altogether one's ideas are totally upset by coming here and going into their homes as we do.

Countess Götzen took us to Charlottenburg and Tuesday we went to Potsdam. Such lovely country! Out of England I don't know of anything so beautiful. The palaces were very interesting, especially Sans Souci, and yesterday morning Carl came for us in full uniform to take us to the Emperor's palace here. We went into many rooms that are never shown to the general public and enjoyed it all immensely, and not a little the constant saluting and deference paid by the servants, and other officers and guards we met with, to Carl. Afterwards we went to the Hohenzollern Museum and Mon Bijou and didn't get home until three o'clock to lunch when Emma met us. Berlin is a splendid city and we both love it. Betty says she would like to live here so we tease her very much because all the officers like her immensely and find her so jolly. The parade here was beautiful but not nearly so fine as at Homburg three years ago, nor can I admire so sincerely the theatrical glitter of the German soldiers after the substantial beauty and pomp of the English, but the Germans ride well and are tall and wonderfully well-built. One sees quite a superior lot in Berlin and in the greatest quantities. All oldish (that is about 50). Princess Thurn and Taxis has taken the greatest fancy to me and she runs in every now and then to see me; as B. puts it 'we actually have to throw her out'. One acquaintance we have made had hunted in Warwickshire and knows some of our friends there. His father always went with the Empress Elizabeth to Ireland and England when she went on her hunting journeys. I don't know whether you would like it here or not, but surely you would if you stayed long enough. German society is a mixture of the sublime and the ridiculous; at a smart luncheon party one must wear gloves.

From Homburg a short visit was made to Copenhagen referred to by Lina as 'the land of our ancestors', though while there it was explained to her that the Sinnickson name is 'really Swedish and only Danish as far as the fact goes that northern Denmark was once part of the Kingdom of Sweden'.

By the end of September they were back in England spending some weeks in Eastbourne to be near Fanny's school where they found her perfectly happy and contented, playing hockey and concentrating 'on her music and French instead of on Society'.

The references to her mother's health continue:

I want you to know, Father, that Mother is fussing away again as she has done for the last few years and B. and I have <u>no</u> intention of letting her come home to go again from Dr. to Dr. and into a rest cure or to upset <u>the whole household</u> until we've tried what it will do for her here; but we have to give up all thought of ourselves in big ways and little ways and <u>all</u> ways to do for her and I really think, and so does Betty, that she can only help herself, and we mean to make her do so with Lewis's aid only and no more monkey-business.

During these weeks they were planning the continuation of their European tour and by 7 December they were in Paris.

December 7, 1900   **Hôtel Vendôme, Paris**

My darling Father,

Your letter of the 26th to Mother distressed us all very much, but by now we are glad to know poor Uncle Tom's horrible sufferings are at an end. I fancy many times since this you have wished us at home, but with Mother so very depressed it would indeed only make matters worse for in great grief one could not stand more than one thing at a time. We spent yesterday morning in the Louvre Gallery and the pictures are so wonderful, and the beautiful sculptures. Fanny's pet Venus de Milo, such a perfect thing! I am so glad if you enjoy my letters. I try to keep writing all I can and let you be quite up in everything and in touch with us. I am afraid when I go home you will not find me half as nice as my letters for I haven't changed a bit. I am quite the same provoking Lina.

Thank you so much for my cards which came this morning. I always have my home address wherever I am, but I fancy, if again in London in Spring that 'Hyde Park Corner, Prince's Gate' will look awfully neat!

During this period Lina reported that her French was greatly improved both in conversation 'as well as other kinds'. 'I do the housekeeping here in Paris, order the meals and make all arrangements for sweeping days, etc.' Betty had taken a side trip to Berlin where Prince George of Prussia had lent her the use of his opera box.

By mid-January they were in Cairo staying at the Savoy Hotel.

January 22, 1901   **The Savoy Hotel, Cairo**

Dearest Father,

I might easily become fascinated by the life an explorer leads who takes great tramps into the desert and finds wonders which defy time and tempests of the past years. I like knowing the rest of the people who are on this earth, their ways and customs, and I find the Arab and Egyptian a capital fellow. Our dragoman has said he would take us to a special service at a mosque if we choose to wear the Arab dress. We could easily do it, I fancy. Betty would be very good without a doubt, but we've not yet decided. Women, you see, are not allowed in the mosques. My only dread would be at having to wash my feet before going through the form of sitting and doing a sort of gymnastics in the prayers. It is, I am sure, one of the very things you would best like to do. Mother was so much better the day we went to the Pyramids but the last two she has been very dull again and it is very difficult to entertain her constantly. I am struggling to get her to go up the Nile as we can go nicely by train much of the way and she is sure to be interested by all she sees.

We are invited to a 'bal poudré' and if the Queen does not die at once there will be the Khedival Ball at the Palace as usual, which I am told is a splendid sight, with all the foreign costumes, the Eastern dress and the brilliant uniforms, but like our Drawing Room it will be 'all up' if the dear old Queen dies now. I don't know whether I have written you that I received word when at Nice that our ambassador would present B. and myself at the early Drawing Room himself, so you can imagine we should be disappointed if now we are prevented by this sad circumstance and yet I should be proud to come back to see Albert Edward's coronation.

Before closing I want to ask if my bonds failed to pay this year the $8.00 I usually get in December?

Queen Victoria died the day Lina wrote this.

January 31, 1901   **The Savoy Hotel, Cairo**

Dear Father,

In a letter B. had from Charlie he mentioned something about the cane work being left off <u>our</u> phaeton. As the estimate I saw called for the <u>replacing</u> of the cane work and there was no such hurry in having the carriage finished before letters from us answering your questions in the matter (and which were promptly sent off after each word or question from you), if the phaeton is finished without the cane work which I like and admire and Betty too, <u>we shall not pay the man one penny</u> and he can give me the price I paid for my phaeton and which was its value when it went to his shop, and I will go to some <u>first class</u> carriage maker and have a phaeton as I wish. I quite know what I want and have a taste of my own in matters which are quite our own, Betty's and mine, and Petzel can either do up our phaeton as desired or <u>pay the damages</u>.

I hope this is quite clear and that the cane work will be on the carriage the first time we see it.

Someone, presumably Father, annotated this letter 'a sassy letter'.

From Cairo they travelled up the Nile by train 'far and away better satisfied than our fellow travelers who have come by Cook's steamers, overcrowded and stuffy'. 'After a rumpus with the proprietor and a little strong language and shaking his telegram at him' they were shown to their accommodations in the Luxor Hotel from which Lina wrote:

February 1st, 1901

Dearest Father,

We spent some two hours this morning at the Temples of Luxor, not five minutes from this house, on the brink of the Nile. They are very wonderful, very, very indeed, grand in their mighty size and dignified in their desolation. But the Copt and the Roman seem to have done for poor old Egypt what the French did for Germany or Cromwell for England.

We drive this afternoon to Karnak and we go on donkeys to spend tomorrow at Thebes. We shall see the whole full moon and have a day of the river life and return on Wednesday to Cairo where we left our luggage and Marguerite [their maid] for this week. But travelling in this country is abominable so we turn our steps with real pleasure and eagerness to Europe once more. We are fortunate to have been able to procure for our whole time here the best dragoman Luxor affords.

I hope by now you will have got my decided letter about the phaeton and the man will put on new cane if the old is not possible to use.

Hotel Savoy

February 16, 1901
Cairo

Dear Father,

All the ceremonies and sights Cairo affords I feel sure we've seen, and this morning we were up early and off to see the Holy Carpet started to Mecca. It is a great day and a great time with the Mohammedans and the Khedive[3] came with his ministers and his court and his whole Army now at Cairo to an open place just below and outside the splendid wall of the Citadel in greater and grander state than we have yet seen him, for his carriage was drawn by four beautiful horses and the coachman and footmen were all in red and gold liveries. The English officers[4] in full dress and swords glittering and gold and gilt everywhere. It was a strange sight. When all were assembled guns were fired and at a given signal from the Khedive the caravan proceeded. It consisted of a rug perched upon a camel and covered with a great embroidered canopy of gold, silver and jewels. A great tassel hung from a moon and star of brass and was the top and pinnacle of this wonderful looking arrangement. This camel was led by several brilliantly dressed Arabians and following were nine more camels in gorgeous trappings, on each of which was a man in some bright costume, then walked some twenty men carrying embroideries spread out on wooden frames, there were some fifty pieces all carried in this way. Wonderful masses of gilt and glitter wrought on silk, black and green and sometimes red with verses from the Koran. The rest of the scene was as usual here, a great mass or crowd or multitude selling, begging, quarreling etc., but all muttering a prayer and silent with awe and respect when the Khedive and holy procession passed.

Mother is little or no better, but Miss Lewis goes when we arrive at Naples, as her six months are up and tho' she understands Mamma and the strain and trial it is for us, she is not able to assist us in any way and is no use as a traveler or a companion for she knows nothing of managing. Why should Mother have so much needless expense? I think you Father are the only person who could ever do for Mamma and be of any comfort to her in doing for her, for I don't believe any doctors or trained nurses or children can do more than they have tried already. With love from all of us to you and the boys and Grandmama whom I hope keeps better.

Two weeks later they were in Italy.

February 28, 1901   **Grand Hotel, Naples**

Dear Father,

The east leaves a strange fascination in one's mind and it is said if you taste of the Nile water you live to taste it again. But, oh, Italy, Italy, I feel sure I shall love it.

Madame Torrigiani comes on Saturday and Lewis departs for New York. She has been good in her way but it is not a great 'way'.

Mother still worries and worries and worries and worries. Every move is a source of bother to her so we make as few as possible and yet in the evening she becomes quite gay and is eager and restless, when chatting with other people, to go about. So B. and I scarcely know just what to do, however we do what we conscientiously think best and shall continue to do so as long as strength holds out. Do not think the fact that Lewis goes to America means that Mother is much better. She goes because she informed us she would stay no longer and she is, she says, not a trained nurse but rather a masseuse and these cases do not interest her, etc., etc. We shall probably get someone else in London, if not in Rome, and old Torrigiani is a far better companion and quite as trustworthy.

                                                          Rome
March 23, 1901   **Grand-Hôtel**

My dear Father,

Fanny is perfectly overjoyed at the prospect of coming to Rome for Easter and of course it is a great opportunity for her. Isn't it nice she is so happy at school?

Our presentation is 'all up', all that's left of it is a lace veil I was to have arranged for my court train and a letter from the Embassy saying, the first 'presentation' made to the King our names are down for, but I want to go home before that can be, if only to give you a good hug and then a big strong shaking for your gallant defense of the Boers; however lots of Englishmen are just as evil with pro-Boer feeling and the uncle of a friend of mine got his seat in the House of Commons just the same in spite of his talking up de Witt, and so on. For myself I am not worrying about the affairs of South Africa, having perfect faith in King Edward and his Parliament. Joe Chamberlain and other politicals equally honest (!) in the other House can do as they choose for all I care. America seems to be adding to her already long list of diplomatic moves for so youthful a country and what are you doing for the 'Nigs' and the Red men now that the Philippine Islanders are the fashion and the Chinese question is a subject uppermost in conversation, according to the newspapers? And I hope that USA will hold on to the whole of the Panama Canal, and manage as they (the Americans) like best the Cuban affairs, don't you?

Lina's rapid review of international affairs at mid-March 1901 covered the following events:

The Boer War (1899–1902) with references to the South African general and statesman, Christian Rudolf de Wet and the British Colonial Secretary, Joseph Chamberlain.

Two events following the Spanish-American War of 1898, namely: the adoption by Cuba on 21 February 1901 of a Constitution containing clauses governing its relations with the United States, and, on 2 March 1901, the authorisation of the U.S. President by Congress to establish a civil government in the Philippines, ceded by Spain.

The imposition on China of an indemnity, the stationing of foreign troops in Peking and other penalties following the lifting, by British, French, Russian, American, German and Japanese troops, of the siege of the foreign legations by an anti-foreign Chinese military organisation whose name translates as 'righteous harmonious fists', more widely known as 'Boxers'.

*And finally Britain's desire that there should be joint construction,
ownership and operation of the Panama Canal.*

*After a month in Rome, during which time a hoped-for audience
of the Pope appears not to have materialised, they went on to
the Hôtel Vendôme in Paris, which incidently advertised baths
in all apartments and steam central heating. By the end of June
they were again in London.*

June 26, 1901   **Walsingham House Hotel**

Well, dear Father,

The last week we've been full up of dinner parties, theaters, afternoon teas and out to lunch, etc., so that after Henley Week I shall
be glad to get out of town. Last Tuesday Lord Berwick sent down
a note to say there was to be an interesting debate in the House of
Lords which if I cared to go to he would like to take me down. As
I was to drive with Mary (his sister) that afternoon that was easily
put off and as you know I love these things. I dispatched a note at
once to say I'd be delighted. The carriage came for me and Tom
and I stopped for Mary at about 4:15. We drove straight down to
the 'House' from here, passing the King in a <u>private</u> brougham and
arriving, found we had to wait as only peeresses can go directly
into this particular august chamber and even Mary who is addressed 'the Honorable' gets no privileges. We both teased Tom
at being such a swell and having no greater influence, etc., etc.,
and then Mr. 'Black Rod', a pompous little gentleman in black
silk knickerbockers and carrying his rod of office in his hand and
a gold chain, etc., about his neck—a Mr. Punch-like looking person, was sent for—and he wrote out an order for the Rt. Honorable
the Baron Berwick's two guests to go in. In the meantime there
was even more waiting so we went to the Terrace for tea, strawberries and cream.

Mary and Tom and myself were the only people on the House
of Lords' side and though we tried to lose ourselves with the

Commoners it wasn't possible, for one of the butlers knew Tom and ran up to know where his Lordship wished his table—even the chairs we sat on were marked 'The House of Lords'—Well, finally we got our order and opportunity to go in and it was such a good sight! It was very full and most of the celebrities were there.

One more letter, dated 9 August, told of their social life during three weeks in France at Trouville-sur-Mer. Lina claimed to have become 'quite a tennis player' and reported that her French was 'so easy to me now I can chatter away at a wonderful rate and shrug my shoulders and use my hands at the proper intervals'.

On 9 October they sailed for the United States.

In June 1903 Lina went by herself to Europe for two months. Despite sea-sickness she enjoyed the voyage. She was instantly recognised as being one of the Sinnicksons of Salem, New Jersey, met a number of friends and made others. Arriving in London she went to the Hyde Park Hotel and straight to bed 'and had a good cry. Just because it is all so wonderful and I love you all so dearly and I feel the distance.' Such expressions of home-sickness reappear throughout her travels and throughout her married life. She made a number of visits to friends in England, went to visit friends in Paris, but could not go to Germany because there was nobody to go with her. 'It is a very different thing being so far away from you all, as I am quite alone, to coming abroad with others.'

The highlight of her visit was a gala opera performance on the occasion of a state visit by the President of France, and Lina wrote a very full report of this to her mother.

9th July, 1903   **Hotel Foyot, Paris**

My dear, dear Mother,

This letter will no doubt seem a little late in arriving as I missed yesterday's mail as I was traveling to Paris and, the day before being the date of the Gala Opera performance, I had nothing to tell you that had not already been told. Well, dear, I have never been to such a wonderful thing in my life before. It was such a sight! The whole house [Covent Garden] decorated with millions of La France roses fastened over a lattice work of green leaves. The Royal Box in the middle was very wide and hung with gold colored satin and long gilt framed mirrors and in the middle of it sat the President of France with the King on his right and the Queen on his left. To the right of the King, the Princess of Wales and I never saw her look so well, nor believed she ever could look so very stately and handsome. Then on her right the Princess Christian and the Duke of Connaught and the Princess Beatrice of Battenburg whom I do admire. She has a charming expression. On the Queen's left was the Prince of Wales, then the Princess Royal of England (the Duchess of Fife) then the Princess Victoria and then the Duchess of Connaught and the Princess Louise (Duchess of Argyle), behind and often peeping over Their Majesties' shoulders was young Princess Margaret of Connaught and then the gentlemen and ladies in waiting, and the servants in the most beautiful liveries and silk stockings and powdered. The King looks so well and so agreeable and is very, very much thinner than when I last saw him and in his gracious way was smiling and bowing to friends all over the opera house. The Queen had such a mass of jewels on, all over her gown as well as her throat and neck, and a large tiara on. Nearly every lady in the house had on a tiara, so had I mine!

The opera was superb, especially the second act of Carmen and the balcony scene from Romeo and Juliet with Melba. I was very amused when the time came for going home they called for Lady Sinnickson's servant. So many people brought footmen, but Lady S. did not, though she got the credit.

Lina continued to visit friends in England, Scotland and Wales; had what may well have been her first ride in a motor car: 'I think really you would love a motor, Father'; commented on the shooting and trout fishing and Sir Thomas Lipton's attempt to win the America's Cup, and returned to Philadelphia at the end of August.

During the next four-and-a-half years there exist less than a half-dozen letters. One, written to her Aunt Fanny Rosengarten, has a reference to Col. Offley Shore, then on duty in Canada.

Thursday, June 27, 1907

**Narragansett Pier,
Rhode Island**

Dearest Aunt,

There is so little in our life here to make a letter out of that I enclose you these few lines more to thank you for your letter with all your home news. We are <u>very</u> glad to hear the invalids are all doing nicely—in spite of the graveness of all illness.

Mother still continues to be exceedingly depressed, nervous and restless—however with Leila as well as Miss Freeman to aid in entertaining her it has been a great help to me. My housekeeping goes on beautifully and I am getting great experience by marketing and learning the 'cuts' and 'sizes' of meat etc., but Mother has an impression I am <u>very</u> much of a novice—and she frets over it and me in a very sad fashion. When the first of the month comes—however—we can tell where I need to be more practical or careful.

Col. Shore has been inspecting a number of camps etc. and playing A.D.C. to the Gen'l. and getting at the same time a little about the country. He took the boat trip from Toronto to Montreal through the Thousand Islands and all over my letter are charming little pictures of island castles—of lighthouses, boats, banks with picturesquely grouped trees and so forth and a very pretty drawing of the Fort on 'my' side of Niagara.

Now I must go and read letters to Mother which have just come from Betty and Fanny.

It was for this beloved Aunt that Lina found time for the following postcard only five days before her marriage.

230 W. Rittenhouse Square
January 24th, 1908   **Philadelphia**

My dearest dear Aunt,

Words—no not even actions could express what I do feel in love and gratitude toward you for all—for so much goodness and generosity to me at this time: not to be close to you as I have ever been by being summer and winter in the same place hurts me deeply.

England and Canada: 1908

After her marriage Lina began her practice of writing weekly letters to her Mother and Father, her Uncle Joseph Rosengarten and her Aunt Fanny Rosengarten from wherever she might be: Britain, Canada, India, California. And they were separate letters to each; once when, short of time, she addressed a letter '———and family', there was great distress and she had to apologise.

The orderliness of this correspondence was made the easier by the regularity of the international mails. Between Philadelphia and London letters took seventeen days, and between Philadelphia and Simla, at 7,000 feet in the lower Himalayas, where much of her time in India was spent, twenty-eight days. Letters were dispatched and arrived on fixed days of the week, so that a well-ordered life style included a set period each week for letter writing, and with such exactness did the replies arrive that on one occasion in Simla Lina recorded with annoyance that the mails had not arrived in time for her to read with her morning cup of tea, but late in the afternoon.

The first of her letters after marriage was a note to Aunt Fanny.

February 2nd, 1908   **'An Bord der Amerika'**

My dearest Aunt,

How kind of you to think of the little note sent to us as we sailed. We got many notes and telegrams but yours happened to be the very first and Offley brought it to me and in his dearest teasing manner asked me 'if I knew who <u>Mrs.</u> Offley Shore was?' As soon as I caught sight of your beautiful and familiar handwriting I knew myself! So there you are dear Aunt Fanny. How you would have

laughed. I really do think I have been a wonderful sailor this time—
not ill a moment though at times I felt very strange in the head but
O. spoils me so. I don't see how I could be otherwise than good.
I keep the 'polie boots' and the little white dressing sacque at my
side and they are really lovely. Though there are but a few people
on board to look at at all (so we think), O. says he knows they all
look at us. Saturday night we thought of you at the Orchestra. Just
as Tuesday will remind us you are no doubt at the Opera.

*In England Offley's mother had received the news of her son's
engagement most unhappily. Between the engagement and the wedding his diary records: 'Receiving anxious letters from Linoschka
about my mother's very cold and extraordinary attitude.—Rachel
Jardine sends kindly note and invite to Dryfeholm.—Had to write
mother an ultimatum and say I merely shall await a "Yes" or
"No" on arrival at Plymouth as to whether we go to her or not.'
No further mention is made of the matter, but it is clear from
the record of their activities during the five weeks which they
spent in England that they did not visit her. Years later, as becomes
apparent from letters, Offley's mother, as a result of intercessions
by friends, became reconciled to her son's marriage. 'She is,'
one of these friends explained to Lina, 'delightful but very autocratic and high tempered—but adores Offley to madness and
always planned a royal marriage or a Duke's daughter for him.'
His father, separated from his mother, and other members of
his family gave them a warm welcome.*

February 9, 1908   **Hyde Park Hotel.**
                                                  London, S.W.

My dear Father,

Here is a letter to you all to yourself, but as we look forward to
having a great deal to do I am going to tell you, hereafter I think
joint letters will really be all one can do. Well, enough for excuses.
We had quite a good trip over. Fair days and fine nights, with many

stars, a young moon and sometimes a passing ship with all the beautiful lighting of any seafarer's hotel of the day. I was not ill, nor
was Offley, but both of us were ready to rest both in body and mind
and found that was the only thing we really could do. Upon landing
we found quite a batch of letters for both of us. One for each of
us separately from his Father and from his Aunt Caroline and from
his sisters and from many friends of his and wires and letters from
many others. We came straight up to town and upon our arrival at
Paddington Station there was Offley's father to meet us! Just as you
would have been, as he had bothered the Agents until he knew just
about what time to count upon our coming. The next day a luncheon
was arranged at Aunt Caroline's that I might meet the immediate
family and one or two friends, and such a sweet house in Connaught
Square as it is. With old Hogarth prints and other delights in pictures,
portraits and furniture, miniatures and medallions. Mrs. Stovin gave
us both such a kind welcome and the old butler and all the other
servants were equally glad to see Offley and 'Mrs. Offley' and I
quite forgot, once or twice, that this referred to me! Among the
luncheon guests were Mr. Shore—Offley's father, Mr. Harrington
Shore, the eldest brother of Mrs. Stovin and Mr. Shore, and Offley's
sister Florence who had come down from Sunderland on purpose
to meet me, and Sir Edward Sullivan, an Irish Baronet, all so very
nice. Mrs. Stovin begged me at once to call her 'Aunt Caroline'
and furthermore is giving a reception for us on Thursday to which
Offley and I may ask any friends of ours as well. The last two days
have been like Spring with real sun and sunsets; so all tell me I
have brought Queen's weather. This afternoon after a morning at
writing notes and unpacking and straightening out our engagements
Offley took me out to call. We went to General and Lady Dorothy
Haig's in Princes Gate, then to Lord Rosebery's, then to Mrs.
Bayly's, wife of Major-General Bayly, now Deputy Secretary to
Government Military Department, Simla, and to others we found
out, then finally to Aunt Caroline's to fetch Florence back to dine
with us, but found the two good ladies were at church, so after
a talk with the old Butler upon the virtue of lifts and telephones
in private houses (I believe Aunt C. won't hear of such a thing as
a phone) home we came and telephoned Offley's father to come
and have dinner with us and spent a very happy evening showing
him your photos; Mother's, Betty's and Fanny's and all the family

portraits. More, just as soon as I have more time to tell it and much love to you my dear, very dear Father from both of us and to each and all and tell Mother the next will surely be addressed to her.

No account of the reception mentioned in the above letter appears in any of the surviving letters of the time, but twelve years later Lina recalled it in a letter to Uncle Joe when the house was sold following Aunt Caroline's death.

July 20, 1920   **Santa Barbara**

... No. 17, Connaught Square, Hyde Park W., dear Aunt Caroline's house, has passed out of our possession and we heard today of our things being sent to warehouse and everything else sold. As I look back to the wedding reception given me there—the beautiful plate—the exquisite old French chandeliers filled with candles—the pretty soft light—the dear old aunt with her beautiful lace and exquisite old family diamonds—the counterpart of my own dearest Aunt, Offley's sisters so pleased and proud of us, Lady Wolseley and Lady Paliser driving up from Hampton Court, the Hardinges, the Bigges, the Stuart Wortleys, Lawrences, General Haldane, the Duffs and General Haig, Lady Sterndale whose husband had been a Governor of Bombay—a cousin or intimate relation of O's Father, Sir Francis and Lady Hopwood, Mary Noel-Hill and Tom—Lord Berwick, and the Rawlins, Sitwells and Cavendishes. Some of the Cokes—also cousins, and a great many more. The dignified old servants—the beautiful plate—the most special pieces out for the occasion, just as Aunt Fanny would have had it, and after it was all over the quiet, intimate family chat—and their great pride in me—and Offley's. From the very first moment our friendship began—she planned I should go on with that house.

During the month spent in England they made their wills: Lina was introduced to Offley's Bankers and calls were made on

appropriate officials at the War Office and India Office. Offley,
writing to his father-in-law, commented on the hours spent

by this little lady in her beloved Bond Street. She talked all the morning
with a Mrs. Daniel, held a seance for tea and chatter all one afternoon
encouraging reminiscences of years ago from men and women of every
description, and smiled like a successful society hostess upon me and
struggled home too late for the hotel dinner saying she had an appalling
headache, and enjoyed such a delightful time! I really do think Lina
is looking wonderfully well, very cheerful, happy, and is fascinating
everyone with whom she comes in contact.

On 11 March they sailed for Ottawa where Offley would take up
his appointment as Assistant Military Secretary to the Governor-
General (Earl Grey) and Lina would start getting used to being
Mrs. Offley Shore and the wife of an Indian Army officer. She
would enjoy and make the most of every moment of it.

It was an important year in Canada's history, being the ter-
centenary of the founding of Quebec by Samuel de Champlain. King
Edward was represented at the celebrations by George, Prince of
Wales, accompanied by Princess Mary. Among those present were
Comte Bertrand de Montcalm and George Wolfe, Esq., descendants
of the opposing generals at the Battle of the Plains of Abraham in
1759, as a result of which Quebec, and Canada, became British
instead of French. Lina recorded that 'the French and English
are greatly wrought up and somewhat jealous of each other as
so many things are planned to be celebrated!!!'

The following letter, on the death of a cousin, is an example of
the close relationship which Lina repeatedly displayed towards all
the members of her family.

April 8, 1908   **The Rideau Apartments,**
                                               Ottawa, Ontario, Canada

My dear, Very dear Aunt,

Your letter of April 6th came this morning and is the first detailed
news of dearest Alice I have had. Of course—I was shocked and I

have grieved myself almost sick as I naturally feel I should have liked to go at once to Philadelphia to be with you, each and all at such a time and in the first days of such a dreadful loss. Offley told me to do exactly as my feelings dictated, but to think it over for he could not accompany me—and as we only came into this little place of our own on Monday and the servants at once proved unsatisfactory and gave me notice and are leaving tomorrow morning, I felt my first duty now is to remain with my husband much as I want to be with you at this time. Somehow I have caught cold and as it is still very wintry here just now, my first housekeeping difficulties and experiences are starting in fairly formidably. However I have the best and dearest husband and helpmate in the world and find him dearer and kinder and kinder and more lovable with each additional worry that comes. Yesterday he brought me lilies and books and telephoned to Mrs. Henré Panet to come and cheer me up and then took me for a walk so that when evening came we were quite gay again, hanging towel racks and talking over things we should do when we come into another country where servants are angels. I am wearing my few black things for my darling Alice— as long as they will serve me—as I felt I must in love and affection for her and at this distance be reminded of her and of you and of what you are suffering with a clearer realization, as I feel there is little or nothing else I can do—and of course I go nowhere these few days—but there are some visits that are demanded of me as wife of the Staff Officer ranking next to the General.

May 4, 1908   **Ottawa**

My Dearest Father,

So many thanks for all your little letters dear. Two came together and I was glad to hear all you had to say about dear Mother and I only hope and pray, as the rest of you do, for her and for <u>all of you</u> that Dr. Mitchell may be able to overcome this depression somewhat.

Offley came back to lunch with the dire news of the attempted assassination of Lord Kitchener and trouble, very serious in India.

Our letters for some time have been full of the unrest which all feel and have felt there for some time now.

Should he have to go at a moment's notice of course I have got to understand. I should myself go as far as I could with him and finally settle in London with Aunt Caroline where one would get all the news daily. Aunt C. has very kindly given me this standing invitation in the event of such a thing happening, but even yet I hope that with a strong man like Lord Kitchener something may be done at once to avert a great war. The government at home in England and Mr. Haldane's policy in particular are not the ones to stamp out this trouble for they have preached and practised peace, with no preparation for such contingencies.

I am so much obliged to you for finding out about the insurances. Billington and Hutchinson at Philadelphia have sent us terms for all accidents in travelling and fire, and breakage by fire, and theft of jewelry only, and unless we find that we can do better with the 'Army and Navy' in London we shall I think insure with them.

Very soon, there occurred other family deaths, that of Lina's eldest uncle, born in 1827, and that of Offley's eldest uncle, Harrington Offley Shore, whom Lina had met at Aunt Caroline's reception for them in London.

May 16, 1908   **Ottawa**

My dearest Aunt and Dear Uncle Joe,

Late yesterday afternoon Father's telegram announcing Uncle Sam's death came to me—and I felt at once I should so much like to be with you, dear Aunt Fanny, could I be of any use or comfort—for you have had so much sadness and anxiety since the death of dear Alice and Mother's poor health and spirits, that I longed to go and comfort you or help you where I could and Offley understood, loath as I saw he felt at having to let me go alone. When we went to the Station and ticket offices we found I could not get a train before this afternoon at 4:45 so I changed the wire I took in my pocket from 'coming at once' to the one you received, and then in the evening yours and Betty's and Uncle Joe's came suggesting it was best not to come, so upon consideration I gave up my journey to you, but you must not hesitate to let me know should you wish to have me later, or if you felt like coming to me.

Dear Uncle Sam. He was so very jolly and nice the last time I saw him, and teased both Offley and myself, and asked me how I found his (O's) relations, and strange to say news came this morning of Offley's eldest Uncle's death.

You will miss Uncle Sam, because I know so well how constantly you thought of him and how often you worried over him when away in the summer and he would not join you, so that since we must all go someday this comes in the light of a blessing to relieve you of further worry and anxiety when the summer time comes and you would feel dreadfully at leaving him behind—and perhaps not do so. I wish I could tell you how ready I am and how equally ready Offley is to let me go to you, to be made in any way useful, as you are both, and ever have been, so good, kind, and generous and so thoughtful for me, and now including Offley too. Please never feel or think I forget you for one moment in my newly found happiness—and we are <u>very</u> happy—for I am in spite of it and with it all—quite the same Lina—the same girl ever wondering how I can be grateful enough to you both and for you both—<u>so much are you</u>, dear Aunt and Uncle, <u>in</u> my life—never mind at what distances.

I hope dear Mother takes Uncle Sam's death calmly. She sometimes realized these things more quietly when her spirits were so down hearted.

The following letter indicates that somebody in Ottawa had reported to Philadelphia that Lina and Offley had been seen behaving unbecomingly, in view of the recent deaths in their families, by attending a State Ball given by the Governor-General and his wife.

June 10, 1908   **Ottawa**

My dearest Aunt,

Evidently you never received a long letter from me—written particularly to you—to tell you <u>myself</u> of being obliged to go to the Court Ball—and bidding you read it with what little description that followed—to my Mother and the others. It seems too bad that you should not have got it and heard as I so wished you to hear and know directly <u>from me</u> of our being there at all. We did not go to the State Dinner as we were able to withdraw from that, but <u>Offley was obliged</u> to go for their Excellencies Entrée to the Ball—which can scarcely be called a ball at all—but a State Reception.

We had both lost our Uncles about two days previous, but I did not go until I consulted 3 elder ladies and told them quietly my position, and when Mrs. Lake came out here to see me and tell me she thought for several reasons, official and rather long to explain here, that <u>I should certainly go</u>. So I made up my mind that my good kind friend knew of what she was talking about and put my feelings down in black and white to you; for I thought you would understand and I trust <u>even now</u> you will give me the benefit of the doubt that I had you and all my saddened dear ones at home much in my mind. However we went at half past nine—Offley in full uniform, looking exceedingly handsome and I in my grey 'Worth' gown (for it was explained we were in mourning). We stood near the throne for the Entrée. Their Excellencies came in preceded by the aides-de-camp and officers and ladies of the Household—while the band played 'God Save the King'. Afterwards the Royal Quadrille in which the Prime Minister, the Minister of Finance and others, and their wives (all had called upon me), and Mrs. Lake and General Otter took part. Then after a short conversation with some of the pleasantest of our friends and their husbands Their Excellencies sent an A.D.C. for us to go to supper—and after a short inspection of Government House Offley and I came away without having danced a step or having had <u>any presentation</u> which annoyed us both—as we were given to understand <u>we were expected</u> to be present. However it may have been that they did not send for us knowing that we wished just to come and go as quietly as possible. Lord and Lady Grey are themselves in mourning for their daughter, but you

see certain people have to go on with their official duties in spite
of these things.

I never met the lady Fanny Gray wrote about nor have I ever
heard of her—and if we were conspicuous it was our last wish, but
a great many complimentary things have reached our ears since. I
am so awfully sorry that you never can have gotten my letter telling
you all this at the time.

*For the Tercentenary Celebrations everybody concerned moved
to Quebec and over a two week period Lina, despite, as she describes, being totally occupied, wrote to her family nine letters
and a number of postcards.*

July 12th, 1908

**Chateau Frontenac,
Quebec**

My very dear Father,

The day has been a most glorious one, but blazing heat. We came
in the afternoon all over the route H.R.H. is to take the day of the
Review—O, with maps and pencils and note-book—and called at
the Mayor's—and having been asked what sort of conveyance I
preferred—4 wheels, motor, or caleche, I chose the latter and we
bumped about in truly first class Canadian fashion.

Offley has this whole show to arrange. Places for the Guards of
Honour, all the salutes, escorts, routes, everything for everything
and he is working like a horse now. I help where I can and just
made some suggestions that have rather pleased O., but of course
I am a 'silent partner' in our trade!

To Aunt Fanny on the same day she wrote:

I think I am going to like myself as 'Mrs. Assistant Secretary to
His Excellency', as the Germans would style one.

July 14th, 1908   **Quebec**

Darling Mother, Dearest Aunt, and Dear Uncle Joe,

A joint letter must do for I am busy in attendance on my good man while he attends the Governor General in his capacity of 2nd Military Secretary, and soon H.R.H. the Prince of Wales. Last evening while I was finishing my dressing to be ready to receive two officers at dinner in case Offley (who is riding the Prince's horses every afternoon now) should be late, Agnes, our maid, said, 'Oh, look Mrs. Shore at this funny ship!' and I turned to the windows to see our fleet glide in quietly, grandly in all their war paint—wonderful and formidable and without a sound—not a whistle, not a gun, for we never salute our own ships. Stately and splendid they looked in the beautiful light of the setting sun in this most beautiful Harbour. Later we heard the band playing God Save the King and the terrace became black with people as soon as the news got abroad.

I was sent for to tea with Mrs. Hanbury-Williams in her rooms at the Citadel, where we should be quartered but there is no room. As a member of the Governor General's Staff and Household however O. tells me Col. Hanbury-Williams has me down for some very nice occasions. First to go with her Excellency and the ladies of the Household to the King's Wharf to meet the Prince and in the same way to several other things.

Offley has drawn me charts and plans of all the war ships coming, even my very own, the New Hampshire, and I now know their size, their tonnage, their cost, the plate armour and their guns. I do wish so much you were all here. The redcoats in the streets, the flags of three nations flapping in the breeze, the guard at the Courthouse for General Otter, the decorations and colour added to the natural beauty and quaintness of Quebec is more wonderful in effect than anything you can imagine and the site for the Pageant and the Review on the Plains of Abraham defies description.

July 19, 1908
Sunday, 4:30 in the afternoon   **Quebec**

Dearest darling Mother,

While I am waiting for Lord Roberts I will send you a few lines.
And doesn't the above sound like nonsense as if we were children
playing at 'Let's Pretend'? Well this time it is really truly true dear.
He is certainly a wonderful little old gentleman and we were all <u>so</u>
sorry that O. did not get back from His Excellency in time. Ld. R.
asked me <u>when</u> I was married, where I was married, when we go
to India, and told me about the Regiment, said it was a very grand
one and that he knew Shore and altogether I enjoyed it immensely
and just as he left he said, 'Take care of that feather if you go out
for it's very windy and I admire y'r hat!' Of course we all laughed.
He asks questions one after another like a quick firing gun.

My cards have come from Their Excellencies to meet the Prince
of Wales on Thursday evening at a reception. O. will be at a State
dinner with him for gentlemen first and afterwards we both stay to
see the fireworks and the ships lit up from the King's Bastion.

Today is very glorious, quite windy and fairly cool, and I enjoyed
driving in and out with O. and having the soldiers salute as we go
into the Citadel or out (when he is with me).

The lights this afternoon are wonderful and the whole city has a
gala appearance, the streets filled with soldiers and holiday-makers
and the river, besides the battleships in it, is gay with decorated
boats of every description. O. has told me a wire has arrived to say
the U.S.S. New Hampshire is 110 miles out and she will no doubt
arrive in the night. O. and Col. Hanbury tease me dreadfully about
<u>my</u> ship!!!

July 22, 1908   **Quebec**

My Darling Mother,

While I have one little moment I mean to try and write to you.
Aunt Mary and Laura arrived and I am more than happy to see

them and have them with me, and for most things we have got them both invitations. Last night the Admiral of the Atlantic Fleet, Sir Assheton-Curzon-Howe, gave a ball at the Parliament buildings to which we, Aunt Mary, Laura and I, went. Offley could not go owing to having to go out to meet P.O.W. in advance. I missed him sadly but we had a perfectly splendid time. For me as Mrs. Offley Shore, wife of His Excellency's Assistant Military Secretary, all is arranged, but as all our friends are perfectly charming to me always, Laura and Aunt Mary were able to be included and at supper, by a little maneuvering and a few polite speeches, Aunt Mary went down to supper with Captain Hughes of the Exmouth and I with Captain Cameron Winslow of the New Hampshire and Captain Chapman of the Venus and beside my place at the supper table for the official guests we tucked Aunt Mary in.

Friday morning, 8 a.m.

Offley and I have been up since six. O. has had to go and hustle the printer for something for H.R.H. and I take another moment to send you a line. I have had my card and my place for <u>everything</u> and I am so proud I can scarcely speak. <u>All</u> admire Offley <u>so</u> much and last night at Their Excellencies' reception H.R.H. noticed me and spoke of me to Sir Francis Hopwood and this will please my dear old father-in-law as it did Offley. The Vice-President [of the U.S.A.] also asked to be introduced to me and so did his wife. I had a long talk with Lord Roberts and Lady Cromer. Spoke French with the French visitors and altogether held my head very high. Offley being 'in attendance' could not look after me as he would like, but I have lots of friends among the gentlemen and The Honorable Hoare-Ruthven, who was in Cairo the winter we were there is here as Lord Dudley's A.D.C. and he helped me arrange my train and was generally nice to me, as all I know are and all I don't know want to be. This morning is the Review and I am to see O. again but <u>mounted</u> this time in attendance on H.R.H.

I had a beautiful seat at the ceremony at the foot of the Champlain Statue yesterday with all the British Navy and Lady Cromer. We got in the wrong place but it was so agreeable we didn't change.

Yesterday the P.O.W. made several investitures and today my so much admired Mrs. Hanbury-Williams and her charming husband are Sir John and Lady Hanbury-Williams. Lady Grey thanked me personally for Offley's constant readiness and splendid attention. It was a <u>very fine</u> sight last night, all the uniforms, full dress of the ladies and Levée dress of the gentlemen. The red lining of the marquee. I wore my wedding dress, my splendid earrings and pendant, (much admired by all especially dear Lady Cromer) and my turquoise necklace as a tiara. Offley said (he was a gentleman in waiting to Lady Sybel as she received us at the drawing room door) that he felt very proud and had quite a heart flutter as they announced 'Mrs. Offley Shore'; but when he found me with Lord Roberts and the Duke of Norfolk, chatting as gaily as any, he wondered if I would ever deign to notice him again.

Of course you'll think my head must be turned, but I assure you it all seems very natural; only when we came motoring home through the little old streets of Quebec, up and down hill with the marvelous illuminations, the soldiers, and Offley covered by his great military cloak sitting in front with the chauffeur, his Eastern headdress silhouetted against the blaze of light, <u>then</u> I felt as if it was a fairy tale or a dream. Aunt Mary and Laura saw the illuminations from our bedroom windows where I had invited several ladies who were not included in Their Excellencies' invitation which was limited to 150.

July 24, 1908   **Quebec**

My dear Father,

Have been on one tremendous rush—but we have had a very gorgeous time. O. constantly with the Prince and I going everywhere on red carpets and in reserved seats. Very royal, very happy, very proud. Last night was the small reception to meet the Prince and see the fireworks given by Their Excellencies. I had to go all alone but found O. part of the Tableaux Vivants and watching me with great curiosity as I made my bow and shook hands with our Prince of Wales with whom I was very much pleased. He looked wonderfully smiling and well after his hard day's work and his long journey. I moved on and soon found myself in great good company . . . At the State Ball we all sat in a row on a dais with our Prince in the middle and our best clothes on while everyone else looked on just as though it were a tableau.

Saturday, July 25, 1908   Quebec

Darling Mother, Father, Uncle Joe and Aunt Fanny,

Just a line to tell you I am just come home into my room for one moment after having been with H.R.H. and his small party on the 'Argonaut', reviewing the ships. Look in the newspapers and perhaps you will see me walking up between the Duke of Norfolk and Lord Roberts, Lord Lovat and Lord Annaly behind. When we landed at King's Wharf H.R.H. was very kind and has said he could not do without Offley, but I am very tired and feel so very lonely without my best companion. I take to Royal Princessing like a duck to water.

July 31, 1908   Quebec

My Darling Mother,

Just a little pencil note to tell you of the last days of our wonderful visit here. Before departing His Royal Highness called Offley into his room and after saying some remarkably kind things presented him with a diamond pin. His 3 plumes, the coronet and 'Ich Dien' with a 'G' underneath to wear as a token of the esteem and friendship he felt for O. I have been extremely favorably impressed by H.R.H. and the gentlemen of his suite. Lord Annaly, Sir Bryan Godfrey-Faussett and 'Hopy' as we call Sir Francis Hopwood, and Sir Arthur Bigge are not only men but gentlemen in the most agreeable sense— not mere men of fashion, and it was delightfully refreshing to talk with any of them. The Duke of Norfolk was exceedingly kind to me, and for some reason or other I seem to attract the kind old man, at any rate on Wednesday evening when dining with their Excellencies he (N.) singled me out very particularly and has invited us to pay him and his Lady Duchess a visit when we go home. I think I have also a really good friend in Lady Hanbury-Williams and Sir John, and Lady Sybel Grey, and this should prove a very happy thing for life and if ever we live at home in England. Of course I <u>know</u> that it is all due to O, but he bless him says it is <u>all myself</u>.

On the day following this letter Offley took a month's leave, a week of which they spent with Lina's Uncle Frank and Aunt Mary in Jamestown, Rhode Island, and three weeks with Mr. and Mrs. Sinnickson, the latter accompanied, apparently as always, by her nurse-companion, and Uncle Joe and Aunt Fanny at Richfield Springs, a fashionable health resort in upper New York State. As a result of these visits Lina felt sure that her family 'all liked Offley the better for knowing him a little more intimately'.

Back in Ottawa, Uncle Joe, Aunt Fanny and Betty visited them for a week; Lina regretted that since she was busy packing up to leave Canada she could not get away to attend brother George's wedding. Offley received reports from his father's doctors 'that he can hardly live much longer—valvular disease of the heart, local dropsy, can no longer sleep lying down'. Lina experienced for the first time what were to become two commonplaces of her life, dreaded separations from Offley, long or short, ordered and sometimes counter-ordered, and repeated packing and unpacking, sorting and storing, at which Offley would later testify she became expert.

October 19, 1908   **Ottawa**

My dearest Aunt,

How good and prompt of you to have sent the luggage labels at your very earliest opportunity—and they arrived this afternoon in the very nick of time as we are <u>frightfully</u> busy packing, sealing and labelling—I must also thank you so much for your letter about the wedding and one this morning from Mother with some details about the presents. How lovely they must have been. A string of pearls!—diamond brooches, a bracelet etc.—do write me more—and all about the clothes. Tell Uncle Joe—very many thanks for 2 'Nations'—but ask him not to send me papers while we are packing and moving.

Offley goes off Friday afternoon to Nova Scotia—to be gone a week—and I cannot accompany him, much to my disappointment. [He did not go. Ed.]

I hope to ship all my cases directly to the Girard Trust and to J. E. Caldwell and Co. and from what one heard today from the U.S. Consul and from the Express agent I think we can do it all quite easily and safely, and when I do come first to Philadelphia we shall come to pay you the promised visit and trust you will not find our packages too numerous and unwelcome—but you see we are utterly homeless and wanderers by force of duty, a duty which requires a certain amount of obligation and clothes and uniforms etc. and my family seem to entirely fail to understand this. I say all this because I today received, in a letter from Charlie whom I had asked to sign, before a notary public, the expediting papers for my cases returned to Philadelphia, a statement saying nothing I might send on ahead of me to Philadelphia to '230' would be received there— only another instance for me to realize that not anyone of them wish me or my things there. It is hard to understand however why this statement was made to me by Charlie, as we have had no intention of sending anything there, but rather of taking away what is there.

On 30 October Offley presented what was presumably his final report on his mission and commented in his diary:

Very peculiar attitude on W. G.'s [unidentified] part when discussing Report on Canadian militia—practically objecting to anything approaching the whole truth being inserted. If our own People are not to know the truth and nothing but the truth—who is to?

A week later they departed for Philadelphia where, apart from a short return visit to Ottawa at the end of the year 'pour prendre congé', they stayed until sailing for England on 5 January. There was time for Offley to learn more about the city which would always mean so much to his wife. He recorded hearing Caruso from Betty's box at the Academy of Music, the opening of the Hammerstein Opera House, visiting the University of Pennsylvania's Veterinary Department developed under Uncle Joe's interest, inspecting horses at the Radnor Hunt Club Races with Betty, and a tour of Powers, Weightman, Rosengarten Co., pharmaceutical manufacturers, conducted by five members of the Rosengarten family, 'all present, each having a speciality and also general control'.

England and the Voyage to India
January to March 1909

They arrived in England on 15 January, there to stay for some seven weeks. It was Offley who first wrote to the families in Philadelphia.

Hyde Park Hotel,
Knightsbridge
London, S.W.

January 17th, 1909: 9.20 p.m.

'I do wish to Goodness she had a telephone . . .'! such, my dear Aunt Fanny, are the words that I have just uttered to Linoshka, when speaking of Aunt Carry. There! She has written us pages of proposed movements and plans,—and we must now (or never) call for a 'taxi' and go right across the Park to 'square matters up'. C'est embêtant, lorsqu'on est joliment pressé . . .

This dear old Aunt of mine tho', is very sweet and charming, and paid us a long visit yesterday—stayed to dinner—flirted away and played with the Little Fat Thing—leaving me out in the cold of course— or winking at me in a knowing sort of way across the flowers—until I wondered what the secret of the spell was that Schatzi seems to throw over all and sundry in her path. Quien sabe? Just pure sympathy and goodness of heart, I believe. Aunt Carry, too, wears all sorts of curious old garments under her best wraps, 'just because they are good enough'—and trusting that 'Offley would not think of looking'.

I have been very busy already, running round my offices and menkind—being received, I must admit, with no end of kindness.

Will anything come of it all, I wonder?

Sunday.

My father was very bright and delighted to see us both again—particularly Lina—but his Dr. tells me he will never be anything but an invalid now—as his heart may fail altogether with the least exertion—poor man.

Schatzi has not quite recovered from the shaking up of this journey yet—but will in a few days be all right again I am sure.

They received us in a very friendly fashion at this hotel: and I must admit things are pleasant and comfortable—if expensive—but the noise at night made by all kinds of steaming grunting shaking shrieking (!) things on wheels up to 2.30 and 3 a.m. is a little disconcerting.

General Sir O'Moore Creagh, the Military Secretary at the India Office, and Sir Francis Hopwood at the Colonial—have been most kind.

A good deal will depend upon one's orders next week—as to whether it is worth while launching out a little bit into Society.

Offley spent much time at the War Office, the India Office and the Colonial Office while his next appointment was being determined. He was finally offered and accepted the appointment of Asst. Quartermaster-General, Training, Army in India, to be stationed at Simla. This would end any chance of his getting command of his regiment. Lina was at first undecided as to whether this was the right course for him to go, but before very long in India she would decide that she preferred life at Government Headquarters in Simla or Calcutta to that of a regimental officer's wife.

January 25th, 1909   **Hyde Park Hotel**

My dearest Aunt,

A letter of yours and one from Uncle Joe just came in—and while I have a few moments all to myself until Offley comes in before dressing for dinner, I will send you a few lines. We are still awaiting further and private telegrams from Lord Kitchener before being positive of our date of sailing etc. and in the meantime I am having a

wretched siege with the dentist—owing to a broken tooth—a loose
filling and 'tartar' which he says needs serious attention. In fact I
have done nothing—nor have I been able to do anything since I
first went to the dentist but go to him every day and suffer with
soreness between times. And Offley has been exceedingly busy flit-
ting about Whitehall each and every day and he has also great anxiety
over his Father's sad condition of health and equally sad position
of his affairs. Aunt Caroline has been kindness itself and wants us
so much to go and stop in her house, but we think we are freer
here and I shall go regularly to lunch and dine and thereby save
any expense possible. We now have given up all idea of taking a
maid out with us and have asked Offley's sister Urith to come with
us—at her own travelling expense—and be our guest for six months.
I only hope she accepts as this would make the best of companionship
for me and be giving her a great treat too. We have not yet got her
answer and I am anxious to have her agree and accept.

All his new letters and titles O. tells me must await his taking
up the appointment—actually being in it. This Offley tells me is
the etiquette. I do so hope all will turn out well, as it is a thing—of
course—to be immensely proud of—to have my husband at five
and forty—A.Q.M.G. Division of Training—on the Headquarters
Staff of the Army in India—Division of Chief of Staff; and Simla
is the best climate in India—and there and at Calcutta our house
and home shall be. I am to meet at tea tomorrow a Mrs. Grover
who is just now in town and wife of Maj. Gen'l Grover—Inspector
General of Cavalry; this has been arranged so she may tell me about
the houses in Simla and the living requirements etc. which I shall
so much appreciate—but I fancy it is all very expensive, rather an
establishment is required for Headquarter Staff officers—but we shall
see. Offley will have to get entirely new uniform as a staff officer
and wear perhaps for the last time his magnificent native uniform
at the King's Levée at Buckingham Palace next week.

*In preparation for this household expenditure she applied to her
uncles to be given permission to draw $5,000 from her grand-
father's trust, to be separately and strictly accounted for by her*

*to show that it was appropriately spent. When in a few days her
Bankers advised her that £1,000 had been credited to her account
in London she asked Uncle Joe:*

was it 5000 dollars or 1000 pounds—as I always keep a strict account
of my <u>American</u> money especially as we shall soon have to think in
rupees and it is much easier to change from dollars to rupees than
from pounds sterling—and had you sent me 5000 dollars it should be
something over one thousand pounds—in fact about twenty pounds
some shillings and pence. I could not make out from the cable.

*She was taken to meet the appropriate officials in various Gov-
ernment offices and to Offley's two clubs, the United Services and
the Cavalry. Her preference was clear. The first she described as
'superb, so stately and beautifully proportioned'. Of the Cavalry
Club she said, 'It is nice for me because I can meet him there to
lunch or just to wait, for there is a delightful ladies' drawing room'.*

*She attended the opening of Parliament and the 'Londonderry
political party', and went to the theatre and the opera and commented that 'Ash Wednesday and the March weather take people
abroad who can go and things will be dull until Spring, but by that
time I shall be seeing India and starting my Simla season there'.*

*At one party she met, and the form of the reference suggests
previous acquaintance with, the Landgraf of Hesse and the Baron
Riedesel zu Eisenbach. The Rosengartens had, in the eighteenth
century, been bankers to the Landgrafs of Hessen Cassel, but
had lost their wealth in the Napoleonic wars. A Baron Riedesel
commanded the Brunswick and Hessian troops forming units of
the British troops during the American War of Independence. Baroness Riedesel, who accompanied her husband, christened one
of her three children 'America'. Lina wrote a monograph entitled
'Frederika, Baroness Riedesel' which was published in the 'Pennsylvania Magazine of History and Biography' in October 1906.*

*The great event of these two months was Lina's Presentation
at Court. Every moment of this she reported with meticulous detail,
including all the preparations, even to including a sketch of the
thrones and surrounding arrangements at the actual moment of
Presentation.*

February 2, 1909   **Hyde Park Hotel**

My dearest Aunt,

A great many thanks for yours of the nineteenth and I <u>do</u> hope by this time that each and all of you are receiving our letters, and now for much and definite news of ourselves (in which I know your every kind interest) and a very agreeable surprise. First, O. is to be attached at the W.O. for the next three weeks and therefore we shall remain in London until our date of sailing, now fixed for the 4th of March and next but <u>not least</u> in a letter from Windsor Castle from Lady Katherine Coke which I received yesterday she says 'The Princess has arranged for the Countess of Bradford, who will attend H.R.H. at the two first courts to present Mrs. Offley Shore. Her Royal Highness will therefore be obliged if Colonel and Mrs. Offley Shore will go to Lady Bradford who is at 44 Lowndes Square' (quite close by) 'and make their further arrangements', and we are to take our letter by way of introduction. O. filled out my cards for the Lord Chamberlain, Lord Alford, and wrote to Lady Bradford to ask when it will be most convenient for her to receive us—and then we both sat down and looked at each other! For of all amazing things— that I 'Dushka' 'Schatzi' 'Natuska' 'Norija' should be summoned to Their Majesties' first Court by H.R.H. the Princess of Wales and in Her Royal Highness's own suite is astounding. O. says it is <u>my</u> luck and I say it is all on account of him, and of course <u>it is</u>. Almost anyone can go to Court, but not every woman can go presented by the Princess of Wales, and also have her husband with her, for we are <u>both</u> commanded to be in attendance, which I do think is so nice. Please read this at once to Mother, but I know she will smile and say '<u>Now</u> the little peacock is happy' or remind you that I was always a Queen of Sheba etc. and tell Aunt Mary who I <u>do</u> wish might be here to help me to array myself or put in the last pin and now I must go and think about my train and my plumes and do my weekly mending and economize in all small things to meet the larger requirements of our lives.

February 5, 1909   **Hyde Park Hotel**

My dear Uncle Joe,

I am busy with my little affairs, gathering together many things for Simla which must be taken out and cannot be got or depended upon to get there so I am wondering if it is not possible for me to have a small sum for <u>my furniture</u> out of Grandfather's estate, or out of my share, as the other Grandchildren have had for furniture for their houses. Yesterday I was lunching with Lady Holdich who was in India 25 years and I often go to the Haigs, and Mrs. Haig went out there much as I go, when first married and never having been before, so she gives me the benefit of her experience and her mistakes etc., but both she and Lady Holdich and Mrs. Grover all tell me I really should take out household things for Simla which cannot be got there or in Bombay. Of course most of these things can be got at Bombay but some <u>important</u> things cannot be got there. All my friends also tell me that even the houses let as 'furnished' are too sparsely so to live in and so I enclose a list of some of the things I have been told particularly to think over. Simla you see is high, very high, and with the best climate in India but varying from an extremely cold to an extremely hot season. The place to go to is an hotel on arrival but we have the refusal of a house now. Shall I then ask you to speak to Uncle Harry and see if $3000–$5000 might not be given to me for this purpose.

Of course you have heard of my good luck and the honour the Princess has done me. I am now practising with a sheet as Lady Bradford suggested and expect she will stop in for tea later and see how I have got on and put me through my steps. She has helped me also to do all as economically as possible and she says she understands they are sending a carriage for us from Marlborough House.[1] I need have no bouquet unless I wish it and then not a conspicuous one as the ladies in Her Royal Highness's suite rarely have any. So O. and I think I had better not have any as this fact was spoken of. I wrote to thank the Princess this morning and to tell her the deep sense of gratitude I felt for her kindness. O. said it was a very pretty note, and of course I hope it was. Now I must close, but oh, I must not forget to tell you we are expecting the

Landgraf of Hesse and Baron Riedesel Zu Eisenbach to tea here with us tomorrow.

February 12, 1909   **Hyde Park Hotel**

I know this is a holiday at home, dear, dearest Mother—for it is Lincoln's Birthday, isn't it? So many thanks for all your wedding anniversary letters. Yes, it is a whole year—think of it and I am so very blessed and happy with Offley. I hope my sisters may soon get such a good man for each of themselves. I have been having <u>such a nice time in London</u> and my friends, old and new, <u>have been so nice to me</u>. The Countess of Bradford has just been here—she is so kind to me about the Court and I only wish you were all here to see the dresses and I wish my sisters were going with me. This Court we go to is <u>only</u> Diplomatic and Official. So it will be very interesting—I shall have to keep my eyes well open and miss nothing there is to see! I wish you could see the cards, they are as large as a sheet of this writing paper opened and very simply engraved. There is no Crest nor Arms or mark whatever on them. Lady Bradford said she knew I would be watching for them and so she just stopped in at the Lord Chamberlain's office and got them herself for us.

You can have no idea how interested I have become in 'our'!!!! Royal family.

Offley lunched yesterday with Mr. Haldane, the Secretary of State for War, and he enjoyed it very much and hopes 'Mr. H.' was also satisfied. Offley works—just as he plays—<u>hard</u>.

Thank Fanny for her sweet letter. Tell her I wish she was here <u>so often</u> and Betty too, but London is not a pleasant climate in winter—it is however very like Philadelphia.

On Thursday I heard Lady Hanbury-Williams was in London having come unexpectedly on a very sad errand—the illness of her young sister—so I hunted her up at once and found she was quite close at Hans Crescent Hotel with her father. I left a note and a <u>few</u> but choice flowers and the next morning I got the sad letter from her which I enclose you. You cannot think how deeply and truly sorry I feel for her—she has been my <u>kindest</u> friend in Canada and promoted my friendship with the Princess which will surely be of great value to us and I feel I have also made a valuable friend in Lady Bradford. She is so like Grandmama. You can have no conception of the kindness shown me—I feel quite at home at 44, Lowndes Square, and yesterday I met the policeman in the street and he spoke to me as if I was one of the family when I nodded my head.

February 17,1909   **Hyde Park Hotel**

My dear Uncle Joe,

Yesterday opened with glorious sunshine and rather warmer and although we had some cloudiness and a cold change in the afternoon it was beautiful weather for the Opening of Parliament and I had a delightful day with the Hopwoods—big and little—at Sir Francis' rooms at the Colonial Office and saw Their Majesties roll by with their splendid escort, and in the beautiful glass and gilded coach—and I have enough of the child and good German sentiment—steeped in 'Grimm' as I am—to love and enjoy it all thoroughly. It was just like one of our family parties—there were the aunts and uncles, the dependents and the little people. Lady Hopwood had such a good picnic lunch—cakes and meringues, sandwiches and tea and coffee and lemonade, to which nobody did real justice with the excitement of the soldiers, the State coaches, and the Royal carriages and the general gaiety in the street to watch.

Today I lunched with Offley and Major Richardson[2] at the Wellington Club and then went to try on my finery for the 26th and saw about having my photograph taken—sent some port wine to my dear old father-in-law, bought Indian underwear and came back to see the housekeeper about cleaning Offley's breeches and gauntlets between the 23rd and the 26th for he has to go to the Levée on Tuesday afternoon.

We are so tired out with the day's work that we have scarcely seen a play, but we shall have to do so before we leave for India and despite the fact that London has its season in June, the theaters are full and overflowing and first nights—tho' plentiful—are booked

for weeks ahead. Aunt Caroline is going to send Aunt Fanny a life
of Florence Nightingale and write her a letter.

February 25, 1909   **Hyde Park Hotel**

My dearest Aunt,

Offley is at the War Office and hopes to begin today to make
his proper official adieux and keep the rest of the time for packing
and dispatching our things. I feel in a great state of 'rush'—we have
had so many things to get for this journey—and poor Offley to
make another change in his packing because of having to be in
uniform. As Offley is 'in Command' of the Ship I hear I shall have
my own stewardess and <u>he</u> his man servant assigned to him, so I
shall put myself into their hands.

I enclose you bits of newspaper cuttings of the Levée etc. and
all I can get after the Court, too. You have no idea how many notes,
telephones, and messages have come to me soliciting my patronage.
'To have the honour of making Mrs. Offley Shore's bouquet'! 'to
have the honour of dressing Mrs. Offley Shore's hair', and just now
'to have the honour of photographing Mrs. Offley Shore'! etc. etc.
I suppose it is because of the Marlborough House footmen coming
here with notes etc., or the servants in <u>this</u> house who take the
deepest interest, deeper since Offley went so grandly to the Levée
on Tuesday. His great blue cloak, scarlet lining etc. and his headdress, 'not uncovering before the King', always excites the greatest
wonder, and now Offley tells me he does not even bow or kiss his
Sovereign's hand, but merely salutes. I hear he was <u>very much</u>
<u>admired</u> at the Levée for his graceful as well as princely appearance.
So you can imagine how exceedingly proud I feel.

Tomorrow night we shall have quite a little party to see us off—
Florence, Urith, Miss Jardine—just arriving—and Aunt Caroline and
3 of her old servants, and 'Miss Elsie' from the Dressmaker.

February 26, 1909

Dear 'Everybody interested!',

The day has come, the great day! Wheler's son—the footman at
Aunt Caroline's has just brought Offley's things that have been duly
polished since Tuesday's Levée. His State sword, his breeches, his
gloves, his kurta, all his beautiful paraphernalia is side by side with
my beautiful wedding dress with its exquisite lace—my gloves, my
slippers and stockings, my best petticoat, etc., and the veil and
plumes, with which is draped a piece of my lace, Mother's gift last
year on that great day. My diamonds are in the top of my little
brown Vuitton box until the last moment. The electric brougham
comes for us at 8.30 p.m. The Palace doors are not opened until
9.30, but Lady Bradford bade us not leave later than 9.00 and the
family—Urith, Florence and Aunt Caroline and the servants from Connaught Square come over at 8.15 as well as Mary Noel-Hill and Mrs.
Kemble, and Miss Jardine arrives at 8.00 to spend Sunday with us.

The Court train has not arrived yet!!! and I am awaiting it rather
anxiously, and Offley to come back from the War Office and the fitting
for his new Staff uniform. We go after the Court to have me photographed at Lafayette's in Bond Street and six of these photographs I
have already ordered to be sent to you, Betty, to be given to the family.

Later Saturday, February 27

The court was superb. The beauty of the whole scene a never to be
forgotten pageant of light, of colour, of sound, of jewels, of, in short,
all that real pomp, stateliness and splendour can be; and Offley, my
Offley, the most beautiful and without doubt the most graceful and
princely man there; and I felt very, very proud and enjoyed myself
exceedingly, but to begin at the beginning. Between 5 and 6 I began to
lay out our things and at 7 the hairdresser arrived. I was all dressed and
ready for him. He coiffed me so well and so becomingly and fitted my
tiara on perfectly. Offley put me into my gown and after I had sewed
on the family diamonds, dear 'R.J.J.' hooked on my train and we
telephoned for the little party in the drawing room downstairs to come
upstairs. They looked me well over, I put them into the care of our good
servant Francisco, the Italian butler. O. put on my new cloak, he has

just given me, and with Mary and R.J.J. as train-bearers we went downstairs. Your old friend the negro footman assisted to put us into the beautiful electric brougham and we glided away to the Palace—a light fluffy snow was falling and the lights and the troops and the other carriages all hurrying in the same direction made us forget everything but the one errand we were bent upon. Arriving in the Mall we found a double row of carriages parked all the way to Marlborough House, and while we moved slowly up we were constantly entertained by a passing State Coach—a Royal Carriage—the footguards and their band passing, later the Life Guards with the Royal Standard; the little electric lights in other broughams and in ours made us peer into each other's carriages and try to see all the 'war paint'. A few interested people were braving the weather to see the noble swells from the sidewalk and before we knew it we were rolling into the Palace Courtyard, a huge place where the bands of the footguards were again playing. We slipped under the broad porte-cochere where many footmen were lined up and soon were in the great carpeted vestibule, where great welcoming fires were burning in the old and beautiful marble fireplaces, and portraits of the Prince Consort, and palms—and the glittering men and women were making their way to dressing rooms. There, rows of nice maids were ready to take one's wraps, to spread and refold one's train properly, put it over your arm, and send you on your way past the Beefeaters, quantities of footmen and gentlemen ushers directed one upstairs. At the foot of a beautiful broad and grand staircase Offley met me, and we were asked if we were the 'private entrée' and taken upstairs to a white and gold drawing room of exquisite proportions in which rows of chairs, like church, were gradually being filled by the marvelous and magnificent men and women summoned to Their Majesties' first Court. There was a murmur as Offley came in! He said it was caused by me and I said by him, and as we went to our seats the Chamberlain and a Captain Campbell of the 11th Lancers and an A.D.C. to the Prince jumped up and came up to us. I stood for a moment with the three most conspicuous guests in the room. We took our places and sat and watched each other—looking at Orders—gowns, jewels, uniforms, flowers, grace or awkwardness, feet!, feathers, and these were arranged in a hundred different ways, on the whole this uniform headdress being very effective. When the national anthem sounded and we knew Their Majesties were passing into the Throne Room everybody rose, and in a few moments the Chamberlains began sending the ladies in for their Presentations in groups.

And we watched everyone, being ourselves on end seats in a row about the middle of the room. Such beautiful gowns, such wondrous jewels, such smart and brilliant uniforms, such quantities of men. A curious wig and gown just in front of me turned out to be a great Law Lord, and Lady Ashburton on the other side of Offley and in black with beautiful diamonds and soft grey hair I admired so much. At last my turn came and the Chamberlain and Offley went with me to the door of the throne room into which we passed through a corridor so full of wonderful pictures and tall candelabra I forgot all about myself. The orchestra was playing delightfully and the diplomats were grouped on the side of a silken cord in front of the Royal party and the seats were arranged like 'Tannhäuser'. One went quietly around single file until one reached the footmen who spread your train. You handed your card to a gentleman in waiting. We swept slowly in and made two curtseys, one to the King and one to the Queen who wore the marvelous Cullinan Diamond, the hugest thing I have ever seen of the kind. I felt reassured when I saw H.R.H., the Prince, looking at me as he recognized me smilingly and felt very like curtseying to the Princess who nodded and I looked for dear Lady Bradford who was quite far behind looking like grand-mama, all in black with three black plumes and a black veil and in another moment I saw Offley standing with Lord Crewe and waiting for me and just as I joined him a kind and familiar voice over my shoulder said, 'Mrs. Offley Shore'. 'I was so surprised and so proud and you look lovely!' It was Ridgely Carter and Craig Wadsworth running after me to speak to me. I introduced them to Offley and we all went through the beautiful rooms one after another and came round into the upper end of the throne room and met the Pagets, Lady Londonderry, Mrs. George Cornwallis-West and her new daughter-in-law and a host of others to whom I was introduced. We watched the last of the presentations and saw the departure of the Royal party for supper and then made our way to the supper room with the Landgraf of Hesse and Lord Aberdeen and Offley and some other old friend of his with a V.C., at supper. We found Sir Francis and Lady Hopwood looking for us, but I was so taken up with the wonderful gold service with its Dresden flowers and painted pictures, the linen, the china and glass, I could not do it justice. Sir Francis walked about with me and said agreeable things, told me this was the room they smoked in when dining with the King, enjoyed the

pictures and the mantle ornaments and gossiped a little with me,
said Offley should one day be a Field Marshal and was amused
when he overheard some lady wondering what sort of coronet my
tiara was, predicted pleasant things for me and then we all said
good-bye and left, going downstairs with the Aberdeens whom we
found were stopping here. On getting our carriage we drove to Bond
Street to the photographers and you shall see the results. Now good-
night. Very dear love and many wishes I had had my sisters here
whom, however, I can now 'present'.

On 3 March, the day before they were due to sail, Offley went:

to have a last chat with his Father. This was a particularly sad parting
as my Father-in-law is in the very saddest state of health and so
unable to tend to anything whatever that he must be provided for
and taken care of, and Offley was much cast down.

On board H.M. Transport Rohilla, *Offley was Officer Commanding
Troops and Lina therefore found herself in the enviable position of
'Senior Lady'. Here she met, for the first time, the British 'Tommy'.*

In the evenings I overhear the men talking and they seem so good-
natured. They sing and they whistle and they chaff; and this is
'Tommy', this is the rough soldier boy. You should see them with
the babies and the mothers in their part of the ship. I have never
seen greater tenderness.

March 4, 1909   **H.M. Transport Rohilla**

My very dear Father,

    While you, at home, are inaugurating a new President [William
Howard Taft, Ed.] we are just sailing away from dear, familiar, old
Southampton for India. Taking over the Military Command as Offley
does is quite a business and I have been watching him with no small
interest. This table was covered with big official envelopes and

telegrams and there has also been a constant stream of officers to report, to ask for orders, all sorts of things to entertain me while I sat here reading of the doings in Washington, the frightful cold in this good land, the King's departure for Biarritz—all the news of the day, in fact the situation in the Balkans and the awful anxiety of Mrs. Taft not receiving her golden-rod gown until almost the last moment before the day of the ball. Just before we moved away from the Empress Docks I went on deck where I found everybody waving to their friends below, chatting and leave taking, some tearful Mothers whose boys—young subalterns—go off for the first time, the 'second cabin' much more cheerful and the soldiers singing.

In a few moments Offley and the Captain came along and took their places beside me just at the gangway—the order was given to sail, and the two Embarkation officers—Admiral and a Colonel—saluted and bade us goodbye and a safe voyage, shook hands with me, went on land and we were off. One might have thought it was Iceland rather than England we were leaving, so covered with snow and so bitter, bitter cold was it. I went to lunch and dinner and felt most cheery, however, and walked about the ship with Offley to see it all, asked some people in to tea with me, but this was not to last. We had head winds and a bad sea and I came to bed.

Monday, March 8

Here in my cabin have I been and as ill as ever you can imagine. The first day or so nothing would 'stay down' and I was ill from 3 o'clock in the night to 3 o'clock the next day continuously. Finally someone told Offley stout and apples was a good thing and, do you know, I have lived on these until I took a little hot soup yesterday—Sunday.

All this voyage the good spirits of 'Tommy' have kept mine up. They shout and laugh and sing—yes, sing and whistle in concert and are a fine lot of brave fellows. Some of them however don't do as they are told and they get locked up and punished and Offley has to administer their 'Court Martial'!!! Some of them get very sick poor things—and many have never been to sea before.

There are 4 or 5 young officers very full of themselves—the

young dogs! And about 22 or 23 charming officers all told—and all most kind and would do anything for you. You should see the drawing room in the evening—the gentlemen in their scarlet mess dress and the ladies, some in evening dress though I did not dress the evening I was there, and as I have the privilege of setting the fashion I do not think I shall get into evening gowns, other than white and blue ribboned!!!!

We have read such a good article on 'Mr. Roosevelt's Exit'. He will be very missed I fear and it will undoubtedly be a long time before we get such another President.

I hope you will like my photographs and each choose what you wish and order from Lafayette at my expense. Were my diamonds not beautiful and very becoming—and several people admired my earrings exceedingly. What a dream it all seems now. I sent our 'Summons' and the Menu to Aunt Fanny that you might all see how abstemious (!) we were, but there were beautiful wines—and some in a decanter for three bottles exactly like Mother's old Sheffield one—only it was gold—all the service was gold or gold mounted Dresden or English china. The most beautiful thing I ever saw. I think you might put these cards in your book you have of me.

Their arrival in Bombay in the last days of March is recorded in a letter from Offley's Aunt Caroline to Lina's Aunt Fanny. It is one of the few letters preserved in this collection of all those that must have been written by Lina's and Offley's relatives. Clearly Lina and Offley could not keep and carry those that they received.

**17 Connaught Square,
Hyde Park, S.W.**

April 18, 1909

Dear Miss Rosengarten,

I feel very scrupulous in writing to you as a complete stranger, though from your dear niece's constant mention of you I cannot feel so myself and I cannot resist her special request that I should 'put aside all scruples' and tell the kind aunt to whom she is so warmly attached how deeply my brother and I feel the extreme kindness shown by all Lina's family from the very first announcement of the engagement of my nephew to your niece, including the most thoughtful act of sending my brother the cable with the good news we could not have heard in any other way: 'Your son and my daughter landed safely and well at Bombay'. I was greatly touched by it.

And all this only makes me wish the more that I could become personally acquainted with those who have shown such a truly kind feeling towards us. Lina won my heart from the very first and I need not say how fully fulfilled my anticipation of the great comfort and help she already has been and will be to both my brother and myself. She is one of those bright loving spirits which shed sunshine wherever she goes and to Offley I am quite sure she will be the greatest blessing for he is devoted to her and she to him.

Believe me, dear Miss Rosengarten,

Most sincerely yours,

C. Stovin.

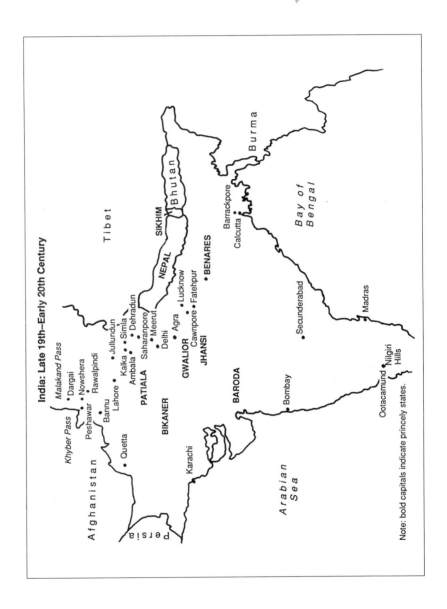

India: Late 19th–Early 20th Century

Afghanistan

Khyber Pass

Malakand Pass
Dargai
Nowshera
Peshawar   Rawalpindi
Bannu
Quetta   Lahore   Jullundun
Kalka   Simla
Ambala   Dehradun
PATIALA   Saharanpore
BIKANER   Delhi   Meerut
Agra
GWALIOR   Lucknow
Cawnpore   Fatehpur
JHANSI
Karachi

Persia

Arabian
Sea

BARODA   Bombay

Tibet

NEPAL
SIKHIM
Bhutan

Burma

BENARES

Barrackpore
Calcutta

Bay of
Bengal

Secunderabad

Madras

Ootacamund   Nilgiri
Hills

Note: bold capitals indicate princely states.

India: April 1909 to January 1912

Offley and Lina would spend the next three years in India until January 1912, when Offley would take a year's leave. Offley, in charge of training, would be preparing for war. In January 1910 there was talk of war with Germany in two years' time with the possibility of an invasion of Britain. International unrest in Europe and social unrest in Britain might make it impossible for George V to attend the Delhi Durbar, the assemblage of Princes in honour of his coronation, set for December 1911.

The marriage would be a complete success: 'It would be difficult to discover two happier than we are: I love my house and my life out here if Offley is with me, and I am very lost when he is not', and often he was not. His duties would take him away on tour for as long as six months at a time. There is evidence that while on these tours he would write to her regularly and frequently, but only three of these letters have been found, written over a period of five days.

Something, however, was missing: 'I long for the most expensive thing in the world, children of our own'. And frequently expressions of nostalgia and home-sickness would appear, particularly on the occasion of family deaths: of her mother, of Offley's father and mother, of uncles and aunts, and she would wish for Offley some appointment nearer home, which would be unlikely since he was an officer of the Indian Army and not of the British Army. Frequently she would invite, indeed plead with, members of her family to come out and visit them.

She would continue her weekly letters to each member of her family: outgoing mails on Thursday; incoming mails on Sunday. To these would now be added letters to her Father-in-law and her Aunt Caroline, both jealously demanding their own. She would

*comment, sometimes with great disapproval, on political and
social affairs in India, the United States and Britain.*

*A few days after their arrival in India Offley and Lina were
in Delhi, where the 18th (Prince of Wales' Own) Tiwana Lancers,
the regiment with which Offley had served from 1885 until his
recent promotion to the Staff, was then stationed.*

*Lina recorded their stay with the Regiment in the following
letter. The siege to which she referred was that of 1857 during
the Mutiny, and the Durbar described to her by Offley and Colonel
Pirie was that of 1903 in honour of the accession of Edward VII,
when Lord Curzon was Viceroy. Lady Curzon, the Vicereine, was
a countrywoman of Lina's, the eldest daughter of Levi Leiter,
co-founder with Marshall Field of the Chicago store of that name.
The 18th Tiwana Lancers provided the escort to the Commander-
in-Chief, Lord Kitchener. The King was represented by the Duke
of Connaught.*

| | **The Commanding Officer's House,** |
| **April 2nd, 1909** | **Delhi, India** |

My dearest Aunt,

At last I actually feel we, I, am settling down and adapting myself
to the place and circumstances for it is a very new life indeed for me
to begin even at my age, or young as I am, sleeping with all the doors
opening on a veranda and surrounded by a garden at one end of which
an army of black servants live. Nothing could be nicer than coming
to see the Regiment and visiting in the Commanding Officer's
bungalow, a long, low stone house white-washed both inside and out.

The Compound, as the garden enclosures are called in India, is
just now brilliant with hollyhocks and many other English flowers.
Yellow roses in vines and all blooming in such mass and luxury
but the grass, grown with such care on a small part of the garden
is parched and yellow already. The glorious green of native trees
is amazing, however. I find Mrs. Pirie and Colonel Pirie most agreeable and almost oracles upon the art and history of Delhi, which is
very beautiful and exquisite. Yesterday we went in the Brake, four-
in-hand, through the City, driving through the great gates of the
Fort after having gone all around the lines of the Siege[1] and getting

Journey

k to see the statue of John Nicholson, a splendid
onze, so calm and dignified. The statue sur-
igh stone base poses the man facing or rather
ward the Kashmir Gate and the beautiful battlemented
walls of Delhi at the part he stormed. The most delightful parks
and gardens surround the many interests and these are constantly
not only well kept, but being added to. We got down and went
inside the Fort and walked through the Diwan-i-Am and saw the
white marble dais where the famous Peacock Throne[2] once stood.
The Diwan-i-Am itself is of an exquisite colour of red stone, the
colour we call Indian red, the Saracen arches, the graceful and light
carving everywhere, the stone fret work in the windows is all superb,
and opposite this is the white and mellow marble palace with the
celebrated Diwan-i-Khas. Nothing, nothing that I have ever seen or
heard of could exceed or match the beauty of this. The same graceful
carving is here enhanced by being overlaid with gold, the borders
or tracery of flowers or birds or conventional designs made more
beautiful than ever by being inlaid with different coloured stones,
or painted in such delicate and wonderful colours that even the most
insensitive are wrapped in wonder, in delight, at their beauty. The
dying light of the glowing hot sun made all a little pink and as
suddenly as it dropped from the horizon the blue light of the moon
and a mist of dust across the land made a marvelous sight. The
dimensions are exquisite, the shape, the colour, the irregularity of
the facade on the river side, here a great bay window of fret-work,
there a balcony, all is beyond description only as Shah Jehan has
written on its walls in letters of gold, 'If there is a Heaven on Earth
it is here! It is here!' For architecturally not even Heaven itself
could have anything more lovely. O. and Colonel Pirie were full of
its history and then they described to me how it must have been,
hung with silks and filled with ladies and noblemen covered with
wonderful raiment and glittering with jewels and pearls until they
came themselves in their gorgeous native uniforms (O. as staff officer
to the Commander in Chief) to the great Durbar. Here in the Diwan-
i-Khas once more hung with many wondrous silks and lit magnificently
by electricity the Duke and Duchess of Connaught held a Court and
beyond, enclosed by a wooden structure reaching from the Diwan-
i-Am to the Diwan-i-Khas a great ball was going on. Imagine the
sight if you can and you can well believe that I stood silent as they

spoke. They described my countrywoman—Mary Curzon—a mass of jewels, sitting there thin and beautiful, for already traces of illness were plainly to be seen and you can know the pleasure and the wonderful luck I call mine—I felt as I stood there.

This afternoon we go to the bazaars in another part of the city and then to Polo in the evening and shall drive if we get tired of that. Tomorrow the Regiment are to parade and do some tent pegging. This the Colonel has arranged in our honour. After it I am to be presented to the Native Officers and it will be a little ceremony generally. In the evening we leave for Meerut to visit Gen'l and Mrs. Nixon and then on to Simla, the 8th, to get settled and any travelling or further sight seeing we shall leave until cooler weather, as the heat and dust have affected my throat and I could scarcely speak this morning and it has been most distressing. The doctor of the Regiment was sent for by O. at once so that with a gargle and a lozenge and some cooling medicine I am already better, but we have decided to make no efforts, however eager I may be, during such heat and until I am a little more acclimated. Very dear love to each and all and tell Uncle Joe to bring you here in the winter. It is well worth the coming and we shall happily see you are made comfortable. The Anglo-Indian newspapers have all the best news of the world, American too, and here we get many English newspapers so, in fact, are little more than a fortnight behind Europe in most reading and intelligence, but the living is very different.

Ten days later Lieutenant Colonel Pirie was promoted to command a Brigade and Lina had this to comment on the appointment of the Regiment's next Commanding Officer:

Major Grimston, the officer junior to Offley has just been appointed Commanding Officer. Offley, had he wished it, would no doubt have got the command, but he is looked upon as far too clever a man to be anywhere but at headquarters and I am much better pleased as I should hate being with any regiment and it would separate us so much more than the present billet. It's a very good thing to be quite content with what one has got, isn't it? Well, I for one am.

Within a few days they had reached Simla where Lina would spend much of her time in India. The seat of the Central Government of British India was then located in Calcutta.[3] In the hot season the Government moved to Simla in the Himalayas. Offley's duties were such that in the cool season he spent many months touring, inspecting, organising and attending manoeuvres. As a result, little time was spent in Calcutta.

From the moment she arrived in Simla Lina began a busy life. There would be the finding of accommodation and then the painting of it, furnishing it and wallpapering it, and the engagement and management of servants to staff it. This would be true even of hotel accommodation, which provided little more than walls, a roof, charpoys and a dining room. There would be the care of clothes: mending, darning, 'sewing new cuffs on Offley's shirts', even making a new evening gown 'over one of my old foundations'. Calling and being called upon. Entertaining and being entertained: 'everyone delights in coming to our dining room and I hear it goes by the name of the most agreeable room in Simla', and her cook the best cook and her gowns the subject of envious glances. These were often presents from Philadelphia and she would have to tell her family that 'I have grown very much larger round the waist, round the hips too a little and across the back'. She carefully followed the fashion magazines from Paris and ordered some of her clothes there: the Paris houses handled orders more promptly and efficiently than those of London or Philadelphia, she found. But it was not only gowns that came from home: a steady stream of requests went back to Philadelphia for everything from sunburn cream through typewriters to bedsteads. Living must have been very much more comfortable than for many of their friends and acquaintances. Finally there was the 'Simla Season' with all the pomp and ceremony centred on Vice-Regal Lodge of which, it will be remembered, Lina had been thinking before she left England. In this she and Offley were fully involved.

While Offley's letters to Lina have not survived, obviously because of their constant movement, those he wrote to her family have, and from these it is apparent that she was an excellent house manager, with everything so organised as to be ready at the shortest notice for Offley to go off on tour or for both of them to make a move. Apparent too is his admiration for her ability to make new acquaintances, to gain people's confidence and to disarm opposition.

Most frequently he corresponded with Uncle Joe. A close relationship had developed early between Offley and Joseph G. Rosengarten. From the beginning he addressed him as 'My dear Uncle Joe' while his father-in-law he always addressed as 'My Dear Mr. Sinnickson'. Joseph Rosengarten had fought in the American Civil War and this formed a bond between them. He had a very wide range of interests and supplied Offley with The Scientific American. *They discussed military matters, social affairs, national and international politics, technical developments and new inventions.*

Lina gave her first impressions of living in Simla in the following letter.

April 11, 1909   **The Grand Hotel, Simla**

My dear Uncle Joe,

Simla is very beautiful—<u>very</u> and I shall no doubt enjoy my new and varied experiences, but big as the billet is I think I shall never really care to live in the East. In the plains the birds and flowers were wonderful. I could scarcely believe it when I saw parrots in all their variegated colouring hopping about on the trees—and monkeys frightening the dear little English ponies by scampering across the road as a squirrel does with us in America—and the quantities of black servants forever salaaming. Yesterday I had a carpenter and his attachés—3 in all—and a curtain hanger with our Rickshaw coolies—5 in all—and some servants to sweep and another lot to push boxes and furniture into place—17 at one time in these rooms—and it took the whole afternoon to get anything done. If 'Memsahib' spoke to one then down comes the carpenter for a little gossip to ask his friend the floor sweeper or the hanger of curtains what the conversation is in their departments. More salaams and they return to their work. Our rooms are beautifully large and have an exclusive view of two different amphitheatres.

Today O. and I went to Church, a quaint scene. The coolies and rickshaws all waiting in a broad dusty enclosure outside the little English church nestled against the hillside—another shed held the

ponies and the syces standing about in groups and Ayahs with their
babies all watching the English crowd come and go in Easter bonnet
and attire. After church we went up the side of Jakko to the Chief's,
Lord Kitchener's, house—a beautiful spot—the best situation possible—
but there are no great houses in Simla—and such houses as we see
at Narragansett or other watering places in America are palatial in
comparison. On the other hand the brilliant colouring, the liveries
and the numbers of servants who always accompany one everywhere
lend an importance entirely undue and yet sumptuous and dignified
for they really are servants. Good-night. Send me any nice French
novels and keep me always in touch with what you all do. Nothing
of home is trivial or dull.

April 18, 1909 **Grand Hotel, Simla**

My very dear Father,

The Ledger [a Philadelphia newspaper—Ed.] can be sent to us
simply addressed 'Simla, India', for Offley, I do assure you, in India—is
as well known as Lord K.

Would you be good enough to buy and send out to us here the
little travelling typewriter 'The Standard Folding Typewriter' weigh-
ing 6 lbs. and costing $50 (it might be less now as it was just out
when we saw it and by now the price might be less I should think).
We saw it at 911 Walnut Street—the Liberty Typewriter Co.—and
as we have seen nothing in London or Bombay to touch it for light-
ness and weight we think we had better have you send us one—
perhaps some extra ribbons would be nice—and let me know our
indebtedness and I will settle with you.

We are packing up to send to you today my photos taken as I
appeared at the Drawing Room at Their Majesties' first Court. The
jewels, tiara, and the beautiful wreath of diamonds and the fan-shaped
brooch worn on the front of my bodice—in the photos—were
Offley's Grandmother's and lent me by Aunt Caroline. They are
wonderfully beautiful and the tiara was re-arranged to fit my head
and suit my hair by the French jeweler 'Chaumet' now in Bond

Street. I wore your wedding gift, my earrings and pendant and the
one or two precious pieces of my own made of my Grandmother's
gift and the little scarf pin the Prince gave Offley. How long ago
it now seems! But the brilliant picture, the sight is still very vivid
in my mind and memory, and I hope I shall go to many more and
have the pleasure of 'presenting' my sisters some day.

The Certificates give us the entrée to any court in Europe or in
Japan or in China.

India—in the few weeks I have been in it—impresses me very
seriously in many ways, but most of all I am struck by the primitiveness with and in which the Anglo-Indians [Lina means a Briton
long resident in India, not someone of mixed birth, a later usage.—
Ed.] are content to live. The bungalows and houses, however much
they appear comfortable, beautiful or roomy or the reverse, are all
alike very poorly and lightly built and the modern conveniences for
baths, electric lighting etc. are nil. One has to have two or three or
even four times the servants one has in Europe, for one fellow sweeps
and the next fellow is a 'caste' above and so he only dusts! Another
waits but does not clean—another cleans, and this one draws water—
still another washes and so on and even in an hotel one's servants
do almost everything, the hotel providing you with rooms and food
and light (the latter very sparsely) and some bedclothes and furniture
which needs much augmenting to settle us down and live. So we,
two in family though we be, have now: one man for butler and
valet, one man, Bearer, who directs the whole family and is to look
after the ponies, Walia, Offley's old servant, a huge grand fellow
dressed entirely in white, he carries a walking stick and smokes a
Hookah. He walks out with me whether I ride, drive, or walk and
I feel so funny and think I must look like a little dwarf and the big
black giant. Offley will make you a drawing of us!

Then we have 4 syces for the rickshaws, a dhobie—or laundry-
man—and tomorrow my 'seamstress man', or dersi, comes. I have not
yet got an Ayah or a woman servant to wait upon me as they neither
sew nor wash nor draw water nor clean, only stand around, brush one's
hair, lay out one's clothes etc., put on one's shoes, and Fernandez, our
butler and valet, does all I need. And when I want a woman I have
for the present secured the services for special occasions of Peliti's—the
proprietor of this Hotel—nice English housekeeper—a very pleasant
oldish woman, and picturesque as an Ayah may be, I do not take

to them and as one's servants—all 7 of them—sit about us in the Verandahs—I feel I don't want, or need, more.

On the 30th the Viceroy and Lady Minto come here and on the 24th of May there will be the Levée and on the 28th the Viceregal Ball, when the Season really begins. Meantime I am getting our rooms in order, buying dusters, and glass cloths, covering furniture, sewing, ordering lamps (which are <u>horribly</u> expensive) and a little linen and a tea-set (China) and such things as Indian 'light' housekeeping requires; beginning to make my visits and my visiting list etc. etc. and also interesting myself in Offley's work and those he is particularly thrown with.

April 22, 1909   **Simla**

My Dearest Aunt,

As the English or foreign mail only goes out from here once a week I am going to scribble a few hasty lines to you! We are gradually getting settled and Simla for grandeur and beauty and immenseness and vastness of mountain scenery I have never seen <u>anything</u> like. The great snow mountains at a distance, Offley thinks, of some 80 or 120 miles are a most wonderful setting for the foreground and the glinting, setting sun turns them many colors of gold and often a pink glow comes just as the sun departs. The bare hills grow darker, those covered with deodars, which are so feathery and graceful, darker still and one just looks in amazement at the beauty, the hugeness and the vastness of such a glorious sight. It is impossible to describe it.

I have nearly 200 calls to make! Think of it, as the newcomers call first, fortunately 'little people' may be called upon by post, but it keeps me constantly on the go, and constantly writing and keeping account of one's visiting list. Then every morning I have to give orders for the day to my servants. Today some window glass has to be mended: small panes were broken by the hail storm a few days ago, and it takes two carpenters and a sweeper for this job. Our horses arrived today. Their saddles and bridles are kept here, to be hung in that part of our balcony we have screened off as a

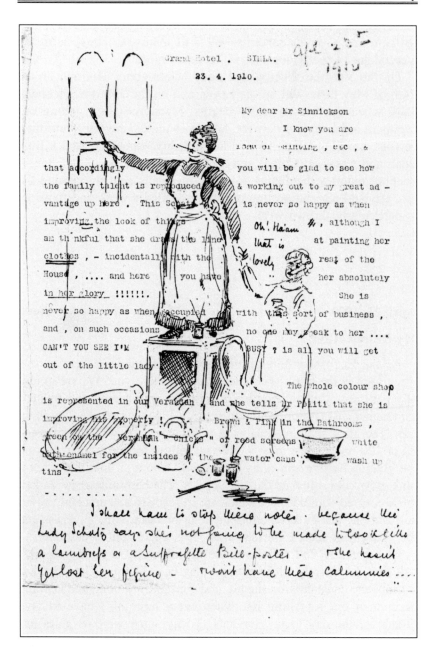

*Lina, on pedestal, and Amy, 'housecleaning and scrubbing' their rooms
in the Grand Hotel, Simla.
(From a letter by Offley to his father-in-law, Mr. Sinnickson.)*

room or office for the servants to clean lamps, boots, shirts, etc. In another corner in a cupboard are kept the tea things, so now perhaps you can picture to yourself a little of the primitiveness of our Indian living, though to come into my drawing room you would think you were in London. Offley is delighted with the way I have arranged it; its clean and bright chintz covers, my baby grand piano, the books and bookcases and our photographs and lamps and tables. There are chairs, tables and lights just where one is most comfortable to read, chat, sew or play, and then I have a table <u>full</u> of flowers and fine brass bowls, two with maidenhair ferns, three with flowers; lilacs are to come today and I have been having yellow jasmine, and then the room is so delightfully large. Most Indian rooms are though Simla differs in this respect so that we are particularly fortunate in ours. Would you be so kind as to order 300 of my visiting cards and 600 of Offley's at Dreka's for me and beg them to send them out to us at once by post?[4] They made our last plates and they also use a very <u>thin</u> card which I like and find most useful.

Gen. Sir Beauchamp Duff went home yesterday and <u>we hear</u> to be made Military Secretary at the India Office. If this is true we may soon hope to see ourselves in another land and in a shorter time than we anticipated. Personally I should like to see O. in Whitehall or abroad as Military Attaché at an important court.

I am <u>so glad</u> to see by Mother's letters she is better and I do trust she will guard against doing any running about. I am so distressed at the court photos being sent out here. I hope when you do see them and get them you will like them and order any pose you prefer directly from Lafayette's.

Letter from Offley to Uncle Joe

May 2, 1909   **Simla**

I wonder whether you can let me know the very latest about progress in the matter of 'Wireless Telegraphy' on your side, and particularly 'Pack Wireless' for the army? Our people here are entirely 'tied up' financially by Morley and his Radicals and we will get no money for anything: India is waiting on England, to see what they evalue, and England with her excellent roads is not so vitally interested as we are in the Pack system.

To my mind, the situation admits of no delay, for this, for a time at all events, will be the only system that the Indigenes are not thoroughly au fait with, and the severance of communications is the all important question of the day, particularly for Europeans in Asia.

I should also like to get hold of the latest ideas of training in the army. I find if we want to communicate with Col. James at Washington, the official channel is Indian Army Headquarters—India Office—Foreign Office/War Office—Washington and vice versa and you can imagine the delay! James is evidently under very strict orders as regards to communications with any 'outsiders' such as we are. Directly we get our Indian section of the General Staff and can get this Imperial G.S. working, we shall hope to abolish all this sort of nonsense.

Of course we are furious about the stupid red tape at Home, but it is very largely due to political control.

My office hours are 10:30 to 4:30, but I ride up for lunch and stay in office till 5:00 p.m. then L. and I go out and explore the beauties of the land, she in a rickshaw and I riding. Yesterday we had a stiff pull up Jakko and stood near the monkey house outside the Patiala and Dholpur houses[5] at about 6:30 p.m. on a lovely sunlit afternoon, admiring the play of light and shade among the Deodars (most graceful of cedars) and ilex: watching the insolent monkey people and gazing down upon Simla 1,000 feet below us as from a balloon. The distant views too were lovely.

We paid a visit the day before to the Kasumpti Bazaar very nearly the most S.E. point of Simla and before that explored Elysium hill and Prospect hill, also dropped down to Annandale, 1,000 feet below and so the little lady is gaining some idea of the place. We have also paid a visit to the tunnel just beyond the Sanjauli Bazaar and peeped out beyond onto the road leading to Mashobra.

The pony I got for her from the regiment seems very quiet and has good paces and I hope shortly may be fit for her to ride. My own Arab is I hope coming up from Meerut, and so we hope to have fixed up the Transportation question. Everything here is taxed very heavily by the Municipality, rickshaws, servants, dogs and octroi duty is levied on every import and relatively to what I remember, the cost of living has gone up to about what we had to contend with in Canada, which for this country is appalling.

Lina has made our rooms quite charming, with her usual taste, but thinks me unnecessarily insistent upon the desirability of economy and self-denial! You can imagine her with her artistic tastes puttering around the bazaar selecting the very best examples of brass, wood carving, embroideries, etc., etc., and wishing to convert the hotel room into an Oriental Art Museum! She is gradually learning something of the art of bargaining with the most expert thieves alive! But she says you would be much worse than she is, were you let loose among all these beautiful things and you know what a first-class hand she is at excuse and repartee!! She has not yet been inside Schreibers, the Far Eastern Art Emporium, or the local jewelers, Hamiltons.

May 16, 1909   **Simla**

My very dear Father,

This last ten days O. has been away with a number of officers to Quetta and to the Afghan frontier to see the Staff College Offley brought into existence and for a Staff Ride and as Asst. Quarter Master General of Training to see what sort of things are being done and suggest others, and how I miss him day or night. I hate going into our rooms even though I have the very sweetest of young companions in Valerie Bingham, a girl of 20 with big brown eyes and golden hair and a genuine delight in everything. Last night was the fashionable night of the 'Gaiety Theatre' and the Simla Amateur Dramatic Society gave a little play (very badly) before the Viceroy and Lady Minto and all of the smart society of Simla. Valerie and I and a Captain Joslin went and it was amusing from beginning to end. The arriving there in our rickshaws, the lights, the lamps, the colour and the babble of the natives and the servants and then looking at everyone in the tiny theatre.

Offley was on the staff of the Indian Staff College when it opened in 1905, but it is an example of Lina's wifely exaggeration to say that he 'brought it into existence'.

May 19, 1909   **Simla**

Dearest Aunt,

Many and many are the thanks and blessings upon your dear head for the weekly letter that I never fail to find in my home mail when the day that brings it—Sunday—comes round. The season has begun in real earnest and one is asked out to dine almost every night. At dinner parties one has either music or bridge afterwards or you go on to a play given by the Simla Amateur Dramatic Society—the theater is a nice, little old-fashioned looking place—red and gold with its royal box in the center and one goes more for the fun of the Rendezvous de Societé than the play or the players—tho' I am told as the season goes on both these last become very much better, even clever. Tomorrow is the Viceregal garden party. On the 24th the Levée, when I hope I shall see the noble swells and the native princes who are here—in their court dress—with the huge retinues that accompany them. Even O. drives up in my rickshaw with the 4 jhampanies in their claret and green and gold liveries and his magnificent servant to be at his side to wait upon him.

As the Duffs are now going home they have offered us the house as it stands—bed and bedding, carpets, furnishings etc.—almost all their Indian curios and collections and while we are undecided about taking any house in Simla just yet or for another 6 months—for various reasons—partly because we are very comfortable in these most beautiful rooms and partly because, unless Betty came out to spend a year with me, I should be so lonely in a house on a steep mountainside all the day long—for Offley could not possibly come home to lunch.

I can't but wonder and wish that Sir Beauchamp Duff will perhaps get Offley into some 'home' appointment before long—oh, if only a change of government would come in! and the 'Literatures' playing at statesmen have done and the socialists grow sensible. I see they are going to tax tea in America—what good then was all that fuss years ago about tea!!? with a King President—as they call it in Europe, and without representation—!!!![6]

I do wonder if you would be so kind as to send me ½ dozen bottles of Morgan's delightful cold cream. I brought out 2 new bottles when I came and we have found it so good and so refreshing and Offley was so soothed by using it after the dreadful sunburn he got when he was away on the staff ride. I also want a good French fashion plate—one of the very latest with pictures of evening gowns and garden party gowns, hats etc. as I can get together my things very nicely sewed etc. by the Durzie or tailor man here if I have a pretty picture to copy. I wrote to Fanny some time ago and asked her to get me a fashion plate she knew of. I used to like the one we subscribed to for so many years, but I cannot remember the name and address in Paris or I should write directly for it myself. It had patterns and receipts and all sorts of things and as my Bearer or Butler speaks French it might prove useful in lots of ways.

P.S. Did I write you of going to the Sipe Fair? when Offley was away this took place at a deep flat place at the very bottom of the steepest 'khud' near Mashobra—a long and beautiful drive of about 7 miles of trees and flowering shrubs and plants and the huge rock sides of the mountain and the masses of splendid colours in the women's clothes and men's turbans, walking in groups the whole way out. Occasionally a local Native Noble or Rajah on horseback with all his retinue following, and when we arrived at the fair the group of natives 'some in rags, some in tags, and some in velvet gowns'—with a quaintly carved old wood temple as a center, and a huge and gaily painted white elephant which had brought a neighboring magnate— with its brilliantly dressed syce and its own scarlet accoutrements. We walked in and out among the booths where native sweet-meats and jewelry and all the ordinary wares of India were for sale, and seated on a bank in the most brilliant of coloured veils and coats and massed with silver jewelry, earrings, necklaces, nose rings and talismans and anklets were the women who had come or were brought to be sold or exchanged as wives.

We wandered in and out of the crowds quite safely and I felt as if I was part of a light opera. The women on the whole were very pretty with monstrous eyes and fine cast of countenance—good faces.

I wonder if Uncle Joe wants any treasures of this wondrous East for any of his museums or libraries.

May 20th, 1909   **Simla**

My very dear Father,

This is mail day so I want to hurry with many letters. Sir Beauchamp Duff has been appointed Military Secretary at the India Office in London. What did I say in my last letter to you! But I believe he was anxious to have got an extension of his time out here and Douglas Haig, Gen'l. Douglas Haig, O.'s friend at home, has been made Chief of Staff, a strange choice for he is, I believe, a most difficult man to get on with men, and I find him good-looking, agreeable, but so dictatorial and tactless, however he is a great Cavalry Officer.

Next Thursday Lord Kitchener's Military Secretary, Capt. Fitzgerald, and an old friend of O's, is coming to dine with us. On Monday Offley goes to Lord Minto's levée in his full dress Staff uniform, wearing it for the first time. It is nothing like so magnificent as his uniform of the '18th' but very becoming, dark blue, and gold lacings and scarlet Staff insignia with a silk sash and tassels, very stately and dignified.

May 30, 1909   **Simla**

My dearest Aunt,

The weather is now warm and the Season is in full swing so that I find reading and writing have to be done with a religious regularity during certain fixed hours or none is done and even these fixed times are open to the frequent interruptions of visitors or servants with notes and messages. Last Wednesday we had the honour of dining with Their Excellencies Lord and Lady Minto and a small but distinguished party. The beautiful fashion in which everything was done, the perfection of an English great house such as Viceregal Lodge is, was I need scarcely assure you fully enjoyed and most thoroughly appreciated by us both. Our welcome was most delightful and the Viceroy introducing me to Lord Kitchener left nothing to be desired. I enjoyed myself thoroughly and as I wrote a long letter to Mother about it I will not repeat that experience to you.

I am deeply troubled at the news Fanny writes me of Miss Freeman and Mother having had a row and parted. Such patience and ability as dear Miss Freeman has shown in these long and trying years justifies some lapses from always controlling one's tongue and temper don't you think? and I suppose that there has been some too plain speaking?

June 9th, 1909   Simla

Dear Aunt Fanny of mine,

Well, we are gay, dining, dancing, picnics, luncheons, polo, cricket, a Horse Show and the day is spent for me changing from one costume to another.

The other day I went to a small Garden Party and met the Native Prince whose house I'd thought I sh'd. so much like to have, and I told the gentleman so and they have offered it to me to live in whenever they are not there! Of course one cannot nor does not, accept such things, but had it been pearls or rubies I don't know that I could so easily have said, 'Oh, thank you, no.'

June 11

This is the night of The State Ball, and O. tells me we must leave at 9 o'clock as it will be one long line of 3 rows or 4 of rickshaws the whole way from here to Viceregal Lodge, or nearly, and from today forward until the 4th of July we have a dinner to go to every night.

I assure you it is dreadful and I am dreading it, but Lord K.'s dinner I am exceedingly anxious to go to, to see his house and his beautiful things etc. The weather is as damp and warm and steamy as Newport ever was.

My dear little pony has a sore back and so I must content myself with a rickshaw drive or a short walk. O. very busy at the office and fuming because he does not get enough foreign news or foreign newspapers and yet he gets special telegrams every day. I hope it will not rain tonight. More tomorrow or next day when I have been to the Ball.

June 15, 1909

Four days after the most beautiful Ball I have ever seen. We started with the heavens full of shining stars, and lightning, predicting a storm, only heightened the beauty of our drive up to the Viceregal Lodge, for it lit up with a marvelous beauty the trees, the distant mountains and the immediate foreground full of uniforms and ladies in wonderful evening wraps with tiaras or headdresses of ribbons and flowers, so much the fashion of this day, and the turbans of our Jhampanis and syces and the variegated liveries, white and much gold predominating. Then there were the ragged rickshaw men of the hired sort and all along the roadside the native men and women and children crouching, standing and some perched in trees to see the huge long cortege of 4 or 500 vehicles and many a gentleman was riding his Arab with his syce at his side. We arrived just in time for the Royal Quadrille which was danced with much grace and dignity by Her Excellency looking most lovely in white satin and diamonds. I was joined by the German Consul General upon entering the ball-room and he was resplendent as the Germans always are in gold lace and orders—a great tall blasé man, who plays and paints delightfully I am told. Then one after another my partners sought me out. The Viceroy sent for me to dance with him and came down from the dais from which Lady Minto bowed me a charming welcome and his Excellency shook hands with me, much to O.'s pride and satisfaction and then we, Offley and I, danced. We were dancing together for the first time and it was perfectly delightful and not yet a crowded floor. Do you know Her Excellency told me later that we had a great many pretty speeches made of us as, 'Such a charming pair opened the Valse'. You have no idea of the fairyland on the Terraces where millions of every coloured lights were hung in the trees and bushes and where the blue silk, draped from pole to pole as a sort of screen was simply enclosing the terrace gardens where roses and flowers and palms and trees <u>really</u> grew. Chairs and tables with cigars and cigarettes with charming smoking paraphernalia were placed here and there and occasionally there was a scarlet or gold-coloured silk shamiana furnished like a little drawing room. The lightning continuing lit up the Himalayas in all the glory and grandeur of the coming storm as well as the uniforms of the officers, scarlet, blue and gold, the Justices in black silk with large rosettes at the backs of their necks and knee breeches, a knight's black velvet with steel buttons here and there or the claret and blue and gold of a Huzzar mingling with the lovely shades of the ball gowns, the glistening diamonds and pearls and the turbans of the Native Nobles and their costumes, like Walter Crane's picture book—here a Bluebird and there an Ali Baba or some other Prince of fairy tale familiarity in silks wrought with gold and sewn with jewels. I assure you I can never forget and am delighted to have seen and taken part in it.

Good-bye for the moment and do try to come out to us. <u>You</u> w'd. enjoy it here above all.

Letter from Offley to Charles Sinnickson

June 24, 1909   **Simla**

My dear Mr. Sinnickson,

At last I feel that I have in part, come up to Lina's expectations of me (of course only in part). The little lady, having got into touch with the Mintos and conquered them with ridiculous ease, attached a few 'members of Council' (equals Ministers) to her train and a handful of Generals with scarcely an elevation of the Supercilious Eyebrow, still looked around for the most difficult old Tiger in the Jungle, to wit Lord Kitchener. I won't say she was exactly petulant because we didn't dine there the night after she met him at the Court Ball, but I could see there was thunder in the air. Well, last night we <u>were</u> at the Maneater's Den, at <u>last</u>!! And despite the fact of our being very little people who had just permission to breathe in a retired corner, this young daughter of yours sidled up to the Man of Cross Green Eyes and gazing up into his ugly face about four feet above her, babbled sweetly to him in French about Art and lispingly plastered him with flattery! I being kept hard at it in the dancing room by the Monster, who hunted me out of comfortable chairs and the restful society of the more conspicuous Dowagers, to trot out all his young lady guests and step up to my chin to his infernal music. You will see by this what the game was! The little lady played it so well, that Tiger-ji capitulated after some preliminary growls and suspicious glaring into the simple and childlike one's entrancing face and finally, contrary to all prognostications, consented to be fed one day soon, in our humble abode.

Up went the winning No. to the top of the Telegraph Board and I had some difficulty in keeping the victorious one within decent reach of earth.

Lord Kitchener, who only consorts with acting Kings and Deputy Assistant Duchesses, over whom all Simla trips over its own feet to get near and catch a cat green glance of approbation, that <u>he</u> should have been lassoed and brought to heel is, you must admit, quite an achievement!! Now, perhaps, I shall have some measure of rest and be allowed a few evenings off in an armed chair!

I expect Lina will be giving you a different account of the whole thing so I thought I ought to let you know the true facts of the case before she got her hand in! Because once she starts talking, there is never a chance of a word in edgewise.

June 27, 1909

Dear Uncle Joe,

A great many thanks to you for your gift and for the many letters and magazines—general information and pleasure and thoughtfulness you bestow upon us. I have already tucked away a number of little gifts I propose sending out to each and all in America—and I am awaiting some pretty things from Kashmir for my approval to send at the same time. As I wrote you, we dined last Wednesday with Lord K. when the great man was particularly charming to me and has consented to dine with us. I had rather hoped it could be arranged for July 4th [American Declaration of Independence], because last year I instituted in our little household always entertaining on that date, and for Offley the 18th of June [Battle of Waterloo] but this year it could not be as the Commander in Chief has so many engagements he reserves Sundays to go to his Bungalow at Mashobra—however the preliminary arrangements are well on the way. One of his A.D.C.s lunches with me on Friday to arrange the date and take my small list of guests for his Excellency to approve or change. Gen'l Sir B. Duff, who is good to me like a father, tells me the honour is a very personal one and we hear the Viceroy has said, 'Why am I not asked to dine with Mrs. Offley!' Very flattering of course. We are in hopes we can tuck a letter in K's pocket to you when he goes through U.S.A. but he is a very shy man and dreads to be made much of, preferring greatly to be allowed to go quietly on his way yet always very agreeable and enjoying people.

June 29, 1909

I am unexpectedly going through what Clara and Christine did when their husbands were suddenly obliged to go to hospital, only fortunately, thank the Good God, it is not appendicitis in Offley's case but a distressing thing known as 'Piles' and not mentioned in polite society unless people are—as I am—7000 or 8000 miles away from those kind ones who help one so bravely over the lonely and anxious days. In Offley's case, he has never had such a thing before and fortunately it is an 'outside' one and only one and the doctor says no danger of any more and that we are wise and brave to have it cut away at once. So last night we drove out quietly to the Walker Hospital after tea at the Hickmans', with Walia and my servants having ridden over earlier with O.'s clothes and toilet articles etc.—and there I left him in the sweet hospital to feed upon low diet and be ready for the surgeon in the morning while I had to come back, dress for dinner and receive 6 guests whom we were taking on to our box at the play. Offley insisted upon me going on with our little party which after all cheered me. The night was fairy like and wonderful in its beauty, half light and half white mist—making a curious effect as if we were dining on clouds—and the play, 'The Country Girl' was exceptionally well done. Their Excellencies greeted me as we came into our box, and bows and smiles from the other boxes and the stalls raised my spirits and I was up and off at the appointed time to O. this morning and was allowed to go to him and found him just coming out of ether—not ill—but a little vague and big tears rolling down his cheeks which he told me afterwards were because he could not remember where I was. I confess I miss your devoted kindnesses at such times but I am very thankful for much, as our friends are legion.

Offley to Uncle Joe

'Private not for circulation'

Sunday, July 25, 1909   **Simla**

My dear Uncle Joe,

A grand consignment of books from the War Dept. and Free Library for which I am very much obliged and will have transferred to the various officers who will be interested in them.

I have been quite busy this last week on the subject of wireless or 'Radio-Telegraphy' as they now call it out here: but the Finance Department are throwing everything out, on the score of no funds. I have also been busy over an automatic scheme for 40 regts. of Cavalry and 150 battns. of Infantry: working out the puzzle with pins and flags and wasting much paper. And just as one has arrived at a Satisfactory Solution—with a colleague, the AQMG Mobilisation, and was hoping to convert the Adjutant General's and Quarter-Master General's people to our side—in pops a finance man who says nothing that costs a single Rupee will have any chance of sanction by Govt.

They won't even feed the horses of the native Cavalry properly—

entirely disregarding the fact that the price of grain has gone up enormously—and 'They' won't sanction money for experimental purposes in wireless—or anything else, (altho. en parenthèse, I have managed to get special facilities put in the way of a Cavalry 'lunatic' who thinks he has invented an automatic balance for aeroplanes!) Still, it's unsatisfactory work these days and one feels that progress is impossible: though so much to be desired.

Of course we are face to face with a very serious problem in re the maintenance of such a comparatively large native Army in these days of unrest: Native Gentlemen and Nobles are demanding a greater share in military appointments and the difficulty is to know how far it is wise to grant them. The Muhammedan Element is, in its own interests—standing by the Government. The large Hindu community are, I believe, hostile and untrustworthy.

It would be better did Lord Morley come out here and investigate matters on the spot and see for himself: instead of blocking everything from an office in London. He is the self constituted autocrat of this part of the East—and his like has never been seen before since India came under the Crown; like most politicians, his ignorance is colossal—and his Council at the India Office, reduced by him to an aggregation of nonentities who may not speak unless spoken to and may not see papers unless he, Morley, decides that they shall. And yet they are former Lt. Governors, Civil and Military officials of high standing! Selected by himself however: and therein is the weakness. On the Viceroy's Council, out here, the members all hold portfolios: but all the same this fool Morley snaps his fingers at what the Gov. General and his Council recommend and refers to them merely as puppets: his puppets.

And we have some very strong men out here too: truly the Evils of undue Parliamentary Control at the Center over far distant Pro-Consulates is being made very manifest and the British Electorate is going to pay very dearly for their misuse of the Power they are so insanely jealous of delegating.

Your letter of 29th June came this morning and we are very grateful for your continued kind thought for us and our well-being: Lina has already told you, I think, of our decision not to take the Duff's house: owing principally to the doubt of your coming out to us (you, Aunt Fanny, Mr. Sinnickson, Betty or Fanny), and partly to the uncertainty as to one's future employment and movements. I do not consider, either, that we are justified in expending so large a sum upon furniture—excellent as it is—which we might not be able to get rid of in a hurry. For this winter we have decided to shift into another hotel—the Cecil—and will quietly watch our chance of getting what we want. This, your last cable, received on 23rd, will enable us to do.

Four guns of a Mountain Battery and the Cavalry from <u>Bannu</u> (S.W. of Peshawar) are 'out' scouring the Tochi Valley for two raiding parties: this may or may not, lead to bigger things. In case of <u>General Mobilisation</u> for a <u>big</u> business—Afghanistan (which was very near last winter) or Russia—the personnel of the Training Branch at Headquarters are made available for general Staff service in the field: and we have always to keep this eventuality in front of us. Our Divisional and Brigade Staffs are all formed and ready: both Infantry and Cavalry: (some 24 Brigades and 6 Brigades respectively)—but the higher staff are only formed on the emergency occurring.

The new Chief of Staff—Sir Douglas Haig—lands in November and will come up here direct, they tell me. Seriously or in jest, he writes me <u>not</u> to leave the Service in May next. This may mean much—or nothing! but I am impatient of the present situation and none too well pleased with my apparent prospects. Schatzie says however that I am naturally despondent and does her stout little best to dispel the gloomy clouds! Bless her good little soul.

I must make a collection of British Military Slang for you: that of your army is very similar to what the 'British soldier' (no longer called Tommy or Thomas Atkins, please note) uses today: but his pigeon-Hindustani beats anything I have ever heard. To properly appreciate it, you would require a knowledge of Hindustani: but only the 'B.S.' and the barrack servants and the invaluable bhisti (water carrier) properly understand it!!

My orderly Wali Muhammed Khan—shortly called 'Walia'—has had the riding of my pony too long: and I hope to be in the saddle soon again. 'Tail' not quite right yet—but I'm glad the Doctor man chopped off the excrescence—as it was in the way.

Do tell Aunt Fanny how interesting her letters always are—and I hope you, Sir, will not miss many mails either—because we look forward with positive anxiety to the Sunday incoming mail.

August 2, 1909   **Simla**

Dear Aunt Fanny,

You must not be cross with me for using this wonderful little typewriter to write to you on this occasion as I want to show you how I am getting on with it and also to have a little practice on it in order to help Offley with his copying. I assure you I have not the faintest intention of doing such an ungracious thing generally. But this I know you understand. I am enclosing you the programme of the tableaux which took place last week and in which Lady Eileen Elliot was very beautiful as Cleopatra and her reciting of her part in Tennyson's poem was exceptionally well done. Everybody was there and we sat just next to the Viceregal party and smiled and talked and criticised with them. Of course there are no end of squabbles among those taking part in the actual tableaux but all the same all have gone to the greatest trouble and we only hope a good fat sum has been realized. I, though not in the tableaux, have lent some of my nice things much to Offley's disapproval!

If my sisters come out one must hear their definite decision, if they come this winter, as soon as possible as they must have a good Bearer and Ayah for them and other arrangements made in advance. In India one must have native servants on account of the language and the caste arrangements. Then, if my sisters come, they perhaps do not know that the time to be in Simla, which is our home just now in India, and therefore the place I should be most desirous of showing them and having them see and be in everything, is during May and June, so they must not plan to leave this country before then nor must they come out too late in the winter to see all the interesting places in the plains. Of course there are a great many primitive and unusual things to adapt oneself to in this country beside the climate. From what I saw in the plains one must always sleep under a mosquito net; yet this does not necessarily mean that there is a plague of mosquitoes. For it would be more likely than not that there would be no more than an occasional fellow whom you had made sure of keeping off. The houses or Bungalows are never very well built and first the heat (like the hottest American summer days) and then dampness bring all sorts of insects and crawling, creeping things in their train. But really as far as my experience has gone this is no worse than the spiders, flies, grasshoppers etc. we get in the foggy days at Narragansett or Newport only that the bungalow, be it a Viceregal Lodge or the best built private house, never seems to be able to shut these unlovely companions out. In the beautiful bungalow, 'Garden House' we visited in at Meerut there were spiders in all corners of my room and a very gay lizard or two always playing on the window panes or walls. In the garden one must be careful for snakes that are really dangerous—in fact even in Simla I have been warned that the pleasures of your own garden are limited for this reason, but one can always call the Mali or gardener. If one is troubled with white ants who eat in to everything, then one's bedstead and other things are stood in little cups of oil to stop the trouble, but this is only exceptional and not the rule and stories of just such sort of things, I think, are so often told about India as if they were common occurrences when I assure you they are no such thing. My sisters or Aunt Mary if they are thinking seriously of coming to see us and India, must be well fixed with trusty and good native servants and must have a clear understanding of the differences in climate which they may meet with. From one's arrival in Bombay during the winter and all through Southern and Central India the weather is like the warm Spring and summer we are accustomed to, but coming up into the Hill Stations, and of course in Simla, February and March are cold and wet—in December we have deep snows and skating and other winter sports that I think people very rarely think of who have not been here or had some near relation or intimate friend experience and write of.

We have been having some of the most gloriously beautiful nights the last three nights with such stars and such a moon and such a heavenly blue-ness and silvery clearness in the atmosphere and crisp air; we thought it meant a long and beautiful break in the rains, especially as this clearing came in time to see wonderful sunsets with rainbows and the moon all making their appearance at the same time, but it is now pouring cats and dogs and pitchforks and so hard and fast you cannot see a yard ahead of you.

August 16, 1909   **Simla**

My dear Uncle Joe,

Last night we went to a most interesting dinner party at the house of a very rich noble Mumtaz Mohammed Khan. Our host having been brought up in England was in evening clothes of the best and smartest of English tailors while his brother was, as he called it, 'old fashioned', but a very handsome man and <u>gorgeous</u> and spotless in the native dress of White Cloth frock-coat, heavily embroidered in gold, white turban, with gold embroidered Mohammedan cap, and the full, long loose white linen trousers and Eastern gold embroidered shoes. His beard was dyed red and so handsome a man was he that even with this bright coloured dye, of which they are so fond here, one could not but admire him. The servants, any number of them, were all in black and gold, with white turbans. I sat next but one at the table and opposite to these wonderfully dressed native gentlemen and noticed the difficulty with which they handled their eating utensils and how they enjoyed the special curry and the sweets, the only Indian dishes we had. The menu for the most part was entirely in French and with courses etc, just as one w'd have in Europe. After dinner we were entertained by Indian singing and Indian music produced by a phonograph!!! These songs especially produced for Malik Khan, who is very rich and we think very loyal and very ambitious.

This week as the 'Good-bye' dinners to Lord K. have brought so many visitors to Simla O. has given me a long list of calls that must be done at once. I have also got to see to my Dherzi for our costumes for the Fancy Ball.

Yesterday I was very homesick. I don't know exactly why, but I do hope it is settled some of you will come and see us and India. Love to each and all.

August 22, 1909   **Simla**

My dearest Aunt,

The cold cream and the writing cards have both come safely to hand and many thanks for both. The cold cream took some time in coming owing to the way in which it was sent, as it came through a broker in Bombay and all sorts of payments had to be made upon it, but we were so eagerly awaiting it and so glad to get it <u>above all other kinds</u> and it was most beautifully put up—the very way which is best for this country and climate. We gave one bottle—very grudgingly, to the Holdiches and I dare say Mr. Morgan will have further orders some day from others—but everything you can possibly send by post is best sent in that way to come to India. Like England they have an excellent parcel post.

We have been at home reading and writing and working all morning and have just hung up Uncle Joe's photo of his portrait in its neat little frame. Everyone admires him so much and all who see it say what a delightful looking man. We are rather gayer again these next two weeks with dinner and a play at Viceregal Lodge. Offley has been out to farewell dinners almost every other night for the past ten days. So I have either gone or given ladies' dinner parties. He has sent most of his menus and dinner plans etc. to Uncle Joe—so you can all see them. A great many people have been brought to Simla, 'pour dire adieu' to the Great Chief—Lord K., whom I otherwise should never have met, and some Offley has not seen for years.

I was very much pleased with a photo of Rebecca's and Charlie's little baby. What a sweet, healthy looking little darling she is. I <u>do</u> wish I had a small rascal boy or girl—as it is I have to borrow the Dick Cunningham's 'Betsy' and make her pink bonnets.

With the coming of the cool season life changed.

On the 14th of November manoevres begin and this will take Offley away—and by the end of the month there will scarcely be 150 white people left in Simla. I dare say Lady Haig will go to Calcutta for a little while, but so I hope shall I—but I am getting very uncertain about going to Meerut and Delhi, and greater journeys I am inclined to forget! Offley will be at manoevres near Delhi nearly all January.

Early in the manoeuvres Offley wrote to Uncle Joe the letter which follows. In his reference to 'Reform Councils' he was commenting on the government of India Act of 1909, known as the Morley–Minto Reforms after the Secretary of State for India and the Viceroy. This act has been described as 'an important step in the introduction of representative government', but at the same time the same writer describes the provision it contained for separate electoral representation for the Muslim Community as 'a device adopted by the new Viceroy, Lord Minto, to win over the Muslims and set them against the Congress movement'. (An Advanced History of India, R. C. Majumdar, H. C. Raychandhuri and K. Datta, Macmillan 1967, pp. 911 and 978.)

November 21, 1909

**Cavalry Camp, Adampur
via Jallundur**

My dear Uncle Joe,

I have been reading your brochure anent the capture of the North Pole[7] with much interest—also the papers about the President's visit to San Francisco and the account of Wilbur Wright's latest flight and decision to confine himself henceforth to motor improvements and manufacture etc.

Your people, always go-ahead, have done marvelously well—and certainly deserve all credit. I wish they would bite some of our officials though, as nothing short of the inoculation of some virus will move them!

We have been experimenting in a small way with an Indian Cavalry Officer's invention for utilising the light Austrian 7 lb. to the mile telephone wire—which can be worked from the saddle—was laid out at a gallop the other night 5 miles in 35 minutes—and we are talking to the Commutator station within five minutes afterwards. The insulation of the 3-strand wire is, of course, very delicate—and I do not know what would happen over damp or wet ground. Each ridden horse can carry 2 drums, holding 2 miles a piece—but many improvements could be made, if the authorities would only take it up.

The Asst. Adj. General of this 3rd Lahore Division put down £400 out of his own pocket—and we shall have the first portable wireless set working in a day or two, at the Divisional period of these manoeuvres—(Again Gov. is sitting still and watching private experiment). I saw the apparatus at the Sapper Center Roorki (near Saharunpore) the other day—entirely put together by the Engineers. They have worked up to 15 miles by day and further by night. And we are hoping to see it go up to 25 miles.

Were our Government to encourage experiment and put down the money in the way yours does, we should have been already far upon our road. There are all sorts of curious atmospherics in this country which must be investigated. Yet they are everlastingly waiting on England.

I need not suggest to you, what a change will come over military movements, once we get a fairly reliable and portable system of this form of communication. To my mind, information, early and accurate, is beyond price and worth its weight in gold. Still, the Powers That Be won't see it because they have never fought and will never fight themselves and it's inconvenient to be asked for the money. There is no way for soldiers to make money or save it—all our savings revert to the credit of the Government—else we would surely work out our own salvation. May I see our Civilians [i.e. Civil Servants. Ed.] being sacrificed by the hundred thousand, before I am finished! Nice pious wish? but it's maddening for those who stand at the door and are going to get shot at first.

I see we are having regular conducted tours of your compatriots now—the so-called American Winter Invasion of India—so you will be having all sorts of experiences and views communicated to your papers by these tourists and it will be interesting to see how the place has impressed them.

Our Reuter's telegrams tell us also of the search for John Jacob Astor who is supposed to have disappeared since the West Indian hurricane—and of the bestowal of the Garter upon the King of Portugal. In regard the latter, I cannot think that our King's endeavors towards an Entente with the Latin Races of Europe is going to be of much value to us.

They are practically decadent nations—and would count for nothing in a world struggle against the more virile northerners.

Transplanted, like the Italians, they may revivify, but I doubt if they are more than mere cumberers of the earth in their own countries. One is ever in fear that one's own people may eventually sink to the same level of dead and dying peoples!

There are men at Home who seem to think that this much talked of struggle with Germany is surely coming: there are men who would welcome it now, before the nation has become too selfish to fight for its name and possessions; there are many who entertain no delusions as to the future, should England get the worst of it.

To my mind also—we had better fight soon—and knock the inflated nonsense out of the heads of all classes: the 'lowest' in particular. Men who require insurance against non-employment and old age pensions from the State and are not prepared to do an honest day's work for the wage they 'accept'—want the only lesson that will ever teach them anything.

I know this sounds pessimistic—but I am inclined to believe things are worse than we care to believe.

As to India—it is difficult to say whether things are improving. The Reform Councils—with a definite fixed Representation for Musulmans will satisfy them for a time and may keep their heads above water in relation to the Hindus, but unless modern education and methods introduce unforeseen changes in character and habits, I do not think the Muhammedan will ever hold his own in the political or mercantile platform with the acuter, milder, but more painstaking, money-making Hindu. The follower of the prophet takes less kindly to education; spends his money freely 'like a gentleman' whilst he has it and much prefers the arbitrament of the Sword—is more force-ful of character—the other is subtler and vastly outnumbers the adherents of the Green Flag.

The general levelling-up which results from Western Education is a distinct menace to the ruling families of today. So far—it is in their interest to stand by a powerful white Government—but a weak one may lose their support. Today I think they are more afraid of socialism and bomb throwing than we are.

It is disconcerting to think how easily a carefully organised Society might wipe out the heads of the whole Civil Government in a day. What we trust to, however, is for the ever-present jealousy among different grades and religions to 'give away' their enemy for their own private satisfaction. The problem is how to identify the interests of the best native Indians with those of the Government and yet retain the ascendancy and direction of affairs.

The cultivators round here seem well to do and friendly—magnificent crops this year and plenty of money in prospect—much jewelry for the women—plenty of babies and cattle, but they merely wish to be left alone with the minimum amount of worry from Government officials.

Of the subtleties working in the minds of the student class, of the Brahmin, of the money people, the Bengalis, who can say?

The training of the soldiers is becoming year by year more difficult owing to the increased areas brought under cultivation and the closer rotation of crops—movement across country is becoming more limited—and as the seasons vary with every few degrees of latitude—simultaneous work in all the Gov. Divisions becomes impossible. Malaria in the plains will probably keep the white troops in the hills until the 1st of December in future and by that time the crops are too far advanced in many Divisions to admit of free movement over them. We shall then have to concentrate masses of men in jungle and uncultivated tracts—and then comes the difficulty of maintenance and increased cost.

So we too, are face to face with increasing difficulties, and your Universal Peace Association had better hurry!!!

The first page of the following letter to Aunt Fanny is missing. The date therefore is uncertain.

. . . and the delightful letters—besides yours and Uncle Joe's, one from Mother, one from Father, one from Aunt Caroline and one from Florence and one dictated to the nurse from my dear old Father-in-law who, after a very serious attack, we thought dying, and he probably is, but seems to have recuperated enough to write us, which is a pleasure to him and he does write such affectionate and charming letters. He has two trained nurses and the doctor <u>every</u> day and so on and poor Offley is so saddened by the sufferings of his 'devoted companion and best friend' as he calls his Father from whom, with the sad vicissitudes in their lives, he has been so much separated. But he is <u>very proud</u> of Offley and very comforted to know he has such a son—during his last illness he sometimes forgot things and thought Offley was Commander-in-Chief in India—so Flo wrote me; Urith, my other sister-in-law, is spending the winter in Nice as the Doctor forbids her return to England during the winter months.

What do you think I have been making! but alas not for myself—'new born' baby clothes. I have been cutting and basting and embroidering little 'festoons' on flannels and other tiny things for Minnie, who expects a little baby in the first week of July.

She does not wish it at all! but I think when the actual Rascal is here she will love it dearly for she has the most kind, impulsive, big heart. She cannot sew as I can and she exclaims when I do the simplest things, 'What would I do without you!' and tells our friends such wonderful things of me—it is very amusing.

How beautiful the materials must be this season—I would dearly love to see the Paris things! I do confess. Here I am sure my own things are the newest anyone has—although Lady Haigh should have had the latest fashions, but she dresses in that decidedly English way and her own prettiness and charm lend all else unnecessary. I have actually made myself a dress—an evening gown—over one of my old foundations and it is fairly successful.

I will have to get something very smart and new for next season—so you must tell me all about the ball gowns and the dinner gowns Mrs. Altemus has. I should like a handsome black satin for the State Ball—so describe all you see, dear Aunt.

I am so sorry to hear of Julie Phillip's separation. What a pity—and why is it?

Thank God in Heaven I am so exceptionally happily married—everyday Offley unfolds some dear trait and everyday I am more proud of him and feel I have so much to live up to and so much that is good in life and of life. Of course we have our differences and sometimes very big ones and very serious—so we think! But we usually feel so sorry for one another that we agree to disagree or I am convinced or he is convinced. I have sometimes been lonely and home-sick and cried and then Offley is so upset. He swears he will leave the Service or do anything to see me happier (and I am not unhappy) and we are better for weeks afterwards. He always thinks of me and puts me first in all things and my one fear is that anything should happen to my dearest on earth, and he is so interested and so attached to all of you at home.

Our lives are always busy for I work with Offley and he plays with me. We ride, read, have a little music or a game of piquet, talk of the times, people, politics, or home and the future, when we plan a home of our own as gaily and happily as if we were just newly engaged and Offley is just as much my lover and more as he was that day he went to tell you all about it. What a long letter I have written about it all. Do forgive me, but I know you will be happy to know this as I am proud and fearless to tell it.

Lina was at this time beginning to anticipate that 'they' would be 'announcing the fact of O. becoming a full Colonel from the date he took up this appointment—at least I have got a bottle of turpentine in the house to rub off the Lieut.; and shortly it will come. I feel no doubt about it, and then there will be a shout for new visiting cards and uniforms.'

Offley returned to Simla for Christmas, celebrated in traditional form except that peacock appears to have replaced turkey.

To her letter of Christmas Day to Aunt Fanny, Lina attached the note which had accompanied Aunt Caroline's present: 'For dearest Lina, the joy and delight of an old Aunt's life.'

In mid-January they left Simla in a snow storm and travelled comfortably down to the warmth of the plains: Offley to return to the manoeuvres, Lina to spend six weeks in Meerut with the General commanding the 7th Division, John Nixon, who had served with the 18th Tiwana Lancers, which was stationed in Meerut at that time.

'So,' wrote Lina, 'I shall always have my place "by courtesy" on the Regiment's 4-in-hand.'

From Meerut they went to Agra, whence Lina wrote to Aunt Fanny on 16 February:

Offley working hard at his report of the winter's manoevres which Sir Douglas Haig wished him to write for the London Times and in order that I should not be disappointed in seeing the Taj Mahal and other beauties of this part of India he has chosen this place to do it in.

*Lina wrote many pages to Aunt Fanny describing the Taj Mahal,
the Fort, Akbar's Tomb, the Shish Mahal, and Fatipur Sikri.*

How you would enjoy this part of India and how we have wished
for you all many times.

While we were there some <u>horrible</u> Americans came in—and I
was very shocked at the pushing way they looked into everything—
and we have seen some dreadful examples of the globe trotter from
the U.S.A. and where and how <u>this</u> class of my fellow countrymen
can afford to travel I cannot imagine—I think they must be shop
keepers or buyers and their families. I was standing looking at some
boxes on the veranda and an American woman said, 'Say, wasn't
you at Delhi? Well you ought to had bought these notions there for
they was a sight cheaper.' I thanked her and came quietly away—
feeling I could never possess that box without the awful memory
of this curious person looking up.

Here news reached Lina concerning her mother's health.

I have been very anxious and distressed to hear how wretched dear
Mother is again. Betty wrote me how ill she had been and you can
imagine how sad it made me and Offley too, who loves my dear
Mother and admires her so thoroughly. You said nothing about
Mother in your letter, dearest Aunt Fanny, but I want to know all
about her—and I beg you to write me of her too.

*By the end of February they were in Peshawar whence Lina wrote
the following letter.*

February 27, 1910   **Peshawar, Northwest Frontier**

My dear Uncle Joe,

Here we are in a very far off corner of the world and <u>I</u> am settling
down to live here until the end of the month, but in the meantime
Offley leaves me for three sets of manoevres, Brigade, Cavalry, and
Divisional and so on, coming in for a few days in between each, <u>I</u>
<u>hope</u>. This is a most interesting station, more than picturesque, situ-
ated on a broad horseshoe shaped plateau in the lower Himalayas.

Broad roads and a beautiful Mall and flower clad bungalows, a big Club—a racing club, and polo club, and the Peshawar Vale Hunt; and an old, walled in native city—teeming with life, full of dirt and filth, but also a mass of colour. An old fort stands picturesquely on the outer or Circular Road that makes an 'enceinture' of the whole of Peshawar, and the whole place is fortified and garrisoned for war—or what Offley calls an equipped War Division—and I confess I feel rather nervous to be so near these war-like people. Every house has watchmen, and officers' bungalows in the Lines are often walled in and with glass broken and stuck in along the tops of these mud barricades or barbed wire trellises here and there to make it pleasanter for the gentlemen to get in!!!

A little further into Afghanistan at the Malakand where they are making some new canals and where Offley hopes to take me later, I was told it was exceedingly interesting to see the Power House with its latest equipment in machinery, electricity etc. etc.—walled in and fortified of course—while outside in the rugged mountain pass two warlike companies of Pathans sit discussing the ownership of a piece of ground that the Government is about to take for the continuation of this canal system—with loaded rifles and sharpened daggers, ready to decide the question after their own good fashion and way of thinking at the slightest opportunity.

There is an archaeological collection in a Durbar Hall here—under the care of an American named Spooner—all are Buddha figures and the life story in stone of this Saint. Some are very beautiful with Greek[8] like features and carving—others less perfect, but exceedingly curious and interesting and the greatest quantity of them.

The more I see of India and Indian Stations and Regimental life, the happier I am to be in Simla with Offley now striking out in an altogether different line—that of a General Staff Officer soon to become the Imperial General Staff—but I admire the Anglo Indian women and the sacrifices they have made to remain here to look after their husbands and to promote the greatest good of the Empire.

The rich native gentlemen in this part of the world are of a very gorgeous and flourishing appearance—driving about in the most elegant of English made landaus—gaily painted and with the brightest of liveried servants, while they themselves are fat and handsome with marvelous fur coats and whitest of turbans. Jewelled tops to their massive walking sticks and magnificent horses.

I have been very distressed and unhappy to hear of Mother's return of her old trouble and it naturally makes my inclinations turn toward home—but I don't see any way ahead just yet of getting back there and we both long for it often.

March 16, 1910   **Simla**

My very dear Family—All of You!

Here we are back again in Simla, after a good two months of touring and seeing a part of the world that the everyday globe trotter rarely has open to him. Peshawar and the Khyber were interesting and delightful and we were fortunate to find a number of friends, official and others, to entertain us and give us the best of everything, yet even so I confess I felt pretty nervous to be right up on the Frontier and among these people who think nothing of shooting you. However they say they prefer to kill a man rather than a woman and I felt as nervous on Offley's account as I was on my own. Of course I always had brave and good servants with me and my little maid has had all sorts of experiences of the Jungle and speaks many kinds of Hindustani, and Walia and the big orderly the Khyber Commissioner lent us spoke of course Pushtu. But I made the most unusual friends among these ruffians! One a Carpet wallah whom I had known in Simla last season and, though I had never bought any thing of him, on seeing me in Peshawar he could not do enough for me in his native city!!! So—he accompanied us on our drives into the native city of Peshawar riding an American bicycle with his large, voluminous trousers full of air as he rode swiftly in front of us, and the dense crowds of natives the like of which I have never seen either here in India or in Egypt, and they evidently thought SOME PERSONAGE is about to arrive; so when Violet Nicoll and I in a little Tumtum, or low pony-cart, with little brown Amy, my maid, arrived, led by my—again devoted—friend, my Tumtum Wallah, who announced 'Rasta chor-do memsahib bahadur', in English 'move off, her honour my memsahib passes', prize fighters were stopped, vendors, letter writers, men old and young and women were pushed aside for us to make our way through this vast throng to the carpet bazaars, to the pottery makers, to the boot and shoe bazaar. Each place young and old, boys and men crowded round us all waving their wares in the air and outbidding each other to try to sell us something. I bought Lungis for my Jhampanis, quaintly embroidered slippers—one pair for a Marani, one for a Maraja, sandals for the man of the hills—all wonderfully decorated with tinsel, pompoms etc. A most lovely coloured blue water jug at the potters and which Amy delighted in, carrying cool water in for her journey home and I succeeded in getting some very precious bits of carpet. One beautiful piece of Punjday. (This is the very finest carpet in the world in the eyes of the East Indian or Anglo-Indian and is of a conventional pattern with wonderful tawny browns, dark reds and blues, always a little mellow white, and the rarest have soft greens—my bit has the green and they are made in Afghanistan at a place almost on the Persian frontier called Punjday meaning Five Villages. 'Panj' is five in Hindustani and 'day' village) and I also got two Purdas or hangings of this same wonderful carpet. These are very, very rare and of a wondrous colouring and design. Dark blue and darkest plum colours or dark pinks and full of exquisite flame or orange browns. In these I know I have unusual treasures in the way of carpets. But, as these are only used in the houses of Khans or Ameers and the better classes, the carpet merchants are very cute and soon learn to charge the highest prices for their really good things so in this case I gave ourselves a treat. So anxious am I for you to see them that I am very inclined to send you one of the pieces home to use until I come back for a visit. The Bazaar in Peshawar with its choice things was irresistible!!!!!!! I think I wrote you about the Pathan knife I got up the Khyber?

On the 12th. Offley got back from the manoevres, and after a hurried packing up we were off by the 9 o'clock train on the 13th to Nowshera (where Offley first joined his regiment in India as a boy of nineteen) en route for a still wilder part of the frontier—to the Malakand where the Chief Commissioner had put the Circuit House at our disposal. It is so changed since Offley was fighting there in '97 that he scarcely knew the place; it is a mass of forts, the Circuit House being within one, and looks very strong and very picturesque. We were very lucky in our weather too as at Peshawar it had been threatening rain for some days. We sent up the cook and mate the day before, took Amy with us and were therefore independent, but having received a wire the day before leaving from Mr. Tickell, the Chief Engineer of the new Malakand Canal, saying he was also stopping there, and if he might remain in the house he would be very glad to entertain us (which we didn't accept as I wanted to see what the cook could do with an eye to taking him as O.'s cook for the manoevres next winter) we had Mr. Tickell's good company and his excellent old fashioned Kitmudgars to serve us at table, having left our Butler to look after the reserved carriage to come to Nowshera and get all the luggage and O.'s camp kit into it for our return here, and Walia had of course to go off with the horses. The cook who was a 'Mug' or as you probably have not heard of the 'Mugs' I must tell you that they are a race or tribe of cooks! Their fathers, grandfathers etc. all have been cooks and they are wonderful and ours proved to be of the best of the kind at that. On our arrival at Nowshera we found the 'Lord Sahib's' or the Chief Commissioner's, carriage waiting for us on the little narrow gauge railway that takes you on to the Malakand so went in style to the quaint little station at Dargai where the booking office is made of old sleepers tarred!!! There we found the Tonga O. had written ahead for and in this rough unpainted wood and iron conveyance we drove up the good but steep and terrible mighty mountain side with the half wild ponies galloping at full speed, swinging round corners, dashing up hill sides reaching the top of the Malakand at tea time. Mr. Tickell welcomed us and put the house and house keeping into my hands—Amy made the beds and arranged everything for us to dress for dinner—to my amazement having brought things enough for us to have appeared presentable had we been dining at the Carlton instead of in the fortress house of one of the outposts of the Indian frontier. Offley immediately went out to see the whole place at once and of course at once discovered old friends. I gave the orders to the cook for dinner at 8.15 and for breakfast, tea and dinner the next day and for a full tiffin basket for the morrow's lunch when Offley and I went on to Chakdarra through the Amandarra Pass and past the village of Khar where O. had seen some very hard fighting. Oh, how glad I felt that these days were over and may they never come again. I hope he will now distinguish himself in other fields. The stern high rocks, the wicked looking tribesmen who stared at me unmercifully, the strongest of fortresses I have ever seen, the rushing rivers, the defended iron bridges close beside bridges of boats, the block houses on every peak and outpost, the cut throat looking savages— I tell you, I am wondering how we came through it alive!!!!!! I am REALLY! Our great safety no doubt lay in the fact that our soldiers have proved themselves the best fighters, and the savage native loves and admires a good fighter and our civil service people have developed their valleys and brought work and wealth into their land. Before our long drive in the morning Mr. Tickell himself took us with his young expert electrical engineer to see the new canal work and the electrical workshops they have set up. It is marvellous to ponder over all that has been accomplished. Here right on the frontier are electric instalments to pump air, water, make light, saw wood, mould iron or work in steel, to sharpen instruments etc.; the natives themselves being levied and taught to use them as well as to guard them. Telephones to the canal works, to the fortifications (all are within strongly fortified places) and this is to carry out a canal, or the new Swat River Irrigation Scheme, which is to irrigate 300,000 acres after the water from the upper Swat has been brought through the Malakand in a tunnel two miles long and at a cost to this government of many Crores or millions of money which, the idea is, will pacify the people who are an agricultural race first and a fighting race secondly. It will increase the value of their land and their work and wages and refill the pockets of the government in time by the small taxes put upon the water supply. We visited the electrical shops and works which the native calls the 'bijli khana' or 'lightening house' and went to the tunnel's head, which has progressed some two hundred feet into the mountain, the power house beyond, and then to see the tunnel's tail—all under the guidance of Mr. Tickell and saw wonderful little electric pumps made by Ingersoll and Rand of New York!!! These things have taken some three years to collect and put ready for use here and in another three years they hope to see the tunnel finished and the scheme in full working order. I enjoyed my whole trip immensely. Offley is an enthusiastic companion and untiring in his efforts to give me pleasure. We delighted in our frugal luncheon seated by the roadside under willows that line the way to the fort at Chakdarra and, with the fortifications perched above us, and having changed our ponies, we drove over the bridge and looked at the fort and fortified barracks where O. had been and he pointed out the new things since his time and then we returned to the Malakand to tea, settled the cook's account and while Amy and I packed up O. went off to see the grave of some comrade who had fallen in '97. He only said he was going

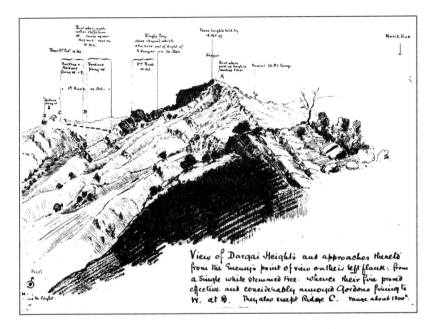

An example of Offley's topographical sketching.
The Battle for the Heights of Dargai, 1897 (original pen and ink colour-washed).

outside and though it made me again nervous I felt or guessed his errand by his expression so said nothing, but you can imagine I was glad to see him come in a little later. We had dinner at six and in the fading light—after some trouble to get out of the fortifications—we were on our way to Dargai, caught the 8.30 train to Nowshera, at midnight found our carriage waiting, had just time to hop in and were off southward bound for Kalka and Simla. The pink of the peach blossoms and the white of the wild cherry, the vivid green of the spring crops and the play of colour and shadows on the hillsides, with the clear green of the water, and the wild ruffians who still stared at me, were immensely interesting, and the clank of the iron tonga bar you read about in Kipling's books[9] and which I heard for the first time in my life was most exciting and kept up my spirits and spurred my courage. And passing troops—Camel Corps and mountain guns returning from ma-noevres were some of the pictures we saw from the carriage window.

We had a dusty and somewhat hot time downwards from Lahore; the night run from Amballa to Kalka was pleasantly cool and the lower hills coming up to Simla looked too lovely and sweet and familiar with lots of peach and cherry blossoms and the Rhododendron compensated for all the distance I am away from you all and gave me a sense of home coming.

Offley's book of official sketches of the topography of the Malakand and of the battles fought there in 1897 by the Malakand Field Force survives. So too does an article on the Malakand torn from the 9 March 1940 number of Country Life *annotated by Lina with a reference to her visit there thirty years earlier. This tour was followed by another eight months in Simla.*

March 20, 1910   **Simla**

My dearest Aunt,

Very many thanks for your last, dated February 15. I found it here awaiting our return home again to Simla and also the two parcels—of petticoats and stockings so beautifully done up. They arrived as safely and neatly as if they had only made the journey from their Philadelphia shops to 1704 Walnut Street. There was also a beautiful parcel of things from Paris—as I find they quite understand sending out to India and my friends the Harringtons get many of their pretty muslins, hats etc. and gloves from the 'Louvre' or 'Trois Quartiers' or 'Galeria Lafayette' and very much cheaper and far prettier than sending to England or shopping here which is horribly expensive. Amy, my maid, was delighted with the things—and has at once appropriated the stockings and petticoats to mark them. She has been the greatest comfort and companion and nurse and maid and general care taker and I am very distressed to have to part with her when the little baby arrives that she had promised to go to before I engaged her, and she too says, 'Dear Mistress, I wish I did not have to part from you and Master for I have been so happy', but she promises to come to me when she is allowed an afternoon off and she is going to clean our gloves for us through the summer and do any little odds and ends she can. It is nice to have her in Simla anyhow for I feel I have someone now to turn to and to help me in all the difficult matters that might arise.

Our rooms in the Grand Hotel are looking so charming with their new wall papers and I am going up there on Monday to hang curtains and get them all in order to go into them. I am so eager over arranging it all—as I ever was!! and Amy has bought me a little machine so we shall thoroughly enjoy ourselves.

I was so pleased and appreciative of your continued interest in the Italian Day Nursery [in Philadelphia—Ed.]. I have so many demands for all sorts of things as a Staff Officer's wife here in India that I often feel I neglect my 'old loves', but one really cannot keep up both sides and my interests here must necessarily deepen the longer I live in the country. I do wish we could bring into being some better work for these awful Bengalis, than their so-called patriotism that leads to this awful sedition. Since I have had my maid, Amy, I know there are plenty of young men and women well worth, and much more in need of, a very different education from that which they are getting. Not that they are not being well taught etc. etc.—but they need a different lot of ideas and morals taught them altogether.

April 14, 1910   **Simla**

Dearest Aunt Fanny,

Two mails—I am afraid—have gone without my usual letter to you—my excuse is that I have been so exceedingly busy getting into our old quarters; housecleaning and scrubbing them—getting the curtains hung and the carpets laid down and the baths and bath tins and bath rooms neatly painted—is all a matter for the occupant to see to in an Indian hotel. Then the rush of people returning to Simla—the visiting list and the visiting to be begun at once. Some old friends going home or a lady with a new baby or in mourning whom one must go to see—take up the days and in the evenings a little reading and sewing or a few friends come in and the days are all too short and Thursday, the home mail day, comes round with a marvelous rapidity. The horses came up again this week, both looking so well, I am happy to say, and now we are fairly settled—yet still a hamper full of sewing and mending and gowns to be done over or O.'s shirts to have new cuffs, all stare one in the face—and each day the gay season draws nearer.

You would be amused at some of the ways the Indian servants accomplish things! My nice young jhampani was told off to clean the windows in O's study and nurse (all the maids—not ayahs—are called 'nurse' in this country) caught him spitting on the glass and rubbing the window with the tail end of his <u>new</u> livery!!! She spoke to him so nicely—told the fellow he didn't look pretty making water falls on the window for Memsahib Bahadur to see from the inside, sent him for warm water and supplied him with <u>clean</u> towels. Fortunately—though I had to change butlers—we have an exceptionally clean Madrasee, always as white and spotless as possible in linen coat and pugerie—and such a nice old thing. He takes the greatest care and pride with my linen and with all my own things but what we are to do next winter I don't know, for his old Master and Mistress return to India and I fear he will wish to go back to them and we hear we shall have to go to Calcutta for the winter. In which case it means a house or flat—not that I mind at all as I am <u>much</u> interested to go to Calcutta, but all tell us it is the most expensive capital in the world for Europeans.

We were both interested in Mr. Hanson's letter and criticisms—poor beautiful little England. What is going to become of her? He also speaks of the very poor way in which the British officer expresses himself in writing and alas it is only too true, with of course some excellent exceptions, but I have been reading over some of the confidential papers to help O. get over a lot of work in the present shifting—as you may not know he has become the Director of Staff Duties, General Staff, India, a very important billet and a very difficult and hard worked one.

This Mr. Hanson would have been pleased to learn that, to quote the Press of the time, the regulations of the Indian Staff College provided that 'An officer will be liable to removal at any time if he cannot write legibly or if he be deficient in power of expressing himself clearly and intelligibly on paper'.

May 11, 1910 **Simla**

Dearest Aunt Fanny and Uncle Joe,

Here we are still thinking of nothing but the death of the King, Edward VII. The loss such a statesman-like King and man is to the Empire and to Europe! for so the Russian Consul Gen'l expressed it today.

Again it seems more personal than I can express because of knowing the Prince and Princess of Wales—now King George and Queen Mary. What a splendid and proud thing it must have been to see our new King and his boys standing with such soldiers as Lord Kitchener and dear old Lord Roberts beside them at the Proclamation in London.

I am so glad you all enjoyed my letters from Agra and Peshawar. I did wish so often you were one and all with me. It has been a wonderful year—this—my first year in India and yesterday O. completed his 28 years of service which assures him a pension of £500 a year if he retires, but I am ambitious and hope he may yet live to be a Field Marshal—and once he becomes a General Officer the pension increases to £1000 p.a. So let us hope that the advent of our new King George is lucky for Offley.

Of course all gaieties and entertaining of every description has stopped—and will not begin again for at least 6 weeks after that; however dinner parties and the play will no doubt resume their usual place in Simla life—and of course as the Mintos leave there will be some farewell parties given for them.

I hope Betty has already started a black evening dress on its way to me as I have been badly in need of one for some time and now could not possibly get on without one—as I am—de rigueur—wearing court mourning like all the other wives of officials—and in fact everyone. Not a soul in the streets does one meet except a few natives—with any colour and the suddenness of the King's death has taxed all drapers all over India to their utmost. Fortunately nurse was having some things cleaned for me and we caught the 'Rauj Wallah' (colouring man) at once and had things dyed. I have succeeded in getting 2 very pretty hats and am doing up myself the things that were dyed.

May 13 and 14

The Proclamation took place yesterday—mail day—and this missed getting into the post as we were nearly all day preparing for it and ladies had to go at least 2 hours before the procession came, in order to get a seat under cover.

It should have been a very impressive ceremony, but with the exception of the many handsome husbands in their full dress—mounted on wonderful chargers—my Offley on his beautiful Arab—the most admired by all—and Lady Minto looking very charming with her pretty daughter driving in State to the Flag Staff—it was disappointing and <u>not</u> well carried out at all.

Perhaps the Viceroy was nervous—at any rate he is not strong yet. I only hope King George will send us a <u>strong</u> man to succeed him.

I am writing by this same mail to the Princess—or rather to the new Queen. Offley sent a kind wire to the King and please God he may be a good, strong King and have a happy reign with all good things added thereto—for the Empire and themselves. The gloom cast over all is dreadful.

Offley is NOW Colonel—full Colonel

Colonel Offley Shore
Indian General Staff

I tell him I should have a pearl necklace to enhance my rank!!!

July 14, 1910   **Simla**

My dearest Aunt:

I have had a very much interrupted morning but I hope this will take to you also my thanks for your kindest gift to me of the evening gown, <u>so much</u> needed as it is. I can only bless you for your <u>ever</u> kind thought of me and say with how much pleasure I shall wear it.

I must tell you what a nice thing O. has done. He has insisted that the money advanced to me from Grandfather's estate for furniture and house furnishings etc. should be kept intact in its original sum, so he has made up the amount I spent last year so that when we do have our own house I may have the whole of the £1000 to

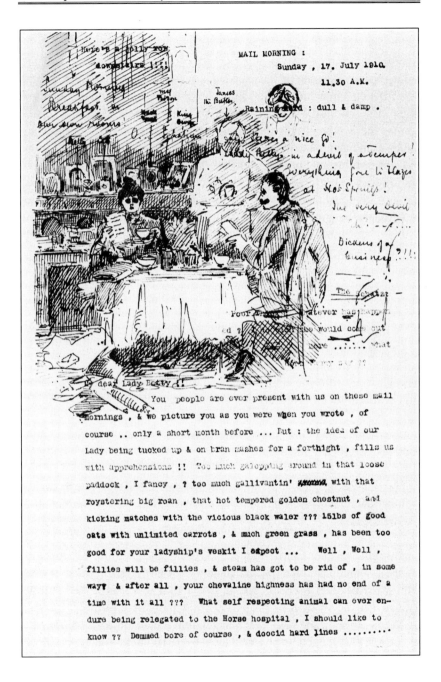

MAIL MORNING :
Sunday , 17. July 1910.
11.30 A.M.

Raining hard : dull & damp .

dear Lady Betty !!

You people are ever present with us on these mail mornings , & we picture you as you were when you wrote , of course .. only a short month before ... But : the idea of our Lady being tucked up & on bran mashes for a fortnight , fills us with apprehensions !! Too much galopping around in that loose paddock , I fancy , ? too much gallivantin' around with that roystering big roan , that hot tempered golden chestnut , and kicking matches with the vicious black waler ??? 15lbs of good oats with unlimited carrots , & much green grass , has been too good for your ladyship's veskit I expect ...   Well , Well , fillies will be fillies , & steam has got to be rid of , in some wayt & after all , your chevaline highness has had no end of a time with it all ??? What self respecting animal can ever en- dure being relegated to the Horse hospital , I should like to know ?? Demmed bore of course , & doocid hard lines ....

Sunday morning breakfast with the mail (Offley sketch).

make use of. This, and other such charming things are what O. is always thinking of and doing for me and he is as pleased as I am with my new dresses or hats, how I put them on, <u>when</u> I wear them etc. In fact when he came riding along with the Chief of Staff the other day, he said, 'Ah, here she is in her new Paris hat!'. So of course there were many agreeable compliments and O. thought no doubt some heart-burnings.

I am continuing in a second class at Viceregal Lodge for 'House Nursing and Hygiene'. This time Her Excellency will be one of our class. I have just sent my subscription for a souvenir from the Ladies in India to be given to Lady Minto upon her departure.

I am studying my Hindustani by myself, each day a few new words or sentences, O. helping me.

In another letter of this period Lina recorded a comment by the Commander-in-Chief on Simla's 'Season'.

The C. in C. told me he proposed leaving Simla 'to get away from this scandalous entertaining for he has scarcely a speaking acquaintance with his bed' but then he is a dull, tiresome old man, and why he ever took this job no one knows—we doubt very much he will last or finish his time.

Her views on women's rights and women's suffrage she recorded when describing a dinner party conversation with a visiting Australian lady:

Last night we had a most agreeable Australian to dine. She told me of their women's suffrage and of her own experience when voting. The horrible part of it all seems to be that the results are nothing gained for the women of property, but rather the enormous increase of votes by women who can neither read or write and whose vote is always influenced—in that class—by their men, whose votes can be bought for a drink. Personally I have no interest in women's suffrage but I think every possible law for their individual rights and their better protection should be evolved.

Blarney Summer Hill,

Simla, the 12 October 10.

Malkani Umar Hayat

request the pleasure of _Mrs_

Shores' Company   at a

ardah party in honour of Lady

'Moore Creagh at Blarney Summer

Hill on Wednesday the 12th October

.910 at 4.30.p.m.

R. S. V. P.
Malkani.

A reception for ladies given by the Senior Lady of the Tiwana clan to meet the wife of the incoming Commander-in-Chief, India.
(It is noteworthy that the Regimental symbols, including the Prince of Wales Feathers, are incorporated in the Coat of Arms.)

Offley during this period, in a letter to Uncle Joe, described an afternoon picnic where Lina apparently on the outward journey had ridden in her rickshaw. At the site Offley suggested that the rickshaw be sent home and that, when ready, they should walk, but Lina complained that:

she would get so hot and assuredly catch cold afterwards . . . and that she ached all over, and how you would be so angry if you thought she was being treated so ill by a brutal and selfish husband!!!!! until at last with many puffs and blowings she bedded her beautiful self down beside the tea basket with a little sniff of content, and busied herself with the spirit lamp, shortly to declare that she was quite glad that she had come to such a nice quiet spot. We watched the setting sun in the west over Viceregal Lodge, under a dark band of rain clouds, and agreed that Simla could be very beautiful, even in the rains. Then after watching the eagles and crows soaring and fighting about over the vast khuds, we picked our way down to the neck again in the failing light, and tackled the stiff pull back to Simla again.

October 14, 1910   **Simla**

Dear Uncle Joe,

Between the intervals of interviewing maids and the hundred and one little things to be done upon returning from our delightful outing in the Hills—and all to be got through before my Amy leaves me on Saturday—and Offley still on a holiday, yet young officers beg a few minutes, and both of us with colds, I failed to catch the mail to you yesterday. I wanted to enclose Lady Minto's charming reception of the gift of a pearl necklace—and Lady Dane's presentation of the same—to you—also to tell you of the gossip and feeling attendant upon the Farewell Ball, by Subscription and much decried by the already heavily taxed Simla official. Subscriptions came often to 100 rupees a piece. They do say that the C's [indecipherable—Ed.] are seeking a Lieut. Governorship—that Mrs. C. who got it up and Sir D. Haig treated all and sundry as though they gave the ball!—that Lady O'Moore Creagh, Lady Dane and the Hon'ble Mrs. Spence, who all rank next to Their Excellencies, though invited guests of the evening, were told to keep away or come down from their usually pleasant perches on the dais because they were not of the receiving party—and that so many left before supper or early owing to the indignities shown them that those who remained to dance on a clearer floor were begged to stay until Their Excellencies left!! A very different Simla from a year ago and let us hope that the pomp and state we hear the new Viceroy exacts—will be really real—for in this land we need it absolutely.

Only this week I am getting off a box with little gifts to you each from us both with best Christmas wishes—the duties should be small as I have now seen the authority that things over 100 years old go in to the U.S.A. free of duty—and my gifts to you and to Aunt Fanny are both rare, valuable, and well over 100 years old. I have just had a gift of a base or capital of a pillar of stone from the Hindu or rather great Buddhist discoveries beyond Peshawar. What to do with it I know not, but I should much like to send it to Mother to have it used in her garden at Narragansett. A sun dial of bronze placed on it would be of the East and will you let me know if there are any difficulties in getting such a thing in to the U.S.

Later Lina explained why she had not been present at the Farewell Ball to Lord and Lady Minto: she had had an attack of bronchitis and Offley had had a bad cold.

Towards the end of October Lina was deserted, as she considered, by her maid Amy but found Mrs. Stewart, who would remain with her for the duration of her stay in India, would prove a great comfort to her during Offley's periods of absence and with whom she would continue to correspond after the termination of Offley's service in India. To Aunt Fanny she wrote:

Wasn't it disgraceful to Amy to leave me? I fear alas—the Eurasians are restless for she has not gone to nearly so good a place. I hope now to get a Mrs. Stewart whom I hear is an excellent woman—she is a Scotch or English woman, not 'native' in any way.

and a little later:

I have a new maid—a very nice elderly woman, kind and attentive and a most respectable woman—a widow with grown up children and they are married and settled with the exception of one young daughter who is studying typing and shorthand. Here in Lahore are the daughters and they seem nice young women and pleased to have their mother with me. She is an English woman and has been twenty years in India so knows the country, its language and ways etc.

In November she reported the departure of the Viceroy and changes in London at the India Office.

Yesterday we bade good-bye to Lord and Lady Minto in the garden at Viceregal Lodge—and saw them drive away with a very sad feeling at heart. I shall miss them very sincerely, but I hope we may meet again. Lord M. made me such a kind little speech that I do feel I could write to him if ever we needed a 'friend at court'. Such an exodus—and it is always so sad—these constant partings.

To meet Their Excellencies The Earl and Countess of Minto.

———

The Indian Community of Simla

request the pleasure of the company of

Lieut Col & Mrs O.B.S.E. Shore D.S.O.

at a Farewell Garden Party at Annandale Gardens,

on September 16th, at 4-30 p.m.

R. S. V. P.

The Secretary, Dilkusha,

An invitation card on the occasion of the departure of the Viceroy at the end of his term of office.

meet Their Excellencies the Viceroy & the Countess of Minto.

The Mohamedan Community

request the pleasure of

Col & Mrs Offley Shore's

company at a Garden Party at Bantony (Nahan House)

on Tuesday the 13th September at 3-45 p.m.

R. S. V. P.

to Khan Zulfiqar Ali Khan,

Bothwell Lodge.

*An invitation card from the Mahomedan Community to a Garden Party on the
occasion of the departure of the Viceroy at the end of his term of office.
The reverse (below) shows a list of the Promoters.*

THE PROMOTERS.

The Hon'ble Nawab, Abdul Majid, Allahabad.
The Hon'ble Khan, Zulfiqar Ali Khan.
The Hon'ble Lieut. Malik, Umar Hyat Khan.
Nawab, Rustom Ali Khan.
Nawab, Ibrahim Ali Khan.
Lieut. Malik, Mumtaz Mohamed Khan.
Faqir, Syed Iftakhar Uddin.
The Hon'ble Lieut. Malik, Mubariz Khan.
The Hon'ble Mian Mohamed Shafi.
Khwaja, Ghulam Sadiq.
Malik, Mohamed Hyat Khan.
Khan Bahadur Maula Buksh.
Nawabzada Umardaroz Ali Khan.
Nawab Saifullah Khan.
Mir Mohamed Khan.

Since writing you last week we have heard officially of Lord Morley's resignation and Lord Crewe's [a very distant cousin of Offley's—Ed.] appointment as Indian Secretary. They say the Viceroy, Lord M., said when he first heard it, 'If only Hardinge [the incoming Viceroy—Ed.] could have had two or three months of Morley!

On 10 November came the first reference to the coming State visit of Crown Prince Wilhelm, son of Kaiser Wilhelm, Emperor of Germany.

Instead of Offley being put on the Crown Prince's Staff, the Viceroy and the Foreign Secretary asked <u>him</u> to provide and suggest such officers as would be available. O. it appears is too senior and too important except should the C.P. go to any manoevres and then it is likely that O., being special officer Staff Duties—would play host to his Imperial Highness. I am <u>very</u> sorry as when I was told by the Military Secretary that O. was a most likely man for it I was in great hopes that it would be a sort of holiday for O. However if Calcutta is not taken off the cards we shall no doubt have the pleasure of meeting the Imperial party there. I am also interested because the new German Consul who is coming out with C.P. is a Prince Henry (XIV I think) of Reuss—possibly of the Riedesel family.

November 29, 1910   Simla

Dear Aunt Fanny,

Please tell Mrs. Altemus that my black satin evening dress in spite of the damage it received on its journey to me was <u>very satisfactory</u>, comfortable and pretty. I have grown very much larger around the waist, round the hips too and a little across the back. Perhaps she would send me a paper with measurements to fill in and would have something to send out to me in February or March at the latest—suitable for the State Garden party—a pretty voile, muslin or crepe and a blue serge jacket and skirt—<u>very stylish</u>, and an evening dress of some colour—say palest blue or pink. This would be 3 dresses. At present I have little but black and will need so much for the next season. However my black things will do nicely for our visit to Government House, Calcutta, where we are now invited to visit the new Military Secretary and his wife—and D.V. shall do so.

I am also sending you two old blouses and a dress shield as I should like some more like them if they are to be had. The white blouse came from Wanamakers and the black and white from Dewees and 2 of each might be sent by post—value not marked. I will be glad to pay for all these commissions on which perhaps you can consult with Aunt Mary, who would choose two hats for the Garden Party and one for the blue serge.

On 1 December Lina left Simla to spend the next three months in Lahore, Dehra Dun and Calcutta: Offley would be on manoeuvres for parts of the period.

December 28, 1910

**Dehra Dun,
c/o Brigadier-General
Frederick Campbell, C.B.**

Dear Aunt Fanny and Uncle Joe,

Here we are in a most lovely spot and with the very kindest of hosts. We came for Christmas and shall now stay on until the end of January as Offley has to go back to Simla where the weather has been very wintery and Mrs. Campbell—nor the General either—will hear of me returning, so Offley will pick me up upon his return and take me to Calcutta where we go to visit at Government House. (Quite the best way to go to the most tip-top house in a place, when you do go!!! eh?) Afterwards we have numerous invitations but I think I shall try to go to see if I can be of some use in helping Lady Lake settle down in Garden House, Meerut, which they have taken at our suggestion and asked our advice and help for servants, furniture—A.D.C.'s—everything in fact—so that I feel as if I was a 'General Officer Commanding'!

This morning they drove us over to see the 2nd Goorka Mess—a charming house and gardens and such treasure in the Mess!! Teapots and temple horses and lamps of massive silver and brass and copper and gold from Thibet and most interesting old prints—a big billiard room and a delightful library. Dehra is the permanent Goorka Station—so, needless to say, their Quarters are all the more cared for. Here also is the Imperial Cadet Corps—or Military Academy for the young Indian princes—and Lord Curzon's hand has created a beautiful English looking type of house for this—or, as someone has called it, a 'Black Forest' house. It is white with beams of dark wood and the thatched roof which is peculiar to this part of India.

I do hope it is true that Betty is coming out to us—and I hope she comes this year—at once. She would thoroughly enjoy a season at Simla and a wind up with the Durbar after some autumn visits. The date is now fixed for the Durbar on December 14th and after that—by this time next year—I hope we shall get some leave for O. and find ourselves making our way home.

In the Mess this morning Offley showed me a quaint old portrait of the only son of the Governor-General, Lord Teignmouth, (Sir John Shore) whose grave we have been asked to look after in Calcutta, and here and there were other Shore presentations or souvenirs.

The first Lord Teignmouth had two sons. In the above letter Lina is presumably referring to the second son, the Hon. Frederick John Shore, 1799–1837, who served in the Bengal Civil Service and is buried in the North Park Street Burial Ground, Calcutta. The elder son inherited his father's title in 1834.

January 14, 1911   **Dehra Dun**

Dearest Aunt Fanny,

We have been having delightful summer days, with tennis parties and rides and drives round the countryside or long walks.

Everyone is talking of preparation for the Coronation Durbar and transportation is evidently to be the most difficult and costly thing if not everything in connection with it—we almost think of buying a motor as one can be quite sure of selling it afterwards. Offley will have to buy a new charger—and uniform and I, evening gowns and court trains have all to be ready. Do make Betty come out—and as soon as she can—as there is not a moment to lose—everyday the passages out are booked up to the limit, and if she is already one of our household she is more sure of being included in all the festivities. We shall have to make every preparation well in advance and have to save up well before hand also as everybody and everything is expected to be very well done.

General Campbell's Brigade is to go—and so they will have their camp—and we hear we should be in the Commander-in-Chief's camp—but of that nothing definite, but if it is so it will mean some house-linen and some plate. I suppose we shall be advised of all in good time. I wish Fanny could come out too. I should be so proud of my two handsome sisters and I know they would thoroughly enjoy it and my friends would fete them too.

January 18th

A letter from O. today tells me the King is to have a great camp—surrounded by the camps of the reigning Indian princes—the Commander-in-Chief an equally splendid camp with all his entourage. We shall buy a motor at once—also a little hooded cart to use my pony in and Mrs. Stewart and I are making lists of the little household necessities that we may order them or get them in Calcutta. Almost any move in India means a big Bunderbust as they call it, but this will be big indeed.

Our evenings have been very gay lately as the General has been reading aloud to us one of Mr. Thackeray's delightful skits on Indian soldiers etc. etc. The General reads so well and now we all understand Hindustani, certainly the terms used in this story. It is brilliant and funny. If you care to read it I will give you a dictionary of the true meaning of the words used in the narrative, for as it is you miss half the fun of the story.

The month of February was spent in Calcutta. Lina described the social aspects of the German Crown Prince's visit; Offley the official.

February 2, 1911   **Government House, Calcutta**

Dearest Aunt Fanny,

Here we are! and oh, such a charming house as this is—great high ceilings and marble floors and real bath rooms such as one has at home. We arrived at 8 o'clock a.m. and our carriage was stopped just in front of the shield of the U.S.A.! part of the decoration for the State arrival of the Crown Prince—so we had quite a triumphal arrival and sped through this interesting old town—Offley pointing out all of interest—as though we were royalties!!! The bridges were so beautifully decorated with palms and the river, full of ships all gay with flags. At 4 the husbands go to meet C.P. while I go at Lady Hardinge's invitation to the State reception at Government House. (We walk across to the house from this wing.) This evening there is a big State dinner and tomorrow they all go out to the Viceroy's pleasure palace—at Barrackpore. More later—I am just bathed and dressed for lunch. I am wearing the little grey and black foulard Betty sent me—a black hat with grey plumes—(All this I feel will interest you).

Later—just before dinner

Offley is in the real bathtub! so I add a little more to you. The arrival of the Crown Prince is over. It was a very pretty sight. All the diplomats and members of Council and Generals etc. awaited the carriage—on the steps of Government House. The Ladies of the Household and Members and officers' wives etc.—myself included—were in the balcony inside the portico.

I was very much taken with the new Viceroy. There is something very charming about him, but Lady H. has not the beauty of Lady Minto—but her manner is very sweet. She seemed awkward to my mind, but that may have been partly due to the ugly (present) fashion of her dress.

Government House is very stately both outside and in. Not so really beautiful as the White House, but of that period. The Native princes had the most splendid clothes on. Oh, such dressing gowns as they would make! and the Nepalese representative had a helmet with a magnificent osprey held in place with a huge diamond and embroidered on top in gold and emeralds—emeralds almost an inch square which we could see and long for from our splendid place.

Thank you so much for the letters with Mrs. Altemus's address in Paris etc. I wrote and asked her to get me an evening dress for the Durbar—a garden party dress—and another morning coat and skirt and blouse for the Proclamation, also a cloak.

I wear your black birthday dress tonight and next week the black satin and shaded jets and crystals Aunt Mary chose me in Paris. Now it's my turn to go to the beautiful bath room.

If only Betty were with me she could meet Rajas enough to arrange to shoot 100 tigers and ride on as many elephants.

February 7, 1911   **Government House, Calcutta**

Dear Uncle Joe,

Now to tell you of our visit here and Calcutta itself. Nothing I have ever seen brings the age of Thackeray so distinctly before one. This is in every sense a Georgian Metropolis and the 'New York palaces' the Rajas build do not take away from the big, stately pillared white stucco houses with their green venetians, great gateways and turbaned black servants. Government House with its lovely gardens is beautiful and this house which is a little Trianon outside is big and cool with marble floors and deep verandahs—most comfortable indeed for this climate. Yesterday Offley and I went out to the old Library, The Imperial Library, a big white place with broad stairs—an iron painted white balustrade with mahogany handrail— huge mahogany doors in white colonial doorways. We went in search of his family graves in the old Calcutta burial ground—as Lord Teignmouth and his brother and their Aunt wish to know that they are in good order. We found them in excellent order—very particularly so now as the Crown Prince was to be shown those of distinction and the Shore grave is one of those.

In the afternoon we went to the Museum—very interesting it was too—and then this morning we drove out to Ballygunge to see the horses of the Body Guard and choose a charger for Offley—and I think we have found a beauty—one of the many out of which the King's charger is to be chosen—and I propose giving it to Offley

as a Coronation gift—using my Xmas gift from you. Everything is
on a big, generous and <u>very expensive</u> scale here and the furniture
reminds me of Germantown—big, plain mahogany beds and ward-
robes and dressing tables and the plain coloured walls again remind
me of the big rooms I remember as Grosvater's, Grosmutter's etc.
In Calcutta, in Bengal India, one can see face to face the age one's
grandparents lived in. Poor Offley is having rather a bad time with
the dentist, but in between times he is making me have the pleasantest
possible visit here—and we enjoy driving about in our viceregal
carriage with 2 footmen to put us in and more besides to help us
out and O. says—'And where is it your Excellency's pleasure to
go next?' and I say 'Mr. Osler the china merchant'—so there we
are let down and I order some old fashioned 'peg' glasses for cooling
drinks on our hot Indian days—and I am told I have been quite
extravagant, and play the part only too well and had best go to tea
with the C. in C.'s lady and see how simple her things are!—and
on leaving there, he exclaims, 'No one has the taste of my Schatz!'
and the tea at Watergate House[10] was atrocious and we came back
and are quite content with <u>this</u> house!!! Tonight we dance at the
Lt. Governor's and I hope to meet a lot of people and old friends—
and <u>wonder</u> if the Crown Prince, who has stayed in bed with a
cold—or a fit of temper! will come.

From Offley

9th February, 1911   **Government House, Calcutta**

My dear Uncle Joe,

We are putting in time here fairly well considering that Youth
and wilfulness have entirely upset the well-laid and carefully considered arrangements for Germany's Hope and Pride. He is out at
Barrackpore, some 16 miles down stream from here, and refuses to
have anymore to say to ceremonial, does not like the look of the
Bengalis, and his mind turns mostly to sport.

Our special staff who are attached to him tell us many things of interest. He certainly appears to be genuinely friendly with Englishmen and very admiring of Indian 'bandobast' as a whole: in fact he has annexed that term to his vocabulary: the German staff seems to be very much at sea directly they are up against new conditions, or anything not provided for in German regulations! and admit being non-plussed and unable to carry on without the assistance of their British confreres. The German Govt. will not fit up the Cruiser 'Gneisenau' for the Crown Prince, as we should have done for our Prince of Wales etc. and he has refused to go home in her, insisting on a passage by the P. and O. from Bombay. He says there would be a question at once in the Reichstag were his father to order special accommodation in this way, and that the radical feeling in Germany today is stronger and more definitely hostile than we have any idea of. He is very greatly taken with polo but says that his father will not sanction it in Germany on account of the expense which officers would incur. Of the men whom he has met in India, he is evidently most impressed with Sir G. Roos-Keppel, and Sir John Hewett, whom he considers to be the two strong men we have in India. He did not see much of our Generals, as he did not want to see any great parades, rather was interested in details of unit working, and Cavalry in particular. He does not seem to be anything like the man that his father is, although he may of course develop when he gets the chance: still he is not the War Lord that Kaiser Bill is.

They do not of course think that his personal inclination for English customs and life will make any difference to the future political relations between the two nations, but that this visit will decidedly strengthen his own feelings about Englishmen.

Last night we went to a dance at Belvedere, the residence of the Lt. Governor of Bengal . . . our hosts being out at Barrackpore, we have been running things more or less 'on our own' with the assistance of such friends of mine as we have come across . . . The little Schatz looked perfectly sweet and very regal in Aunt Mary's last dress, and attracted much attention and secured many more partners than I had ventured to expect for her; the house was admirably adapted to entertainments on a large scale, and the new ballroom a distinct success. I believe the magnates of the Commercial society were present, but we were not impressed with their external appearance or style . . . for a more ordinary or commonplace looking lot I never beheld. The supper to my mind was that sent in by a second class restaurant, and the servants and waiting not what one is accustomed to see in an establishment of the first class. The truth of the matter, to my mind is, our big civilians of today are not of the class to which most of us belong, and these second rate people do not know how to do things, albeit they are plastered with high decorations and occupy great positions under Government. The world is changing, and I do not think for the better in these respects.

Court Mourning [for Edward VII—Ed.] prevents any dances being given at Govt. House, so that we shall not see much in that line while here.

There are to be special races here on Saturday, at which the Viceroy attends in State: Capt. Keighley comdg the Body Guard, of my regt, has kindly arranged for us to go to the special enclosure, and we hope to meet many people there whom we have so far not run up against. People are saying that the 18th King George's Own Lancers are getting things very much their own way, since the following officers hold some of the best appointments.

Myself; Gen. J. Nixon, Comdg the 1st Division; Major Maxwell, Mil. Secty to the Viceroy; Capt. Keighley, Comdg the Bodyguard; Major Wigram, Pvte Secty to the King; Capt. Fitzgerald, the favourite A.D.C. of Lrd K. (now with him in the Soudan) . . . we say that if we have been able to collect a really exceptionally good lot of boys in the past, our predecessor's selection has been justified. We are anxious to get the Regt. on to the King's special escort for Delhi: there are many claimants, however, and everything depends on the King's personal choice. From the admiration with which he expressed himself to me at Quebec, when talking about the Regt, I am inclined to think there may be some chance. There are however many King's Regts in the Indian Army.

I am glad to hear that the new Viceroy cannot say too much for his personal Body Guard, and seems to be perfectly fascinated with it.

Schatz will have told you all the other and more interesting social news.

Ever very sincerely,
Offley Shore

Offley in the above letter uses the Regiment's new title, 18th King George's Own Lancers, granted in December 1910, following the accession to the throne of George, Prince of Wales. As hoped, the 18th was indeed chosen to provide the King Emperor's rear-guard escort at the Delhi Durbar.

Government House,
Calcutta

February 14, 1911

Dear Uncle Joe and Aunt Fanny,

Every day this place gets hotter and though we have comfortable rooms I am very anxious to get away—for everything is exceedingly expensive and we have done most of the sight-seeing and are bored driving every evening on the river side—and seeing Rajas stuffed in—six and eight of them—and their offspring, in brilliantly painted landaus.

A huge row and noise of sort of singing and shouting is going on under our windows. Offley looked to see the cause of it and discovered about eight coolies dragging an iron girder! They always sing, shout or groan over their work in this country and when the weather is very warm it aggravates one extremely.

I think I have made good terms with some people here for a motor during the period of the Durbar—or rather for the month of December—also with the same firm—carriage builders—for a light victoria or cart in which we can put the pony. We make the final settlement tomorrow. This with clothes and uniforms are a pretty penny for one's King—eh? However we hope it will all pay in the end. I only pray and hope one or both of my sisters will come out for this great occasion.

Offley saw his name selected among some 30 out of 85 to be gazetted Substantial [*sic*] Colonel and to be published any day now, and ante-dated we hope, as he was promised or led to believe. This means the actual possibility of seeing him made a General Officer if he remains in the Service—and I do want a 'Field Marshal Sir Offley' before we finish with India.

We are just off to the Fort now so I must close this dull enough letter. We are both so sorry to hear poor Mother had to go through another operation for her eyes. I was glad to have heard at one and same time however that it was all safely over and trust she is enjoying health and happiness now.

'Substantial Colonel': Lina meant 'Substantive', i.e. permanent, as against for the duration of an appointment.

February 18, 1911   **Calcutta**

Dearest Aunt Fanny,

Mrs. Grover is here staying with a Mrs. Fanshaw. Mrs. Fanshaw is an old friend of Offley's Mother and she has taken a great fancy to me and has probably heard a great deal about us. Anyhow—she is going to tell O.'s Mother what she misses in not having our friendship etc. etc. She tells me O.'s Mother is <u>delightful</u> but very autocratic and high tempered, but adores Offley to madness and always planned a royal marriage or a Duke's daughter for him. When I told her I had never done anything since her abrupt letter to me and that Offley had had no further correspondence with her since he wrote to say she must apologize profoundly before he would ever write or see her again, Mrs. F. said we had done <u>perfectly right</u> and I know from what she told Offley that when she goes home this summer she will enjoy telling his Mother all about us. So I wonder whether anything will come of it. O. speaks with great appreciation of all his Mother ever did for him especially in the matter of his education etc. etc., but Mrs. F. says they are very alike and both have loyal, devoted natures until some particular clash comes and his Mother always feels she should direct him in all great steps etc. etc. and of course, Offley, equally decided, thinks she should not. More tomorrow.

On their return to Simla they rented for a year Wildflower Hall which Lord Kitchener had used as an unofficial week-end residence.

They had been for some time considering this and Lina had se-
riously considered buying it, but had been dissuaded by Uncle
Joe. In hindsight this would have been a profitable purchase, but
it can be understood that this would seem a dubious proposition
viewed from Philadelphia.

March 6, 1911   **Simla**

Dear Uncle Joe and Aunt Fanny,

We have taken 'Wildflower Hall' the place Lord Kitchener had
for 7 years—up and out beyond Simla and a 1000 feet higher. I am
now making great alterations that the place may be brighter and
have more sun and air. Lord K. paid no attention whatever to the
house, never even sleeping in it more than half a dozen times—but
in the garden his skill and work and care knew no bounds. So I am
turning my attention to the house and hope with much <u>white</u> paint
and simplicity to make it not only <u>livable</u> but very attractive. I have
chosen my dinner and breakfast service—a white china with a tiny
little vine with a 'bluet' or cornflower vine-like border. It is an
inexpensive reproduction of a service made for Marie Antoinette—to
use perhaps at her farm at Versailles. The cooking utensils are all
so Indian you people at home would not understand, but though
they are called 'Degchies' and are of various sizes and shapes etc.
they are all made of aluminium! Then there will be glass to be got
and trays (these will be the carved wood of the Hill people here)
and Chota Hazri sets. For no good old Anglo-Indian could live
through the day were he deprived of his early morning tea or Chota
Hazri = Little breakfast.

If only some of you could come out and pay us a visit. Betty
and Fanny I so wish and long for, but even them I begin to despair
of. If they would only start in September they could spend the most
heavenly month—October—here with us at Wildflower Hall and as
for you two dear people—once we got you out here you would
forget all about Narragansett and politics and parties and such like
distractions.

March 18, 1911   **Simla**

Dearest Aunt Fanny,

I have not been unmindful of this date today and of the death of my beloved Grandfather on this 18th of March some twenty years ago. By a curious coincidence we went to take possession and give directions for improvements to our house—'Wildflower Hall'—and I felt all the time this is just the sort of lovely and unusual spot that Grosvater and I might have played at giving and taking from each other as we used to when driving in Newport. I say 'playing' advisedly as one can scarcely realize that so far away here in India—where from our verandahs we look to the snow clad hills of the Roof of the World—I make my home.

Private

April 2, 1911   **Simla**

Dear Uncle Joe:

Your letter of March 7th with its enclosures for me from The Pennsylvania Company—authorizing me under Uncle Sam's will to have $10,000—under the conditions provided in the will—was received this morning. I have a copy of Uncle Sam's will, but I had quite forgotten that we had this privilege. However—after talking things over with Offley and thinking them well over myself I feel I do not wish to do this—nor ever should wish to resort to it unless very hard pressed—and especially as the sum we should require would not be greater than $2000, or $3000 all told and not that at one time.

Offley and I always try to look ahead to live within our joint incomes and to keep aside a sum of money for the journey home at any moment. This we have so far managed to do—and Offley also wishes, if possible—to put aside a little each year that should anything happen to him I might continue to have an income equal to his pension on his retirement. This last we have not attained. But though ever most generous and kind he is very positive in his adherence to these principles. We both thank you extremely for your kindness and thoughtfulness in reminding me of this matter—as it is a good thing to know—and I had quite forgotten it. I shall keep the paper safely by me and should I ever wish to use it I will follow your instructions, but for the present we think it is best not to avail ourselves of it as the thousand a year (or $998 something) is always an agreeable 'yearly' addition to our income.

Your generous Christmas and Birthday presents and my Father's annual Christmas gift—have each added to our necessities and our pleasures of Life—and though I long for 'the most expensive thing in the world' i.e. children of our own! I am happy to say—with all my tastes for beautiful and costly things—we are not in debt and please God, even with the changes and chances of this Indian life—which is expensive—I hope never to be. Of course I miss much all those at home have with theatres and operas and motors and then the constant companionship of their Mothers and Fathers and their good Uncle Joe and Aunt Fanny and the many little requirements of everyday that it was ever your pleasure to give me—but I have so much in Offley and you are all so ever kind and thoughtful for us at home—that much as one has to be on one's own—for everything out here—I have nothing to grumble about.

I have marked this private as you said you had spoken of it to no one and preferred we should not.

Letter from Offley

5.4.1911   **Grand Hotel, Simla**

My dear Uncle Joe,

With regard to your very kind thought for Lina in respect of 'ways and means':- I think that we can get along all right just now, without taking immediate advantage of it.

Since one never knows however, when new and unexpected demands may not be made upon one in this most exigeant of government services, or when sudden misfortune may not befall . . . I think it would be as well to keep your arrangement as a reserve. It was just like you to have kept this contingency in mind, and we are both very grateful.

Believe me, ever very sincerely.

Holy Thursday April 13, 1911   Simla

My dearest Aunt,

I have not a moment as we have been busy with other letters since our sad news this morning and with the preparations for going out to Wildflower Hall today. My dearest one is very brave but <u>very</u> sad. He loved his father deeply—and together they were like two boys. In the last two years since his Father's health had been broken down entirely Offley had given his father every comfort and it was out of his purse (Offley's) and the depth of his generosity that the last few years were made peaceful and comparatively happy. He was one of the most delightful of men and devoted to me.

April 14, 1911   Wildflower Hall, Mahasu, Nr. Simla

Dear Aunt Fanny and Uncle Joe,

I am afraid our letters yesterday were hurried—as we were coming out here—and we were both full of our distress at the sad news that reached us with yesterday's early breakfast.

It is the best possible thing that we have this place and that we can come straight away now and pitch in to some absorbing work—and also be quite by ourselves.

(Offley continues later)

Since Thursday evening last we have been continuously at work superintending the washing of furniture out on the lawns, beating and airing of carpets and bedding, the selection of trash in the way of tables and chairs, the checking of wines, stores, china, glass, lamps and a thousand little things indoors, surrounded by carpenters, paper-hangers, brick-layers, hod-carriers, etc. etc. (for we camp in one bed-room) and in the garden, I have been hunting the gardeners (malis) to get the most important work at this season completed—the sowing of seeds and clearing and pruning of the 4–5000 rose bushes which Lord K. has established all over the place. After that will come the tidying up of the lawns and paths—the erection of espalier for the rose garden and lower lawn and a thousand other things. The crocus are over. Daffodils and hyacinth up in limited numbers in the beds in front of the house, on the slopes facing it, and all the way up the ¼ of a mile of steep ascent from the Hindustan–Thibet road.

The lawns and grass slopes are looking delightfully green—ox-eye daisies about to appear in myriads, the young amber fronds of the Schatz's favorite maidenhair fern and the chestnuts and wild apricot and walnut just bursting into life. In fact one doesn't know all that is struggling up to have a look at the sun through the snow drenched ground—surprises meet one every morning! NNW, N, NNE,—across a tremendous 'Khud' some five miles rise the towering masses of perpetual snow with peaks at anything about 23,000 and over.

Westwards from the rose garden, through the pines a divine view of Simla and the Sutlej winding through the lower Siwaliks far out into the plains—50 or 60 miles in a straight line. The garden is most beautiful of course in the afternoon light about 5–6 p.m.— and the deepening shadows falling on the marvellous range upon range of spurs, with the valley 2000 feet and more below us, are so fascinating and entrancing that one stops to gaze at the glories in silent wonder.

How my father would have revelled in all this if he had been only well enough to enjoy it! I fear however that the cold winds of the snows which have not even yet stopped—would have kept him indoors, poor man, and he is not here to share all this with us! Lina is desperately busy planning the general arrangements of the interior, and clever little thing, is being I hope, repaid for all her extraordinary imagination and foresight. She certainly is on her little legs a good

14 hours a day and has barely time to report that she is tired! The progress we have made in 3½ days is wonderful, and I must say James, the 4 Jhampanis, and the workmen generally have all worked like Trojans. This has been one of those rare occasions when the native forgets to say So and So is not his work. Cheering little exception to their customary attitude of always appealing to 'the other man'. I shall be very loath to return to Simla and the office on Tuesday morning! and henceforth only get out on Saturdays about 2 pm: back again early on Monday mornings.

Still—the little visits will be, I hope, as pleasant and as healthful as these few days have proved. The air is simply gorgeous! Mrs. Stewart has forgotten all about her back-ache and is looking tons better. My orderly 'Walia' has proved immensely useful, as he always does in emergencies, and hunts his brown brethren famously—besides riding in and out of Simla for the mails, or anything else that we require. He has just lost 2 nephews and so is, like me, sad and out of sorts rather. This interest is just what Linchen wants in the shape of an occupation. She now definitely announces that she is going to settle in England, and find a house to hold all her worldly goods! I demur and say I refuse to live in a nasty dark damp climate. Then we begin to fight—in our amicable way—and call each other by pet names—she's a desperate little obstinate pig sometimes and of course says I'm impossible and don't know my own mind!!! Poor little fattling—but she is enjoying her small self and no mistake about it. One or two people have already dropped in upon us—just to see how we look—and are amazed at the revolution she has created in the interior of old K's dismal den.

Offley

And now goodnight. We both wish so much you were all here to enjoy this beautiful spot—to smell the pines and to just be with us. I have been sewing curtains in between running to look at this and that in the gardens, and it is all heavenly and so good for my dear one—so sad at this time. This morning we both had letters from the devotedly attached Father and Father-in-law. It is all so hard to realize.

Lina

The following is the letter Offley received that Easter morning from his Father.

St. Faiths
Mount Park Road
March 26th   **Ealing**

My Dear Old Fellow

I was, indeed, glad to hear <u>at last</u>, that you were <u>Full</u> Colonel. They have taken their time about it and you have a lot ahead of you on the list but somehow I have always felt that 'they' have their eye upon you and altho Seniority cannot be altogether ignored, that they will manage to find a special opportunity of making use of your valuable services and I know how valuable they are from others who served under you!!—<u>so there</u>—

Your last most interesting and I am sure you are right in your views about India but it's hard to get the Parliament at home to agree to leave the Country to those on the spot who know. Keir Hardie has once more been making an ass of himself about India, and now Morley has come back temporarily one doesn't know what they will do!

Poor Ena passed away on Friday night (24th) after having been tapped in the chest 3 times in so many weeks but I believe she had pneumonia at the last. All we old ones must go and are going. I was nearly bowled over this last week by a dog—and found out that my heart is as weak as possible still!

The very attached old
Gov

April 27, 1911   **Simla**

Dear Uncle Joe,

Thanks for your letters and kindest appreciation of ours. I am so glad you write to Offley as you ever have and he values your letters and now that those of his dear Father can come no longer I see he will look all the more eagerly for yours and my Father's. It has been very sad to get his Father's letters week by week and to read them—as we do—on the lawn, at breakfast—at Wildflower Hall— and to try and realize each time that this must be the last.

The Orderly rides into Simla and brings the mail out. Last Sunday the bags were stuffed full and I received two from Mr. Offley Shore and O. one—such a charming one from his Father. I could not help wondering if the cable had been correct.

Last evening a lady in the rooms next to these played most beautifully on the piano—Chopin and the newer French composers and Russians. Offley went on reading, but enjoyed the music too; while Stewart and I sat in chairs near the door from whence the music came. She told me quietly how her Scotch husband had had her taught to play and how she loved it, but she had no great talent and too many babies so gave it up. However her daughter sings very nicely and her daughter-in-law is a 'gold medallist'. She is so glad because she thinks it adds to the love of one's own home. I like to hear her tell of India 20 years ago and more. She came out here as a little child, Motherless—and married at 14!! She helps me so much with my house and all our interests and daily duties here in Simla and I hope she may soon get well and strong again.

May 1st, 1911   **Wildflower Hall**

Dearest Aunt Fanny:

We read your letters at breakfast on this lawn yesterday morning, but you must not feel sorry that we have taken this place for it will not keep us in India a single day longer than we have got to be. This year you know they refused Offley any leave whatever, but even now his application is in for leave immediately after the Durbar, and we do trust they will grant us this privilege. When Offley was so ill last winter at Dhera Dun, I made up my mind that I would never go home and leave him behind in India, and we have only taken the house for a year and with the first refusal to take it for another year if we are obliged to stay in India. I am sure if you could only be with us you would certainly share our delight in so lovely a spot. Yesterday there was a coolie strike in Simla—and as the coolies are the people who draw the hired rickshaws or local 'cabs', we have been wondering what we shall do about getting in and out from here.

I am enclosing you samples of the wall paper in our room which is so pretty and bright—from the windows you get the most superb view of the snow covered mountains and the now green and blue hills in the foreground.

Last night we heard that 2000 coolies had left Simla and it is all because a tax of 2 rupees per head has been put upon the lazy rascal himself, who comes to Simla to work, instead of putting it on us, the masters. This civilization or education of the masses of natives in India is a most dangerous and impossible thing, especially as their views and codes and creeds are quite different from ours. To me, I believe East and West are impossible to bring together in this way—neither black and white nor oil and water ever mix well.

I had such a sad and touching letter from Aunt Caroline telling me how my father-in-law had talked of me and of Offley and his happiness in ours, and that night he passed peacefully away. He had already addressed the envelopes for the following mail day to go to us and Aunt Caroline's letter was sent in the one addressed to me.

June 15, 1911   **Simla**

Dearest Aunt Fanny and Uncle Joe

You must <u>know</u> what my feelings were the night I received Betty's cable that dear Mother's condition has become serious and how sad and anxious we have both felt ever since. As no further cable messages have come I am hoping that she is better again and that she will steadily improve and be able to go up to Narragansett and enjoy her sweet new house.

We much enjoyed a visit from the Lakes who came on to us from the Commander-in-Chief and revelled and delighted in the beauty of Wildflower Hall. They walked as you and Uncle Joe do— quietly leaving the party of chatterers and finding their way in every direction, and with wildflowers and butterflies they return to ask questions about all the birds and trees they have seen. I think they really did thoroughly enjoy their visit and so did we in having them.

Wildflower Hall is looking very sweet and green in these fresh rains and I only wish we could send to you and to Mother some of our splendid roses. This is a dull letter but I am thinking so much of Mother and wondering what the trouble and suffering she has really is—that I cannot easily write today. It is dreadful to get but a few words in a cable and to try and put two and two together for more and then give it up, only to hope and pray things are better.

From Offley

June 19th, 1911   **Simla**

My dear Uncle Joe,

We have just come in for a day or two, after three positively delightful days out on the Mashobra Hill—where many have been so pleasant, none have been more successful. Possibly this has been the direct result of pleasant company, good weather, and congenial occupation? Anyway, the net result has been quite charming. There were drawbacks, of course, but they faded into insignificance beside the glorious views, wonderful light and shade, the superb air, beside which that in Simla seems heavy and inert . . . Wildflower Hall is the gem of all the places around here.

Last Saturday they had the Coronation Fête away down in Annandale, the most—to my mind appalling democratic and mixed nationality hurlyburly imaginable—but we decided that our sylvan retreat would be a better proposal and now we are hearing many and divergent accounts of that same festival. You can never mix up natives with Europeans in shows of that nature with success: some of the more advanced of our legislators think that the time has come for attempts in that line . . . but they are mere vain theorists, without any knowledge of Asiatic human nature.

Today, the 21st June, the precious box of plated things arrived from Karachi—enclosed in a rough crate. On being opened by Schatz,

Charles Perry Sinnickson, 1844–1925.
Lina's father.

Emma Sophia Rosengarten, 1847–1911.
Lina's mother.

Joseph G. Rosengarten, 1835–1921.
The 'Uncle Joe' of the letters.

Fanny Rosengarten, 1833–1925
The 'Aunt Fanny' of the letters.

Lina's room at Rittenhouse Square, Philadelphia.

Annotated by Lina: 'Offley on his beloved Arab'.

The wedding of Offley Bohun Shore to Caroline Perry Sinnickson in Philadelphia, 29 January 1908.

although the outer crate was in perfect order, she found that the lock, special catches had all been wrenched open, the Caldwell box with nearly every part of it broken, and the contents in the most unholy mess you ever set eyes on. She telephoned to me at the office, and on my recommendation, sent over to the Commerce and Industry Dept., who kindly sent an official to examine into the state of the damage. The beautiful Indian Customs are under that Dept., fortunately. Every single article in the box was badly dented, broken, or damaged in one way or another . . . the candles which Aunt Fanny so kindly put in I believe, were strewn about among the broken glass, things had been put back into their bags two and three together, and no attempt made to repack. Net result—things had been jostling around all the way from the coast and their condition defies description. What the bill for doing them all up will come to, the Lord only knows and I very much doubt whether we shall ever get any redress out of either Forbes Campbell and Co., the agents at Karachi or out of the Govt. of India. One never does. This is as you know the fourth time that we have suffered at the hands of this precious Govt.: the effect is therefore cumulative, so to speak, and neither of us are fit to hold any conversation with. One way and another we have not been fortunate this year, and we are, I think, quite prepared to leave the country for good and all at the first opportunity. (Aunt Fanny will say 'Hurray!'?) Poor little Schatz!!! and the hot weather does not tend to make her take things easier.

The pig-devils have shot another civil officer, and a police officer within the last two days . . . and every one is shouting for severer repressive measures. I think our political governors, who at present are intent upon reducing the army, and at the same time giving universal compulsory education to the masses, are out of their senses. It is about time we went elsewhere? The meanness of the Govt. to their servants is indescribable, and the class of servants is not improving. Can they wonder? Apparently they do not care.

The military camps for the Durbar are being run on the cheapest possible lines, whilst the civil and political ones are to be done 'up to the knocker' with everything found free: we have to pay for nearly everything. Military men are not what you might call pleased. I have been trying to get decorations for certain officers who I know have done magnificent work for India, and I am told that they are quite well enough paid and don't deserve anything. When one knows the enormous gazette of civil honours that is being prepared, it makes one perfectly sick. Favorites too are being given everything, under specious arguments, and the really good men are being left out in the cold. I suppose it is the same in every country in the world, but I have not been brought up in this manner.

Everything at home is of course Coronation mad. We are looking for some good from the Colonial Conference, and are delighted to see that the rough young element is not sparing some of our so called Ministers and may stiffen their weak resolves.

You evidently saw a good game of polo the other day and I expect our people learnt something—the tendency in England and out here is to get hidebound and tied to ancient customs and I expect their defeat will do them a great deal of good. I wonder what the total value of the ponies on the ground was? Lady Betty no doubt saw the game and will give me a spirited account of it. Both sides played like demons I expect? Precious near a fight?

The monsoon looks like failing if not altogether—temporarily. What it will mean to this hand to mouth country, if it does fail, I don't know. If it holds off and then comes along late, the camping grounds round Delhi won't be fit to touch. First of all they feared plagues—now it's the rains with possible rise in prices. Will the Durbar or the manoeuvres ever come off?

There are odds offered against—just now.

June 22, 1911   **Simla**

My dearest Aunt—
Dear Aunt Fanny—

How can I write to you and begin to tell you what I feel—how stunned this news has left me. To realize my darling Mother is dead—dead ere I could ever see her again—or touch her hand or hear her voice or sit to comfort her or be her companion through anymore gray days or good days to come and we have been looking forward to having those good days together—talking of leave and pressing for it. The longing to go home has been so keen—but how could you all know—we are so far away—so far away. If I only could fly to you all now—to comfort and help you all—who have been through so much by her side, by her dear side. Instead Offley and Mrs. Stewart are doing all they can to soften this blow, to console me in my grief. Offley has been gentleness and consideration all through and we are in the midst of Coronation festivities—and fetes and 'by command'—and so all my friends know—and they have been so good and kind and all this in a far off land helps—but oh, I wanted to see my Mother again. I wanted her to see how happy I am—to see my house and my home and all the things she provided for me and you too and Uncle Joe. If only you would all come to us in India you would love it at Wildflower Hall—and the journey in the right season is not so trying. I cannot write more dear Aunt Fanny. God bless you and comfort you and my sisters and my Father. How wonderful Mother ever was. I think I understood her and the load of sorrow she had. I remember her long ago when she was young and merry and we were little things. I can see her playing for us to dance in the old drawing room at Rittenhouse Square. I remember her the day she came back from the Alaskan journey. I thought no one ever looked so pretty. She wore a hat and such a pretty lace coat—things I think she had got at Guerins and oh—it was so good to get back to her. I remember how we loved to kiss her soft white neck when we were children.

Oh—oh dearest Aunt Fanny you must know the memories that surge in my heart as I write. Offley is just coming back from the Coronation Service so I must stop, dry my eyes and try to be brave and thoughtful for him. We go tomorrow to Wildflower Hall and shall stay there until I want to come back.

God comfort you all.

July 12, 1911   **Wildflower Hall**

Dearest Father,

We are going into Simla tomorrow for the day so I am writing my mail letters this evening. Your last letter dated the 6th of June and which reached me only last Sunday, July 9th, tells me of your bitter anxiety for my darling Mother. Poor dear, eager Mother always so alert and so alive in all her interest and energy for each of us. How hard, how dreadfully hard it must have been for you and Betty and Fanny to see her so ill and listless. Offley and I have been so sad and heavyhearted, aye—broken hearted at all our news from home either in England or in America. But we talk of you and Mother and of our beautiful and happy wedding day and it is such a glorious memory of you all at home. The lovely day—the beauty of the house and the generous, splendid spirit that pervaded everything because of you and Mother and how nice and dear you both looked. I have such a good kind tender husband, dear Father, in Offley and, but that we are so far away from you all, we have nothing to wish for in each other. You would love this place and I should be so pleased and proud showing you all Offley has done himself to add to the loveliness already here. I am so glad the tea arrived safely. You must tell me if you really like it or not.

July 17, 1911.   **Wildflower Hall**

My dear, dear Aunt Fanny,

Your letter of June 20th telling me of my dearest dear Mother in her last ill days reached me yesterday and I am so thankful to you for writing it and for knowing that you were all with Mother and that she knew you all—but it is very dreadful and terrible the grief and heartache I feel—to have been so far away. There are days when I cannot realize it all even yet—and I fear from your letter that it came as a great shock to all of you—for Father's last letter was so hopeful and happy as there was such a change for the better.

How much and how often I wish and long to be with you. Offley does too. My dear, splendid, loving Offley to whom every day I become more deeply attached and every day too I look at him in wonder and amazement for his tenderness and devotion to me—and I have so many times wished my Mother would come to visit us—if only to see the esteem in which he is held. How very proud she would have been. I try to be brave and cheery as Offley is and to have consideration for others as he does—and my friends have been <u>very kind</u>, but you can understand how much I wish it might have been my part to have been with Betty and Father and Fanny and <u>you</u> and Uncle Joe at this time. How much in life one has to learn to take the bitter with the sweet. As Mrs. Grover said, the Easter is our great consolation and Mother had such a sure faith. God bless her and bless her. She was very wonderful and the memory of our last days together and of that last afternoon in Philadelphia with her is very present in our minds and hearts and <u>very sweet</u>. Stewart has been very comforting, poor old soul. She has seen a great deal of trouble in her life and I think I shall bring her home with me when I come. I hate changing and I like to have my people remain with me as you all have for many years. Even our Indian servants are very faithful and the old Madrassie butler had a chance to go to the Commander-in-Chief's the other day, but he said, 'No. I stay with Missus and Master. They very good to me.'

Throughout September and October Lina was very distressed; everything appeared adverse.
Her youngest sister, Fanny, was ill:

I have felt so distressed that in all my letters there never comes any news of Fanny having joined you. However to us it seems she would recover her strength so much better in the heart of her family especially having gone through such a sorrow and now that you all lead such a quiet life. I do not agree with doctors wishing so constantly to separate the family. One must live a family life in this world in any walk of life and I think the idea of taking people so much apart is <u>very wrong</u> in most cases.

The international situation in Europe was disturbing and there was social unrest in Britain.

The war clouds look very black over Europe just now, don't they? This materially interferes with the question of 'leave' and it often looks as if the Delhi Durbar was a very uncertain thing—at least so runs the talk today. The Labour troubles at home and the war scare make everything look very much against the King's coming out. Emperor Bill seems very bullying and grasping. Why should he devil poor France to death? Frighten Belgium and Holland and most of the rest of the world in the bargain?

> *Lina did not mention as a reason why the King might not be able to leave Britain for the Durbar the looming Constitutional crisis over the powers of the House of Lords to defeat Bills passed by the Commons, which Prime Minister Asquith threatened to resolve by recommending to the King the creation of an adequate number of additional Liberal Peers. Had the House of Lords not given way against this threat the presence of the Monarch in the country would have been essential.*
>
> *Then for a month Lina's mind was fully occupied with business matters: their tenure of Wildflower Hall; her family's plan to sell 230 Rittenhouse Square; her own finances.*

September 24, 1911   **Wildflower Hall**

My Dearest Aunt,

I am for once ahead of everyone down to breakfast—but we get up very early here. You would not know me at Wildflower Hall—for we are all called at six a.m. and I am always up, bathed and down about 8 o'clock.

Today is Sunday and such a day. The snows lie deep and white on the hills that surround us some 6 miles away while our gardens are blazing with dahlias and cosmos and the grass green and beautifully kept and cut. The deodars full—crammed with young cones. The place is so lovely this glorious weather that we are feeling very sick-hearted at going forever next month. To take it only for one year has been a great expense—not that we have not had great, great pleasure in it, but with Uncle Joe's advice always in the top of my mind, I/we decided not to buy it and so it has been sold over our heads and we are homeless in India—or even worse than homeless for we feel so sore and sad that the place we love here and made so much of is lost to us forever, and Offley is an Indian officer—not a British—so our lot is cast in this country if he keeps on in the Service—and having come so far it seems a great pity to give up now. We are offered a place for which they ask a lakh of rupees or in dollars about 33,000, while this place with its 24 acres went for less than 12,000 dollars.

I am feeling sad and sick over it all. It would have been such a sweet place to bring you all to.

God bless you and keep you all and may it please the same good God that we all meet again soon.

October 12, 1911

Wildflower Hall

My dear Uncle Joe,

Very many nice and charming and kind letters we have constantly to thank you for—and Offley last night on giving me his long letter with its pen and pencil sketches for you said, 'Bless the dear man, I have the deepest affection for him and I only wish these poor pictures were worthy of the good kind man to whom they go!' We so often speak of you and Aunt Fanny whom we both look upon as a second Father and Mother to us. All sorts of things come on to the horizon to make 'leave' look very uncertain, however we are packing to get off immediately after the Durbar (now a very sure thing in spite of all said and done and the serious conditions at home—and even here).

I am most anxious and interested to know several business matters.

1. What are the taxes per annum of Mother's house—now ours—at 230, W. Rittenhouse Square?

2. What has become of my income from Uncle Sam's estate?

I did <u>not</u> take my ten thousand—but I have only received $500.00 and some dollars <u>this</u> year, while last year I received nearly a thousand dollars. You wrote me some time ago that with the re-adjustment of investments it would be augmented etc.—but now the year is almost over and one's income is less by half? Will you tell me what you know of it. I have written to my brother Charles, but neither of the boys ever write to me; at least not for over a year or more have I heard from either of them. I suppose I am too far away and they forget my existence, and their interests are self-centered in their own particular families, but as Charles and now George both have business interests in which I share—I hope they will not forget me. Poor Betty has been through so much and has had so large an amount to do that I do not like to ask her for anything further in my behalf, but I do think Charlie might keep me a little posted on these business matters for which he is responsible. I am really quite annoyed, not to say hurt about it—however you will know how to quietly tell him to be so kind as to let me know what I am to expect. I am afraid in any case we could not get home until Spring—if it were not for this Durbar we could start now.

October 12, 1911   **Wildflower Hall**

My darling Aunt,

How the time does fly—days and months pass—all too quickly. I am ever thinking of my Dear One, my darling Mother whom I have lost—the awfulness of any home coming for me—only perhaps the blessing to share my grief with you and my Father and sisters. I do confess I am greatly distressed at the idea that they wish to sell the town house. Where will they go? Where will they find or keep a 'Headquarters'? It would be far better to rent it—if possible—it seems to me. I would so gladly buy it myself for them—Father and Betty and Fanny—to have to make their headquarters—if I could afford it—or if the 3 girls could just buy the boys' share—so that Father, Betty and Fanny had a place to call home. What are the taxes? I have written to ask everyone and get no answers and I am so concerned. I feel sure my Mother always intended us to keep this house unless we all married. And it is our most natural center.

Why should we not rent it rather than sell it? or what are their plans? Of course I am far away and therefore realize am not a capable judge—but I see homeless people every day of my life and feel the bitterness of it. In fact I am so sorry now and deeply regret not having bought this place. The new owner wishes to come in as soon as possible even before our time is up, if we will allow it—and perhaps we shall, as we must go down to Delhi in November. The Durbar, having been somewhat curtailed in numbers will now be more expensive for the fewer members than ever—and fall even heavier on us—those of middle rank—than the very high or the quite low officials etc.—and with the hope and possibility of a journey home ahead of us we feel very shocked at the amount of round dollars—or pounds and pence needful. English officers get their way to England paid for them, but Indian officers do not. I have been in correspondence with Messers Thomas Cook and so has O. and these journeys home are as Offley says 'the very devil for expense' so my dresses will be of the very simplest for the great Durbar.

On the subject of Wildflower Hall Lina finally wrote even more strongly to Uncle Joe.

In another fortnight now we leave this sweet place—in any case that would make us feel very sad that so soon the summer was over, and such a wonderful summer as far as weather and climate have been! But, with the sale of this house to an hotel proprietor it is lost to us forever and we are regretting and grieving more and more that we didn't buy it ourselves—$10,000 is not much for a place of this sort in the best climate in India and I am sorry to let myself be influenced so strongly by your wish that I should not buy myself a house—nothing we see suits us now! and the breaking up of one's household and habitation so constantly is an unhappy thing and a horribly expensive one. I should have insisted upon O. buying it—but I wanted to have it out of my 'trust' so that it would not deplete our or rather his small income. However the deed is done and we are left disconsolate with every other owner of a fine country place anxious to rent them to us. I must say we have got a good name for taking care and interest and after all let us hope all is well that ends well—but I feel very unhappy about it all.

By the last week in October all minds were occupied by the approaching Durbar in Delhi and the subsequent festivities in Calcutta.

Everybody is bustling round trying to get their clothes in final order for the Durbar. I have not even a hat, but one I trimmed myself. Black clothes in the presence of their majesties has been forbidden, or even black and white—but in my case I have a special dispensation from HM—however I suppose as we have a most considerate Queen all people in mourning will be excused.

All sorts of electric things we had in Canada are to be set up for me in my tents for the Durbar and Stewart and I are taking all the pretty things we can to make the tents look smart.

Offley in a letter to Uncle Joe had a paragraph on Lina's managerial skills:

The past week has been one of packing up, evacuating, and redistributing luggage to three destinations at once. Shall we ever re-unite it all again!? What Lina has learnt about administration and 'bandobast' you've no conception! Ditto finance and audit. I hand all the accounts business over to her. She keeps a firm grip on the purse strings—so firm indeed that I can't spend my own money! But, all finance ministers are like that? She fights me over 5 rupees to a servant or cooly, but trots off and gives a thousand for a carpet! They are really marvelous these women? However, I am very grateful and the subdivision of staff work is necessary—and things 'go' alright—on the whole. She has got to land me in America and bring me back to India—if we decide to return to our chains—with some balance to start afresh or I'll twist her beautiful tail.

Lina outlined their own movements over the next two months and detailed her own responsibilities.

November 1st, 1911   **Wildflower Hall**

My dearest Aunt,

This will probably be my last letter from this sweet place as by the next mail we shall be moving into Simla and on the 15th we leave for Garden House, Meerut, to stay with the Lakes until time to motor into Delhi for the great and long looked for Durbar. I have been busier than the proverbial Bee—with this house to close and to pack for the big house in Calcutta where I shall have a household of six—O. and I and Sir Percy—General Kitson and 2 A.D.C.s. I am to be Chatelaine or hostess and always have a luncheon or dinner table ready to receive any of the Great and Big of this Empire who may drop in during the festivities at Calcutta—all my silver has to go down—and linen for the table etc.—to me falls the duty of catering and ordering (or at least to Stewart and James). Such is the wish of Sir P. and Offley!! However we are not frightened, Stewart and I, but you see we shall have our hands full. Lady Lake is very frightened and of a most retiring nature on these occasions, but she has consented to come to the Court and wishes me to present her. It is now almost certain that we shall get leave early in the new year (and go to America)—on condition that O. returns to a much higher General Staff appointment here—D.V. I am very pleased at this as I do not wish him to resign the Service and I know it is Sir Percy Lake's wish that the Service should do anything rather than lose my husband. So I hope I do my part well in Calcutta this winter—as you can imagine.

We are having the greatest difficulty to make sure of a carriage etc. to leave Delhi at once the Durbar is over and get on to Calcutta and make the house ready there. The railways will all be over-filled and over worked and we must take all our luggage actually with us—if we ever expect to see it in time at the other end. If Offley was only Chief of General Staff or Commander in Chief he would have his own rail car!! and then these difficulties would be solved—but now the railways are so congested that even if one is quite willing to pay for one's own carriages (and we always do this) there is not one to be had because of the arrangements made a year ago at least for the noble swells who come out to this occasion only. We hear some Americans have ordered whole trains for themselves—but they will not be able to get them—no matter how many dollars they are willing to pay—because there are not enough to go round the great officers of State etc. in the Indian Empire.

*Offley and Lina described the Durbar in several letters, each
from their own point of view, and with some repetitions.*

From Offley

**Army Headquarters Camp,
Delhi Durbar,**

December 7, 1911   **Tent No. 50**

My dear Uncle Joe,

The Badshah is at last in Delhi and the Royal Standard floating
north of the historic Ridge.[11] He is actually here!

This morning Lina insisted on having her dozing-hour tea at 6
a.m., was ready dressed and jumping with excitement to be off by
8—just because ever since dawn motors and regiments of foot and
horse and Escorts and Native Chiefs' retinues and carriages had
been on the move en route for their respective rendezvous on the
State Entry Route. Why wouldn't I hurry up! Breakfast? she didn't
want any! I reminded her that HM would not arrive at the ridge
(just above us and ¾ mile away) before 12 noon: that we shouldn't
get back till 2 or 3 p.m. (which was exactly what we did do)! Bless
you! she didn't require to stoke-up like a blessed old warship and
I was merely wasting valuable time and making myself objectionable
. . . The police arrangements are not good here, and the place was
not originally planned for a great ceremonial; the 'communications'
are narrow and bad and few, and as a matter of fact starting as we
did at 9 a.m. to go such a short distance was none too early. We
had seats under a canopy at the Reception Pavilion on the ridge,
and for 3 mortal hours amused ourselves strolling about and talking
to our friends and acquaintances, of whom there were v. many. Then
a bugle went, and everyone settled down in their chairs and the
leading notables, Governors and Lt. Governors began to arrive from
the Fort where they had met the Royal Party as they got out of their
train.

Shortly afterwards the head of the Royal Procession began to
appear and finally the King on horseback and the Queen in her
carriage pulled up in the midst of us. We were a little far back to
clearly distinguish people, but we made out the Royal Personages.

Lina's invitation to the State Entry by King George V and Queen Mary to Delhi in December 1911.

The Queen looking v. regal and imposing in appearance, King George mounted. A very gay throng.

After they moved on, the Native Chiefs' Processions, 1½ hours long, followed, until the eye was tired of watching them. Every conceivable combination of uniform, color of trappings, garish appointment and escort, from modern escorts to the Negro-Arabian Hussars of Hyderabad! White dolman, Prussian blue breeches, scarlet tunic and white facings! Sun-shades of golden embroidery, fly whisks of every imaginable shape and kind; silver coaches, barouches, out-riders, coachmen, British and Native, followers on foot and mounted, in the old padded and chain armor, banners of yellow and green and gold, horse drummers, state bands, performing horses richly caparisoned, that walked past on their hind legs. Rajahs asleep or bowing solemnly to the clapping of the European guests; all this mingled with the blaze of every European uniform and Asiatic dress, the costumes of the ladies, the scarlet gowns and wigs of the Justices of the Chief Court, green and

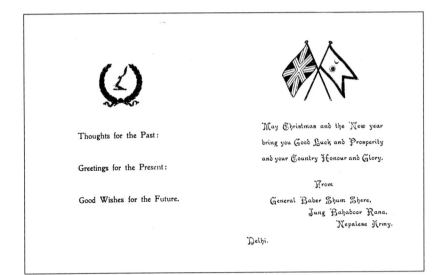

*A Christmas card from General Baber Shum Shere, Jung Bahadoor of the Nepalese
Contingent, showing the outside (left) and inside (right).*

gold of the Royal Archers, the silver lace and scarlet of the Lord
Lieutenants of English counties, French and Japanese, Nepaulese,
Burmese and Chinese, and Foreign Office delegates, the cuirasses
of the Household Cavalry and the enormous helmets and plumes of
the Gentlemen at Arms—all made a kaleidoscope of colour which
fairly dazzled you. It was a brave show, but somewhat lengthy.

Lina and I are both obstinate in our way, but we found my little
thermos basket containing biscuits and chocolate uncommonly apropos about 1 p.m.! Not only for ourselves but for some surrounding
friends.

We eventually found our motor and reached our camp by a long
circuitous route about 2:30 p.m. You have no idea what a relief and
convenience the Schatz's motor has been! In fact we should never
have seen as much as we have done without it.

We have two or three days in which to recoup from all the
labour of 'shows' and sightseeing and then the week begins in
grim earnest.

December 13, 1911   **Army Headquarters Camp,**
                                                            Delhi Durbar

Dear Father, Aunt Fanny and Uncle Joe, Betty and Fanny,

The Great Durbar has taken place and we have seen and taken
our small part in the most magnificent ceremonial that has assuredly
ever taken place in this world. The King and Queen in their coronation robes with their jewelled crowns on, arrived amid the cheers
and enthusiasm of their people in India in the most exquisite state
and pomp one could possible conceive. Their Majesties held 'Durbar'
under a canopy of scarlet and gold of exquisite design and beauty.
They walked, they sat, and they received the homage of the kneeling
Princes and Chiefs of India, of the Church and of the high courts
of India, of their Members of Council, with a regal splendour that
no description can picture to you. It would need the pen of Bea-
consfield to paint in words the ropes of pearls, the glitter of diamonds,
rubies and emeralds, the velvet and silks, the beauty of stuffs, the
elaborateness and uniqueness of dress of the Rajas of Burma, or
Thibet, of Central India or the Punjab, of Madras or of Rajputana—
pearls and diamonds were sewn into coats of velvet and brocade—
emeralds almost the size of eggs were hung and draped in turbans
of every intricate and imaginable shape and fold—all the magnifi-
cence of an Emperor and Empress and the greatness of the greatest
Empire that God has ever given on this earth. The solemnity of the
ceremonial, its beauty and its radiant colour and its reality are beyond
the possibility of words to describe. The Durbar held by their Majesties, with 60 thousand troops from the King Emperor's camp to
the Durbar amphitheater, and some 100 thousand people in the two
stands, was a marvelous sight. Not an elephant to be seen and yet
in all Asia such a thing of wonder and glory has never yet been.
Spellbound one rose or sat according to the ceremony—at the arrival
of the King-Emperor and the Queen-Empress cheers so great and
loud that it seemed as though they shook the earth and at the end
every voice in that huge assemblage sang the National hymn.

After the Durbar the ceremonies surrounding Their Majesties'
visit continued at Government House, Calcutta, after which Lina
and Offley would start their year's leave, a round the world tour
visiting both their families.

Watergate, Fort William,
Calcutta

January 7th, 1912

Dear Uncle Joe,

The Imperial festivities are over and a green card for the special
entrée (which I will enclose before I mail this letter) takes me to Government House tomorrow to bid good-bye to Their Majesties. It has
been a wonderful and glorious visit and I think impressed all Hindustan.
The Court was a magnificent sight—the throne room a beautiful picture
of brave men and fair women—with all the oriental glories of every
colour and every jewel that exists. The native ruling princes and the
native ladies that were present outdid each other in cloth of gold and
glittering jewels while the Queen never never looked so well. H.M.
wore yellow satin and a court train of exquisite Irish lace, the gift of
the Irish ladies at the Coronation. The Duchess of Devonshire had
rows of lovely pearls and Lady Shaftesbury is so very like Mother
when her hair was soft and brown—she has the same lovely skin and
colour that dear Mother had. I knew nearly all surrounding the throne
and everybody was charming so that as I came by I felt as much at
home as though I had been bowing to the King and Queen in my own
drawing room. Th. M's both knew me and the Queen smiled so kindly—
while Lady Hardinge and Lady Creagh I saw were looking at my
dress—and my lovely head dress of old pear shaped pearl earrings
arranged in my hair. Lady Lake whom I was presenting never looked
better and she had a most beautiful dress on of blue and gold brocade.
We sat in the splendid old State dining room with its graceful old
French crystal chandeliers—and the huge great busts of the Roman
Emperors that stand against the walls and we chatted and talked and
admired all our friends until our turn came to go into the throne room.
After passing the throne we could have gone to sit with the private
entrée in a little opera box arrangement from which we could see the
rest of the ladies come through, or up to the ball room up stairs where
people were assembling until Their Majesties came up, or to have

supper in the verandahs. We went upstairs where with Offley and Sir Percy we wandered through the lovely, stately, white rooms with their quaint old silver candle light over the old mahogany doors and we saw every one. Later the Royal party made their stately parade through these rooms and Their Majesties went straight off to bed, while the rest of the Court stayed to talk and enjoy the supper and the company. The little native pages were nodding their bejewelled little black heads almost off with sleep when I met Sir Henry MacMahon carrying one small rascal off to bed. Sir P. and I were amused to see brown elbows showing above white long French evening gloves on ladies in golden 'sarees' and satin gowns. One sees the quaintest mixtures of East and West in India today.

I did my hair myself—Stewart proudly adding the finishing touches and standing off with Offley to have a final look round to see if I was all right and Sir P. said he studied all the dresses and thought none handsomer than ours—Lady Lake's and mine—wasn't it nice of him. For myself I was immensely taken with the beauty and style of the costume of a Belgian Countess. She had a remarkable dress of flame colour and blue and such unusual diamond ornaments and tiara. She thought I was a French woman!

To this letter Lina added a long postscript covering the whole of the Royal Visit.

The persons of the King and Queen were never for a single moment in danger and the King walked about at Polo in Delhi and rode out to the Camps, quite simply and only a few attendants and here also rode out in the mornings like all the other Calcutta people—before breakfast. Offley and Sir Gerald Kitson with him with the Duke of Teck about 8 a.m.

January 18, 1912		**Watergate, Fort William,** **Calcutta**

Dear Uncle Joe,

This morning a wire came telling us of the death of Offley's Mother. Poor fellow he feels the widening of ties and the breaking

up of those houses he called 'home' in England. During the year
O. and his Mother had taken up their correspondence again and I
feel sure it was illness and a more than usual admiration for Offley
that ever caused those unhappy letters to have been written at the
time of our marriage. In her last letters she always spoke of me or
sent some message or asked after me. Mrs. Fanshaw, whom I saw
so much of here last winter, <u>did much</u> to bring about these letters—at
any rate I am glad for Offley's sake that such has been the case,
and though it is sad that no meetings took place for five years, I
am happy to think that they were friends at the last and O's last
letter must have reached just before the very last and final illness.
This will mean a good deal of business for O. in England as his
Mother kept all the family plate, portraits—some 18 of them—and
diamonds. These must be stored or disposed of and then there are
his Mother's marriage settlements which can now be arranged to
help out his two sisters somewhat.

I hope I wrote to thank you for all our gifts for Christmas etc.
also for the care of my boxes at Girard Trust. It is so good of you.
I long to have a home of my own and have all my lovely things
about us—and visits from you and Aunt Fanny and my Father and
sisters and Offley's sisters, but I am at the same time <u>very</u> ambitious
for Offley in his soldiering career and Sir Percy thinks he is sure
to go <u>very far</u> and that must needs mean India—and for another ten
years or so <u>at least</u>.

It is very warm here now—and our journey to Ceylon, via Madras,
Madura, and Tuticorin will be a hot one I fear—however it will
give us a little of Southern India to see and know before we leave
her shores and lots to tell you of when we meet <u>in California</u>.

Don't disappoint us—for we shall hurry along with the idea of
being together on the American continent.

The Japanese Military attaché here has given us a charming itinerary for Japan and proposes giving O. letters to the Japanese Chief
of General Staff—so that we ought to see and do things under unusually good conditions.

Round the World Tour: 1912

They started their year's vacation from Calcutta on 1 February, accompanied by Mrs. Stewart, and by 7 February were in Colombo at the Galle Face Hotel, where they were met by a deputation of relations of their servant James, who had clearly warned his family of their coming. Their journey would continue by way of Malaya, Singapore, China, Korea, Japan, Honolulu to San Francisco, where they would arrive on 28 April. There they would be greatly disappointed that, despite having given plenty of advance notice of their arrival, they would not be met by a deputation of their own relations. Three months would be spent in the United States, followed by five months in the United Kingdom, after which they would return to India via Brussels, Paris, Rome and Naples and arrive in Bombay at the beginning of February 1913.

Lina's first letter of the voyage was written aboard the S.S. Yorck, 'off Penang', and was not a happy one.

Offley has written you such a comprehensive letter, dear Father, that I only put in these few lines because of the opportunity. Never again shall I come this way and risk or brave this awful heat. I should rather roll up in rugs and furs and try the Trans-Siberian R.R. Surely it would be far more interesting than any of these tropical countries. I hope a little trip in China and a pleasant journey through Japan may repay us for this wretched part of it. But Europe has far more charm for me than any of this side of the world. No more hot seas and small fortnightly steamers for me! More when I feel cooler and with much love to all.

At Singapore they toured the Island and Offley reported at length to 'My dear People':

Of course Mistress Schatz wasn't ready, the dilatory little animal, and we were the last to leave the ship about 11 a.m. She missed the usual crowd of enterprising touts of every description who rush up the gangways; and I had been able to telephone from the dockgates to the motor firm of Wearne & Co and had a 4 seater ready for Her Excellency to step into, when she had recovered from the annoyance and shock of having to change her cabin, consequent upon the arrival of favoured passengers who 'had already von Bremen aus their cabin registrirt'. She put up quite a good little fight with the bland German agent who—though full of apologies—had us out of our little dog-box all right and we sailed out of the docks, bound for Johore (18 miles to the ferry via the Botanical Gardens) with annoyance stoking up her feelings, and raising the body temperature to fever heat! The sight of the pretty red roads, lined with leafy trees, hedgerows of Ruigalls (Chinese or Japanese bamboo), plantations of grown rubber trees interspersed with pineapple and cocoanut—the undulating country with European 'residences' perched high up amid tropical foliage was delightful and she began to fan herself less vigorously as we swung into the Botanical Gardens, which—even with the sun at high noon, were very attractive and refreshingly cool to look upon.

When they arrived at the Johore Strait across which lies Johore Bahru 'where the guide book said there were Gardens, a Mosque, the Sultan's Palace and Gambling Rooms to be seen',

Mistress Schatz discovered that she and her motor were not to be ferried across as she sat—but that she would have to alight and get into rickshaws or another conveyance on the far side—she refused absolutely to move! 'She wasn't an American tourist! She felt perfectly convinced that the place wasn't worth seeing', as it was not, we afterwards heard; 'that it was far prettier seen from a distance! besides who wanted to see a stupid old Mosque?' (I had unfortunately told my lady previously that she would have to remove her shoes if she went to see it, which may have had something to say to the sudden contempt for such places of interest?)

By 5 March they had reached the American Legation in Peking after an alarming journey from Tientsin, where they had landed, through shooting, rioting and looting. Lina in her letter of that date reported seeing detachments of Russian, French, German, Italian, Japanese and Chinese troops at Tientsin railway station and that the railway line from Tientsin to Peking had been guarded by British troops. They had arrived in the middle of the Chinese Revolution. On 30 December of the previous year Sun Yat-sen, who had recently returned from Europe, had been elected President of the United Provinces of China by a Provisional Assembly; on 12 February the Boy Emperor, Henry Pu Yi, had abdicated and on 15 February Yuan Shih-k'ai had been elected Provisional President of the Chinese Republic in place of Sun Yat-sen. The situation was still unquiet and rival parties were jockeying for power.

Yuan Shih-k'ai had, prior to this point, held military command and Offley secured an audience with him.

On 19 March they left Peking and ten days later they were in Kyoto. They had travelled by rail to Mukden where Lina admired the Ming Tombs, on towards Seoul through the battlefields of the Sino-Japanese War of 1894/5 and the Russo-Japanese War of 1904/5, which were of great interest to Offley. In Seoul Lina was amused by the large European palace of the old Emperor—furnished by Maples of London. As for the Koreans 'with their quaint dress and hats, O. seemed to admire them. I can't say I did, but they say they are not at all a bad people'. Then on to Pusan to cross to Japan at Shimonoseki. Lina covered the whole journey in one account, again venturing one combined letter to the whole family.

In Tokyo Lina had this to say concerning the modernisation which she saw developing in Japan:

The mixture of European and Japanese is very curious and I don't think it quite agreeable to meet with a people, not a dependency of an English speaking people or subject to them in any way, giving up and over so much of their own ways and means and manners to develop on utterly foreign lines—however there is a good reason for it all—as we are told the Japanese language would not carry

them far enough and it is necessary for them to take up another to
express themselves in science etc.

*The voyage across the Pacific on the SS. Korea was apparently
not pleasing.*

In another four days we should reach Honolulu which will be a
very grateful break in this monotony: too much sea on a great big
badly arranged ship full of noisy Americans of the very worst class
and type—however, we have found some congenial friends among
the really nice few.
    We have had to pay $4 per head to enter into the United States.
All this seems to me so utterly ridiculous for a country and a
nation to exact. They tell us, the Americans themselves, that it
is because they are ridden by politicians. What dreadful times we
live in! when such classes rule! Poor old England, ruined with
strikes, and America fighting over its elections or rather men of
the same party squabbling.

By radio they listened to reports on the sinking of the Titanic: *'the
horrors seem to increase with every fresh wire.'*
    *And again the request to be met in San Francisco: 'All the
time I am writing you in Philadelphia I am hoping that you,
Father and my sisters are meeting us in San Francisco.'*
    *On 29 April they reached San Francisco and immediately ca-
bled Aunt Fanny: 'Arrived Hotel St. Francis today, Sunday. Deeply
disappointed you did not meet us.'*
    *San Francisco was not to their liking. Their impressions in
summary were contained in a short letter to Father:*

We feel still very, very far away—we would feel much nearer in
fact—and more at home, in London than in this bustling, swindling,
extravagant and ostentatious part of the world—where men and
women wear diamonds to breakfast . . . the Newspapers give no
'world news'. Everything is 'Boost California' but we are not in a
'boosting' temper!

The details were included in a long letter to Aunt Fanny:

Sunday, April 28th   **San Francisco, California,**
and Monday, 29th, 1912   **St. Francis Hotel**

My dearest Aunt,

We arrived here this morning and 'docked' about ten o'clock. From an early breakfast hour (8 o'clock) until they were finished with us at the Customs we were subjected to every imaginable indignity that one could well arrange for travellers in this mundane sphere. Two utterly farcical health examinations—an immigration and customs examination etc. before landing at all—and these, added to the time they kept us after signing papers and making every possible and conceivable declaration, took something over four hours to accomplish. We had nothing whatever in the way of difficulties in the matter of duties and declaration etc. only there were not nearly enough men to inspect and appraise the boxes to be opened of so great a number of people. Otherwise they were rather more agreeable and civil than the people in New York—not that the Americans one has met with so far are civil—for they are very far from it—in fact I am shocked and ashamed—at least twenty times a day—of the vulgarians we have been thrown with—even American travellers intend to report at the steamship offices tomorrow of the treatment they have received. On board the 'Korea' the food is frightful, and the service, exceedingly bad, while Stewardess and Captain and other officers seem to be so hurried they have not time to be civil and one has been ordered about more like a pack of sheep or cattle or prisoners than 1st class cabin passengers on a conspicuous steamship line. Fortunately the sea was smooth—like glass—and the ship a good, old, sea-going craft that went steadily on and I never had one moment of illness on that score, a most unheard of thing for me! Especially as I was very sea-sick almost all the time from India out to China and Japan.

We looked at least for letters to greet us on our arrival, but not one from anybody. Feeling weary and tired we did not realize at once that we arrived a whole day ahead of scheduled time and on a Sunday! so could not get at the mail at once.

Monday

Today, however, such a delightful package of letters, and Betty's and Fanny's wire made me very homesick for the America I ever knew—quite as different from this side of the continent as though another nation entirely. We spent the best part of this morning at the Atcheson, Topeka and Santa Fe R. R. Offices and hope for a somewhat rapid journey via the Yosemite (where O. is very eager to see the big trees)—two days at Santa Barbara, two at Pasadena, and at Los Angeles and then on to the Grand Canyon and directly through to Chicago to reach Philadelphia on May 16th to have a fortnight in your house in Philadelphia and up to Narragansett with Father, Betty and Fanny and you 'dear Two', making the journey in Uncle Frank's and Aunt Mary's new motor, as they invite us to do.

How I can accomplish all I want to do in Philadelphia I don't know. I want to go to Salem to see dear Mother's grave and my Aunt Fanny Sinnickson—and I want to sort out some of my household things to take back to India. I also hope very much that Betty will give me such personal things of dear Mother's as fall to my share. I should so love to wear and use anything of hers that I may inherit. Then I <u>must</u> get some clothes—for I am, quite honestly, in rags and tatters—travelling is so hard on one's things.

Thank you for such kindness in your preparations for us. Stewart would like the little room next to us—and she will eat with your servants. She is quite pleased at being so considered—dear old thing.

This has certainly been a <u>most wonderful</u> journey for us and one which we hope to appreciate again and again as we think of it and talk it over. We heard the <u>awful</u> news of the 'Titanic' at sea—receiving daily wireless messages with their increasingly horrible details. As some one said on our ship, '<u>The Public</u> demand these ships that cross the ocean in such rapid time—bridging the distances like lightning—making "records" etc. and <u>The Public</u> are therefore to blame'. The rush and haste we meet with here is very shocking and I am sorry to think that this bustle and racing and 'to-get-there—first anyhow—by fair means or foul' is an American creation. The hurry one has met with and the curious methods of these people make one shudder. I only hope we shall find Philadelphia as slow and charming as we left it.

The next three months were spent with Lina's family and the next letter was therefore written while at sea, crossing the Atlantic to England.

August 3rd, 1912   **S.S. Kaiserin Augusta Victoria**

Well, My dearest Aunt Fanny and Uncle Joe,

We must take up our regular letters again and keep in close touch with each other in this way until our meeting which I trust will not be very long off. Thanks for all you both did for us during our visit at home in America and thank you dear, dear Aunt Fanny for saying what you did about considering ourselves always as having a 'home' with you at 1704 Walnut Street.

I think almost the most difficult sacrifice I have to make is giving up—for the present at least—all idea of a <u>fixed house and home of my own</u>. I always had the greatest ambition—much as dear Mother had—to have a sweet beautiful home where all were welcome and where all should love to come. To have all my tell-tale treasures of many years collecting, pieces of furniture, books and pictures valued by my people and Offley's take their places in a house of mine. But if I want Offley to go on and become a general officer—to fill someday some big appointment, if not Commander-in-Chief-in-India, I must put these ambitions in some pigeon hole. Our visit to the Henry Shore's[1] is partly in the interest of storing Offley's pictures, plate and household treasures inherited from his Father and Grandfather, as the eldest son of Commander Shore and next Lord Teignmouth is Offley's heir, after his sisters. I am so glad we had the greater part of our time in America together for I think you know Offley better for it and feel with me what a truly <u>remarkable</u> man he is.

It seems incredible that we are arriving in England tomorrow morning so short does this journey seem after all our others and so perfectly comfortable are these boats.

Judging from the opening lines of the next letter, they must have disembarked at Plymouth.

Mount Elton, Clevedon,
August 10, 1912   **Somersetshire**

Dearest Aunt Fanny,

Here we are being made so 'at home' by all the family that I feel as if I had known these charming cousins always. We made a long but <u>very interesting</u> day of it yesterday by landing early enough to catch the 8.30 train to Dawlish and going to Offley's Mother's sweet place in S. Devon and seeing all his pictures and his beautiful old silver. The day was happily bright and sunny and we found a sweetly and beautifully kept house with the old butler 'Davis', though not expecting us, delighted to see Offley and equally me. The house was <u>full of treasures</u>— old china, old silver, old furniture, books, pictures, miniatures, such a beauty of O.'s great grandmother—such lots and lots of sweet photos of Offley from the time he was a very little boy all along when he must have been such a handsome young officer—how I should have loved to have known him then too. The portraits and pictures are all very interesting and the silver beautiful—unusually beautiful—and the china—such Crown Derby! teasets and dessert sets and lovely pieces— a splendid piece of 'Boule'—I am not so sure that this is the correct spelling—and some lovely mirrors. It was rather touching to hear the butler say that O.'s Mother had put away the Shore diamonds and some of the silver for me, during the early days of her last illness because she felt sure I would like to have them in India, where I should have occasion to wear them more often than she should. I am <u>so</u> glad of those letters O. and his Mother had this time last year from each other.

We spent some time in the garden and then came away in an afternoon train, getting here by tea time. So kind and charming the Henry Shores both are. Their eldest son is at home now from Madras on a year's leave—such a nice fellow—just 31 and this house is full of beautiful things too, such lovely gardens and grounds and trees. It was built sometime about 1840 by Mr. Shore's aunt, Lady Mount Elton, when she had to leave her old home 'Clevedon Court'— the <u>big place</u> here, as it went to the heir, and she must have been a woman of great taste and a capable builder, for the house is so delightfully arranged and many things in her old home are reproduced. Mrs. Henry Shore is sweet 'Cousin Mary'. I can't think who she looks just like unless it is a little like your neighbor Mrs. Conrad. She is so pretty and fair—now gray—and so interested in all of you—my people—and they are so deeply attached to Offley. They say <u>he</u> is the distinguished one of the family and must become Commander-in-Chief. Their three boys we've decided shall be an admiral, a future Governor-General and the one in the Police—Head of the Indian Police!!! We take long motor drives each afternoon and in the evening sew and chat and listen to all sorts of glorious music on Lionel's new phonograph. I hear all sorts of family history from Mrs. Shore and she tells me O.'s Derbyshire home is full of history and the Sir John Shore of that day was a staunch Royalist and hid King Charles for days in his home and later Cromwell discovered it and confiscated this seat and lands. She says we <u>must</u> see it.

On Monday we go up to London to meet Offley's sisters and he will have much to look after. He is to meet Sir Beauchamp Duff in town on the 17th. Letters and telegrams announced to us today the appointment of General Sir John Nixon to be Commander of the Southern Army—the biggest thing, but to be Chief, in India. Letters and invitations from everyone. The Norfolks are in Scotland so we may see them. The King is to be in town for a few days so I hope Offley may see him. If only his leave is extended. Everyone very much down on Lloyd George and the weather cold and autumnal, but the country looking so beautiful and so invitingly home-like.

The next three weeks were spent in London, as usual at the Hyde Park Hotel where:

We are delighted with our quarters. They are expensive, but it well repays one for we have the loveliest park in the world to look abroad over; just now trees and flowers in perfection and grazing sheep and the greenest grass and the glittering Serpentine.

Offley made the rounds of the War Office, the India Office and the Admiralty; in company with his sister Florence he spent much time settling his father's estate, visiting his grave and calling on the two nurses who had looked after him during the last two years of his life.

Lina received from the Bank Offley's grandmother's diamonds. To Aunt Fanny she wrote:

Our great pleasure in having them is to see how proud Aunt Caroline is in my possession of her Mother's and Grandmother's things. She is the dearest old lady and we talk constantly of you and Uncle Joe and of Mother, Father, Betty and Fanny.

Aunt Caroline wrote to Aunt Fanny:

August 14, 1912   **17 Connaught Square,**
                                        Hyde Park Hotel, London, S.W.

Dear Miss Rosengarten,

I cannot resist writing a few lines to tell you of the arrival of my nephew and his dear little wife. It is such a real joy to see them both looking so well and so <u>unmistakeably</u> happy. I can only say your niece has brought very real sunshine into my life—her affectionate nature and loving ways attracted me from the very first and if for no other reason I should feel grateful to her, for all she is and always <u>will</u> be to Offley. Their devotion to each other is delightful to see. Lina has made me long more and more to come to Philadelphia to make the acquaintance of all those she loves so dearly. They did indeed enjoy their few weeks with you all—everything was so beautifully and carefully arranged for their enjoyment and it will be a most happy recollection to take back with them to India.

Believe me dear Miss Rosengarten—Most Sincerely
Caroline Stovin

With Aunt Caroline, Lina went 'to look over the Florence Nightingale Hospital to which later O. is going to let me give his picture of F.N.'. Florence Nightingale had been aunt and godmother to Florence, Offley's sister.

Together they went to visit Lord Kitchener at Broom Park which he was renovating.

I told Lord K. my great ambition was to see Offley a Field Marshal and to have a sweet house of my own and all our things about us and he said, 'Well they rather clash—those two things—but you must keep at it!'.

The political and social situation gave cause for alarm: 'Everybody is terrified at the conditions in this once Merry England.'[2]
From London they went to stay with Rachel Jardine where they were joined by Florence and Urith, and there has survived a letter Florence wrote to Aunt Fanny:

Dear Miss Rosengarten,

May I introduce myself—I am Offley's sister—and I thought perhaps you would like to hear that I have been spending a fortnight with Lina and Offley at Miss Jardine's—I was so glad to have the chance of seeing so much of Lina. We had a delightful time together.

I thought Lina was looking very well, in spite of a tiresome cold in her head, which fortunately was much better before I left. We had such long chats, and she told me so much about you that I just long to see you and feel quite as if I ought to call you 'Aunt Fanny' too. Offley told me how awfully kind you have been to him. I am so glad you like him so much—for he really is a dear boy—and he has worked so hard. It is so nice to see how devoted he and Lina are to each other. I do wish you did not live quite so far away for I should so much like to have the pleasure of meeting you.

Offley engaged himself in the settling of his mother's estate.

August 31, 1912

**Dryfeholm, Lockerbie,
North Britain**

Dearest Aunt Fanny and Uncle Joe,

I make this a joint letter because I have scarcely enough news to put into two letters this week and because I fear I have missed today's mail steamer. This morning we waked to see the sun streaming in our bed-room windows and the glass which we have been watching for days with disgust began to go up considerably yesterday—so we hope for better days to come—with some sincere trust that they may.

Offley is very busily and quietly going through all his papers and has already arranged to see his Edinburgh lawyers from here which will be much easier for him in every way. You will be interested to hear that they say all is in excellent order and most of their small inheritance is in excellent securities, British and colonial but he—Offley—will have between 1200 and 1400 pounds to pay in death duties—which is a big bite out of some 7000 or 8000 pounds and then that must be divided among the three of them!!!!!!

We are going to Derby to see the old Shore manor one day next week.

Among his pictures there are several by such well known artists as 'Phillips', 'Webster', 'Lilly' and 'Romney' of whose there are still some four or five left, but they have been left in care of cousins that inherit them if Offley has no heir—and we don't suppose we could sell any one of them for this reason. Offley's Great-Grand-mother seems to have been a beautiful woman and painted by all the 'big' artists of her day—she was Mary de Bohun—and the co-heiress with her sisters of a great estate. We have an exquisite mini-ature of her which would certainly fetch a good price at Christies. It is also by a well known painter—but I cannot bear to part with it and it is small enough to take care of ourselves. They say that American wives hold on to houses and heirlooms and make a greater fuss about things than any of the English ladies, who usually take their vicissitudes with a wonderful courage. Anyhow one never wants to buy or sell one's ancestors at Christies or Maples—do you think so? If we get a house we can keep them all—and what would be better still you can see them and meet them, such as we do keep. Some Offley will certainly send to his cousins who have houses to hold them.

Miss Jardine is as kind and dear as ever. She looks older and not nearly so strong, but she has had a severe illness since we were last home. Thank you for your birthday letter. It arrived in the nick of time. Offley made no gift and no festivity for me, as I particularly did not wish it—until all his affairs are settled we mean to strictly economize and then we can have all the better gifts and fete days at Christmas. However in the evening the kind hostess had well remembered me and my health was drunk in champagne—and we were all so very happy to be together again. The sisters-in-law join us here this evening, and so I have told you all. We walk, drive and enjoy a wonderful old walled garden and a park of 600 acres together with farms and prize cattle and sheep and fowls so we are never without something to do. I have arranged to send Mrs. Stewart to India on the 20th of September and she will come back to me when we come back to India. We want to try and pay the biggest part of death duties out of joint income.

Lina's account, in this letter, of Offley's 'Great-Grandmother' is incorrect. Mary de Bohun, c.1700–40, wife of Joseph Offley, was his great-great-great-grandmother who was an only child, and does not appear in a 'List of Family Portraits Extant', compiled in the nineteenth century. It would seem that Lina was referring to Urith, 1736–81, daughter and co-heiress, with one sister, of the above Joseph and Mary Offley, who married Samuel Shore, was painted by George Romney and was Offley's great-great-grandmother.

Once again Lina found herself rebuked for sending a joint letter to her family.

September 18, 1912

**Dryfeholme,
Lockerbie**

My dearest Aunt,

I am more distressed than I can tell you to think that any letter of mine should have put you in an unhappy position. If I addressed my letter as I did to you 'and family' I felt you were so exactly the person—as next to dear Mother—who would have shared it in the household—and I thought—if Father happened to be in Philadelphia—as he was so likely to be—that addressing it to you—you would open it and read it at once and send it on. I am rather surprised that the others should be really indignant at anything sent you in this way. I really do try my best to write to each and all and not only very especially in acknowledgement and gratitude for all they did for us during our visit at home, but because of my deep affection and interest in each one of them. But they said to me many times when last at home—'I don't see how you manage to write so many letters!' and you said 'Be sure to send your weekly letter' so I felt they were not so dependent on my letters as long as they knew we were safe and well—and as I have told you in all my letters how extremely rushed and busy we were both in London and the whole time on the steamer—how hard we worked to get Offley's papers and plans in order—in case the 'leave' should not be granted.

I am glad you wrote me frankly about the little matter I have tried to explain away. I want you to do so—and feel you must blame and admonish as occasion demands, though it caused me a great deal of distress that I had brought such a thing about. I had a letter from Father yesterday dated Sept. 8th. Yours was dated the 9th and as he said nothing about it I conclude and hope it has blown over. We sometimes find great difficulty in finding time to write—visiting and moving about and living in boxes is not conducive to regularity in such things as weekly and frequent letters.

Offley is very anxious to see his sisters settled together in a house and home above all things before we leave again for India, and after we did a great deal of hunting about in town they changed their minds and elect to live in the country. I am very fond of them—but they are very trying and would altogether monopolize Offley if they could. I love Florence very dearly and she is sweet and charming and practical and would—I am sure—make a charming home; Urith is a beautiful pianist and very proud of her birth and name and all that sort of thing, and to me—this is to the exclusion of many good things she might have and attain in life if she would only come down a little. I should like her to dinner but not to live with!!!!!! It is so very kind of Rachel Jardine to have invited us all to rendezvous here—for much has been gained under this most hospitable roof and under R.J.J.'s kind sensible guidance that I feel sure would never have come about elsewhere. I have little or no patience with a proud old family maid of 5 and 40—always thinking in castles and family names—'Our good name etc. etc.' on £500 or £600 a year. Well, I must not criticize them anymore. They have had sad lives and not the love and affection I have grown up with, but I find it very trying to stay clear and you can understand. So does R.J.J. and this comforts me as I would not hurt Offley for the whole world—and he holds me up as a <u>marvelous</u> example to the sisters which again is awkward. With Offley the sun rises and sets in me and with them it rises and sets in Offley!

Three more months were spent in England mostly at the Hyde Park Hotel, Offley constantly reconsidering his future, learning to drive a car, visiting friends, as he relates in the following letter.

October 28, 1912

Hyde Park Hotel
London

My dear Uncle Joe,

All my spare time just now is being devoted to tackling motor car construction and driving. I have already had 3 lessons and feel I am really beginning to get a grip of the mechanics of the thing— once one fully realises the reason for everything on the chassis and the resultants of applied forces I think I am going to progress. One has hitherto been so ashamed of one's ignorance of such things that I am glad to have been able to put that behind me. The Wolseley car people have me in hand: the managing Director married one of the Teignmouth Shores, and so takes some slight additional interest in a 'family pupil'. He at least has put his best Chief Instructor on to me! and of course hopes that I may purchase a car very shortly.

You may imagine that my applied mechanical and chemical knowledge of one's school days is being rudely recalled to mind! but I do find that my military training in drawing and plans, sections, elevations etc. does help one enormously to understand mechanical plans—(to my instructor's astonishment apparently!).

I have seen Sir Francis Hopwood—now a Junior Lord of the Admiralty—about getting into the Colonial Service: but he sees no openings at present though I know he would help me to an eventual

Governorship if he could. I have intimated to certain commercial acquaintances that I am 'open to an offer' of employment and I am still waiting to hear from Sir Percy Lake about the prospective Brigadier Generalship on the General Staff in India.

Lina wants me to apply in the right Quarters for an appointment on one of the Young Prince's staff, and I will certainly do so.

What an upset in the diplomatic world these Young Bulgarians and their friends are creating! There is much anxiety in this country as to the final outcome of it all, but personally I think the final disappearance of the Turk from Europe[3] will be a great step in advance. I also think we can tackle our Muhammedans in India and Egypt should they be inclined to give trouble, and I doubt that the expulsion of the Mussalmen from Europe would bring about a Holy War against the Infidels. They are not sufficiently united.

They tell me that Sir Douglas Haig failed signally to electrify military men with his Cavalry at the recent manoeuvres in Cambridge, and that he showed up very badly at the final pow-wow before the King, through his inability to speak clearly and concisely. He was, as you know, regarded as our great theorist and army trainer.

Lord Roberts has again been trying to awaken the nation to its military responsibilities, but they only laugh at the old man!

Lina and Offley were 'of course deeply interested in the European situation which is certainly very grave' . . . 'The Servian and Montenegrin Peace delegates[4] are lodged in this hotel—but it still looks as if war in Europe was inevitable' . . . 'We feel a little uncertain about going to Germany at this very critical moment.'

They were planning their return journey to India and finally decided to travel via Brussels, Paris, Rome and Naples.

In Paris they heard of the attempted assassination in Calcutta of the Viceroy, Lord Hardinge. Rome was 'of course full of memories of my darling Mother—every street and place we went together'. Here letters reached them, telling of Offley's promotion to Brigadier-General.

At Naples where they were to board the City of Glasgow *for the final stage of their journey Lina wrote:*

I am more homesick than I care to admit. So many ships take one straight to America from here and one dislikes the sea so much that one wishes it were to some dearer place than India. However we have had a wonderful holiday and we <u>both</u> hope and pray—and that <u>very sincerely</u>—that the next return from India will not be far off and then that it will be <u>for good</u> and <u>for always</u>.

India: January 1913 to August 1914

In Bombay they were met by Walia and Mrs. Stewart, both very proud of Offley's promotion: 'Every one calls him "General Sahib" so easily,' wrote Lina, 'but I can't recognize it at all yet.' They refused all invitations to visit in Bombay; were advised not to go to Delhi unless they were obliged to and went straight to Simla. Lina quotes Lady Hardinge as writing, 'The Viceroy has been a very badly wounded man' and adds, 'along the roads and in the post offices in great big print are the notices of rup. 100,000 reward to the man who threw the bomb.'

In an early letter Offley reported to Uncle Joe on the state of his health, physical and mental, and his thoughts for the future:

Extraordinary to relate, the staff surgeon passed me yesterday fit for active service, and so I am safe from being thrown out, medically speaking, until the next winter confidential report is due—barring accidents in the meantime. It would almost have been a relief, yesterday, had Mr. Pillbox recorded it as his opinion that I should leave the country at once. I am not looking forward to succeeding Brigadier General Headlam on the 2nd April: it means too hard and too continuous work of a kind that is not in the least congenial and for which I do not consider that I am especially fitted: however we have determined to tackle it and hope for the best. Something better may turn up. I shrewdly suspect that my little lady would like to return to you with the title of Lady Offley Shore—just to show you that she has made a success of her matrimonial venture from a worldly point of view and in order that you would say, 'Well done, you little scapegrace'. I only fear that this cannot come about for a very long time, and would be quite prepared to waive such doubtful honours. If these should eventually fall to us, they will be worthless if you are not alive to share them, accordingly you and Aunt Fanny must make up your minds to wait for this military Knighthood for Schat's sake. I regret to say that many annoyances are not improving my usually fairly respectable temper, and I am exhibiting signs of unusual irritation, which poor Lina has to put up with: I tell you this, as she would never do so herself.

Their first need was to find a house, which, in view of the greatly increased demand and rise in rents, due, Lina said, to the transfer of the seat of Government from Calcutta to Delhi, they were fortunate to achieve quite quickly. The cost of their year long vacation forced them to live as cheaply as possible.

Offley had been appointed Director of Training and Staff Duties. Lina would enjoy the enhanced standing that his promotion would give her.

One major change in her household, compared with her first years in India, would be a close relationship with Mrs. Stewart arising from the fact that Mrs. Stewart had now been 'home' with her and that they could now talk together of family and Philadelphia.

February 20, 1913

**Faletti's Hotel Cecil,
Simla**

Dear Aunt Fanny and Uncle Joe,

Again it is mail day before one has time to think! We have been put to a good deal of worry and trouble by hearing that the house we thought we had taken 'The Mythe' is under consideration by the Government of India for offices and so we cannot know definitely for another ten days or two weeks whether or not we can get it—and there is but one other that we can get and that—though very pretty and nice—is small and frightfully expensive to rent.

The hotels will be impossible as they are both making huge additions and up to July cannot give us more than bedrooms and a drawingroom—no study for Offley which he must have—so I am a good deal upset—however it must turn out happily as we must get something by being early on the spot.

Offley is very hard at work each day and Stewart and I are equally busy, though Offley won't believe it! arranging household matters, interviewing servants etc.

Would you be so kind as to order for one year 'The Ladies Home Journal' and have it addressed to Mrs. F. M. Stewart with Mrs. Offley Shore or c/o General Offley Shore, Simla, India and let me know how much it will be and I will pay for it, as Mrs. Stewart liked it so much and felt that it would be full of most useful receipts and patterns for us in India. It is most amusing to hear her enthusiasm for America—poor woman—and need I say it gives me infinite joy! She said to Mr. Clark, the <u>best</u> haberdasher here—'Oh! You should see the shops in America—why they're palaces—palaces indeed and like Museums at that—with everything in 'em like Museums indeed, it would pay you to take a trip to America to see "Wanamakers" at Philadelphia or "Tiffanys" at New York—nothing but marble and marble and splendour!' and so she goes on.

We talk constantly of home and of the wonderful journey and of you both—and it does make such a difference here, so far away. I should very much like to see 'Vogue' now and then—but only now and then. Now I must close. We are all very interested in the situation in Europe though here we hear very little of it. The principle topics of conversations being the Viceroy—if he will go or stay; how weak as a Viceroy he is though so charming a man; the conditions in India etc.

I heard a very good story yesterday; we went to tea with Lady Ker—and she said when the Viceroy took her in to dinner last Summer he told her he heard constantly from Lord Curzon, who always told him how he should govern India—so Lady Ker told Lord Hardinge that Lord Curzon told her, when he once took her into dinner, that he had <u>only once</u> been properly received in India and that was in a native state where, when he arrived, the band struck up the music of 'Holy, Holy, Holy, Lord God Almighty'. Last night's papers announced the Viceroy would remain in India so I suppose there will be a great season here.

I have written to Father to get the new President to ask for Offley as a Major-General for Military Attaché. You see O's next appointment could be nothing less—could it?

**The Cecil Hotel,
Simla**

February 24, 1913

The lovely miniature of dear Mother came this afternoon Aunt Fanny dear, and a thousand, thousand thanks to you. It has been snowing again and all our Christmas boxes arrived from Betty, from Fanny and from you. My precious miniature. So we had a real Christmas time over the tea table opening our parcels and we were delighted with the things. We have put the miniature on the writing table where we can see it and study it all the time—and tonight, as I look at it, I feel very pleased with it, and dear Mother seems to smile. Just as she often did at me and my ways—and I do love it already. I wish so much I had one of you. Do sit to Mrs. Taylor—and let her make a really good one of you. How sweet the little light brown curl is—of hair at the back. Oh, I am so happy and pleased to have this lovely little picture of Mother—how can you ever know how much I thank you for it.

We think we have at last got a house. A very pretty little place—with quite a lovely view of the snows on one side and some flowers and fruit trees—peaches—in the nice bit of garden round the house. It is called 'Dormers' and belongs to Mrs. Cotes: 'Sarah Janette Duncan' the authoress. It is prettily furnished too—and very clean and nice and central—that is near enough to the offices that O. could come back to lunch quite easily. They asked an enormous rent for it but, as all say, we are lucky to get a house at all. I suppose we must consider ourselves fairly fortunate.

You ask me how to address us now. Well just the same as before only

> Mrs. Offley Shore
> c/o General Offley Shore D.S.O. etc.
> Simla, India

instead of colonel as before. I am very proud of having Offley a general officer. He always said they would never make him one—he would never be one etc. etc. and here it is! But the appointment is a big one—and one full of hard work and sometimes when things look rather formidable and difficult we wish ourselves back with you—and as we both so often long for America now—I don't think it will really be very long before you see us back. Offley's new appointment carries with it the private entrée at the Viceregal Court—which is always nice—and I believe—or so I am told, the Viceroy will take me into dinner on some occasion during the season and in my turn.

Mrs. Stewart seems quite pleased at the idea of the house and we are planning how we shall arrange all our Chinese things. The drawing room will be yellow and gray—a pale gray—more like Aunt Mary's drawing room curtains—of neapolitan satin and the yellows the beautiful, brilliant Imperial Chinese yellow table covers of which we have 6—like the one I sent Uncle Joe. The dining room will be very simple—but with my Italian majolica and plain white Venetian glass. O. bought me some lovely old plates from Serico in Naples. The walls of the dining room are green—and the curtains a quaint flowered material half silk, half wool— very soft and pretty and there are one or two good pieces of old English Jacobean furniture and some very nice engravings. I shall have my own carpets—as far as they will go—O. will have a sunny, charming little study with a lovely view through some deodars of the hills and Viceregal Lodge. His wall paper is brown and there are some quaint Persian tiles in the fire place and I shall put our Mogul miniatures on his walls and our Indian things in that room—for the rest it will be books and papers and maps. I must get him a big writing table as there is none—and he always wants lots of flowers too—so we must fill the windows and have bowls and vases for these lovely things everywhere in his room. I must send you when we are finished with it—a wonderful literary production of the orderly's and the gardener's—written in English—probably by a paid writer, telling us what is in the garden now.

In a letter of 11 May to Aunt Fanny, Lina gave a description of their financial situation. They were spending a few days for a change and a rest, at a small bungalow close to Simla and having described how 'we have only brought out 10 of our servants!!! and Mrs. Stewart, and we only had 19 coolies to carry out our things!!!!', she continued:

I only got 2 dresses in Paris and 3 hats and some gloves. I really couldn't afford more—and I had two old ones done up—and they seem very successful. Travelling and sight-seeing interested us much more and things for my house.

We had the expenses of the journey back to India and the possible setting up of our house and after payment of the 'death duties' before leaving, and deduction of the income tax every month one feels dreadfully poor!!!! Then everything in Simla has increased so much in price—rents, servants' wages, and Offley's predecessor went home on 3 months' leave at the expiration of his appointment, which meant that Offley takes up his new appointment for the first 3 months on half pay!!! Thanks to Stewart's conscientious assistance we are quietly coming out 'square' as they say. I am trying hard to save up. There is always—according to Offley's strict orders—there must always be 'put safely aside' the passage money home—and in our case he also always insists that must be the sum it requires to take one to America—until this is accomplished—no shopping luxuries or otherwise can be indulged in.

We have lately been hearing a good many sad stories of officers and their families leaving India with large sums of money which they could not pay—standing behind them. This is all very dreadful, but it is now being recognized that it has been the government, and the Civilians[1] that have brought this about—not the military or soldier people whose rates of pay have never been adjusted since the Mutiny, while all the Civilians have very large salaries and these are adjusted from time to time. Offley is making a great plea for re-arrangement in these matters—for the soldiers—for Simla anyhow—just now. The Financial Secretary to the Government is our neighbor and with tea and tennis we have become great friends!!! Let us hope O. may make his point.

May 14, 1913   **Dormers, Simla**

Dear Uncle Joe,

Last night in the face of a thunder storm Offley and I started out to dine at Viceregal Lodge. We hoped to run over the little distance between this house and the Viceroy's palace before the rain came on, but as the 'darkies' say, 'that didn't occur!'—however we were protected in our rickshaws and only the jhampanies got a good wetting which must have been well worth the good things they got while waiting for their 'Sahib Log' dining in the palace. It was a dinner party of 54, as one of the A.D.C.s told me afterwards—a little conversation and a little dancing.

The whole thing missed the charm the Mintos always lent to all they did—at least so we felt—though Her Excellency, Lady Hardinge, did look most lovely in an evening gown of cloth of gold with turquoises, pearls and diamonds. The house is much improved by a number of beautiful and interesting portraits brought up from Government House, Calcutta. The company consisted of Railway Magnates, Bankers and Civil and Military 'Big-Wigs'—and their ladies—wives or daughters or both. I went into dinner with Major-General Aylmer V.C. and sat very close to the Viceroy, but my gallant officer was a dull companion and General Stanton on my left was not much merrier. I heard no good news and no good stories, though I told off all of mine I could think of, apropos or otherwise! They rushed us through dinner and then the Viceroy took at least 20 minutes or ½ an hour to make up his mind to get up. One felt sure his Ex. had lost a slipper or something.

Later I enjoyed dancing and also enjoyed knowing I had on the prettiest of dresses and my lovely old 'Shore' diamonds—or rather the 'Offley' diamonds. Young Astor, A.D.C. is such a nice boy although not good looking and I wished for Betty and Fanny a hundred times.

There are seven vases full of lovely roses in this room and one large bowl of all pink ones—while the house is covered with them— trellises and roof gables and every conceivable corner is draped with masses of yellow, white and pink and salmon shades.

I am keeping my best bib and tucker for the Court or the State Ball, and the lovely Tiffany diamonds.[2] Offley danced with a series of fat ladies last night, which amused me immensely. I believe he was told off to each in turn and had no choice—however they proved to be agreeable.

May 21, 1913   **Dormers, Simla**

Dearest Aunt Fanny,

I am so glad that you like to have my, or rather, our regular letters and that you do think I write regularly. I try to do so, because I know so well the eagerness with which I await those dear, dear letters of yours every Sunday morning and which never fail. I see right through your letters into your life and all surrounding you at home. I only wish my two sisters wrote to me regularly— even if only a few lines—but I suppose they belong to the new generation that have so much to do all the time and lots more in between!?

By the time this reaches you it will be again an anniversary of dear Mother's death. How I miss her and how I love the many things she taught me and the clever insight into many ways and means she unfolded to us. Offley loved and admired Mother so truly and we often talk about her just as if she was still there at home. How proud she would have been when Offley became a 'General'. I love my miniature—the face and sweet fairness—and the expression. I only don't like the breadth of shoulders and the ugly, stiff fichu arrangement—but I now don't see that as I love the half merry half sad expression and Mother's very own colouring that Mrs. Taylor has most certainly caught. Oh, please do have your miniature painted, dear Aunt Fanny, sitting with a book or your work in the corner of your library sofa or one of your usual chairs—as I see you now—as we sat together this time last May. Do have it done.

Next week we begin with 'the Bust' O. calls it!!

27th May	State Garden Party
29th May	The Levée
3rd June	The State Dinner
5th June	The State Ball
9th June	The Drawing Room at which I am presenting

a large number of ladies. The wife of the present Quartermaster General in India—has never been presented at Court at home in England which makes it impossible for her to 'present' any one here at the Viceregal Court, and I have been selected to take her part, as it were, as Lady Lake is presenting for Lady Creagh who will be absent with the Commander-in-Chief in the country at Mahasu. I think I am the only one of 3 ladies now here who have the private entrée and privilege at St. James too. Naturally I feel rather important, but O. takes all my pride down, by saying it is my stout dowager like appearance or my soft heart that appeals to them etc.

June 9, 1913   **Dormers, Simla**

Dearest Aunt Fanny,

The past week has been one mad rush all day and each day. Beginning with luncheon parties before the Horse Show, the polo games or the races and then returning, always feeling a little belated and hurried—to go out to dine or to dance or to the State Ball. The latter was brilliant and the Military Secretary told me about 1100 people were present. We were asked to the private supper in the dining room which was especially good and very jolly. Tonight is the Court and there is much gossip and anticipation and excitement. Many have never been before—among the younger women—and a big General Officer, commanding one of the Divisions, divorced and remarried a divorcée and they have appeared in Simla and push themselves everywhere and <u>she</u> has contrived to arrange to be 'presented' tonight! In this <u>big</u> little place—where we all know each other—officially anyway—you can imagine the way tongues wag over this. I for one have known the lady <u>and the General</u> when I thought by their exceedingly intimate appearance that they must be sister and brother or cousins at least, though I first took them for husband and wife. So I shall not receive her or him as their pushing and impertinence is very disagreeable to me—but what they do at the Court where perhaps their trials and tribulation with the 'Number Ones' may be better understood—is quite a different matter.

I was very pleased with the little notice in the Ledger of Offley's new appointment—and one of the pleasantest things about it all is that everyone seems to feel that he—O. is exactly the man for the place. The work is interesting but <u>very hard</u> and very continuous.

At the State Ball I was introduced to the German Consul General, Graf Luxburg, with whom I danced 'the Berlin'—to the polka being played. I enjoyed it immensely though I felt rather conscious and conspicuous—especially when I saw her Excellency and her companion—the gentleman talking with her on the dais—stop their conversation and turn to look at us. Tonight is the Drawing Room and it is a dreadful day—raining and mist. I fear we shall all look very bedraggled by the time we rickshaw to Viceregal Lodge. I am wearing the beautiful black and white frosted-beaded dress I bought from Mrs. Altemus—the Offley diamonds and my own, although we left my tiara in England this time and I shall wear my hair simply dressed with an amber comb in it. I think I shall be quite splendid enough without my beautiful crown and it will leave something for Lady H. and the others to wear!!!! More tomorrow when it has taken place, this Drawing Room.

June 16, 1913   **Dormers**

Dearest, Dear Aunt Fanny,

You said your letters must be dull, but I love every word of them and the beautiful writing and even the spaces so even and delightful between your lines, but I often think mine must be very dull—for it is so difficult to write of people and places and things you don't know, yet in a fashion you do know Simla as you have heard and read so much about it—at any rate I am constantly wishing you knew my house and garden—the road leading to it—the Mulberry tree under which we sit and the lovely deodars and the snows! and oh, the snows at sunset—when they glow and glisten in every light and I wish you could know our friends—for some of our friends are delightful—interesting and agreeable. This morning I began for the third time with my class in 'First Aid'. Every year one seems to learn something new and useful in it. Now those who have passed the exams successfully are formed into Brigades and are allowed to wear the St. John's Ambulance Aids' costume. The brigades attend in this nursing 'Kit' at all the big Fêtes or occasions of various kinds and polo games and are available to act and attend accidents. Both at the Birthday Parade and at the Big Fête held at Annandale

last week, these ladies proved of great assistance as there were two
bad cases of sun stroke and several faintings.

June 18th, 1913

Two ladies yesterday attended the class in their nursing costumes
and they <u>did</u> look <u>so</u> pretty—pale gray gingham dresses—white caps
and aprons and little white cloth, short shoulder capes, and white cotton
gloves. One of them is a great and an old friend of Offley's and to me
she looks very like Alice Ashton—so much that I call her 'Alice' and
she is one of those capable, delightful women, who ride well and dance
well and shoot straight and don't seem to neglect their houses and
homes or husband and children either.

Yesterday the parcel with <u>3</u> pairs of stays and 1 pair of bedroom
slippers arrived and many, many thanks. It came in a tin box which
we have immediately put into commission for the sugar! The rains
have begun in earnest—and one can now do nothing <u>for certain</u>
except play bridge or some amusement within doors although many
who ride treat this monsoon weather quite as a matter of course and
go on whether it rains or not. We are very sad over the lameness
of our pony, and I fear it means we shall have to get another, in
fact two more, as she is all we had upon returning to India.

You speak of the arrival of Miss Jardine's maid in Philadelphia and
also of dear Miss Jardine's death which you say we did not mention
in any of our letters. I <u>feel sure we did</u> as we were greatly grieved
and shocked ourselves, but we did not hear of it for some time after
it occurred and then only by a short letter from Jim Richardson who
it was always understood was to inherit the place from her. At the
last moment—eight days before she died—and when she must have
been very ill—under pressure from her brother—already a very rich
man with a huge place and over 30,000 acres of lands, she changed
her will!!! Jim Richardson wanted Offley to go to him at Meerut
before he sailed and talk things over—Offley was also remembered
in the original will—but O. could not go as he was just taking over
his new appointment here—and we have not heard from Jim since
his return to England—or rather Scotland—and none of her friends

or relations had the kindness to send us even a line or a newspaper. I wrote to some old maiden ladies, cousins of Miss Jardine's—and had an old fashioned, long letter in reply which however carefully avoided any news of the will or poor Jim in any way whatever. We have lost a dear and delightful friend and what we cannot understand is how anyone with all her character and life and health could ever have been prevailed upon to change her will as she did even on her death bed. We miss her and her letters dreadfully.

In the following letter news has reached them that Aunt Mary, wife of Lina's Uncle Frank, was ill. Subsequent letters, for a long time, discussed her progress. It will have been noted by now that, in Lina's family, no illness was ever named nor indications of the nature of it given.

July 14, 1913   **Dormers**

Dear Uncle Joe,

This is your birthday! and many happy returns of the day—I am sending you and Aunt Fanny one small piece of ivory—one of those I had already written you about—in spite of Offley's feeling that they were none of them good enough. I felt it was the only way you could tell at all what you think of them. This one goes as my birthday gift to both you and Aunt Fanny.

We have had Miss Impey staying with us for the last few days and she is delightful. I wish you could meet her. She lives in India with her brother who is the Political officer in Baroda. A big native State as you know. She tells most interesting tales and experiences of her life in India and discusses all the interesting and difficult questions of the day with Offley. She is so popular that we have only lunched together once and only dined at home altogether one evening since she came. We too have been out to a number of delightful dinner parties.

We went to a delightful dinner party last night at the new Lt. General of the Punjab. Sir Michael and Lady O'Dwyer are most agreeable and in the party of 20 I found myself to be the Senior lady, when Sir Michael took me into dinner. There again we had music after dinner, but not so good as at Count Luxburg's and I was feeling rather tired after 5 nights running, out very late and looked round to see if there was no move among the ladies to depart, when I realized no one would go until I did—so I asked my old friend Major Bailey A.D.C. who in the most natural way in the world (for an A.D.C.) took out his watch! and said, 'Yes, no one should go until you do Mrs. Offley'. Thereupon I turned to say goodnight to Sir Michael and thanked him for giving me the pleasure of feeling like a princess for the first time in my life in Simla. He seemed delighted and we bade goodnight or rather I did—for O. had not noticed it at all—and I walked the length of the big beautiful drawing room with Sir Michael and the two A.D.C.s feeling very much the peacock, very proud, very royal!!!

I am utterly delighted to hear of George's promotion and I shall write to congratulate all, Father who must feel very proud and also Louise. They will feel sorry to leave their charming house at Haddonfield I am sure but think of having a private [rail road—Ed.] car! Just think of it!!!!

We had a sad, sad letter from Uncle Frank. I can quite understand his anxiety and his great loneliness, but I suppose it is far too hot now to attempt to go home with Aunt Mary no better than she is. We both feel very distressed about poor dear Aunt Mary and for them both.

July 23, 1913   **Dormers**

Many, many thanks my dearest Aunt for your generous gift and also for the charming songs and Mrs. Towne's list and all your trouble to secure a list of new and pretty songs for me. I have at once arranged to have Mademoiselle de Taranle Coates—daughter of the Madame de T. Coates who comes to me to speak and read French—come every Tuesday now that my First Aid classes are over—to accompany me and help me a little bit with my singing.

We are very distressed at dear Aunt Mary's condition. Her last letter made me feel very sadminded, but she particularly asked us to send it on to you and Uncle Joe—so I enclose it.

Simla now has its electric light and lighting everywhere and it is much cheaper and cleaner than lamps and candles—though my dining room is entirely lit by candles and so is the drawing room and in the dining room anyhow I think I shall keep that on, but through the rest of the house—electricity would be a very great boon. Now I must run away to dress for dinner and finish this tomorrow.

July 24, 1913

Dearest Aunt,

Again I put in a few lines just before closing this to catch the mail. As I date the above I remember what tomorrow's date—July 25th[3]—always means to you. How much more I too can realize and sympathise with you now. These partings are so little thought of and understood except by those of us who have been blessed with the marvelously tender care and interest in each one of us as our two darling Mothers ever took for us and in us. Poor Betty—I see in her letters and between the lines how much she still grieves and misses dear Mother.

On 11 September Lina wrote to her Uncle and Aunt:

Alas and alack—Offley goes down with Sir Percy Lake—on his great tour of Inspection—all over India—on the 14th of October, and cannot return here for a halt until Christmas. I shall indeed be lonely—and after Christmas he will be off again until March!!! We have not been successful in sub-letting this house so far and I don't relish the idea of going to Delhi to wait for his comings and goings as even then it will be but for a day or two at a time.

and in the letters which follow she detailed the preparations to be made for Offley's tour and gave an indication of his itinerary.

September 23, 1913   **Dormers**

My dearest Aunt,

I am as busy as the bees this week. Mrs. Stewart and I getting together all Offley's camp kit—or Field service equipment. It is a job, I can tell you, to provide for months of living in a tent or a train—bedding and cooking things—all his uniforms—full dress and otherwise to be smart and perfect. Soap, dusters, brushes, canvass pails and baths that fold up etc., etc.—a hundred and one things little and big to be got together, verily it is like setting up a house. He goes off October 14th with Sir Percy Lake who takes Lady Lake with him! Offley and Sir P.'s A.D.C. to have a carriage to themselves on Sir Percy's train—also a car for their horses. O. takes 2 horses. Kind as Lady Lake is—she is not a manager—in these instances. Offley is wonderful in such matters and so is Mrs. Stewart—so between them he should come out on top in the matter of arrangements.

September 24, 1913

Tonight we all dine at Viceregal Lodge and tomorrow night and the next and the next for five days running—then a break and then the first week in Oct. another set of dinner parties, dances and quite too much for our pleasure.

We were a great success at the fancy dress ball which was beautiful, more beautiful than ever before even! I—in my wonderful Japanese 'Court' costume of 200 years ago—the wig and the toed stockings and the quaint little Japanese shoes held on by my big toe. The dresses were old. We bought them from a lady of the Shogun family and all the other accessories and paraphernalia Offley ordered through an artist to whom we had a letter of introduction and we know they belonged to the Japanese wife of a Chinese Ambassador. So Offley wore the beautiful Chinese coat of blue and gold and silver that we bought in Peking and Laura may remember. He had a Chinese headdress and was so disguised nobody knew him. Most of the people were in powder and patches as Lady Hardinge had got up a Gavotte, which 64 ladies and gentlemen had practised for weeks and it was most beautifully done. She, herself, Lady H. looking most lovely as 'Perdita'. Is it Romney or Gainsborough? At any rate her Excellency was an exact copy of the portrait.

September 25th, 1913

I must close my letter today as it is 'mail day' again. I left it open to put in anything of interest about the Viceregal dinner party. We all went—the Campbells and ourselves. I had a rush—and felt we were a little late—as Offley came into my dressing room to sit and talk while Stewart and I were putting on the finishing touches—fastening on my lovely diamonds etc. but we arrived in splendid time and I was greeted by the A.D.C.s in waiting at the porch with Ohs and Ahs and 'Mrs. Offley you were ripping at the fancy ball!'. A big dinner party—I went in with old General Hunter whose wife—about 80 years old and the greatest of matchmakers was there in a splendid yellow brocade decolté dress, fan and mitts (!) and a lace handkerchief on her beautiful snow white hair. Both their Excellencies talked to me and admired our magnificent fancy-ball costumes and Lady Hardinge gave me the programme of the music which I enclose. After dinner I was one of the ladies sent for to talk with the Viceroy. One feels very like my old nickname 'the Queen of Sheba'—being taken up by a young A.D.C. The Viceroy then rises as you make your curtsey—that over, both sit down. I never feel Lord Hardinge is at ease. Lord Minto of course I knew better but he was always the most charming of men. We talked away. I asked him about Paris—and he said much as he would like to go to Paris as Ambassador he had no wish to leave India sooner than he was 'obliged' to—'obliged'—mark the word! I told him Offley was to be a Field Marshal before he had finished at which he laughed and commended my ambition. He very, very much admired my Japanese costume and my patience in carrying out the part. (I could not dance you see—as I wore the Japanese footgear.) We talked of Rome and Simla and then came back to Paris and people, when it was time for me to make another curtsey and go.

The orderly is sewing bags in the veranda for Offley's tents and tent furniture, the gardeners are chopping up boxes for seeds and seedlings for the gardens while Stewart is sewing and cleaning and mending and counting to get Offley all in order for his tour—and I have blankets to bind and handkerchiefs to mark—so my letters must be hastily written. No decision as to who the next Chief will be and a deplorable state of affairs in England and Ireland isn't it?

October 14, 1913   Dormers

Dear Father,

Very many thanks for your last letter in which you gave me such a clear account of the payments—with all details regarding the sale of the house 'Die Rosen'.

I am so very sorry if you were disappointed in not receiving a cable from me to say 'Fully satisfied—feel you have acted for the best' though I do feel sadder than I can tell you that you and Aunt Fanny and Uncle Joe should not have that sweet house that dear Mother so beautifully arranged for you all—until the very end of your days—but of course there was a good deal else to consider I am sure. I depend on your good judgment to act for me in any of these matters.

Offley has been worked day and night for the last month and left me today for his long winter tour with Sir Percy Lake. They go first to Quetta to inspect that division and to see the Staff College. How I should have loved to see them there. The Staff College is Offley's own creation and the work for which L'd Kitchener specially picked him out. I believe they are to get into full dress and regalia to be received by the Commandant and students. They also inspect all the Quetta troops—then on to Peshawar and up the Khyber in motors—when the Pass straight away to the top is to be specially picketed and they—O. and Sir P. go in plain clothes with the Frontier commissioners, political agent and staff etc. That part I should love as I liked the frontier with all its attendant excitement. Then to Pindi to inspect that Division, 'The 1st', and always kept fully ready for war—then a Staff Conference, Staff tours and manoevres on a biggish scale from Lahore, and then Delhi—there 2 days halt and off to the Southern Army!! I now expect to remain here quietly until December 23rd when I go to Delhi to meet Offley and we shall stop there quietly for Xmas and perhaps the 2 Shore boys will join us over our plum pudding.

Die Rosen, referred to in the above letter, was a summer residence built in Narragansett by Mrs. Sinnickson and always referred to as 'Mother's house'.

Again will be noted Lina's wifely exaggeration of Offley's part in the establishment of the Staff College.

The theme of her loneliness without Offley runs all through the following letters. She reports to her family on his journeyings and at the beginning of December on her preparations to join him in Delhi.

October 16, 1913   **Dormers**

Dearest Aunt Fanny,

You will know how lonely I am as I wrote of Offley's departure to be on the 14th in my last letter. The daytime is so full of occupation I do not miss Offley so much but at tea time—when it grows dark it is very, very lonely—even to come into the cheery and pre-lit study all alone—so I now ask Stewart down to tea with me. On Monday the Campbells come for ten days—and I must say all our friends have been very kind in asking me out to lunch and dine with them, but the great distances and the nights growing colder and colder—do not encourage one to accept dinner invitations. Yes, the weather is beautiful now, but October is the best month almost anywhere in the world, I think. If only Offley could have stayed at home a little later to enjoy it here. The roses are lovely and so are the early autumn flowers and today the gardener is planting sweet pea seeds for next Spring, and Offley has left about 30 boxes of seedlings of every variety for the gardeners to set out now from time to time under my direction to make this place bright and charming for next year. If only you could come out to see it—and us!

We are also busy with the Autumn cleaning and Stewart and I hope to do a little preserving! It will be great fun I think. Thank you for having my commissions done. I only wish one was not so dependent on Europe and America for so many things. I am afraid I give you a lot of bother. I am racking my brains to know what to send you all from here for Xmas—as I fear I have exhausted most and certainly the best of India's productions.

October 23rd, 1913   Dormers

My very dear Father,

After guessing the whole summer long who was to be the next Commander-in-Chief of the Army in India (The biggest Military appointment within the gift of the Empire)—I had a telephone message last night to say the telegram had just come saying Sir Beauchamp Duff is appointed. Colonel Bruce Seton telephoned me as he knew Offley would be pleased. You wrote to Sir Beauchamp— one of those many letters for 'a character' for Offley when I became engaged to him and he wrote you a long letter, which you may still have? He is a very strong man—and was Lord Kitchener's choice last time for Chief. Intellectually a very clever, brilliant man, a good speaker and will be quite the best man on the Viceroy's Council—an Indian Officer and knowing India very thoroughly. So I should think all is well—but many names were in the running and there are assuredly many disappointments. As I wrote to Offley, 'This should be a good thing toward my F.M.!' but Sir Beauchamp is not a man to advance a friend or a soldier for anything but his own ability or fitness for an appointment.

I miss Offley dreadfully—oh dreadfully and when the Campbells go next week I shall be lonely indeed. My bed is still on its way from Calcutta. I do hope it arrives before I leave here! but as we are keeping this house on another year—it will find a place in my room as I originally intended.

November 12, 1913 **Dormers**

My very dear Father,

Thank you for thinking of me, to cable me about dear Aunt Mary's death—you know how well I loved her. What friends we always were and you can understand my grief and sorrow, now to know that she is no more. Uncle Frank wrote us very regularly and sent us many little snap shots of dear Aunt Mary—very, very changed—and yet—somehow her wonderful energy and splendid spirit had carried her so well through other illnesses that we thought and hoped constantly it would through this, for many a day to come yet. What a happy day that was we spent all together at 'Die Rosen' the Sunday before we left—when we had our photos taken and how sweet and gay Aunt Mary was. You have no idea—how sad these breaks in our family make me and how I think of and long for dear, dear Mother—and now Aunt Mary.

I feel <u>so sorry</u> for Uncle Frank. What will he do without Aunt Mary!! and the two boys—they were more dependent on their Mother than they realized.

I am most awfully lonely without Offley and I may go down to Delhi sooner—if he has any change in his plans to bring him there earlier or longer.

Write to me often dear Father and oh, if you would only pay us a visit! How welcome we should make you and how happy we would be to have you.

On 4 December Lina started a letter to Aunt Fanny with:

It is a beautiful winter day—clear and sunny—perhaps not quite so cold as it has been—and now I am packing vigorously to be off to Delhi to meet Offley!!! Hurrah!

and continued with New Year greetings to the family and finished with:

I fancy you are all pretty much bothered over the income tax in U.S.A. Surely it cannot be exacted of me? I have received already any number of papers and booklets upon the subject but not one paper to fill out or show that I am a British subject. I cannot understand why they have sent me these things at all. Offley holds some American bonds and he has not received any of these notices. However—Uncle Joe and Uncle Harry will look after my interests I feel sure and hope, and I have written to Father and to Brown Bros. and to others also to do so.

December 10th, 1913   **Dormers**

My dearest Aunt,

In another week or little more we [herself and Mrs. Stewart] shall be off—and happy as I am in Simla and much as I like it in the winter when we are a little colony of pleasant people—all rather more friendly than there is time for in summer—I shall be so glad, so very glad and happy to see Offley again that nothing else will matter. I leave here on Monday the 22nd to reach Delhi that night at one o'clock mid-night. Offley comes Christmas Eve so that gives me a good day to get our quarters at Curzon House in order so that our address from now until February 22nd (for me) will be 'Curzon House, Delhi'. On the 22nd of February I leave for Agra to go to the 'Highland Meeting' with the Campbells—who join me there—in Agra, at the Cecil Hotel—and on the 1st of March I expect to go back to Kohat on the North West Frontier with them for a month. Whether I will pay Miss Impey a visit in Baroda or not I don't know.

I received such a kind and sad letter from poor Uncle Frank by last mail—written very shortly after dear Aunt Mary had passed away. This was so thoughtful and kind of him and I was glad to know she died so peacefully and calmly. It must have been God's comfort for them—the two tired and anxious watchers, Uncle Frank and Clifford. I also felt that it was a deeper touch of affection for me and for Offley loving Aunt Mary as dearly, dearly as I always have—and Offley too—that he—Uncle Frank—should write to me so soon and in this way. Oh, how I shall miss her! It is a great joy that Stewart and I can talk together of 'home' as we now can.

I hope to get your letters regularly. There has been a great deal of trouble with the post office here, in Simla, and there is all over India more or less trouble with the native employees. I was 8 days without any letter from Offley—though I know it takes 5 or 6 days to come from Southern India—I also know he writes me every few days—if not every day at times and we discovered that his letters to me were being sent back to Delhi! You can well imagine there will be a Big row made by me! and I hope to some good.

By an odd coincidence it is from precisely this date that come the only letters from Offley to Lina that have survived, written during that part of his tour which took him to Southern India, from Ootacamund in the Nilgiri Hills and dated 6, 8, 10 December. They are detailed accounts of his travels. His absorption in topographical detail, so apparent in his official sketch-books, comes out, as does his interest in trees and flowers and shrubs. He gives distances covered, he lists the altitudes, to the nearest foot, of the eleven stations on the rack railway up to Ootacamund from Metapalaiyum and notes the steepest gradient at 1 in 12.28. And he draws a small sketch of the route.

At the end of each letter he becomes more personal:

You and I must come here together, before we leave India. If we had been together here, tonight, how we should have talked over the glories and wonders of this day. More tomorrow—much love little one.

How you would enjoy the pleasant part of this touring! But what squeals there would be of the heat and dust and bustle. Looking forward, as ever, to seeing you again. From Secunderabad onwards to Bombay and Delhi you will not, I think, get any letters.

I do hope things at Delhi will work out to your satisfaction; I have every confidence in your judgment. I am glad Mrs. Clark has been friendly. You are a splendid hand at getting things out of people! That wonderful persuasive manner and faculty for making people think they are in the wrong and not Mistress Schatz—a very great gift. Much love little one.

The 'Curzon House' to which Lina refers in her letter of 10 December and from which her New Year letters were written were staff quarters in the new Government buildings in Delhi named for Lord Curzon, Viceroy from 1899 to 1905.

December 31, 1913   **Curzon House, Delhi**

Dearest Aunt Fanny,

Last week I missed the home mail and wrote no letters to anyone—as I travelled down here from Simla on the 22nd—reached here at 1:30 a.m. and became entirely engrossed in arranging our quarters all the next day to receive Offley that night, the 23rd at mid-night, and the next day, the 24th, the two Shores—Hugh and Noel arrived, again about mid-night, to spend the Christmas holidays with us, and Mrs. Stewart left on the 24th by a midnight train for Lahore to spend Christmas with her daughter who has since been so ill that Mrs. S. is staying on with her a little. I hope she recovers shortly as Offley leaves me again January 5th to be away until the 29th. Not so long this time. He looks very well and in spite of the dust, heat and difficulties and trials of such huge journies he has seen a great deal of interest and met a great many people and the Lakes have been charming and kindness itself. He brought me back all sorts of quaint and unusual things from different far away places and gave them to me all at once—9 packages as a great surprise on Christmas morning.

We took Christmas dinner with the Lakes and I sent her our plum pudding from home—England—and it was delicious and we had great fun with some marvellous crackers she had. The next day we lunched with the Commander-in-Chief and Lady Creagh. I shall be most sad at parting with her. I am very attached to her and she has been extraordinarily nice to me. On New Year's night we dine with the Chief Commissioner of Delhi and Mrs. Hailey. These holiday parties are not big festivities but we are asked quietly and in this way we enjoy being with our friends. We spent Christmas day motoring and taking our lunch basket with us, we spent the afternoon at the Kutab[4]—just the two boys and ourselves. Another day we did the same thing and wound up at the Fort—where the Pearl Mosque and the exquisite palace—the Diwan-i-khas was a jewel of loveliness in the sunset light and its restored gardens—now green with the softest of grass and waterways and splendid trees of poincettias now in full flower. It is truly splendid and beautiful at this time of the year and as I say in its present setting. On Sunday afternoon we motored out to the site and work at the New Imperial Delhi. It was very interesting and we had of course a plan of the Imperial city that is to rise in a few years in the midst of the seven Delhis that still proudly hold their sway—though in ruins.

We have been trying to settle the question of a motor—or some sort of conveyance for me particularly, and for ourselves, while here. The tourist globe trotters make Delhi a very expensive place during the season and the price asked to hire a motor by the month is fabulous—and yet the distances are very great. But one has to remember our expenses in Simla for 9 months of the year are very great so I want to live as quietly and economically here as I can. Then there are Offley's travelling expenses and the horses this winter and next year, 1915. I want so much to go home again and see you all in Philadelphia. How is one to plan all this ahead—and 'finance it' as Offley suggests I shall do?

January 1, 1914   **Curzon House, Delhi**

My very dear Father,

You will know ere this what a New Year we have begun. Last night after dinner Offley told me the Military Secretary had told him he was to have the C.B.—Companionship of the Bath—the soldier's order—par excellence of Great Britain—conferred upon him in today's Honours List. Imagine then—how pleased and proud I felt when our first official notification came early this morning and was brought in with the 'early tea' at 7:30 a.m. in the shape of a telegram from the Viceroy. We spent a very happy quiet day—motoring in the afternoon and returned to receive the splendid news this evening that Betty is coming to India.

All day long telegrams and letters and telephone messages and visitors have come to congratulate Offley—God bless him—and I know you and Uncle Joe and Aunt Fanny and all my people at home and Uncle Frank will feel pride in this last new honour for Offley and for me. Someday your Son-in-law—who never thought to be more than a Colonel Sahib will surely be a big General or perhaps a Fieldmarshal—and if not—'the Admiral of the Queen's Navy'—at least he'll surely be a K.C.B.!!!!!! I am so proud and pleased over Offley and so excited and delighted at the thought of seeing Betty in India. So much for one day—that I must close without saying more this week.

I am delighted with my bed, dear Father, and I shall have some further correspondence with those Rascals in Calcutta and would you at once ship me another bed only this time a double one of the very same pattern and with the same height head and foot boards.

We have just written out a cable to send to Betty. Of course we shall meet her in Bombay—and how pleased we are is difficult to express.

I am sure she will like it in India—and we shall do our best to have her enjoy it.

This letter was clearly written late on New Year's Day. On 'New Year's Eve—1913-1914', Lina had written to her Aunt a much shorter letter which contained the following paragraph:

Offley came into this little drawing room with me just now after dinner and kissed me and told me. Isn't it very splendid? The best part of it is that he is my husband—My wonderful and my most devoted husband—this distinguished Offley—Brigadier General, D.S.O., C.B., etc. and God bless him as I am blessed in him.

*Early in the New Year, on hearing of a broken marriage in Phila-
delphia, Lina reviewed the six years of her own marriage.*

How blessed one really is in a happy marriage, it is indeed a Heaven
on Earth. My own for instance. How wonderful it is. I often wonder
if I am sufficiently appreciative of all Offley does for me—all he
is and means. He wrote a little note with my Christmas presents
and put 'For the dearest creature in the whole world'. And now
after six years close together, closer perhaps because we are so alone
here in India, there are no illusions shattered, and as affection constantly increasing and a confidence and trust made stronger every
day we live.

*Lina's letters from this point through early April are almost
entirely concerned with the visit of her sister Betty accompanied
by a friend, Bessie Hays. Lina had expected them to stay much
longer than they did and was most disappointed that they did
not. She seems to have packed into their stay as much sight-seeing
as could be. She commented that they thought they knew all about
India because they had bought guide books.*

January 27th, 1914   **Curzon House, Delhi**

My dearest Aunt,

I am looking forward so much to Betty's coming. Just now I
have given up my motor for a little while and begin again the end
of this week when Offley comes back for a few days and in order
to have it when Betty is with me to go about in—and perhaps to
travel into Agra and Lucknow. It is so <u>very</u> expensive to hire a
motor by the month with chauffeur etc. and as our winter expenses
seem to increase instead of decrease—with Offley's touring and me
coming down here, and the house and house rent and some servants
in Simla going on all the time, one gets very little chance of being
quiet and economizing. However as the setting up house and beginning over again in Simla last summer was a very expensive
thing—I am <u>determined</u> to be as quiet as possible now and get ahead
a little before Betty comes. Of course I shall go down to Bombay
to meet Betty and with the greatest pleasure in the world—but I

don't suppose she realizes for a moment that it is a journey of two
nights and a day—and one upon which I must take Stewart and a
native servant as well—and also to have a sleeping carriage to ourselves we are obliged to pay double fares—that is, as the carriages
hold 4 one must buy 4 tickets or else run the risk of others coming
in the train with you and not necessarily Europeans! So the journey
to Bombay and back costs about 500 or 600 rupees—or something
like $200. I will see that everything is as comfortable as possible
for Betty. I am only sorry Offley cannot come with me. He of course
knows so well how to do things properly in this country. I have
never before taken these very long journeys without him—but Stewart
is a good traveller.

I hope when Betty comes out she will see all she can of this
country—and if we could sublet the house in Simla later, Offley is
quite willing we should go to Kashmir—he will try to go with us
but if he can't we can go. It would amuse you to see an Indian
journey's arrangement. If to the South and warm there must always
be an ice-box taken and some cooling beverage, for the dust and
heat parch one so much and if to the North all sorts of warm things
and more bedding. One always travels with one's bedding in this
country and many of us—most of us with our own food. Tiffin or
lunch baskets are as common as birds in this country. Just now I
cannot get any quarters here in this house for Betty but I hope to, or
to put her in a tent next to or with Stewart and I will let her describe
that to you herself. I feel sure Betty of all people will like India immensely. I wish I knew more about her coming but I've had nothing
but the cable and I don't know if she is bringing a maid or not or if
she comes with friends. If she is coming with friends of course I can't
take them in here as this is only my official abode—and if she comes
with friends then she would certainly need a native Bearer and I
have—not knowing anything—done nothing about one for her—as
when with us our servants would gladly do all and anything for
her—but it would be quite a different matter if she has to go into
an hotel as she must then have a good servant of a certain class
and caste—and such things take some time to arrange—however I
will do my best whatever comes—but my house in Simla has only
one good spare room, and if the family came I could arrange to
double up more than we do, as Offley now uses a bedroom for his
dressing room and we use another bedroom for the tennis days—

when the officers come straight from the office to play tennis but you won't understand why this is unless you come out to India and see how different our mode of life is—bath-room arrangements etc. being very primitive! No more tonight dearest Aunt.

Please don't read this to anyone—it must be quite entre nous—as I should not like anyone to misunderstand, <u>but</u> you to whom I write as I think or would talk, dear Aunt Fanny, you know people are often quite unprepared for things travelling in an entirely new country.

February 4th, 1914   **Curzon House, Delhi**

My dearest Aunt,

I see by the calendar before me that <u>this day</u> next week I shall be starting on my journey to Bombay to meet Betty and Bessie Hays. So you will not expect any letter from me next week—as I fear it will be a long, hot and dusty journey not conducive to writing in the train. I have made every arrangement for their comfort I can think of when meeting them—engaged a room at the Taj Mahal Hotel—pre-arranged a reserved travelling carriage to come up country here and have told everyone I know they are coming so that they may have plenty of invitations and I hope all will go well. This afternoon I took tea with Lady McMahon, wife of the Foreign Secretary and afterwards we motored to a lovely garden in the cool of the evening. She will help me to take Betty about—as we are not <u>always</u> asked to Government House, for instance, each one of us being invited more or less in turn here as the Viceregal Lodge is not big enough to entertain any great number—so that Lady Mac—as her friends familiarly call her—will take Betty—and she is the wife of a 'Big Nip' in the Civil Service here. She is also going to try to get Betty into one of the camps for the 'Kadir'—the most Indian race in the world—where they ride on racing horses to stick a pig—a wild pig—and the sight-see-ers or audience go on elephants. All the riders in the race are cavalry officers—and these sort of <u>unusual</u> things are rarely if ever seen by the 'globe-trotter'. I only

hope it all comes off for Betty. How she would love it. At Agra
we will 'sight see' in between the 'Highland Meetings' as we go
there for the week of 'The Gathering' of Scotch [*sic*] and Scotch
Regiments and I think Betty and Bessie will both thoroughly love
the fun—and Agra with its beautiful Taj Mahal and the Fort with
its Palaces etc. etc. They have both been asked to the Impeys which
would mean a visit to a Native State—always an interesting thing
to do but as Miss Impey is going home—they are just too late to
accept this. I am so sorry they did not come out earlier—but as
they have come out when they have!—you must understand it is
almost <u>impossible</u> to have them return in April, May, June or July—
or August. The heat of the plains is appalling and the Red Sea!
Anyone not used to this tropical climate could not possibly brave
it—or would be worse than a fool to think of it and no doubt you
and Fanny and Uncle Joe and Father will find some pleasant place
to sojourn in during the summer months—Newport or Bar Harbour—or
Lenox or all three. Fancy me! arranging your summer for you! You
will say, 'how very cool of her'. Now I must close with dear love.

February 18th, 1914   **Curzon House, Delhi**

Dearest Aunt Fanny,

Thank you for your letter and for the lovely dress sent by Betty
and which I wore last night and everyone said how very becoming
it was. Not a hook to be changed—not a stitch needed! It felt a
little wee bit tight at first but it soon was as comfortable as possible
and it <u>fits</u> one so prettily all about the 'decoltés'. As you can imagine
we <u>do</u> talk and Betty is the same Betty all the world over and quite
orders me about in 'her Excellency's' own particular fashion, motor,
menservants and the household generally and we all feel a little
bouleversé in our joy at having them. Last night I had a very large
dinner party of 18 in their honour—and it was the merriest (my
friends said) in Delhi for many a day. Now I must run away and
dress for dinner and a concert I am taking them to, but more tomorrow
if I have a moment. How I wish you could see us, dear Aunt Fanny,

but you will when Betty returns and through very straightforward, true eyes—and I should like to hear Betty telling you of me, of us.

P.S. She sightsees in her big goggles, red guide book in hand, a topee or Indian sun hat and a big tourist's umbrella. Too funny.

February 24th, 1914   **Hotel Cecil, Agra**

My dear Uncle Joe,

Many thanks for many letters. I know Offley will do his best—all he can—for the University books you wish—and if he is too busy, upon my return to Delhi on Friday, I will see if I can do anything in the matter myself.

I think Betty and Bessie enjoyed their visit in Delhi—but we of the lazy, indolent East do not bustle enough for them!!!! perhaps it is that Betty is nervous and excitable. One thing I do feel sure of and that is that the longer she remains with us the more good it will do her. She is difficult to advise and direct, but she has profound admiration for Offley's judgement and he has advised her as far as possible—in the little time we were together. She and Bessie get on most happily together and tho' there are some awkward and unpleasant things to overlook, one cannot expect everything! I have secured a good servant for them and they like him which is a great thing.

Betty sightsees very intelligently and I've put my motor completely at their disposal ever since they arrived (Offley's Christmas present to me—that is one of them). They will write for themselves, no doubt, of the 'society part' of their visits to Delhi and here. Cards have just come for a ball at the Willcocks—Sir James Willcocks commands the Northern Army in India—and they are invited to all the festivities going on in connection with the Highland Gathering.

From here they go to Calcutta, Benares, Lucknow and Cawnpore, returning to Delhi and going on again from there to Lahore and up to Peshawar and the Khyber Pass. I hope all will go well with them. I must return to Delhi to be with Offley and to pack up and send back my few household things to Simla.

I do hope Betty will feel like staying the summer with me and also that Father will consent to her doing so. She is very conscientious I must say and anxious to do what is best. [Betty's age at this time was 42—Ed.]

March 4, 1914   **Curzon House, Delhi**

Dear Uncle Joe,

We came back from our gaieties and the wonders of Agra last Saturday—Betty and Bessie Hays to go on the same night by mail train to Calcutta and I to take up my daily life here—with Offley however, this time, I am happy to say. I think Betty and Bessie enjoyed Agra with all its Mogul glories now in their loveliest settings—parks and gardens arranged to be kept up by Lord Curzon's intense interest. They will have written of the Fairy Story likeness in everything—of the Tattoo in the Fort when Bengal lights and little lanterns lighting up the palaces of marble and red sandstone made one gaze in wonder and stretch one's eyes as though one had been asleep and dreaming. Then the reception in the palace of marble with supper in the Jasmine Tower—fountains playing and the tinkle of water in the decorated marble gardens. Highlanders everywhere and their exquisite regimental silver set forth in the loveliness of candle light with its background of mellow marble. They were lucky to have got in for such a time.

Today began with an avalanche of duty. The memorial service for Lord Minto—I have felt very sad all day as he was really a very good friend to us and one felt one had in him 'the friend at court'. Up at 6:30 to have breakfast and be dressed in parade clothes— mourning dress—at Church at 9 o'clock and back again for another little breakfast, only to be off again by 10:30 to bid good-bye to the C. in C. Sir O'Moore Creagh and Lady Creagh. I felt very sad and sick hearted at saying good-bye to them and to their Military Secretary, General Peyton and his wife, but I enjoyed driving through the roads lined with troops and bowing and looking at them and walking through the Station with its scarlet carpet to the train. The C. in C.'s own Special all white and gold. At the Station the scene was wonderful. The different officers all in their splendid uniforms and the Native Chiefs in gorgeous array and then came the departing old Chief and Lady Creagh over whose heads and round whose necks were flung gold tinsel necklaces and garlands of roses, and baskets of flowers were brought and as the train moved off and the band struck up 'Auld Lang Syne' some native servants flung showers of rose leaves over them as they stood on the little platform of their train. He looking an old man and she feeling it all deeply yet trying not to cry. I gave her a little fan and she kissed me goodbye. A real friend I have but just made and she must go. Our lives are full of partings in India.

In a letter dated 5 September 1913, Lina had written:

I shall miss dear Lady Creagh when they do go. It is sad—her husband as Commander in Chief has been anything but a success—but she is so charming and one feels sad—as I am sure they hear a great many unpleasant things that are said of him.

April 14th, 1914   Dormers, Simla

My dear Aunt Fanny and Uncle Joe,

Tomorrow Betty and Bessie leave by the one o'clock train and you can imagine how sad I feel at parting with Betty. It has been splendid seeing my darling sister and I cannot make enough of the pleasure it has been to me, to us—both of us. Offley as well as myself, is deeply attached to Betty. I hope she will try and arrange matters that she may come out again and perhaps bring Fanny—if Father too cannot be persuaded to come. I shall be very, very lonely when they go as Offley is away, as you know, and does not return until the end of this month. Oh, how I hate to see her go home. It has been such a short visit—and I have no one but friends and when Offley is away I am desperately lonely.

In April and May, Offley wrote two long letters to Uncle Joe: one on the future of the British Empire, the other on his own future.

April 26th, 1914   **Simla**

I have a feeling that things are likely to be troublous this year—and that we shall enter upon an anxious time. The Home Country is going through a most serious social revolution—which of course will be reflected out here—and most of us think the party system of Government must surely end by disgusting the people as a whole, or by disrupting the Empire and bringing about its downfall. Being a practical nation, I suppose some sort of compromise will be arrived at—as far as the Ulster question is concerned—but Home Rule for Great Britain or a Federal Council for Imperial affairs seems bound to come—if we are to hold together at all.

India, even under British rule, is feeling that there is too much interference from London, and wants to be more independent in matters concerning her own self: but—like the Dominions wishes to be consulted in the greater affairs of State policy.

At present—you will scarcely believe it—the Viceroy in Council, can only sanction an expenditure of 50,000 rupees without reference to the Sec. of State for India—which means the British House of Commons! We are bound hand and foot by regulations and decisions dictated by our working classes, socialists, and Exeter Hall. I know you are watching these things with close interest from your side: and, I expect, with no little dismay.

May 3rd, 1914

There are many changes on the tapis—this year and next—and I have been told that I shall probably be recommended for a Brigade Command 'down below' [i.e. in the plains—Ed.] directly: which may mean 1915 or 1916, since I fancy they will soon be trying one with troops to see if one is to go any further, and so, Dormers may not see us again for a while. If tried and a failure, of course it means 'outside'—on a pension—but thank goodness one has—or will have by the 10th of this month, May, have completed 32 years active soldiering and be entitled to £700 p.a. whatever they may say about one's fitness for further advancement. I feel free! and I don't care one hang what they do!!!

Quite a satisfactory state of mind—Eh?

In early June, Mrs. Stewart was rushed to hospital for an operation.

June 9th, 1914   Dormers

My dearest Aunt,

Last night was the Court—a very ceremonious affair—not quite so pleasant as last year's I thought. However perhaps I was in no mood to enjoy it—as my dear old Stewart who had told me of a curious lump in her breast (and I wrote for Colonel James to come and examine it at once) has just left me to go to the Hospital and to have an operation tomorrow for tumour. You can imagine how upset I feel. She runs my house entirely and so smoothly and beautifully.

June 11th

Offley has been my lady's maid and I have been very busy with my housekeeping—and especially as my head bearer, 'Gulab', took leave to go to his Father's death bed!

Mrs. Stewart was very brave and stood her operation wonderfully but in the doctor's note to me he said 'The growth turned out to be true cancer so I removed the whole breast together with some enlarged glands which I found under the arm-pit on that side. And I have every hope that we have eradicated the disease as the growth was still small.' But how I feel—you can have no idea. Stewart has been home with me—we can talk about you all. She has cared for Offley and for me in our turn when we have been ill and she serves

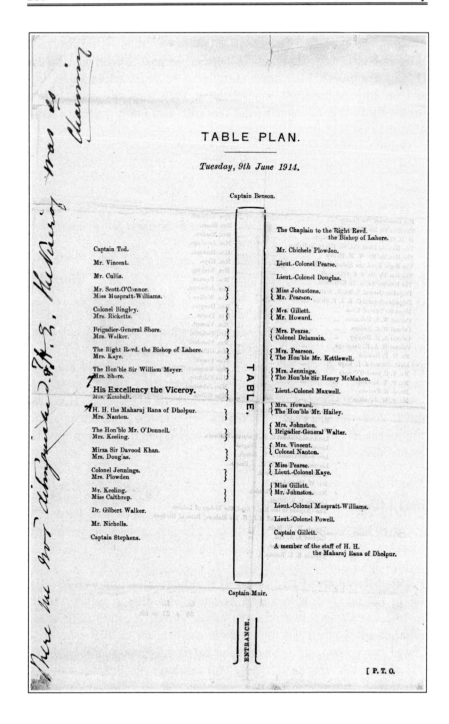

TABLE PLAN.

Tuesday, 9th June 1914.

Captain Benson.

Left side (top to bottom):

Captain Tod.

Mr. Vincent.

Mr. Cullis.

Mr. Scott-O'Connor.
Miss Muspratt-Williams.

Colonel Bingley.
Mrs. Ricketts.

Brigadier-General Shore.
Mrs. Walker.

The Right Revd. the Bishop of Lahore.
Mrs. Kaye.

The Hon'ble Sir William Meyer.
Mrs. Shore.

His Excellency the Viceroy.
Mrs. Kemball.

H. H. the Maharaj Rana of Dholpur.
Mrs. Nanton.

The Hon'ble Mr. O'Donnell.
Mrs. Keeling.

Mirza Sir Davood Khan.
Mrs. Douglas.

Colonel Jennings.
Mrs. Plowden.

Mr. Keeling.
Miss Calthrop.

Dr. Gilbert Walker.

Mr. Nicholls.

Captain Stephens.

Right side (top to bottom):

The Chaplain to the Right Revd.
the Bishop of Lahore.

Mr. Chichele Plowden.

Lieut.-Colonel Pearse.

Lieut.-Colonel Douglas.

Miss Johnstone.
Mr. Pearson.

Mrs. Gillett.
Mr. Howard.

Mrs. Pearse.
Colonel Delamain.

Mrs. Pearson.
The Hon'ble Mr. Kettlewell.

Mrs. Jennings.
The Hon'ble Sir Henry McMahon.

Lieut.-Colonel Maxwell.

Mrs. Howard.
The Hon'ble Mr. Hailey.

Mrs. Johnston.
Brigadier-General Walter.

Mrs. Vincent.
Colonel Nanton.

Miss Pearse.
Lieut.-Colonel Kaye.

Miss Gillett.
Mr. Johnston.

Lieut.-Colonel Muspratt-Williams.

Lieut.-Colonel Powell.

Captain Gillett.

A member of the staff of H. H.
the Maharaj Rana of Dholpur.

TABLE.

Captain Muir.

ENTRANCE.

[P. T. O.

me so faithfully and we have been so much alone together—that this causes me the greatest anxiety and sorrow for her. However as O. says and as the doctor told me—I have probably saved her life by acting so promptly in calling our excellent and kind doctor, Colonel James.

In the early 1920s, some years after Lina had left India, she was still corresponding with Mrs. Stewart in service in India.

In addition to being very anxious and very distressed about Mrs. Stewart's condition Lina, at this time, was becoming concerned about the general state of Offley's health. He was having high fevers at night.

July 2nd, 1914   Dormers

My dearest Aunt,

Offley is better I am most happy to say and poor Mrs. Stewart is back again here, after 3 weeks in the hospital, but neither my darling Offley or Mrs. Stewart are quite right yet. Offley looks very thin and pulled down and I try to feed him up all I can—but he is very busy at the office these days and it is a great strain, when one does not feel perfectly well—and especially now the rains are upon us. While Stewart is still feeling the shock of her operation—but is so eager to do what little she can, poor old dear. I, thank God, have been keeping very well through all these bad days for them.

What a tragedy! The assassination of the Austrian Archduke and his wife! The poor old Emperor has indeed been spared nothing.[5]

If Offley could get a little 'leave' next summer—would you and Uncle Joe come as far as England or the Continent—say Switzerland—and meet us? I feel as if he should make a great effort for some leave out of the country, but it is but the barest chance of getting it and then, he says, it would be but for a very short time, too short for us to take the two months it would require to journey to U.S.A. much as we would both like to do that.

We feel pleased to hear how well Betty enjoyed her visit to India. She assuredly gave us the very greatest pleasure by coming. I am glad that Bessie Hays too has acknowledged the kindness she received from Betty. She never did while she was here.

July 23rd, 1914   **Dormers**

My dearest Aunt,

Rumour has it that they want Offley to succeed General B. as Commandant of the Staff College at Quetta—but O. will not do it even if he's offered it. He wants very much, if possible to get away to the Continent, at least for a little change—if it's possible—as the next move will probably be to send O. to [command] troops and in that case it would be wise to have a good breath of European air and ideas before settling down to the plains of India for an appointment of any length. So do make up your minds to meet us in some pleasant place—perhaps the Tyrol next year.

This house will of course have to be given up, but it is very expensive for little more than 5 months out of the year to live in it, and all Offley's big winter tours are to be made. I should like to be able to fly off at a moment's notice—as we soldier people have to do when leave is granted or any changes come about.

I fear Stewart's usefulness is waning since her operation—though she is wonderfully well—but she appears to coddle herself rather and be too old for this or too old for that—and I must not rely upon having her always—though she is excellent in the house and with housekeeping—but I am sure you understand what I mean.

How lovely it must be to have beautiful houses—like the others have at home. I am often tempted to agree with Offley that it is time to go but I feel so very ambitious for him and such confidence in his ability.

July 30th, 1914   **Dormers**

Dearest Aunt Fanny,

Everyone's interest is now turned upon Europe. Again the Near East—as they call the Balkan States—is the center of excitement—and we look eagerly for every telegram. Will diplomacy fail and Europe be involved in a great war? Russia seems very anxious for war—and no doubt wants Constantinople. All this has a very serious effect upon India. What is going to happen? The Irish question is small compared with the issues at stake on the continent today. Offley and I are much interested as you can well understand.

I can quite sympathize with the Austrians <u>against</u> the Servians for the assassinations at Sarajevo were not the act of a madman, but a deeply laid political plot—and it would be very wrong indeed were it to pass un-noticed, unpunished. How far has the old Emperor got his <u>own fingers</u> in this matter? I do hope all will soon be settled, but things look very grave, do they not?

To turn to more personal matters—It may prevent Offley from getting any leave—and we have and are still planning for that. Please God all ends soon and for the best—<u>the better</u>, for all these terrible things must have some outlet. Just what part it will be given to England to take—one scarcely knows.

Will you again be kind and get me some more 'corn plaster' from your special man. It is of the greatest balm to me and saves me many a bad ache, by way of using it as a precautionary—and would you also get me half a dozen petticoats—white muslin of a not too expensive kind—with a little embroidery. Wanamakers[6] is no doubt the best place for such things.

August 4th, 1914   **Dormers**

My dearest Aunt,

I am afraid I have never written last month so as to reach you with birthday greetings on that day. I am so sorry and particularly annoyed with myself that I have not done it!

Our days now are so full of excitement and suspense and anxiety. One literally 'lives' on news, telegrams and cables. War and rumours of war.

Since Austria's ultimatum to Servia and the outbreak of war between that country and Servia, and Germany's declaration and Russia and France mobilizing, Belgium, Holland and Switzerland doing the same, and with the 'Alliances' and 'Ententes' so established in one's head, the position in which Great Britain is, we are hourly expecting to hear: what she is doing, what she <u>has</u> done. Never have I lived through such days as the last four or five. The Viceroy has returned and everyone is hurried and calm, but suppressed excitement must exist. It must.

August 5th, 1914

The news came early this morning that England had declared war. You can imagine how my heart flutters and how one prays God to give one strength and courage to act as one sh'd when the moment comes that O. and I must realize that we may have to part. He for this war, and I to wend my lonely way to meet him. Where??!!! and when!!!

I am now <u>so thankful</u> that Betty went home when she did. It would have been a great joy and a great comfort to have had her here with me this summer <u>and now</u>, but I realize how lucky it is that she is at home. I am wondering if Charlie[7] and his family have returned home safely and if Clara[7] and hers have got back.

We have the most wonderful lilies, 'Jersey lilies', now in bloom and lovely begonias and the morning glories on the lattices above the tennis court are charming, but the weather is but rain and fog and dullness, until evening when we get a marvelous sun-set, glorious in cottony mists and gold hues and snow peaks, and one looks upon this exquisite land and so heaven like it is at these moments, but one can only think of War! War! War with its devastations, its animosities, its horrors. War! But I must write no more.

Offley, on 4 August, began a letter to Uncle Joe:

A good deal has happened within the last 10 days to upset most calculations—! our news is limited to what Reuter gave us before Censorship was established and now, to what the Censors allow to pass: so, since censorship probably is thoroughly established all over Europe, I do not suppose we shall have the least idea—from now on—of what is happening.

So far England does not appear to have declared war on Germany— Germany is said to have invaded France, Russia to have invaded Germany, Austria to be fighting Servia—Norway, Sweden, Denmark, and Italy neutral and diplomats are apparently still babbling. New York, Paris, London Bourses closed—English Bankrate 10%! We expect important and exciting news hourly—which does not come— So much for the situation.

What England will ask us to do, is 'in the air'. We know absolutely nothing: but our imaginations run riot. Anyway—it's no more interesting to be at a H.Q.rs. these days than with the army down below.

Aug. 5th

Today we hear it is War between England and Germany, so we are all in the Dogfight: and a thundering good thing for the English people who just want something of this sort to pull them together and stop all their infernal political nonsense. There'll be lots of fur flying around and I don't fancy much mercy for the dogs that go down!

When you will receive this letter, I can't imagine—what with fleet actions and commerce destroyed and censors and privateers— mailboats may have a lively and precarious time. Already our newspapers contain nothing! not a decent word about the Austro-Servian campaign—nothing from Russia or Germany—cable interrupted through Persian Gulf, Turkey–Russia: so far Suez Canal seems intact and its cable route working. What of the China Sea side?

If Lady Betty had consented to stay the summer through, she would have been bottled up in this country! tho' I confess I now wish that had so happened—as the 2 sisters would have been together.

My personal chances of going with any troops anywhere are small indeed—as I doubt the Chief sparing any of his headquarters staff, who have so much of the direction and preparation and watching developments to do—but you never know!! Training for war (my business) now gives way to the real thing—but I have new formations and the supply of staff officers to handle, and so may remain on my office chair.

Aug. 6th

Nothing of interest seems to have come over the wires last night! We are expecting news of a fleet action either in the North Sea or the Mediterranean—we want to see the flags walk across the war maps like insects, and are irritated at the slowness of their progressions. We wonder why so and so doesn't do the obvious thing: we try and forecast the opponents' movements—but we don't know how long it is taking certain nations to mobilise because in several instances we are ignorant of the first date of mobilisation. They have been at it for some time, partially and stealthily.

All routine and ordinary work now loses its interest by comparison with the Great War—and no wonder.

Every officer we have, is dying to be off, and afraid of being late for the great battle!! I tell them, when they are in it, they will only see their own limited battle front, but they want to be there.

I am glad to hear your report of the Baobab seeds, and hope many will survive and live to grow up. I have some others here with skins like armour plate—which I brought from Ceylon and also some Tamarind seeds—hoarded against the day when I might have a greenhouse of my own: as there seems little present likelihood of such good fortune, I think I shall have to 'convey' these also to you—in some manner.

When so many of the family are cruising about England and Europe, it seems a pity that we cannot get over there and fore-gather—probably those of them who have managed to get into Germany, will find it difficult to get out again! and you will have some vivid word pictures of mobilisation and popular feeling. We shall probably find our future mails will be delayed—if not altogether inter-rupted for a while—and so I don't know when you will get this.

India: August 1914 to March 1917

War between Britain and Germany, with the United States remaining neutral, aroused problems of loyalties difficult of reconciliation for Lina.

Her much beloved maternal grand-parents, the anniversaries of whose births and deaths she remembered in her letters every year, were German. Her favourite correspondents, Aunt Fanny and Uncle Joe, still had family connections in Germany, and new friendships had been made as a result of marriages between Philadelphians and Germans. On the other hand her husband was British and an officer in the Indian Army. She developed a mental division between the bad Germans, headed by the Kaiser and his generals, and the good Germans, represented by her re-lations and friends. She could not understand how the latter had been so misled by the former, and was worried about their fate.

The neutrality of the United States evoked her anger and scorn. As submarine warfare developed and American vessels were torpedoed, her criticism of President Wilson and his neutralist Secretary of State, William Jennings Bryan, grew fiercer and fiercer and as the Presidential election of 1916 approached she hoped that the Americans would choose for themselves a stronger and more 'patriotic' President.

Indian troops took part in the war in France and Mesopotamia, the land between the Tigris and the Euphrates, and for the first eighteen months of the war Offley remained at Army Headquarters in India, in charge of the training, the organisation and the des-patch of forces to both these theatres of war. At the outbreak of war he was aged 51, had never commanded troops, and was, by all the available evidence, an experienced and efficient staff officer. Lina recognised the validity of his constant complaint that if he saw no active service during the war, he would have no further career in the Army at the end of it. She was ambitious for his rise to high rank, but in constant fear of losing him.

Under the territorial division of responsibility between the British and Indian governments at that time, the Mesopotamia Campaign was an Indian operation.[1] It began in November 1914, when Turkey entered the war, with the occupation of Basra in order to protect the oil pipeline from Persia. In June 1915, with Sir John Nixon in command, an attempt to advance to Baghdad was begun, but was halted at Ctesiphon. A force of 10,000 men under General Charles Townsend retreated to Kut-el-Amara where they were besieged by Turkish forces. Three relief attempts in January, March and April 1916 failed and on 29 April, after 143 days of siege, General Townsend surrendered. (See Appendix B.)

In January of that year Sir John Nixon had been withdrawn on the grounds of ill health and replaced in command by Sir Percy Lake. Offley accompanied him as his Chief of Staff. After the surrender of Kut, Sir Percy Lake was withdrawn from command; Sir Stanley Maude was appointed in his place; a Commission was appointed to review the progress of the campaign.

At the end of October Offley developed jaundice and was invalided back to Simla, arriving there at the beginning of December. The results of an examination by a Medical Board a month later would severely limit the future of his army career.

International matters, other than the war in Europe and in the Middle East, which concerned Lina were what she called 'this Irish wickedness'—the Sinn Fein rising at Easter 1916—and the state of war between the United States and Mexico arising out of the Mexican civil war following the revolution there of 1911. Pancho Villa's forces raided New Mexico in March 1916; American troops forced the raiders back across the frontier and sporadic hostilities continued until early 1917.

In Simla, Lina became very busy with sewing parties producing clothing to supplement the official provision for the troops. Her sister Betty organised similar working parties in Philadelphia. As prices rose and taxes increased she became ever more anxious about their financial future. The mails became irregular as the result of submarine activity and the delays resulting from censorship, but gifts of clothes continued to arrive from her family in Philadelphia.

August 6, 1914

Dormers

My love to you, dear Uncle Joe,

I am very depressed these days. One minute it is likely O. may be sent off with a Brigade or to Staff duty in the field. The next, it is not at all likely. 'No! He must be kept here.' In one's <u>heart</u> one is praying for courage, one is full of ambitions, and one is choked with distress. The <u>most conflicting</u> of emotions are mine. In the meanwhile, I pack and pack, or read and sew, all night one dreams and one awakes tired out, but I feel no lively excitement, a curious calm, a great amazement at the hugeness of such a calamity. War in <u>the whole of Europe</u>. A great war with modern war equipment and my Best Beloved a soldier. It is horrible.

August 12, 1914

Dormers

My dearest Aunt,

I wonder if this letter will ever reach you? <u>Someday</u>, perhaps! and I know how anxiously you will all be thinking of us, of me—at this time of great stress and excitement—each day one says good-bye or rather 'au revoir' to some soldier boy or man who leaves to join his regiment should his Division be called for or sent off—but where that might be to or when—even he himself does not know! There is strict censorship upon all news—<u>all mails, all cables</u> in and out of the country, and our news is therefore of the scantiest and the excitement is intense among us all. Anyday one's husband may be off. This morning I began my day by having my early tea at 6 o'clock—and going to church to the Special Services for our soldiers and sailors at war and about to go to war. Already there were many women there whose husbands have already left Simla.

We are very well, barring little colds now and then—and that is not to be surprised at for the weather has been so wet. The monsoon so strong. We have quite decided to give up this sweet little house— not altogether our own idea but the landlord, looking well to the fatness of his pocketbook and without the slightest pretense at courtesy, 'wishes an answer as soon as possible'. Some civilians are after it and they, the civilians, not being soldiers are not likely to be shifted. Scant return for the trouble and care I took for him when the electric lighting was put into the house just after Betty left. However, price of living is going up these distressful days—and the rent is very high and it will be best to live quietly in an hotel and O. thinks more diverting for me as he is away all day now—never getting back for luncheon. In fact all at Headquarters are overworked and many work day and nights as well. Eleanor Davis came to lunch with me today—her husband left last night for his Div. If there are victories or defeats—we know not—all we do know is that the High Seas are unsafe. Should Offley leave me and I am able to get home to London I should I think want to be there where news is procurable. If there are no steamers in which we women could go—then here we must stay. However one has many friends and I am 'at home' with sympathetic neighbours on all sides. Of course you will send nothing—no clothes—nothing—as mails and parcels are all so very uncertain. The best assistance—so the Bankers tell me—is to have plenty in an American Bank—as American cheques are at premiums.

I am sewing hard—making a dress and making over dresses and Stewart is doing some underblouses and petticoats. I often wondered why I bought so many stockings etc. in America when I was last at home. How lucky I now feel to have them! as well as to have a precious 'piece trunk'—or part of one filled in that way. How glad I am to have learned so well—almost by heart—of the courage and fortitude of Baroness Riedesel. It should help one—when in a far off land under such circumstances—but I long more than ever for the comfort and blessing I feel a child would be.

It is sad to think how degenerate the Germans have become in their lust for World Power—and to hear of such behaviors as they have shown to the departing French and English Ambassadors. In Civilized Europe! In Intellectual Germany!!! We don't expect these things. Owing to the strict censorship—news is hard to get with us—so you must write us all you hear—all you can tell—as you in America will hear much no doubt. I shall look so much more eagerly—if that is possible—for your letters.

August 16, 1914   **Dormers**

My dearest Aunt,

On Friday afternoon last Lady Buller had a meeting at her home
to start work among us for the sick and wounded soldiers. There
was a good deal of 'feeling' and a diverse opinion among everyone
as to the place of organisation etc. and 'if this was the best and
most desirable assistance'—i.e. a scheme they had already arranged.
We were asked to come and discuss the best means for providing
and increasing comforts for our soldiers at war. There was no discussion however and the plan of action was announced all cut and
dried! This was not really what it should have been as many felt
and very rightly so—that the things called for on the lists circulated,
which was to be an auxiliary box of comforts and accessories for
a Govt. hospital of ten beds,—such things as Govt. does supply—
many thought ought not to be included at all. Offley was very much
averse to this scheme—and so were Sir Percy Lake and many other
officers of experience during the South African War. Well I thought
we all wanted very much to do something and to begin at once. I
was put on a committee to collect funds etc. and ask for helping
hands to sew etc.—among the clerks' wives and families—I know
what a hard time many of them have to live on their pay (Govt.
clerks)—so I gave the necessary funds to buy everything and then
Mrs. Crowe, Mrs. Spence and I got between 30 and 40 women to
come together and sew last Tuesday afternoon at the Convent school,
where they very kindly lent us their big room for the children's drill
and entertainment. This Mrs. Crowe and Mrs. Spence, both being R.C.s,
got from the sweet little Mother Superior, and these good women old
and young and some of the Convent school girls made all the articles
on the enclosed list [shirts, socks, caps, mittens, jersey, drawers,
mufflers and gloves sent to the 1st Gurkhas and 15th Lancers—Ed.].
The women who had machines brought them along—and so we had
nine machines going full tilt and with an interval for tea—during
which Mrs. Spence and I told them all the reasons for this war etc.
etc. It was a curious sight, that work room with the diligent workers—and two or three nuns looking in upon us, and lending a hand—
the Native bearers' faces—looking at us all as they brought in big
lamps, for it poured in torrents and grew very dark. Today we pack
the box at Mrs. Crowe's and later—as soon as we can fix upon a

day—we are to have a workshop party once a week in my big drawing room. Nothing else is talked of but the war—and it is horrible. The partings—the anxieties and what is to become in the near future for any of us—soldiers' wives—Offley has told Uncle Joe of all the news. We really enjoyed Sir Beauchamp's dinner party—it was a relief and a break in the midst of all this war and one met the big civilians and soldiers and heard their opinions.

How sad this all is for Germany—I cannot but think—and how deplorable—whether victor or vanquished. I will not believe the Emperor himself wished it—though I feel sure those Prussian officers and the Crown Prince did. You will be most interested in New Poland.[2] Long may it live and prosper—but I fear the next generation, if not the next to that—will have an over powerful Russia to fear.

August 27, 1914   **Dormers**

Dearest Father,

It is most difficult to take my pen in hand and write you anything worthwhile. We think of nothing but the War. This horrible War— and our news is <u>so little</u> and so uncertain. We have said 'Good-bye and good luck to you' to many of our good friends—some were off to the Mediterranean this week—some only leave Simla to join their regiments and 'stand fast'—as the term is. The hotels are practically empty and we try to cheer ourselves by little dinners—6 or 8 of us. The death of the Pope seems to pass almost unnoticed. This is the end of an era—I feel. Offley with all others at Headquarters is very hard at work—long, long hours and under great strain and tension. The Commander-in-Chief has issued an order that all officers holding appointments here are to remain in their appointments until the end of the War—upon the very heels of this announcement comes Lord Kitchener's speech in the House saying he wants at least thirty Divisions!!!!! Where will the officers come from?!! <u>India of course</u> and of those officers—capable, experienced men that he, Lord K. <u>knows</u>. Oh—what days we are living through—what dread and fear and anxiety—is ever in my heart. All our officers are naturally longing to go—to be off—and we women—soldiers' wives and mothers are naturally proud and ambitious to see them go—but if it must be to return 'on their shields' rather than—with them—that is the great pain at one's heart—and God only knows the end of all this horrible business.

We have been very hard at work, over hospital supplies and I believe we are to have regular 'working mornings' or afternoons, but none has as yet been settled. I am packing continuously as one does not know and cannot tell whether we shall come back here in the Spring or not—and we go to Delhi—'Curzon House', the 2nd of November.

The day before yesterday several Germans were sent off from here—men who have shops or cafés or work in music shops. They and governesses are all taken to a safely fortified place—a fortress—I think at Ahmadnagar. The young German Vice-consul we liked so much is there too. I believe they had all played their part as spies and many have tried to incite natives. But they will be kindly and well looked after.

There is much criticism of the Viceroy as he will not allow his bandmaster to be treated accordingly—and he, the bandmaster, is also a German. It is a mistake—I think—and we hear that even English travellers are held in Germany or by Germans anywhere they are met with!!!!! Surely we should play the same game?!

Today is my birthday. I thought of course Offley had quite forgot about it as he has been through such anxious tiring days. But I had instead a charming surprise. He made me a gift, upon waking up, of a handful of gold sovereigns and Mrs. Stewart brought in a beautiful basket of magnificent dahlias and a parcel from her daughter Peggy—a lovely teacloth with crocheted corners and lace edging—her own handiwork.

I was reminded so much of you—dear Father—when Offley gave me the gold. It was just the sort of thing you might have done at the time of a great war.

We hear of great casualties to our troops—one must know so many of the officers now in the field—and every time we get a little news, we long for more. The poor Belgians.[3] I feel so sorry for them and one hopes and prays the Allied Armies are strong to defeat the Germans. Yet one knows how well trained and strong they are known to be. The very flower of the British Army are now at the Front and I believe it is the same with the enemy. But it is all so horrible I will close for I have said enough.

September 3, 1914   **Dormers**

My dearest Aunt,

No letter from you has reached us for over a fortnight—or nearly three weeks—but we received one from Uncle Joe—and we know you are well and safe in America—and I feel sure you have written and that sooner or later your dear letters will turn up. The days fly by and our all engrossing interest is <u>this horrible</u> war. Our telegrams and news are the scantiest—but we have big maps pinned up on the walls and follow as best we may—pinning in flags as the operations go on. What carnage! What ruin! Are there in fact words to express the awfulness and horrors of this war? The Germans have behaved like such brute beasts and it not only makes one's heart ache for those who are the innocent sufferers among the Belgians, the French, and our own English, but for those Germans—of whom we have been privileged to know not a few, who so bitterly deplore this. Surely it is not in the hearts of our friends and relations to behave as General von der Goltz and the others of the Germans. It makes one's blood boil.

I hear in London there was the greatest excitement the night war was declared. We had a letter from a young friend telling us all about it. She and her husband went up to town to hear the proclamation and arriving at 11.30 p.m. at Victoria Station—they were in a taxi and crawling about at snail's pace until three in the morning and reached the Palace and saw the King and the Queen appear on the balcony etc. and she said the singing of national anthems was wonderful and flags—everyone had flags. They met one taxi full of Japanese. They also had flags and were singing 'God save the King' and the Marseillaise. We had a meeting of our little French Society, 'Les Amies de France', and we sang after a little address by the Foreign Secretary, Mr. Grant, and a 'thank-you' from Madame de la Batie, the French Consul General's wife. We sang the Marseillaise and the Russian National Hymn, led by the Russian Consul General, who sang it in Russian—and 'God save the King'. I can tell you even these meeting are stirring at such times, for one returns only to bid 'good luck and God speed you' to some friends just off—and all <u>so keen</u> to go. Our orders, O's, are 'to remain here' i.e. at Headquarters, until the 'end of the War'—but we know Lord K. and he knows Offley and I dare not think of <u>the</u> day that may come. Of course Offley would much like to go and everything is being got ready. His uniform and his small kit allowed for War!!!! While I am packing up this house, every day a little. They get but 12 hours notice when it does come.

September 13, 1914   Dormers

My dearest Aunt,

Another Sunday and Offley off immediately after breakfast to the offices—also Colonel MacAndrew who is staying with us until he sails, with the Cavalry Division from India for France. Such a very charming man—and very good looking—an old friend of Offley's and they talk over all and every side of this awful war. However the news for us has been good all through this last week, but oh! such horrible losses and casualties. It is said that the (Gay) 'Gordons'— the 92nd Highland Regiment has been wiped out—not a man—not an officer left! They were coming along a road at night, in Belgium, and thinking they had come upon some Belgians not 3 yards off they called out, 'Nous sommes les Anglais', and at once they were fired upon by Germans. It <u>is awful</u>—and many a man we know has been cut down. We hear the Crown Prince of Germany is dead—that the news of his having been wounded was true enough but they did not—for various reasons divulge the truth—the whole truth that is, that he has been killed. We also hear that the poor old Emperor of Austria is dead—but one sees it in the papers only that it is a 'rumour'. General Headlam whom Offley succeeded here as Director of Training and Staff Duties—we hear has been wounded at Mons,[4] I believe. Yesterday I saw the Viceroy for the first time since Lady Hardinge's death. He was as charming as ever and rode alongside my rickshaw for a little way—he seemed very pleased poor man, because I told him I saw a future Commander-in-Chief in his young soldier son—who has been severely wounded in both arms. Everyone is giving and giving and working and working. It's wonderful but I wish that they would send—without [being] asked for—a larger force from India—also that the Chief would allow Offley to raise new regiments and train them at once.

Poor Eleanor Davis I hear had a dreadful time on her journey down country from here last week—and then upon arriving in Bombay in all the dreadful heat—she found the 'Troopship' in which she was to sail on the 9th would not leave until the 18th and that she would share a cabin with three other women and a baby! She very sensibly took passage in a P. and O. steamer and was to sail today. A great many women—soldiers' wives—have bought return tickets via the P. and O. liners—and having a ticket ensures one being found a cabin. O. thinks I should be in possession of a 'return ticket to England' that in case of any emergency I could quietly go off when necessary. However I shall do this of course as it seems wise, but at present we see no sign of Offley's being sent to the War. However there is also always the chance of Lord K. when in need of experienced officers—remembering his old, old ones in India—and who were under him in South Africa.

Thank you so much for all your trouble for me re the dresses. If they cannot be got off now I shall quite understand and do without them. Many of us are giving up different things—in order to give to the war funds of various kinds—and in nearly every house you see large Red Cross boxes standing in the Verandas.

September 14, 1914   **Dormers**

My dear Uncle Joe,

You are not doubt following this horrible war almost as closely as we are—and though we have had good news all through this last week and one hopes and prays it may soon be brought to an end—a successful end for the Allies—yet I very much doubt if it will be over for a year, if not two years, and two years is the time we hear Lord K. has given it.

It is wonderful to see and to hear of the way in which everybody is doing and giving—Everything—and here too—it is magnificent. The Natives from Prince to beggar are willing to give all they possess and the civilians and the soldiers too. The soldiers who are already giving their lives—officers and men—are all doing their part—and indeed more than their part in giving. Yesterday we had a week of editions of the daily London Times. It is all old news but fuller than any we get and with a good many interesting articles. We were most interested in receiving the 'Evening Telegram'—New York—of August 4th with its big headlines and cartoon of Emperor Bill 'Run Amuck'.

I was told yesterday by an officer who is high in the favour of the Great at home that he knows that Offley was shortly to be wired for from home by name. If this be true—then I shall return to England when O. goes. I have not told him—Offley—that this was told to me—as I know he would like much to go, but thank God he is not fussing to be off, as many are, but his keenness is just as great and his spirit and interest in his profession—as a fighting soldier—is perhaps greater than ever. I shall feel it very deeply—when it comes—if it does come.

I had great difficulty in cashing an American cheque here the other day—as the exchange is so very great at present and not in my favour—losing ten pounds in every hundred, so I am going to ask you to kindly deposit $5000—or £1000 in my name with Messers Brown, Shipley & Co., 123 Pall Mall—that I may draw on them as may be necessary and pay yourself back with my quarterly income from Grandfather's estate—or let me know what the exact amount is and I will send you my cheque on my Philadelphia account. Will you be good enough, dear Uncle Joe, to arrange this at once my letter reaches you as the delay will be great and I shall have to draw on England should I require to buy a passage home. I don't quite understand these differences in Exchange, but the manager of Brown's agents here—the Delhi London Bank is most kind and though I sent him my American cheque here for deposit, he said in my own interest he preferred not to cash it for me unless the money was urgently required—and so I have with his kindness decided to

ask you to arrange this better way—which you will no doubt quite
understand. I hope Clara has safely returned and all their party. I
wonder at them going on so far into Germany at that date if all we
hear of German preparations is true. I had six young girls to lunch
with me last Sunday in honour of Maisie Campbell who is staying
with Lady Lake—all but one had been at school in Germany—and
were very glad they were not there now—and very sorry for the
good German friends. One—Nancy Birdwood—a very sweet and
pretty girl—had lived with the Reuss for a winter—Regina, Sybel
and Viola Reuss—nieces of the Prince Reuss who was out here as
Consul General and 'they are nice Germans' she insisted! as did
we all, of our friends! One girl, Margaret Grover, said that two
years ago she and all her companions at a school in Dresden—were
all packed up ready to go home—as War was expected then. This
time, alas, many young girls whose parents are in India—have not
been heard of at all—from Germany. Is it not dreadful! Much love
to you and to all and thanking you beforehand for some prompt
arrangement I feel sure you will make for me about the money.

Undated   **Dormers**

Dearest Aunt Fanny,

I was very sorry to hear of the death of President Wilson's wife.
It is very hard and very sad for these big men in their 'lonely jobs'
to lose their best loved companion. I shall always miss Lady Hardinge
and feel for the Viceroy, but these strenuous days are a 'God send'
to him. I only hope he will be strong and act wisely, but I have not
much confidence in him as far as that goes. He is but a diplomat
and diplomacy has failed—failed perhaps for lack of strong, straight
men. I am very, very, very thankful we have Lord K. where he now
is! and the King—God bless him—for all his constitutional hedging,
I believe him a very true, very courageous man.

Offley, writing to his father-in-law on 21 September, considered his own war-time functions:

Schatz and I are gradually packing up everything—prepared to go when we are ordered: at a moment's notice. I may be stuck at Army HQ the whole war through, or I may have to go to some ungodly spot to relieve a more fortunate Comdr who is off to the war—still it is all in the country's service—and one must take one's luck as it comes, without grumbling. Of course waves of intense disappointment come over one, which have to be put aside. We must feed the fighting line, if the country's armies are to remain in the field to help to win. We don't know how the native of India will stand a Continental winter with its damp and wet—we don't know how they will face shrapnel and rifle fire—but we hope they will give a good account of themselves.

Enclosed with this letter was an order by the Commander-in-Chief in India, issued that day, reading:

The following gracious message from his Majesty the King-Emperor to the Princes and peoples of the Indian Empire is published for general information:

During the past weeks the people of my whole Empire at home and overseas have moved with one mind and purpose to confront and overthrow an unparalleled assault upon the continuity, civilisation and peace of mankind. The calamitous conflict is not of my seeking. My voice has been cast throughout on the side of peace. My Ministers earnestly strove to allay the causes of strife and to appease differences with which my Empire was not concerned. Had I stood aside when, in defiance of pledges to which my Kingdom was a party, the soil of Belgium was violated and her cities laid desolate, when the very life of the French nation was threatened with extinction, I should have sacrificed my honour and given to destruction the liberties of my Empire and of mankind. I rejoice that every part of the Empire is with me on this decision. Paramount regard for treaty faith and pledged word of Rulers and peoples is the common heritage of England and India. Amongst the many incidents that have marked the unanimous uprisings of the populations of my Empire in defence of its unity and integrity, nothing has moved me more than the passionate devotion to my Throne expressed both by my Indian subjects and by Feudatory Princes and Ruling Chiefs of India and their prodigal offers of their lives and their resources in the cause of the realm. Their one-voiced demand to be foremost in conflict has touched my heart and has inspired to highest issues the love and devotion which, as I well know, have ever linked my Indian subjects and myself. I recall to mind India's gracious message to the British nation of good will and fellowship which greeted my return in February 1912 after the solemn ceremony of my Coronation Durbar at Delhi, and I find in this hour of trial a full harvest and a noble fulfilment of the assurance given by you that the destinies of Great Britain and India are indissolubly linked.

October 1, 1914   **Dormers**

My dearest Aunt,

We hear from friends of some most dire and awful experiences of English travellers in Germany. We cannot understand or conceive how they can be so unkind and unjust and even cruel, as they have been to mere travellers. I heard of 2 young French boys travelling in Germany with their Mother in order to perfect their German and when they were trying to return home and reached the Frontier, the German officer in charge, seeing the young men might be of military age—shot them dead then and there—and let the poor mother and a little girl struggle on to Belfort as best she could. This Madame de la Batie told me of and gave also the names of the people. I wonder where the Lippens are—poor things! and many other Belgians—and what of the Countess Borchgrave and her little children? It is all so horrible—and everyday almost we hear of people we know among the dead and wounded British, besides as often as not meeting sorrowing friends on the way home in the evenings who have heard of the death of their loved ones—nephews, brothers, etc. and it is worse and worse for the Emperor and Germans to make out that other nations brought on this war! It has been brought about by Germans and Germany and by them only, and every fact and every date and document prove this, over and over again.

We are as busy as busy can be—sewing all day and every day, and besides my sewing parties we are very busy putting all of Offley's things in order and in readiness. His room is full of khaki and all his swords and revolvers being oiled and cleaned and things being weighed. I do not like to think of what might come—all I can say is I <u>do</u> feel so thankful he is still here with me.

Offley, writing to Uncle Joe on 2 October, gave some thought to his current duties and his future prospects:

I think I have been instrumental in getting a very large number of our Staff College officers away with different organisations—and fear I shall myself be left to continue improvising staff and training formations to the end—however, somebody has to do it! though I fear one will be passed over by the war heroes, when they return, fresh from the Great Conflict.

I should like to go with the next Army Corps to leave, in a big appointment, and even a Command if I could get one—just to see what this war of masses means—though I know one would never actually have any knowledge of anything outside the limits of one's own battlefront, and when the war is over, then the time will have come to retire for good and all. I'm not hankering after military titles or military jewellery! and shall be quite content to be, like you have been since 1865, plain Mister——

He also reported on Indian reaction to the War:

Thousands of men out here are shouting to be allowed to help the Empire—Native Chiefs have placed their own services, treasures and men at the disposal of the Government and many have already taken the field in person. Even the wild frontier tribes have volunteered! and I pity the Germans if the Gurkhas and Pathans ever get into them with the kukri and heavy knife: because these people know no mercy.

We are accustomed to the idea, in our frontier Expeditions but civilised European troops are <u>not</u>. If the border men get into you, it's a clean wipe out of everything breathing.

And on 11 October he wrote:

I understand it was the King who gave Asquith [Prime Minister—Ed.] his ultimatum on the subject of fighting or keeping out—he (A) was ready to skulk: W. Churchill promptly resigned: the King sent for this wretched lot and said so long as it was merely a question of their poisonous politics he wasn't disposed to interfere—but now that it became a question of the nation's honour, he, the King, told Asquith he had got to fight: and that ended it.

October 15, 1914   **Dormers**

My dearest Aunt,

It is difficult even in these most stirring times to write you much of any great interest. We live from day to day in the same simple way ever studying and changing our war maps—hoping and praying to hear of successes and only to hear of the Fall of Antwerp, and that we—our troops—and the allies are going well and bravely, but the Germans seem to be over-running Belgium and their papers are big with their constant successes. Please God the Allies are now to have their turn—and to drive the enemy out of Belgium at once. Every day more and more officers and men go from here. The enthusiasm and loyalty is splendid—but oh, how horrible it all is—horrible! For the last few days Offley's fate has been under consideration and I sat dreaming over my work—fearing the worst and hoping he might have his chance in France and feeling sick at heart lest it should come true—all too suddenly—when he came in yesterday he told me he had been offered his choice, almost, of the Brigades and he had refused. He knew the Chief of Staff wanted him here as long as he could have him and 'if it isn't France, I prefer to work on here until it is' was Offley's answer. We hope it is all for the best—but as the situation changes every day—these things may come yet—and all too soon. So far we are not to go to Delhi this winter—that decision may too be changed.

Last Monday I went to Annandale at the Viceroy's invitation to judge the doll dressing at the Fête to the Girl Guides and the Boy Scouts. It was a lovely day and I had tea with His Excellency but no chance for a quiet talk—which I should have liked. He looks aged and sad, but on the whole he is wonderful. He said he was sorry to hear we were not coming to Delhi—and I am sorry in some ways too.

October 22, 1914   **Dormers**

My dearest Aunt Fanny and Uncle Joe,

Everyday more or less I dread the order coming that O. may have to go. Last Thursday my heart sank when I was told that the M. S. wanted to put his name down for this next Cavalry Division to go. No more has been heard of it, however, as they have not decided yet to send a whole Division. We read with interest and eagerness our own English papers, The Times and others, and the American papers you send, also a number of German papers O. gets, and a Vienna and a Swiss paper. Have you seen Punch since the War began? If not I think it is well worth looking at.

Last night the Lakes dined quietly with us alone, Sir P. and Offley having a good talk in the dining room over their port— while Lady Lake and I hugged the fire in this room, the Study, with our knitting. She is very pleased we are going to Delhi—which is now fixed that we are to do—after having changed us round to go or not to go for the last month. Curzon House will be our address where we hope to have 'double quarters'—(Betty will understand—four rooms and Stewart's hut). Even at this it will not be very luxurious. However I am taking some extra comforts—bed curtains—tables etc.

I fear I shall find it a very long, dull time there—but I shall hope to be able to move round with O. more than last winter. We are in some doubt about getting a motor—which is indeed essential in Delhi—but as all these things will be so very expensive—and last year it was even a shocking price—we may have to do without, but I hope not, for my own sake as well as for Offley's, as I found it such a pleasure motoring over the warm and too often dusty roads and especially in the evening when I got O. back from office. We recommended the excellent Rascal we had as chauffeur, for the war, and I am afraid he has been taken.

We were very sorry to see in the London 'Observer' of young Baron Riedesel of Eisenach (the one we knew in London when we were first married) having been killed in action at Kiaochow in China.

We feel we hear so little of the French in the war and poor Madame de la Batie, the French Consul General's wife, gets no news of her two brothers at the war. The American papers you send are better—with all sorts of bits of news from all parts—than ours are.

October 25, 1914   **Dormers**

My dear Uncle Joe and Aunt Fanny,

Yesterday I took my knitting and spent the evening with poor Sir A. and Lady Ker. They have lost their only son—only child—very grieved indeed they are and yet it seemed to me wonderful how they would go on talking of this horrible War—and of regiments and their losses just as we do and Lady Ker still working and knitting as we all do. I tried to cheer and to console—but indeed they were so wonderful I could but listen to them in amazement. Another of our letters today brings us news that O.'s young cousin Lionel Shore—the Naval boy—was in the action of Heligoland and his account of it is to follow. We are glad to know he is safe—please God he may live through this awful calamity.

Offley's name went up to the Chief for this last Cavalry brigade going—but H. E. would not let him go. There were a few days of suspense and anxiety—on my part—I said nothing and was surprised to find myself getting his things ready with him and Stewart. We two women sometimes drew long sighs—but beyond that my prayers were one repetition that God would safely keep him. One cannot realize these terrible days and times and what they bring in their train.

Before leaving Simla for Delhi Offley took time to write a couple of letters to Uncle Joe.

October 28, 1914   **Simla**

My dear Uncle Joe,

We have today heard of the baptism of our advanced Indian troops near Ypres. They seem to have gone in with a Swing and done well and I hope, if Lord K. is satisfied, that we may be honoured with a demand for many more. Every officer and man is <u>dying</u> to go—the restraint is from above. I hope the brown and the white and the black will all fight like blazes for the flag! Irishmen, Dutchmen, Islanders, Sikhs, Gurkhas, Pathans, Rajputs, Mussulmen, and Hindus!

We've trained them, all we know: and it should be all right as long as our officers last—only—we seem to be losing them so fast—and the class from which they are drawn, is not inexhaustible.

If I have to go, Lina will, I know, accept it in the right spirit: poor little thing! I know she is hating the day when the order may come—but she is very brave—and says nothing.

She could of course go to England or America, if I did go. Government would pay her passage home from here—or at least give her part of it.

November 2, 1914   **Simla**

My dear Uncle Joe,

This is our last night in 'Dormers'—we go down to Delhi by the midday train tomorrow and the house is being left by Mistress Schatz like a new pin. A great deal of luggage has gone to Delhi—since one never knows what the next move may be—a great deal more stored at the Delhi-London Bank here. We have been steadily and surely packing up for the past two months: and now, at the last moment—everything is ready and all kinds of arrangements made. Bills paid—servants settled up with—careful lists of everything prepared——and all done by that little wonder, herself—for I have now been in office every single day including Sundays from 9.45 a.m.—4 and 5 and 6 p.m. and have been obliged to leave things to her. She has been most clever in selling what we did not want, or could not carry away, and the only thing we have not been able to find has been a winter tenant for the house which of course is ours till the end of February 1915. We have been very happy and <u>very</u> comfortable here, and have I think dispensed a considerable amount of hospitality in our small way—and the only single point which has, in its own way been regrettable has been the expense—the burden of the endeavour not to exceed our income has entirely fallen on my sweet Schatz and she has managed magnificently, all honor to her charming personality and capability, and to her upbringing!

Well—someday you may know what we have accomplished in the way of the dispatch of troops, to many diverse theatres of war: and although this achievement has not come up to what many of us would have hoped for, at least in the face of the grinding down at the hands of the Civil and the Finance prior to the war, one may say that we have perhaps done something to help to feed that great firing line at the front.

<u>Had</u> we been able to look forward and prepare for 'the Day' as our 'friend the enemy' has done, we might have startled Europe. I have struggled in my small way to get our authorities to look forward and think on great broad lines; but with no success: in fact many look upon March 1915 as the utmost limit of the War and when the men at the Top adhere to such a line of action, one is helpless.

Day by day we read the heavy casualty lists in Reuters, and wonder how we are to meet the drain!

The unworthy thought also crosses one's mind of the ultimate honor and promotion that will come to those more fortunate officers who have been allowed to go to the front and may 'stand up' at the end of the business, and contrast this with the undoubted supersession of those who have not been 'spared', and have had to remain behind.

November 5, 1914   **Curzon House, Delhi**

My dearest Aunt,

I read all your enclosures with interest among others Mr. Rinald's plea for the Kaiser and Germany! I am afraid he knows little of the true facts of the case. Of course we all realize that this war had to come—but there is no hatred among the English of any class—of the Germans—while there is a very great deal of hatred—nothing more or less—on the part of certain classes of Germans against England and the English. This is an undisputed fact—and the atrocities too <u>are facts</u>. Our troops and the French, both officers and men, have met with these dreadful horrible cases—and our British troops and officers—to a man—would never dream of inflicting such cruelty upon the old—or women and children. No one has for a moment denied that Germany has been wonderful in the past 20 to 40 years in trade, manufacturing and development etc. nor has anyone denied that she has had the finest and most efficient fighting force in Europe. Her wonderfully trained Army—and that she has the greatest amount of extraordinary and valuable war material. But that she has broken <u>every international law</u> in War—that she has lied and spied and bribed—<u>Who can say</u> she has not? We see and read the German papers—even now—'Berliner Tageblate' such papers and the exact truth is not given their people. Germany has over run Belgium and ruined Antwerp. Her excuse was that it was the only way into France! Since when must one go to Antwerp to get to France? I cannot understand why Mr. Rinald has not returned to Germany to fight for her if he feels as he does. Daily our list of casualties becomes more and more horrible. And now Turkey too is dragged into the struggle—as though it were not already big enough and terrible enough. Alas! I think this Kaiser is mad and I fear he has made many of his people mad too. With jealousy and hatred and malice. We may win or we may lose. The end is not yet. But whatever the result is for the people of Germany—and Germany—can she ever forget what will—until the end of time—be attributed to her and to her army when fighting in Belgium?

Curzon House, Delhi

November 15, 1914

My Dearest Aunt,

In writing the date upon my letter I am reminded that this is dear Mother's birthday. What changes since those days when we were all about returning to town [from their summer residence at Narragansett—Ed.] and beautiful chrysanthemums and flowers were arranged for this special date—and our beautiful house and home so charming. Here—every day sees the break-up of homes right and left.

Offley went to the station early yesterday morning to see the regiment—the 18th Lancers off—for France. He said the men seemed very fit and well and very pleased to go.

They gave O. a great cheer as the train moved out and begged him to follow soon.

Poor Offley—he longs to go but he is sticking bravely and steadfastly to his work here—and with every dawn that breaks I dread the arrival of a wire or word that might take him. Later—perhaps—if there is an army of occupation—as there should be in every place and corner of Germany to drive home to these wicked people the ruin and havoc they have caused. Perhaps O.'s ability in languages etc. and command of men and administration may be used. I am reading this book 'Pan-Germanism' with horror and amazement at their policy and creed. But however deeply and strongly we feel—they can but reap the reward they so well deserve and that whether 'they' are victor or vanquished. A better hated people never lived. A people no nation—no one can trust. Individuals—yes—fortunately—but as a people who can trust or believe in them? Not for generations can they live down or wash out the blood stained hands they gave themselves in Belgium and in France.

We are not surprised but rather appalled by the income tax. Two and sixpence in the pound will lower Offley's pay alone to such an extent that one must arrange to do without many pleasant little luxuries, not to mention servants etc. and what life in England will mean! This all so sad and so unnecessary had there not been a wicked war-like and war-wishing Germany.

November 19, 1914   **Curzon House**

My very dear Father,

This is to reach you at Christmas time we hope. No one here feels merry or like celebrating a Festival other than as a Church Holiday.

Our news from France and elsewhere—brings with it lists upon lists of casualties—sons, cousins, brothers killed—every one of us has some loved ones far or near in the thick of this horrible struggle.

Not a breakfast, lunch or dinner do I sit down to without hearing of some one gone—some one dear to us or close and dear and near to our best friends. This morning we went to the Memorial Service to Lord Roberts—and it was amazing just to look round among those in the church and count the number one now knows have lost their brothers or sons.

We were much interested in your account of the Sermon at the Special Service for Peace held in America. If, as you say, we can sheath the sword with honour and assurance that the Germans are crushed and their wicked warring creed is forever disposed of, then indeed shall we be pleased and thankful for peace but it looks like such a long war. Millions of men, millions of money and greater sacrifices are daily being asked. I live in dread and fear of Offley going—and I know how much he wants to be at the Front—but oh—dear Father it is horrible—horrible to have to contemplate. When I hear of the devoted husbands killed and the young men and boys—in the Navy a lady we heard of lost her two only sons, the youngest a midshipman of but fourteen, both on the 'Crecy'. And the poor Belgians—so brave in making the stand they did—and the French—we hear nothing of their losses. Why, oh why, would our people not have a great army—and the Belgians too—and listen to Lord Roberts. In America too, they should look well to their Army and Navy and be able to protect and maintain their Peace or neutrality or Monroe Doctrine, whatever the case may be.

November 29, 1914   **Curzon House**

My dearest Aunt,

After lunch I wrote notes and at 4 o'clock went for Offley to the office—dragged him out for a long two hour drive all over New Delhi. The lights were so pretty—the fields are looking so green with young and very promising grain and the great tombs of Humayum and Safdar Jung stood out well against the afternoon skies, and pools of water still standing since the very heavy rain of the last Monsoon reflected the clouds and trees or the coolie men and women. Today the great tombs and their gardens were alive with people and gay with colour—as it is the 'Muharram'—a Mohammedan holiday and celebration of the killing of the Prophet's Grandsons.

O. is much interested in Hilaire Belloc's articles in 'Land and Water' on the present War—while I read the '19th Century' and the 'North American Review' and the 'Nation'. He is amazed at the Germans being so deceived by their political leaders—the Kaiser at their head—but one is also amazed at the deaf ear England turned to the warnings of war with Germany. Offley often feels very disappointed that he has been allowed no chance at or experience of this war—this great and awful war—and now he says he feels there is not a ghost of a chance for him now. When it is all over, having done his best out here—he means to resign at once—and I confess I think conditions have become very hopeless and unjust. The whole of this Government is in the Hands of 'Finance' and their actions are scandalous, but who will hang the Minister? and his colleagues? Who?????

The 'Queen Mary's Guild' to which Lina referred in the following letter was a working party established in Philadelphia to provide similar comforts for the British forces as were being produced by the ladies in Simla. In another letter she wrote: 'It is amazing and most splendidly generous—all that is being done for the many victims of this war by Americans too. It is splendid of Betty to arrange working parties—and why does she not have acknowledgements sent directly to her? She should have.'

December 10, 1914   **Curzon House, Delhi**

My dearest Aunt,

This week has been very uneventful—news from France being about the same—our work goes on steadily and upon a suggestion of Offley's, Lady Carlyle has already started work among the native women of the Indian regiments for their husbands and soldiers at the war, and this is an excellent thing, a great step in the right direction and which one hopes will last and continue on beyond the war.

We have had a great number of letters from France written 'in the trenches' or with the Staff Headquarters. I am afraid they—poor brave fellows—are having awful weather at the front. You must tell Bessie Hays and Betty that we have heard from one officer, wounded and in a London hospital, that he is wearing pajamas made by members of Queen Mary's Guild and he says 'they are beautiful, but the buttons all fly off like shrapnel the moment you touch them! Do tell the good people who made them to sew on the buttons well.' Does Harry make vaseline at his factory? and if so I do wish so much he would send a great quantity in small packages to our officers' and soldiers' base of supplies—or in your Relief ships—for 'The Indian Officers and Soldiers'. We cannot include this to any extent in our parcels from India as it all comes from Europe or America. Carbolated vaseline or cosmoline for their feet—as they suffer from the long marches—the change in weather and frostbite. I know this to be one of their crying needs.

Last week Mr. Porter got up a 'Smoking Concert' at the Delhi Gymkana Club in the evening. Everyone engaged tables and sat in little groups in the big room—Betty will remember—where we went to concerts and plays and dances—and we had some very nice music and some lively songs and choruses and Monsieur Mabakoff, the Russian Consul General, recited the poem 'The Day' which I think I sent to you. I thought it was a wise and healthy break in our gloom and unflagging interest in the War—but I was amazed to find quite a number of people were a good deal upset by this little gaiety. Many of the regiments have lost such a number of officers and those who have lived with their regiments as with a family—feel it deeply. I think it was that and also the strain all have been undergoing.

On Christmas Eve, 1914, Offley wrote to Aunt Fanny:

I have a lucid moment, on this Xmas Eve, in which to catch the outgoing mail in the early hours of tomorrow morning—and just want to thank you and Uncle Joe for your unfailing thoughtfulness in writing to us as regularly as you do, and have done throughout this eventful year. Deprived of your letters, the weekly 'English Mail' would lose its interest—as it is, we look forward to it, with unabated keenness, and should your letters ever fail, we begin to get fidgetty and wonder what has happened. My Schatz is, thank goodness, as bright and cheerful and resourceful as ever—supporting me in many moments of discouragement, manfully taking her own big share of our combined business, and more of a companion than ever—and as she often says, if we haven't got all we would desire, at least we have got each other—and we cannot be sufficiently grateful for that. Of course I often fret—for a time—at my enforced retention here, when hundreds of my seniors and juniors are in the field, actually <u>doing things</u> for the Empire. I equally realise that from the point of one's subsequent career, it is ended with the conclusion of this war: and I know she had hoped I might go far. There will be no place among the General Officers of the future for the man who has not seen any of the present fighting. But after all—that is perhaps too selfish a view, and one may be happy in being any use at all to one's country in such a crisis—and when it is over—well perhaps one may have done enough, and be glad to join you all again, as a free and independent individual—satisfied with the knowledge that one had done one's best. Someone has said, 'one merely gets one's deserts', and perhaps one may not have deserved as much as one sets one's heart on.

Removed as far as we are, from the war, things naturally pursue their wonted way—more or less—and I think it is an undoubted fact that to many, the conflict is scarcely yet a reality. Whilst there is much paper speculation on the probable duration of the war, an idea out here seems prevalent, that it will be all over by the Spring. It may be.

Meanwhile we are waiting with some interest to see whether Italy, then Greece, and perhaps Roumania join in, in their turn. Turkey's participation has of course increased our responsibilities and troubles—and a certain reflex action is to be expected among our border tribes and neighbor, Afghanistan.

Still Moslem Africa and Egypt appear to be satisfied to stand aloof—and for the defence of the latter, we are not wholly unprepared. What the New Year may bring one cannot guess: but, as I have often said to Uncle Joe, I am sure we are all prepared to see the thing through to the bitter end.

It had to come, evidently: and we may better go down fighting, than sink to the level of a third class world power.

If we, as a nation, have done our task in the great scheme of things, we shall go under. I expect that's about the strength of it. If not, and there's still work ahead for us, the other man will—and anyway, we don't feel yet as if we were finished or didn't wish to live any longer! Now and again, an interesting letter reaches us from the front—or, shall I say, from one of the many 'fronts'—where our people are engaged and they are human documents of much interest. Still we realise that probably only the men who stand round Lord Kitchener's flagged maps in the morning, actually realise how things, as a whole, are going. Gen. Joffre, or the Russian C. in C. are equally seeing things from a viewpoint unattainable for any General in the field—far less to the ordinary officer or soldier, or even to the staff of a tributary or dependency. You probably have a far wider view than we have.

A few days later, in a letter to Uncle Joe, Offley continued his musings as to what life after the war might be like for Lina and himself.

December 29, 1914   Delhi

Lord knows how any of us are going to live, when the thing is finished and the war taxes have to be paid! or whether the country will be able to afford payment of full pensions for years to come. They are already talking of an income tax alone of 4 shillings in the pound and we have only been at war for 4 months!

Whether the general expenses of living will come down all round or not, I don't know, but for the elderly people I fancy the result will be, at least, the loss of ¼ of their incomes.

However, many of us will not be alive to bother about it. The women will, for them one is most anxious. Still, even that is risked cheerfully by the classes who are not commercial, and have most to lose.

Schatz and I are hoping for our release from service, after peace had been declared—or rather—as soon after it, as we can be relieved which is quite another matter! Not having been able to participate in the Great War will make it impossible to remain when it is over, and we are prepared to burn our rubbish and retire into private life and make way for the more ardent young spirits who have acquired recent experience and exalted rank at an early age. So you can look out for a humble dwelling in a nice bright climate with plenty of sun-light where we can spend our summers—and we are still counting on the 3rd story of 1704 for the winter season and with you.

A pleasant dream enough—but what of the reality? Could we lift the veil and see, should we be content, I wonder?

December 30, 1914   **Curzon House, Delhi**

My dearest Aunt,

We expect to go back to Simla in April. We have not taken 'Dormers' on again for next year up to date and just what we shall do I don't quite know. In the uncertainty of things Offley wants me to arrange to go to the Cecil Hotel but if we could find a small suitable house—naturally I should much prefer that—and especially as I have all my good servants and a very good cook—all ready and anxious to come back to us.

This morning's news tells us that a Turkish Army is said to be within 20 miles of Port Said—and that elsewhere we are 'holding our own'. Not very definite and always such lists of casualties—and so much suffering and ruin in Europe—and people here beginning to feel and realize the changes in incomes etc. and an uncertain future before them after years of good and faithful service. Lady Suffolk (who was the youngest Miss Leiter—Daisy) has come out to join her husband who is commanding one of the Territorials—now hopes to spend the summer in India—and wants 'a big house in Simla'—having brought out with her her children and numerous cows and a cow-man, motors and chauffeurs etc., etc. There are no really very big houses in Simla—bar those appropriated to the Viceroy! the Commander in Chief!! and the members of the Viceroy's council. So we shall watch with interest what she acquires! I hear she offered a large price a month for the C. in C.'s house! Tomorrow there is to be a New Year's parade—Offley has to ride out to meet the Viceroy—in full dress etc. while I shall go in the motor and look on.

I do enjoy your letters so much. Never fear they are dull to me, who looks so eagerly for all your details of home news and all you do. When you go to Uncle Harry's and Aunt Clara's or to Father and Betty and how and when the different members of the family come to you. In these depressing times, when our home news from England is all so full of sadness and sorrow, it is very good to hear of the ordinary and happy family life going on with you and of all your great sympathy for a people—for the people I should say—who are trying to establish justice in Europe—or such justice and liberty as is possible with the varied people of a great continent. Much dear deep love to you all—we shall think of you this evening and our hearts will be with you.

January 14, 1915   **Curzon House, Delhi**

My dearest Aunt,

I went on Tuesday to the First Council Meeting opened by the Viceroy, who spoke—and I enclose you his resumé of the last few months in this country. He is not in any way a strong man—nor does his speech from the throne—or on any occasion impress one particularly. He is, however, always the typical English gentleman

and always one is impressed I think, by the conscientiousness of
the man. Lord Hardinge is ever striving to do his best after his
own way of seeing it. He reads his speech so charmingly. There
is no hesitation, no repeating any phrase or part of it—that it
appears almost as if he spoke entirely from memory and there is
never any fussing with his papers or any undue mannerism or
nervousness. His accent and manner and voice are all so agreeable
and so dignified.

I am just getting over a nasty attack of bronchitis and last night
while dressing to go out to dine I had to pick up my curling tongs,
which were 'cooling'—by the hot iron end and burned myself badly
up and down the forefinger and thumb of my left hand. Fortunately
it was my left hand. I suffered in agony for a few moments but
thanks to Stewart's care and Offley's prompt attention (he found
carron oil in his medicine chest) my hand was dressed and bound
and we went off to our dinner party—only a half an hour late—and
I am much better this morning but I think the dinner party saved
me from being worse as I was obliged to use my self control.
Today I am bandaged and though the blisters are big and bad to
look at, it is not serious, but I can't knit or cut out just now for
a bit.

Yes, I am afraid Lord Kitchener's own fear that the war will last
3 years is much more nearly correct than those who think it will
be over in the Spring. It may be so in France—but in the Western
theatre of war—and please God it will be—but this war has so many
other theatres of action and increasing complications arrive every
little while. I have had letters from Lady Edith Legard who has
been with her Mother in Yorkshire and though 20 miles inland at
Lady Liverpool's place they heard all the firing and guns at Scar-
borough and Hartlepool and the windows and doors of their house
rattled and shook the whole time. What will these Germans do
next—bombarding an undefended town!! Have they no humanity—
whatever!!!! Who would have imagined they could become such
devils incarnate.

January 18, 1915   **Curzon House, Delhi**

My dearest Aunt,

The beautiful pair of 'Poly boots' <u>knitted by you</u> for Offley came to hand this morning and they are charming and look so very comfortable and nice. Thank you so much for them. He is very pleased and is writing you himself.

I was very much in agreement with 'John Cadwalader, Jr.' in his letter to the Public Ledger, December 19th, and much and deeply as I love and admire all the good things and the good people we know and have known in Germany—I think she—Germany—should be brought up for her present behavior on many occasions lately. In another letter in the Ledger of December 22 someone writes in reply to Mr. Cadwalader—and says he is so manifestly unfair and later goes on to say that Lord Kitchener like the Kaiser and Count Reventlow will wage war ruthlessly and quotes Lord K. having said, 'We must fight to a finish'—but he does not (the writer) remember that Lord K. spoke to the Army when they went off to war on the continent and admonished them to be courteous to women—not to pillage or loot and not to drink—and we have so far no evidence that they have not so conducted themselves. What may happen <u>now</u> if they get into Germany—God only knows for they will feel a mighty vengeance after what they have seen. But I have a great confidence in the British Thomas Atkins—he is made of manly stuff—and I have seen a good deal of these men since I have been married and more lately—since the war.

January 21, 1915   **Curzon House, Delhi**

My dearest Aunt,

We have had a real tragedy in our everyday life in poor Stewart's sorrow. Her eldest daughter and the great 'Lady' of her little brood was returning from England after a year at home to put her children—3 little boys—at school. She wrote regularly to her Mother and up to the very last mail before she should arrive spoke of her own renewed health—yet—on her arrival in Bombay she was unable to go a step farther—(Her husband and home is in Lahore) but put herself into a hospital and wired of her illness. The husband hastened to her only to find her very, very ill, almost dying—but longing to get to her own home. He endeavored to bring her thinking it would improve her to grant her great wish. He is a doctor—in the Subordinate Military Class and lent to the big Railway that has its headquarters in Lahore where he has a house given to him and 2 nursing sisters living in a dispensary next door—but his wife, my poor Mrs. Stewart's daughter, died on the train on the way between Bombay and here. I did my best to comfort the poor woman and we packed her off in the train, when it came in here that night—only to see her girl in death and to bury her and do what she could for her grief stricken husband. She is still away—and we have told her to stay as long as she likes. Her younger daughter 'Peggy' whom Betty saw, was here. I sent the motor to the offices and telephoned to Offley to get her 'off' from her work at all costs. I knew she could comfort her Mother—in fact I had to tell her the awful truth—but she was wonderfully brave and womanly and I was as kind as I could be and so was my ever splendid Offley—who wouldn't be! but there is so little one can do at such times. I do not know, but I much fear I shall have to try and replace Stewart, as this may break her down utterly. However, I will not think of that until needs must.

The mail here does not leave until six in the morning and Offley and I always have our Thursday evening writing 'bee' together, but this week I have a host of letters to answer and always so many condolences and occasionally one of congratulations.

I enclose you a little slip with some commissions if you can get them for me at that excellent emporium, John Wanamakers—I often wish I could do just one day's shopping there!!

In a letter to Uncle Joe dated 24 January, 1915, Offley wrote nostalgically of all the hard work Lina had put into improving Wildflower Hall and expressed concern over a chronic health problem of Lina's to which she only occasionally and lightly referred:

I am glad that pencil panorama has reached you—Schatz made me work at it in the early mornings before I left for office in Simla—and I shall never again look out upon it—at all events from <u>our</u> old Wildflower Hall. When I remember what she did to the place, and how we appreciated our time there—the re-turfing of the slopes, transference of the roses, and all our plans for its improvement—the only residential site worth talking about up on that Range, I <u>cannot</u> go there under present conditions and live in the modern hotel. I am in rebellion against all I see—except that glorious view—which is too good for the vulgar crowd who now possess it! It's rather sad, but I don't feel I belong to the present democratic generations— I've come along 50 years too late. Confounded nuisance?

I think a hut somewhere in California after the war, may be the best solution for <u>us</u>. Schatz has been suffering from the most obstinate succession of colds and inflammation of the mucous membranes of the head and chest—and I don't like it at all. The rains are her worst time—and somehow the change to the drier climate of the plains this winter has not benefitted her in the same way as it did last year. I am accordingly most anxious to leave this country, fi- nally—in addition to one's feeling of disgust at the unspeakable meanness and short-sighted un-imperial policy of the Indian Gov. with which I have been closely associated since 1909. Of course, personally, I am 'tied up' until the end of the war—but if we have enough to live upon in your country, at the end of it—I feel we should 'put in our papers'[5] and come away, while we can. I am not keen about orders and promotions now —i.e. not so desperately desirous of rising in the service, as to be prepared to sacrifice all to <u>that</u> ideal—and after this war, I anticipate the Civil Gov. of India will be less generously minded towards the army, than ever. It is nearly intolerable now—their meanness—what it <u>will</u> be, the Lord can only imagine. However, our views will probably be largely in- fluenced by the way things actually go.

February 3, 1915   **Curzon House, Delhi**

Dear Uncle Joe,

Your very nice letters with Aunt Fanny's in one and the same envelope came promptly to hand this week—and we both note with deepest interest your interest and sympathy and criticisms of the awful war. It is so hard to be temperate over it all. One has naturally a very strong affection for Germany and a great admiration for the people and country as we knew it—and Offley feels the same—a great admiration for the thoroughness and industry and strides in the world's progress they have made in the last generation. He was very happy as a boy when attached as a young page at the Court in Dresden. But how is one to stifle the feelings that rise with the awful inhumanity shown upon such occasions as this last exploit, sinking merchant ships and so on without a moment's notice and the utter disregard shown on all sides on the part of the Germans for non-combatants. I have tried to read and interest myself in books quite other than those of today and to get away entirely from the constant thought of this war, but can I do it? Not for a moment. I find myself reading between the lines of whatever my book may be some present day parallel.

February 18, 1915   **Curzon House, Delhi**

My dearest Aunt,

This morning instead of sitting down to my home mail and writing letters, we were much shocked to receive a cable from Woking Cottage Hospital telling us that Offley's favourite sister Urith was danger-ously ill with meningitis. She had been working among the soldiers in a great camp there and I am afraid in her eagerness and energy the work has been too much for her.

It has been very hard to know just what we could do for her from this great distance. Florence is in France—in charge of a 'base' hospital and Aunt Caroline is such an old lady—and the men of the family are all abroad—and their wives or mothers or sisters scattered to do what work they can in this Great War. The immediate family is so very small and you can imagine how very distressed we are tonight and Offley very deeply feels his sister's loneliness. He bears it with a splendid courage and I bade him cable to the hospital and to his bankers and to Aunt Caroline—more out of comfort to himself to have done something than anything else—as Aunt Caroline will surely have been informed.

February 24, 1915   **Curzon House, Delhi**

My dearest Aunt,

I know you will all be very sorry to hear of the death of Offley's youngest sister and I may say always his favorite one, 'Urith' whose letters I had sent you telling of all her work in the 'Emergency Corps', in which she became so deeply interested that we fear she quite forgot herself and over taxed her strength. She seemed so very happy in her work and had reached the very pinnacle of her desire—to be at work among and for Lords K's new army—dispensing warm clothes and comforts to them and looking after their welfare in a great camp at Woking—when the cable came to say she was dangerously ill with meningitis at Woking Cottage Hospital—and shortly after a second cable came saying she had died that night. Poor Florence came back from France but was 'too late'.

Offley feels it deeply—he had hoped and planned these two sisters should have some real happiness in a home of their own as they grew older and for the comfort of their old age. Urith was a beautiful pianist and was clever and accomplished and an excellent linguist. She was one of those very reserved very proud English natures, that it is so difficult to know and understand. Very, very sensitive, and she adored and admired Offley extravagantly. She was very petite and with a marvelous quantity of brown hair, and there was always a sense of brilliance—real brilliance in this delicate little woman. Ugly—and yet not really ugly—more plain—but always with an alert eager expression that was very charming. I was very attached to her—and she to me—and yet I never felt I understood her—and I should have liked to so much.

We are both deeply interested in the present situation this awful war has created between America and England. Please God all will come out happily between the two countries. The Spectator of 23 January has an excellent article on the subject—and does some very plain speaking—and today's Pioneer quotes a long letter from Mr. Bryan [Secretary of State—Ed.] to a Mr. Stone of the Foreign Office—setting forth many difficult questions with replies to the same but, I am afraid we badly need a great character, a man or a woman in great place who would use a restraining hand and be such an influence as the Queen or Lincoln were in those former days of trial.

Things still continue to look the same—very serious and awful—but with the coming and settling in of Spring weather I fear there will be tremendous forces brought together and awful battles to have to hear of. How terrible this way of waging war on all at sea—regardless of what the craft may be or whose—by the Germans.

In my last letter from Florence, my sister-in-law who is nursing in a Red Cross Hospital in France—and among French—writes—'Do you know anyone who will help us along—we are badly in need of funds to carry on and we should be glad of gifts—of socks, pyjamas and dressings.' Algerians and Arabs and not English at all—and she says they are very plucky. Ask Betty to send to her direct and perhaps Uncle Joe will drop a line to the right person and ask them to send to Florence's hospital.

Offley reported to Uncle Joe on 18 March that possibilities of a more active role in the war for him had arisen but come to nothing:

There is little to tell you of interest from this country except that I have actually been asked for twice by subordinate Commanders in the field—and am not allowed to go—'cannot be spared', so I hear, and it is a very sore point although I quite realise that someone has to stay at home. Still I have sat here steadily since the war began—4/5 August—and no one wants to be in the coal cellar whilst things are being done in the street! Poor little Schatz is relieved, I know, and in a perfect terror lest I should go one day. There was a first class chance of it, the last few days, but I'm done now—my immediate Chief has told me so an hour ago. Aunt Fanny sent me a charming note—and it was very sweet of her, and I quite realise that she can't enter into a soldier's feelings about being left out of the greatest fight of the century.

March 25, 1915   **Curzon House, Delhi**

My very dear Uncle and Aunt,

Well, I have had some sleepless nights since I wrote last week— and although Sir John Nixon asked for Offley as his Chief of Staff and made a fresh point of it—the C. in C. refused to let him go—and told Sir J. he, Offley, was too valuable—all very well, but none of them—either Sir P. Lake or the Chief were gracious enough to mention it to Offley.

I am sorry to say I found Offley looking very, very thin and tired upon my return from Jhansi where I was so happy with the Kemballs. We leave here for Simla on Saturday and shall go first to the Cecil Hotel before taking over Mt. Pleasant. I know we shall feel very lonely and strange in Simla this year. All our good friends have left. But I shall be busy with work and Offley alas—will I fear be much too over-worked. However I am glad our house is central and perched high up on the very top of a hill above the Cecil Hotel— between that and Viceregal Lodge and we shall enjoy being there and looking at the snow and being all by ourselves.

I fear that summer will be a long and anxious one. The Spring and hot weather will make such awful and fearful fighting possible in Europe where the sorrow and sacrifice has already been appalling.

The fall of Przemysl [Poland] to the Russians is great good news and we are daily hoping to hear we are in Constantinople.

On their return to Simla they had to move into another house as the owner of Dormers had returned.

April 15, 1915   **Mount Pleasant, Simla**

My dearest Aunt,

At last the back is broken of the work getting into this little house and I am able to sit down and have the pleasure of writing to you my regular weekly letter. Both Stewart and I have worked like two horses, and so has Offley when he had a little respite from office and so have the rest of the servants—and now the place is sweet and clean and looking quite pretty—but our young friends the St. Johns left it for us to take over in an appalling state of dirtiness, not to call it by worse names. The site is beautiful—high, high up on the very top of a hill from which we look down upon all the rest of the world—even H.E. the Viceroy. Next to us lives a member of Council and Offley had already diplomatically arranged to share his (the M.C.'s) tennis court and that and the garden will give him exercise and pleasure—but only such pleasure as is left for a bitterly disappointed and ambitious soldier man. That they have not sent him or rather allowed him to go to the front upon any of the 3 occasions upon which he was asked for—and not even told him that he was particularly asked for, first by Gen'l Rimington commanding the Cavalry Division (Indian) in France, and to be Chief of Staff upon two other occasions—one, when Sir John Nixon was sent to the Persian Gulf—hurts and depresses O. exceedingly. I, in the depths of my heart, am glad he is safely here and I try to cheer and encourage him—but he feels it very very deeply—and I can understand and sympathise and feel very deeply grieved for him.

The weather today is quite lovely and we had breakfast in the garden, where later I intended to take my writing things and go on with my letters, but no such luck! The tailor for the servants' clothes. Before he left, the man to fix the electric lights and so it went on and it is now lunch time and I am just begun.

The awful things one hears (which are true) in one's letters. A friend of ours who was taken prisoner by the Germans—an officer—was kicked by the German officers!!! A thing that is punishable if an officer did it to a soldier in our army—besides they made him—a gentleman taken prisoner after the way of war—surrendering, giving up his sword etc.—and he was then turned on to cleaning streets. Such are the present day Germans. I wish a few of the people in Philadelphia whom you say are pro-German could have a little taste of the German officer and his ways! A more non-manly, caddish lot could not be found than the Prussian officers. It is sad—it is appalling.

May 12, 1915   **Mount Pleasant, Simla**

My dearest Aunt and Uncle Joe,

I have been so incensed with rage and indignation and horror at the sinking of the Lusitania[6] by the already more than infamous murderers, the Germans, that I can scarcely write to you—my dear ones in America—and very real and true and devoted Americans in spite of your name—in any possible or temperate frame of mind. What do the Americans mean to do? And why do such a people put up with Wilson and Bryan—where so much is at stake? What kind of language and what sort of meaning is to be drawn from such a statement as 'don't rock the boat!'—Surely the Government of the U.S.A. are quite justified in putting the man, Bernstorff [German Ambassador to the U.S.—Ed.], in irons, at once and expelling all Germans from the country—and all those of Pro-German sympathies—old or young—as they are indeed dangerous to the State. God help our brave ones and our allies fighting an enemy who are devils incarnate. More, oh, much more would I say and even that would not suffice for there are no words in our language or terms equal to express what these people and all or any who sympathise with them <u>are</u>.

We went last night to a soirée musical at Viceregal Lodge. The music was <u>beautiful</u> and <u>beautifully</u> played—it soothed one—but among all of us was suppressed rage and excitement—I know. The song 'Crepescule' of Massenet—I used to sing—and the lovely 'Unfinished Symphony'—how familiar. I sat very quietly trying to listen (people did talk so) and it carried me back to my old home and the wonderful music we had such opportunities of hearing. Ah, how one misses all this sort of thing in India. The Viceroy spoke to very few. He came toward me—but I turned away and hoped to escape. I felt very wrought up. I dread the everlasting questions

'What will America do now?' Her honour, her humanity—where and how will it be upheld? The Kaiser, Tirpitz and the man Bernstorff are murderers of American men and women—are they not? A naval battle—a great fight between battling armies—one understands, but there are rules from time immemorial that have been cast to the winds.

We are both well and both very busy—and both equally <u>very</u> <u>unhappy</u>. Today at our Red Cross we worked for the Servians. We have our working meetings in the Council Rooms, Viceregal Lodge. I was asked to stay on to lunch—all our working parties bring about little luncheon groups later which are very pleasant and I think friendships do come about over our common work.

I go to tea on Tuesday with Mrs. Cotes—at Dormers. I believe she was very gratified at finding the house had been kept in such beautiful order and the electric lights so well and prettily arranged by me—and we have made friends through the sweet house—but this one is far prettier still—the garden is a blaze of wonderful rose-pink double poppies, cornflowers, larkspurs, stock, periwinkles, roses, gold gorse and such views!!!!! of the hills and the snows and such birds!!! and such butterflies. Offley works hard in the garden over things to flourish in the rains. We have put in bushels of gladioli and mignonette and ageratum and white and gold and pink cosmos—and dahlias and the servants say 'the Sahib does too much garden work!'—'great work of gardener!' which is amusing as one knows it saves them from really being lazy and just sitting in the sun.

Do you remember in the Germantown house[7] the light with a bowl of water near or under it for insects and creeping things—well in this room the flies and butterflies and green glistening beetles and the moths and 'bugs' and insects are all over the lampshades and on the white walls until one might almost take it for some Chinese or Japanese embroidery.

Very dear deep true love to you both and to all at home in sympathy with us. Stewart very much appreciated your kind messages to her. She is a dear old thing but no longer strong, but she loves the house and garden and works away in affectionate interest in it all and in us.

June 13, 1915   **Mount Pleasant, Simla**

My dearest Aunt,

No doubt these Daily Mail articles are reproduced in the American papers—and you and Uncle Joe should see them—they would interest you. 'The Tragedy of the Shells' and the 'Shell Scandal'.[8] Then there is a painful, well-told story of the dreadful carnage wrought by this war, headed, 'A Caravan of Agony' by an American correspondent. If only this war would end—and end for the happiness and liberty of the people of Europe and in fact the White races on this Earth. But what is America going to do? Only write letters and talk? Are Americans who plead that their cause is liberty and humanity and the development of industry and commerce and peaceful relations with the rest of the world—going to stand by and talk—when hundreds of lives are taken by a people who only understand 'Force'—are the people in America content—pleased to go on without greater remonstrance for the outrages perpetrated upon all nations of the earth as they are doing?

Alas, alas what is this world coming to with such principles at issue and men still preferring to go on money making—until their turn too comes to be over-run by the barbarians. These ruthless Germans, the people now making this awful war. It is sad enough to find the big men that we have pugnacious and pig-headed over serious points at issue, but it is sadder still to see a people unmoved—however surely the Right will triumph—God grant it may be soon.

We are very glad indeed to have Lord Hardinge's time extended for 6 months—when perhaps the war may be approaching its end. There is a great deal to upset things if every one right and left is changing at such a time—and nearly all H.E.'s Council come to the end of their time this summer and autumn. But Lord Hardinge himself is very anxious to get home—as one can well understand after all he has been through. I fancy our next letters from you will be from Narragansett or some summer sojourn you have taken. I hope your cold has disappeared. Do write me all about your very dear self for I am ever and always thinking of you and with a great anxiety when I know you have not been quite well.

August 3rd, 1915   **Mount Pleasant, Simla**

My dearest Aunt,

Tomorrow being a year since the war was declared there is to be a service all day, all over the empire—of Intercession for our troops. Our letters from England are very, very, very depressed and sad. Sir John Nixon has done very well in Mesopotamia and had real successes in spite of the many difficulties to be overcome and not the least of these being the appalling climate. He wrote to Offley how pleased he was to have had a letter from someone named Nixon in Charlotte Va. U.S.A. saying that he and 500 Americans of his name were watching the campaign with deep interest and sympathy. It is a great comfort to me to hear of the over-whelming sympathy of my countrymen and women in America for the cause of the Allies—and of all their great generosity and assistance, but many here are very ignorant of the American people and speak hardly of them as 'mere money loving'. To sit still under such indignities as the 'Lusitania' incident etc. Do ask Uncle Joe—who writes so much of interest and sends us so many books and pamphlets which we much enjoy—If U.S.A. went to war with Germany—am I not right in believing she would then have to stop all supplies and exports of the many things—ammunition and others—which have been of such valuable and real assistance to the Allies?

It is the greatest pleasure having Miss Impey staying with us. She is an older woman than I am by 20 years or so but very alive and intelligent and full of fun. Her Mother was Lord Lawrence's sister, as you know, and so many of that family are old family friends of the Shores.

Have I thanked you for all you have done and are so constantly doing—but how can I sufficiently my very dear, dear Aunt. I hope you are out of town and well.

October 7, 1915　　　　　　　　**Mount Pleasant, Simla**

My dearest Aunt,

Offley is busy with the ink so I can but resort to pencil—as I want to write to you and Uncle Joe at once to tell you our great good news. I have felt instinctively for a month or more that something unusual and long-wished for was about to make itself felt and so I wrote a little note to Colonel James to come and see me. He came and we had a little talk and he said he'd like to come again about a fortnight or three weeks later and so I sent for him again to come in today or tomorrow and see me for I am now v. busy with our preparations for the move to Delhi and he assured me today, after a very simple examination that I might expect an 'heir or heiress'—as Offley calls it—early in April. Offley had to go to the office without waiting to see the doctor and it was not until he, Offley, came in at tea time that he knew that, if all goes well we shall become 'Papasha and Mammasha' in the Spring! We talk over many things and way into the future (!!) already, and in any case I have made up my mind whether the child is a boy or a girl to have it named after you, principally and as my part in its christening. The Offley Shores all have lots of names so this little person will no doubt continue to follow the family precedent.

I believe we shall have something very large to pay for the family pension dues as they rate the amount according to the age and rank of the Father and O. is going to look it up as he thinks it is something like £300–£350!!! so no pearls or bracelets for Madam Mère!

I have written to Betty and Fanny and Father and I have asked Betty in conjunction with you dear Aunt Fanny (and to whom I always turn) to get me some things that are not to be got here and also because I am not at home with such shopping in London and I would like [here follows details of a maternity outfit—Ed.].

Now I must close—with my dear love and eagerly awaiting yr letter upon the receipt of this and assuring you how well and happy I am. All so wonderful. With dear dear love.

It is just like the joy of a new doll only better—a very real gift of God.

October 14, 1915   **Mount Pleasant, Simla**

My dearest Aunt,

Here I am flat on my back—having been put to bed on Tuesday afternoon—the 12th. I came back on Monday just before lunch from my Red Cross working party where we have been rushed and hurried, packing and filling the extra boxes and the last to go from here for this season—and I felt somewhat exhausted when I came in—though I had done no leaning over or actual packing. My work was—for that day—calling off lengths of material for various swabs etc. However I <u>felt</u> very tired, but otherwise was quite well. The next day I had a 'Dherzi' (the man who acts as seamstress in this country) in to do some work for me, and Stewart and I were directing him—when I again felt rather unusual—Stewart at once put me on the bed and telephoned for the doctor, who was out at the time, but he came up here about 6 o'clock and said I must go to bed then and there—as he feared a 'faussecouche'. So far I have had little or no pain and nothing has happened but it is trying—and with the lovely weather to be locked in one's room in bed.

This morning I did have a shock at morning tea-time. O. received a cable from Sir John Nixon saying he had asked for him—Offley—to be his Adjutant General on his staff—and so it is. Offley left me for the office and he may or may not hear anything further about the matter—as this is the way he has been treated by the C-in-C and C.O.s on three previous occasions—as they do not seem to be big enough minded—or generous enough to tell him frankly either that they can't spare him or that he is too valuable where he is. If they decide to let him go, oh, how lonely and anxious I shall be—but I am only 8 days away from him by letter and here I am surrounded by friends and near my good kind doctor. Of course we hope for the best and that all may go on well with me—and if Offley has to go to Mesopotamia then I must be brave and take things as God sends them. No more now. I shall keep you regularly informed week by week. Stewart is devoted to me and Offley. He has my room full of lovely flowers from our garden and even arranges the door and curtain and screen that I may see out and have all the sunshine possible.

October 18, 1915   **Mount Pleasant, Simla**

My dearest Aunt,

All my high hopes are dashed and shattered. The Doctor told me this morning what I feared from the morning I was put to bed—and I am very disappointed—however we must think of <u>how blessed</u> one is in so many other ways—and one must rise above all these chances in life and take every comfort and pleasure in what one has got. Offley is my very all and no one could have a better or more devoted or more wonderful husband, lover, or companion. He and Stewart have done their utmost for me and I must be brave and resigned. It is God's will—but I could cry and did last night. I miss you all so much—kept so in one room as I am. I think of all those heavenly days when <u>you</u> dearest, dear Aunt Fanny used to come and read to me and devote yourself in a thousand different ways to me and I bless you now for it all and the memory of it all is very precious. I hope in a few days to be about again—on the couch or in the garden. Offley has worked so hard for me.

Dear deep love to you and to Uncle Joe—my heart was bounding and leaping with so much happiness and such plans. The child's name and so much more.

On the same day in a birthday letter to her Father Lina reported:

I was told by the doctor this morning that I can not now look forward to a child. It has been a 'faussecouche'. However, I am very blessed in so much else I must take things as they come—or do not come! and as God wills it. I will not write more now—I grow easily tired.

November 5, 1915   **Curzon House, Delhi**

My dearest Aunt,

Here we are and almost settled in, and though plumped into great heat and feeling it is very wicked of the Viceroy to order his Govt.

to Delhi before the middle or end of November, we are so delighted with our new quarters here—No. 11—that we are behaving with less temper over it than we otherwise should have shown.

I had rather a hard journey down as my head ached and I was very sea-sick in the train, but on arrival here the servants we had sent ahead had everything ready and exceptionally nice for our reception.

The bed-room is very bright with 3 windows and so is the drawing room which I have made old-rose and greyish white—the colours Aunt Mary loved so well—and with a few photos and pictures and my Persian carpets that Stewart would bring—for my greater warmth and comfort when it grows cold—it looks delightful. Offley ordered 25 to 50 palms and ferns and flowers every week and the new motor too is very comfortable and a great pleasure. We have a number of pleasant people in Curzon House this winter and more of my old friends than ever before. I think it will do me good to have come here—as at first I felt such reluctance to meet people and when they ask how I am and what was the matter—I feel I could burst into tears.

Sir John Nixon seems to be winning great honour in the field. He is a clever, careful man and an excellent soldier and I hope to see him win out extraordinarily well. He has again asked for Offley to come out to him. We hear now that men with brains are badly wanted at the War Office at home and I wish very much Lord K. would remember Offley. It would be just the thing for him—but I know how overworked the great K. is—and utterly unlikely to think of O. much as I know he likes and admires him. I must just pray for it.

Florence is with the English Red Cross at Boulogne. She had a little holiday at home and resigned from the French Red Cross and was sent by the War Office to her present position.

On 19 November Offley reported to Uncle Joe on the progress of the campaign in Mesopotamia.

November 19, 1915   **Curzon House**

My dear Uncle Joe,

As you say, Sir John Nixon's 'show' is the one which looms largest in the local eye out here—for 2 reasons. One—it is a force under the orders of this Gov. and two—we do hear a little more about it than of other forces. So far Sir John has been remarkably successful and I trust may continue to be so: but we are quite alive to the chances that the Turk under German leadership will make a great effort to prevent the capture or the retention of Bagdad by our troops. Hence fairly severe fighting is more than likely—and on a bigger scale than heretofore. The worst of the country is that its climate is too hellish for words. Some of our officers who have returned sick, say the heat, at its worst, is something unbelievable: and the bad water, dust and dirt and bad food in addition has knocked out the majority of them sooner or later. At this season of the year, climatic troubles are not so bad—and beyond Amarah (which is 100 miles N. of Basra) it is drier and more bearable than lower down. I don't think anyone who has been there, is over anxious to return unless for the fighting's sake, or in hopes of advancement.

We see that you people are gradually unearthing a pretty widespread plot on the part of the German and Austrian diplomatic representatives, to hamper your output of war munitions for the allies: and from all accounts you have to deal with a pretty pack of unscrupulous ruffians. I can understand such action in a country hostile to the warring nation—as being a mistaken notion of patriotism—although it is a disgraceful violation of the protection offered to the supposedly innocuous foreigner: but to foment that sort of thing in a neutral country where these ruffians pose as being citizens—seems — — — —? We know by now that the Germanic people recognize no code except their own: and I certainly would treat them like mad dogs if I had anything to say to it i.e. something so dangerous to the Community that they had to be extirpated.

Our 'overland' car really is a blessing and enables us to fly out of cantonment limits and get about generally in a way that one cannot be sufficiently thankful for. Our present one has a self-starter, electric lights, and I am in hopes Miss Schatz may one day find amusement and healthy exercise in driving it herself. Can you imagine her turning into the professional chauffeur? There will be no doubt about her <u>style</u> when she <u>does</u> do so! Perhaps one day she will drive you and Aunt Fanny about?

November 26, 1915   **Curzon House, Delhi**

My dearest Aunt,

Your letters and Uncles Joe's come so full of interest that my weekly screeds must seem very dull. Our lives—though very busy are so much the same. Last evening Father's cable asking how I was came in—we answered it at once—but it is hard isn't it to have come so very near to having had one of the most longed for and dearly desired wishes of one's life—however I must be thankful for so much I have got in this sad world—and there's an end. I want to try and forget the bitter disappointment in all the other blessings. I had every reason to have such high hopes and I was very ambitious. I intended asking the King and Queen to be Godparents with Hugh Shore—O's cousin—and Clifford and to have named the child after you and Uncle Joe—whatever the child had been. Offley and I were looking over his family names the very night before I was taken ill—and Offley has long liked the name of John—and I said, 'Well then we'll have all the names we both like and those of people we love' and I made lists—such as

Fanny	Joseph
Elizabeth	Francis
Josephine	John
Urith (O's sister)	Charles
	George etc.

and read them over and rearranged them and at dinner Offley and I almost always talked of the child's name—often and often I rather felt I should like my darling Mother's name and Sophie is also a Shore name—and then Offley would say, 'Alright—have your Mother's name too!' One plans in such leaps and bounds. I wonder what it was all meant for.

Lady Suffolk brought some things out for me—very kindly—but as one of the clerks in O's office has just had twins—I can dispose

of the things to them as Christmas gifts and there are a number.
Thank you again for the dress and coat—I look forward to them
with great interest.

It will be remembered that in her letter of 14 October Lina
had reported that Sir John Nixon had requested that Offley be
appointed his Adjutant-General. On 10 December she reported
that another officer had been appointed instead and commented:

The history of the whole case is decidedly curious, but the fact
remains that O. was appointed and we had begun to pack and arrange
his small allowance of luggage when certain circumstances over which
O. had no control, but a certain set of very ignorant people seem to
have—(or appear to have it in their hands for better, or worse)—decided
that the climate, which is a 'Hellish' one, was not the place to sent
O. and thereupon the C. in C. changed his mind. They are obviously
a swindling lot, the doctors, and happy as I am to have my Best and
Dearest safely here I feel that these people have cut short a brilliant
career and have lost an invaluable officer in the field.

Offley, in the New Year's Honours, had been awarded the C.I.E.
for 'Meritorious Service during the War'. According to Lina: 'We
believe it is for all his hard work and push for aviation, wireless,
and mechanical transport'. She suggested that the award had
been on the recommendation of Sir Percy Lake.
At this time Lina, particularly in view of the Presidential elec-
tion forthcoming in November 1916, was becoming increasingly
concerned about the American attitude to the war. 'I, an American,
feel in a special way that USA is taking the blows and insults
heaped on her by Germany in a shockingly casual way, and as
Mr. [Theodore] Roosevelt says, appears "too timid" to protect
her own citizens from outrage and murder, or to speak on behalf
of the Belgians. I hope when the new President is elected God
may give you a man that will put some pride and principle and
patriotism into America and Americans and sort out the European
American from the real American'.

Since Lina was a grand-daughter of immigrants from Europe one wonders where she drew the distinction between 'the European American' and 'the <u>real</u> American'.

Then on 7 January she wrote:

O. when he came in at tea-time told me that he is ordered to leave on Monday with Sir Percy Lake for Mesopotamia, for the Front! It gave me a great shock, I confess, but one must meet these things bravely in such times as these and hence we are <u>very busy</u>, although a great deal that was got ready a short time ago has never been unpacked. Sir Percy goes to take command from Sir John Nixon who has been there a year and who feels the strain and climate and is coming back on leave for a much needed rest.

I know how much you will all feel for me, but with it all I feel so proud and glad for O.'s sake that he is to get his chance and may God bless him and keep him and all good luck attend him.

On the night of his departure for Mesopotamia Offley wrote to his father-in-law to let him know what Lina would do in his absence.

January 10, 1916   **Curzon House**

My dear Mr. Sinnickson,

I am leaving here tonight with Sir Percy Lake for the Persian Gulf—at rather short notice.

Lina has been wonderful and quite splendid in helping to get me off and make all arrangements. It has come just at a moment when she has been very seedy with an atrocious and most persistent cold, but I am relieved to think she is already much better.

What she will decide to do about the house at Simla remains to be seen, but she is levelheaded enough to make the best arrangement, I have every confidence in her ability—no one may say how long this separation may be for, of course. My appointment is Sub. Chief of the General Staff, General Headquarters, and I am fortunately accompanying a General Officer whom I know well, and is also a great personal friend. We naturally look forward to success but it won't be obtained without overcoming most unusual difficulties.

I shall hope to send you messages thro' Lina, if I cannot write any to you directly.

With every good wish for 1916.

P.S. I sent you the following telegram this evening—'Sinnickson-Phila—ordered front line Lina remaining India' which I hope may have conveyed the situation to you.

Lina added her own P.S.

I cannot write more to you my very dear Father. I feel this separation deeply but I shall just wait quietly here—to be near Offley until he comes back—and please God safe and sound and covered with glory.

January 21, 1916   **Curzon House, Delhi**

Dear Uncle Joe,

Your letters have just come dated 17th December. Of course we have all lost mail in the 'Persia' and what a horrible, horrible thing that was! Such a number of young officers and their wives and children returning to duty here, many of them after their year in France, recovering from wounds, and coming back to light work with their depots here, perished. We are now beginning to hear the awful details from survivors.

Well, my Beloved has reached Basra, and proud and confident that I am for him, and in him, I am very lonely and very very heart-broken without him. Even after a long hard day he could always come in with a cheery word and eagerness to be at home again. In the mornings here, when he either rode early or walked in the Gardens on the river bank, he always brought me a young rose, a leaf or a sprig of something lovely in nature and to him so deeply interesting. When there was stress of work I worked with him and he always made much of my poor bit of assistance. We literally lived together in the utmost happiness and joy, and this makes the room, the house, my life, the lonelier and I am restless and uncertain except for the things I can do for him. A parcel every week and letters, but I can only hear from him once a week.

Our friends here are very kind and Lady Lake, my near neighbor, and I do much together and lonely though I am, I feel equally very glad, very proud that it is my O. that is the long, longed for Chief of Staff on this Expedition. May God keep him safe and well and bring him back soon.

The new Viceroy is the all engrossing topic here just now and the changes in the Viceregal Staff. Lord Chelmsford seems to be a man of promise and all who knew him in India where he had been as a Captain (!) of Territorials since the war began, feel confidence in him.

The surrender of Montenegro[9] is a sad, very sad, piece of news, and sometimes one wonders how it will be possible to break and crush the Germans with all their powerful preparations and equipments. Who, God knows who, wants to be under their hellish yoke! but as the Neutrals are pouring in supplies and adding to the increasingly difficult task of the Entente Powers,[10] it is difficult to see an end, or a peace or any horizon.

O. bade me tell you how greatly your wireless books have helped him and how much he values and appreciates all you have done to help him in this particular and many others. You must write to him in Mesopotamia. At parting he came across the enclosed advertisement of a Garden book in one of the Philadelphian books you sent him and I found this note afterwards on my table and feel sure you will kindly get it for me.

I am keeping on our house 'Mt. Pleasant' and shall live there and have my friends come and visit me, and work in the garden to have things kept up for O.'s return, please God, and pay visits elsewhere as I feel like it and already I have received a great number of letters inviting me to visit all over India, but for the present I shall stay here quietly until my letters begin to come from O. and then go to the Impeys' in Baroda, and on to Bombay, and I may go South to the Madras Presidency to the Hugh Shores. My letters would be safer sent c/o Delhi and London Bank, Simla, or to me at 'Mt. Pleasant', Simla, in any case in Simla I am known to all and when I leave here it will be to the Simla Postmaster I give directions.

❧   ❧   ❧

January 27, 1916   **Curzon House, Delhi**

My dearest Aunt,

Think of it, it is already growing into 3 weeks since Offley left me. The daytimes when there is much work to do and people to meet and the sunshine to cheer and sending the motor here and there to give a lift or a run to my less lucky friends—all keeps me up.

We have had a slight trouble, which they choose to call a 'Petrol famine'—so every one has to be a little careful how they use their cars and keep them for emergencies.

I am afraid Sir Percy and Offley take over from Sir John Nixon at a very difficult moment—and that they will be so fully and constantly occupied that Lady Lake and I can scarcely hope for many letters. I know they will write to us any and every moment they can find time.

Both Lady Lake and I have been so harassed the last week and more by this hateful Govt. who can't leave us a moment in peace and want our quarters and our telephones and to disturb us generally. Today—the mail day—when one wants to sit quietly down to write letters we have both been worried with visits from the various public works people—to know when we will and if we won't give up our quarters. To take out our official telephones etc. and to change the numbers and what not. So we had a long talk with each other— Lady L. and I—and have determined to possess our souls and our 'Suites' in peace, or until we are bodily kicked out. I am better off than she is as I have a smaller set of quarters and therefore not so much in demand, but I believe she—dear Lady Lake—is to have 2 of the rooms in her flat lopped off. Betty and Bessie will understand how these can be thrown into the main building by changing a partition. But isn't it annoying and despicable of them. I too am better off as I know the Viceroy better and easily laugh and chaff with him so that I should simply tell him—if I am turned out here—His Ex. must take me in!

I am better but still a good deal troubled with my ears—whenever I feel tired they ache. With the warmer weather no doubt I shall be better. We are very, very busy with our work: Red Cross and comforts. We need funds. I had wanted and hoped to give them—the Red Cross—£100 myself, by the 1st of the year, but Offley's sudden departure cost so dearly—2 horses to get—9 servants to be given each an advance and certain affairs etc. to be bought and settled at once, cooking utensils and camp kit of various kinds to take to such an out-of-the-way place—amounting to little less than 10,000 rupees or $3000 (horses are very expensive and two to be bought at once), that I feel I cannot do more than give my time and work. India does not pay for her officers in these instances. They simply order them to go and give them their passage money to the place of joining the appointment, but their equipment they supply themselves—the consequence is that in a headquarter staff billet—where one does not require chargers etc.—Offley let his horses be taken to France last year when they refused to let him go—but in fact he could not have kept them had he liked to do so—at the time—and when one wants these good animals quickly— you pay the price.

February 17, 1916   **Curzon House, Delhi**

My dearest Aunt and Uncle Joe,

Now you will be addressing us as Major General and Mrs. Offley Shore!! or directing letters to Offley as Major General Offley Shore, C.B., C.I.E., D.S.O., for tonight he is in the Gazette as above. God bless him and keep him—for many an honour and any rank—it cannot change him from the gallant, lovable fellow he ever is and was from the moment I first met him. I know how pleased and proud you will all feel with me.

This afternoon I went to the opening of the Lady Hardinge Medical College for Women by H.E. Lord Hardinge. It was most interesting and most touching the way in which Lord Hardinge alluded to his sweet and lovable wife whom we all miss as 'Her Excellency' among us and whom he so adored. There was a huge company of distinguished ones—The Begums, The Maharajas of Gwalior, Bikanir, Patiala and a long list were I to put them all down, besides Lady Willingdon and Lord Carmichael and the Commander in Chief and Members of Council and Sir Valentine Chirol and Lutyens and Baker, the architects of New Delhi. I felt a very great swell when I stepped out of the motor in my lovely brown coat and was taken up to one of the very front seats.

February 25, 1916   **Curzon House, Delhi**

My dearest Aunt and Uncle Joe,

Your <u>very dear</u> letters give me such very, very real pleasure—and it is <u>so good</u> to get them regularly. Offley's lately have come quite regularly—once a week—and then a little batch of two or three at a time. It must be a most awful part of the world to work and war in—and climatic conditions so treacherous it makes one very, very anxious. God grant that he comes out of it safely and well. He writes that the Staff are a charming lot of men to work with and work is very strenuous. Erzerum[11] gives great satisfaction to one and we trust this may shorten the time in reaching Baghdad—but the difficulties—physical—are so hard to overcome and push things on under such circumstances.

Last Monday—just as I received your letter—Uncle Joe—of January 14th, Miss Gertrude Bell, who is a young Englishwoman traveler and writer came to see me. They sent her over from Vice-regal Lodge where she was staying with H.E. and she goes shortly to M.[esopotamia] under the Foreign Office—or in some sort of semi-official way. I read her your bit of the letter in which you spoke of all the savants of your Oriental club dinner and she was most interested. She took a little tea-pot and basket for me to O. and how I wish I might have gone off with her. I questioned her as to my being of any use—if I went there—and as I neither speak Arabic or stand intense heat very well—it seems to be best to remain here—though I can do many things to help in a hospital and hold a certificate of the Red Cross—and I can type—but it might make Offley very much more anxious. My good woman, Stewart, is quite willing to go with me.

It is reasonable to assume that Offley received the 'little tea-pot and basket' for on 9 March Gertrude Bell wrote to her mother:

Today I lunched with all the Generals—Sir Percy Lake, General Cowper, General Offley Shaw [*sic*] and General Money, and as an immediate result they moved me and my maps and books on to a splendid great verandah with a cool room behind it where I sit and work all day long (*The Letters of Gertrude Bell*: Selected and Edited by Lady Bell, D.B.E., Ernest Benn Ltd., London, 1927).

Before returning to her house in Simla Lina visited the Impeys in Baroda.

March 18, 1916   **The Residency, Baroda Camp**

My dearest Aunt,

As I date my letter I realize that it is twenty-five years ago today since dear Grosvater died. How many changes since then and how sad he would have been to see Germany wreak her own ruin as she is so steadily doing.

I should much like to see a good Academy Exhibition after all these years! But here in Baroda with the temperature at 108 in the shade and a hot wind and a very small community of Europeans, even in so advanced a place as Baroda I realize that I have never known what exile in the real India must be—with only a month or two at best in a hill station and constant separations of either husbands and wives or children and parents. Simla and Calcutta or Simla and Delhi are not to be compared to such places as these—for they are big communities and to which all the best men and minds lead.

I have quite given up on going on any further visits at present, as the heat is even greater than usual this year, and I want to keep well and ready for anything, so that on Tuesday Stewart and I return to Simla to 'Mt. Pleasant'. I know how deeply I shall feel the lonely return home there, but it must be faced and there are so many women whose plight is less happy than mine.

March 28, 1916   **Mount Pleasant, Simla**

My dearest Aunt,

Your dear letter of February 15th and Uncle Joe's equally precious one of the 17th greeted me on the breakfast table this morning.

My little house is gradually getting in order and looking very sweet and homelike and the garden is exquisite. Masses and masses of stocks arranged so charmingly by Offley in the loveliest of colour schemes. There are three long rows on the terraces to the South E. of the house—a line of purple against the white washed walls of my wee house and in front of that a lovely pink row and the same on the other side of the path—pink and purple and then at the top of the terrace a line of white—on the next terrace there is the same arrangement in lilac and crimson—and so on. In the bed toward the North of the grass terrace where Offley and I used to breakfast there is lilac and white and all the beds are edged with forget-me-not—just coming out. In the rose garden the beds are all carpeted with pansies just coming out and all the wild cherry and wild apricot trees are in bloom and the rhododendrons. Offley will be delighted to hear that when some friends came to tea this afternoon, they said they had never seen anything so lovely except in the Great English gardens! The roses he pruned and worked so hard at last year are all looking so healthy—and in my verandas I have masses of blue, purple and crimson cinerarias and the tenderest of primulas and pink hyacinths—by Easter it will be like a florist's show—as for the hollyhocks and foxgloves coming on and poppies and cornflowers and the bamboo bushes we transplanted, they look gloriously healthy and happy and some little trees Offley grafted. I do so wish he was here, and God grant he may come back soon.

Yes, it is very gratifying that Offley's excellent work has been acknowledged and I hope it may be even more so for he had given his very best energies and devotion.

P.S. We are anxiously awaiting news from Mesopotamia daily, but the relief of Gen. Townsend looks very uncertain so everyone says. Isn't it awful? You've no idea how heavy my heart feels, but I know how much you sympathise with us.

On April 1st Offley wrote a long letter to his father-in-law on the Mesopotamian campaign and his own activities since his arrival there at the beginning of the year.

Indian Expeditionary Force 'D'

April 1, 1916

Basra

Dear Mr. Sinnickson,

In reply to yours of the 18th of January, 1916, received through Lina on March 3, 1916.

Since I landed in this unwholesome spot, I have paid two visits—one to Nasiriyeh on the Euphrates via Qurna and the Hammar Lake, and one other—with the Army Commander up to Sheik Saiad, just behind the fighting line. I saw the trees of Wadi in the distance—that's the nearest I have been. On the two occasions when riding out with the local Generals discussing problems of attack and defence, our escort was fired on—but I never heard it—and now the Army Commander has gone up stream to witness the final attempt to relieve Kut—and I am left behind in the infernal office—principally because a British Liaison officer from home had to be accommodated, and there was a shortage of accommodation on the G.H.Qr. river steamer.

There is little likelihood of any big fighting after this attempt, and I am more put out than I can say—but it's all in the day's work I suppose and one was lucky to get out of India anyway. This place is the very worst I have ever struck—or ever hope to—the so called cold weather is one continuous series of bitter cold, hot sun, howling wind, damp heat, dirt and filth of every description, and rain every week which converts the country into an india rubber bog! It's blowing a howling gale from the Gulf tonight and the Tigris is like an ocean in a stiff breeze—devil of a tide—tugs and boats and barges swinging all over the place threatening the big ocean-going steamers moored in the centre of the stream. It rained hard this morning and as bad luck will have it—they have had the same storm up at the front. I suppose the infernal place will, what with the rains plus the river floods, be simply impossible for days to come—and this just as active operations are about to take place after infinite pains in preparation—248 miles by an erratic river though illimitable marsh and alluvial flats isn't a satisfactory Line of Communication, is it? Especially with the confounded enemy upstream of you.

The marching road which had been made with the greatest of labour is breached and flooded at least every 10 days! and wind driven flood water over thousands of acres is apt to come along at you, like a river 'bore' and will eat away any kind of earth-work, revetted or 'protected' as you like. The problem of feeding the army at the front with a heterogeneous crowd of antediluvian groggy old tugs, paddlers, sternwheelers and barges unearthed from forgotten Indian waterways, and shaken to bits in the voyage up the Gulf—is an anxious one—and you must remember we are only a 'side-show', and must therefore be content with any scraps and rubbish that is thrown at our heads! The country produces dates—date palm wood which won't float—grain—reeds—sand that won't make cement—water that won't do for mortar and there's no rock or stone. We haven't a railway and all our Musulman troops regard the pestilential country as 'holy ground'—and consider that they ought not to be caught dying when fighting in such a sanctified locality. It doesn't make any difference to the illogical hounds that this is a Shiah country, and they are for the most part Sunnis. They just hate being here and the good old British soldier is the only man who can be trusted to fight anywhere and fight solid. The Arabs call him the 'Lion' and the Indian soldier 'rubbish'. We look upon the Arab, as do the Turks, as a murdering thief and jackal—with no principle or honour—and they say, the Arab is not in the least keen for our administration, because under the hated Turk, he could at least buy immunity, whatever the crime—and he much prefers this to what he has heard of the Pax Britannica.

I only mention a few of these little points to show you the class of thing we are 'up against' so to speak, let alone an enemy who is almost European and is led by German officers. In the first year of this fighting our enemy was largely Arab regulars; now we have divisions of Anatolian and European Turks against us—a very different class of men—and they dig like beavers—they are always digging and have criss-crossed the country for miles and miles with trenches and redoubts on the most recent Hunnish plan. They float their supplies and reinforcements down-stream. We drag ours up mile by mile: — however, we hammer away, and stick to it, and no doubt Mr. Baggy Breeches[12] will get tired of it before we do, particularly if the Russian keeps him busy in Anatolia. The marvel is where they get the men from and the guns! If we put up 25,000 and 70 guns, we find they have 23,000 men and 50 guns behind earthworks. When we increase to 30,000 they appear to have got 28,000—and so it goes. These deep 'low command' trenches— invisible at 2–5,000 yards, 9 ft deep, 1st line, 6 ft deep, 2nd and 3rd offer no target—and are most difficult to range on and the beastly country is as flat as a pancake for miles and miles and miles! We always have to attack—mostly frontally—because we haven't sufficient land transport to move wide of a flank with a strong enough force—and when we make a night march round a supposed flank, we find it thrown back with a series of invisible trenches and 'refused' and are in for another frontal attack, and if it happens to come down in deluges whilst this turning move is in progress—every da—d thing sticks in the mud!

I should buy the d—d country, but not fight in it.

Summer temperature gets to 126 in the shade! and it's getting hotter daily. Chief ailments—dysentery, fever, jaundice, heatstroke— all pestilential in their way and I have forgotten 'mirage' which would deceive an archangel! The only fellow who can laugh at it is the aeroman—there is no mirage from above! but it's the most weirdly deceitful thing you ever struck—a dog will look like a great yellow galloping cow! a line of camels like a lot of palm trees, miles and miles away, and they are neither of them 3–4 miles off.

I want to know where Adam and Eve spent their youth, that they thought such a d—d lot of the Garden of Eden.

Per contra—if you're not fighting you understand, you will find quince, pomegranate, figs, grapes, oranges, lemons, wild apricot, myrtle, growing under the date palms, the latter in flower just at this particular period—all in a carpet of green wheat and barley in a crisscross of green, muddy yellow water channels—willows, poplars, persian lilac, scirrus, babul, along the banks of the creeks— throwing the most beautiful reflections in the water—meaning that with controlled irrigation, almost anything could be raised in this alluvial soil. Vegetables do splendidly, shaded by the palm trees from the sun—as also lucerne—what you call alfalfa—but there is one peculiarity about the Sun—it gets up hot—no hour or hour and a half before you begin to feel its power—it just stabs you straight the minute it appears above the horizon. If you've got any friends who aren't satisfied with their lot, send them along, before it's too late. (I haven't mentioned, fleas, flies, lice; frogs, snails, mosquitoes, dust, wind and glare—nor locusts—everything seems to bite like the very devil.)

I expect one ought to dress in rhino-hide? There are lots more things too, but you will get tired of hearing of Egyptian plagues—and you will never come out and see us in the East, if I continue or overdo it!

Just wanted to let you know a point or two about the place.

Lina I hear today has got back to Mount Pleasant and Simla and I am glad of that, because she can't stand the heat at all, and it must have been heating up down Baroda way. They do say that India is in for one of the hottest summers on record, this year. I wonder why? What has come over the world? England under snow in March after a promise of a delightful Spring. Must all be Kaiser Bill's fault.

I am glad to hear from Uncle Joe's letters that all goes well with the large family circle and I hope they are, individually, sufficiently thankful, and I must say I wish I were with you all again. We're coming anyway, directly we can get our 'discharge'.

April 14, 1916   **Mount Pleasant, Simla**

My dearest Aunt,

The hot weather which is so killing in Mesopotamia and all the difficulties of the situation there make me very depressed and anxious about My Best Beloved, although Offley writes as regularly and often as he can and such delightful letters full of little sketches, also full of directions about the garden and gives me many tasks to work out there and he has sent me a most beautiful old Persian box—still, he is far away and the indefiniteness of his return is always an unconquerable ache at my heart. When will this war end! and when will these degenerate Germans see the wickedness of their ways.

News from Mesopotamia has been more encouraging lately, but they've not yet got to Kut to relieve Gen'l Townsend and the floods season has begun! One therefore is very very anxious and on a great strain. I find I sleep so badly and think so much—but I am blest with the most devoted and kindest of friends here.

The following letter from Offley's Aunt Caroline to Lina's father indicates that he had sent her the article on Offley which had appeared in the Philadelphia 'Ledger'.

17, Connaught Square,
Hyde Park

April 15, 1916

Dear Mr. Sinnickson,

I was much touched by your so kindly sending me the interesting notice of my nephew which I should not have seen if you had not done so. I have told Lina how much I should like to have the pleasure of making your and your family's acquaintance. Lina speaks of them all with such sincere affection. I wish I could tell you one half of what I hear of your daughter in India. She is so devoted to Offley and so perfectly fitted to fill her place as his wife. I often say he is indeed a fortunate man tho' I can hear her say 'Not more so than I am as his wife!' and one's only feeling is 'God grant they may be long spared to each other'. I cannot tell you the comfort she is to me. Owing to circumstances his was rather a lonely life and it is your daughter who has brought the sunshine into it and made it what it so truly is, a perfectly happy home. I know I need not make any apologies for all I have said about your dear daughter and I only trust I may be spared to welcome them back to the old country and Offley with the additional honours he so richly deserves.

April 17, 1916   **Mount Pleasant, Simla**

My dear Uncle Joe,

It is difficult to thank you and to thank you <u>enough</u> for your gift to me so thoughtfully deposited at Browns and of which notice has just come, but I do thank you with all my heart.

Offley bade me to come back to this house and just try how I should like it before I did anything definite about giving it up or subletting, and I am so glad I have come, for my friends find their way here, someone every day—and I am kept busy with my house-keeping which my excellent Stewart does the brunt of and I enjoy looking after and working in my garden which is beautiful. If I can get anyone to take some snap shots I will certainly send you some, but I fear they will give one no very real idea of the exquisite colourings as well as the masses of bloom. The birds love our garden and such a chatter and titter as is going on there now. Our newspapers are full of the departure of one Viceroy and the arrival of the other. Their speeches etc. seem to have been very well received and Lord Chelmsford to have made a pleasing first impression.

April 28, 1916   **Mount Pleasant, Simla**

My dearest Aunt,

Hardly enough happens week by week to make my letter of any real interest. We wait as patiently and eagerly as possible for news of the relief of Kut-el-Amarah and yet one knows the difficulties are so enormous—so great that if it is possible at all it must take time and cannot be done in a day or a week or even a month, which is heartbreaking. Wireless messages from General Townsend continue to come to us and to the people at home—all very cheery, very plucky and reassuring yet we have also heard of the death of officers from disease and the filth and food, which is not suitable to our soldiers and officers under these conditions. The lists of casualties have been very great among the forces fighting there and now one meets more and more of those wounded and ill who return to India and come here to be in the hills and good air—All tell a sad, sad tale—although this is not the time to criticise and quibble when there is still a task to do—and the Army are doing it—doing their very best bravely and splendidly and forgetful of themselves. The Government of India and those persons in authority—the Finance Member and even a higher in authority—have much to answer for. The 'Morning Post' in London has some very interesting articles on India and statements by Sir John Hewitt—and Sir John Nixon's dispatches are deeply interesting reading.

May 4, 1916   **Mount Pleasant, Simla**

My very dear Aunt Fanny and Uncle Joe,

Since I last wrote we have had the sad news of the surrender of 'Kut-el-Amarah' a more gallant stand has never been taken—and with the abnormal rains and floods, in a place or land that in ordinary times presents more physical difficulties than any place one's ever heard of, I think it is marvellous they held on so long. The gallantry and pluck and bravery displayed by the forces that went to their relief and the many young and valuable lives given in this endeavor and cause—it is sad to think of—and now all this Irish wickedness, paid for to a great extent no doubt by Irish men or women out of their wages earned in many a good American home. Verdun not yet ended and talk of a greater and more titanic struggle on the Russian front by the Germans. Is this war ever going to end? I hear thinking people in England have settled down to the fact that it is to be a long war—longer yet by another year or two!

I found the article about Offley in the Ledger—it is very flattering to be noticed and thought of, as I know he will feel—but it is an awful bungling of fact and fiction and no one seems to have the very faintest knowledge of his orders or appointments. To you dearest Aunt and Uncle Joe—really and always so interested in the English, 'Who's Who' or any Peerage and Companionage will have a little description of Offley and his service etc. In addressing him his orders come not according to the order in which he got them but according to their seniority as orders—for instance the C.B. comes first as it is the oldest and most distinguished military order—and C stands for Companion not Commander. The King is the head of this order. The C.I.E. (the Viceroy, who'er he may be, is head) comes next—and again is only a Companionage (in which however the Companions are often promoted to be Knights—so also in the C.B.) like the old fellow in Pinafore 'who polished up the handle so beautifully' that they 'gave him the order of the K.C.B.'. I only hope my Best and Dearest will polish up something so beautifully that they give him the order of the K.C.B.—the soldier's most coveted order. So when addressing Offley—very politely and properly—one puts Br. General Offley Shore, C.B., C.I.E., D.S.O. The Distinguished Service Order has no head or companionage but is like the V.C.—given for just what it stands for—Distinguished Service.

I went to tea and tennis with Their Excellencies at Her Ex's invitation on Thursday and had a pleasant talk with the new Viceroy who left a very pleasing impression and is certainly a very, very agreeable type of man—simple, dignified and serious and the young daughters are all delightful. As I said to them 'you are like the charming rhyme in the Nursery Song, "One can dance and one can sing and one can play the violin".' One paints very prettily and one plays the violin and the eldest has spent this past year as 'house-keeper' in a hospital at Fécamp in France, 'an experience' the Viceroy said 'in which one sees how much English women have to learn from their French sisters'.

People look for great things of Lord Chelmsford—it is too soon to say what the years and the man will make of the post. The new Military Secretary to the Viceroy is a Verney—Col. Ralph Verney—whose grandmother was, I believe, the sister of Miss Nightingale.

Offley wrote me upon the fall of 'Kut'. He hadn't expected anything else—but speaks in high terms of the gallantry of such a long stand—143 days—in such a climate etc. etc. He says you write him the most wonderful letters and it gives him the greatest pleasure to get them. He also writes me very fully in regard to this garden—and sets me such a task remembering each nook and flower arrangement—I only wish he could see it in its present glory. Every morning such sweet baskets full of sweet-peas or roses or pansies or larkspurs etc. go to my friends in hotels or hospitals and Stewart takes great pride in seeing me off in my rick-shaw with such lovely bouquets.

June 9, 1916   **Mount Pleasant, Simla**

My very dear Father,

This is sad news about L'd Kitchener isn't it? What an unfortunate ending to a great career. I hear he had lost to some extent the great influence he possessed at first and had become latterly the subject of attacks in Parliament—and that people at home, in England, no longer had the same confidence in him—and that Robertson was the man to whom the public looked. He is now Chief of the Imperial General Staff in London—but no doubt more than was possible in any one man was expected of K. of K.

We lose a valuable friend—and Offley will feel it deeply as also the death of Oswald Fitzgerald, K's beloved young officer and Military Secretary who was one of the old 18th Lancers—the Tiwanas—with Offley. He it was who always answered letters to K. if he did not write himself and Offley thought a great deal of him. This awful calamity and the cost of the big Naval victory in valuable lives quite mars any joy of it, glorious as it <u>really</u> is.

Offley has been busy with a Russian Cossack Squadron which made a gallant ride down through the Pushti-Kuh to join them—Sir P.L.'s forces in Mesopotamia.

I see Yuan-Shi-Kai is dead too—and what will China do for <u>a man</u>? a man of sufficient force to carry the Chinese to stable govt. etc. etc.

They say Lloyd George will succeed K. as S. of S. for War—but long ere this reaches you, you will have all the news and many details that I expect we never get.

To amplify some of the events Lina referred to in the above letter: Lord Kitchener of Khartoum, then Secretary of State for War, and his Military Secretary, on a secret mission to Russia, were drowned when the ship in which they were travelling, H.M.S.

Sir Percy Lake decorating the officers of the Cossack Squadron which had ridden down from the Caspian to join the British forces on the Tigris: Offley reading the citation.

Hampshire, *was torpedoed off the Orkneys on 5 June. David Lloyd George succeeded him as Secretary of State for War.*

In writing of 'the old 18th Lancers—the Tiwanas' Lina was referring to the fact that the extended family name 'Tiwana', introduced into the Regiment's name in 1903, was dropped when in 1910, following the accession, it became the 18th King George's Own Lancers.

The Naval Victory referred to was the Battle of Jutland, 31 May—1 June in the North Sea, a major naval engagement of the War. Each side lost six ships, but the British tonnage lost was double that lost by the Germans.

The arrival of the Cossack Squadron on the Tigris was an element in a Russian advance westwards through Persia, begun in 1915, to block a Turkish advance eastwards.

Yuan Shi-Kai was appointed the first President of China in 1913 following the fall of the Manchu Dynasty.

June 17, 1916   **Mount Pleasant**

My dearest Aunt and dear Uncle Joe,

I must not neglect to wish you, dear Uncle Joe, many happy returns of the day for the 14th of July. God bless you and keep you long to be with us.

Offley writes that the heat is something <u>terrific</u> but fortunately he keeps well. God grant he continues to do so. He has had the Russian officers who rode down through the Pushti-Kuh to join their forces (the British forces) in Mesopotamia to look after and he has had to talk Russian and make a speech in Russian—also to translate Sir Percy's speech made to them when he decorated the 3 officers—and the enclosed photos, are some that I have just received from an officer on the Headquarters Staff—of the investiture—which took place in the little garden of Messrs Gray Makenzie and Co. one of the big firms in Basrah. It was strongly urged by O. to decorate these officers immediately and they wired home for permission which was granted. Of course Sir P.L. gets all the glory of it but O. is content that he advocated it and that it will have a good impression.

I have had some <u>very</u> anxious moments lately as when I last heard from Offley he told me he had been recommended for a certain Cavalry Brigade. This meant a fighting command and one that was bang up at the front. My heart sank and for a few days I did not seem to hear anything anyone said to me. The next thing I heard was that an officer from here had been put into the command and General Kemball who told me—said Offley was far the best man for it, but evidently Sir P.L. wanted him where he is. He—O.—was not exactly flattered by being considered for such a thing so late in the day, but he was quite ready to take it and do his best, but I am glad for the present he has other and just as important work to do. Sir Percy does not speak French, German or Russian. O. speaks all three—and he has now been sent up the Tigris to where the Russian column is, to decorate 5 of the rank and file—and to look into certain questions regarding them and certain other inspections are to be made. My last letter was dated 'May 29th'—now nearly 3 weeks ago—so I am looking forward most eagerly and anxiously for my next one.

I am <u>very</u> distressed and so are most people here to see and hear the criticisms made of Sir John Nixon. He and his men under him did splendidly and it was the most successful and brilliant campaign from its start under Sir John and up to the moment when this Govt. or Lord Hardinge withheld the troops promised them—in fact stopped them actually embarking at Bombay. I simply worship all their splendid gallantry out there. There is a story going round that Gen'l Townsend did not want to go on or rather disagreed with Sir J.N.'s order to advance on Baghdad (before Ctesiphon) and from a most reliable source I am told that this is an utter untruth. Whatever he may have said in his letters to ladies or to anyone—at the Council of War—held by all the officers before hand and under Sir John Nixon—they all agreed that they must push on to Baghdad—it was a risk—they must take their chances, etc. etc. but this was war—and they must do or die—if they succeeded—well, and if they failed some one else would take their places and carry on to the same end and goal.

We all know how gallantly and bravely they did—and we all know why they failed. India whose campaign it was—went back on them—did not support them. Lord Hardinge—then the Viceroy—failed them. Lord Hardinge was frightened to send men, money, or guns—in fact anything out of India, though he talked constantly in public places of the loyalty and quiet of India. I like him much as a friend and he is undoubtedly a man of ability, but he is sadly pugnacious and proud and a politician, I am afraid. But he and his lot should be blamed—not the Army Commander in Mesopotamia or any of the gallant fighting men who were out there. If only we could see some end to this cruel war in sight.

July 25, 1916   **Mount Pleasant**

My dearest Aunt,

I have had either letters or visits from a number of young officers who have just been serving under Offley and all speak with such admiration and affection of him and this morning at the work party just as Her Excellency was making her round of inspection and I at my table—where I list all the parcels going forward—some 400 or 500 per day—a young officer helping us (from one of the convalescent homes just opened here) came up to me and asked if I could point

out to him Mrs. Offley Shore. Before I had a chance to say anything
he said, 'I'm just back from Mespot and have been serving General
Offley Shore as his engineer officer at Nasiriyeh and he's magnificent
to serve! I should like so much to see Mrs. Offley Shore'. Of course
I was most awfully pleased and asked him who he was—and we
had a nice little talk. It was a Captain Lilly.

July 27, 1916

Just this evening I received yours and Uncle Joe's letters of June
20th and 23rd and your gift to me of $500 deposited at Browns for
which many many grateful thanks—but tell Uncle Joe—who feared I
might still be living on my good credit—that I wrote Offley about it
and he wrote to the Govt. authorities at once and also arranged to send
me a most generous share of his pay. But things here are most awfully
expensive—and in Mesopotamia the price of everything is <u>frightfully
exorbitant</u>. O. has about 7 private servants—4 syces or grooms (native
Indians of course) for his 4 horses. An orderly servant—a man I am
glad to say who has always been with him off and on for 27 years—
'Walia', and a bearer, or personal servant, a sort of valet, and his own
private cook. Of course you quite realize these are none of them quite
like European servants and they have to do their work under the most
difficult and trying conditions—but when the wages of these necessary
followers become doubled or trebled it becomes a shockingly expensive thing for the officer on service in such a country—and just now
there seems to be no way of stopping it.

August 25, 1916   Mount Pleasant

My dearest Aunt,

I work hard at my garden here to keep it looking bright and gay,
but perhaps more than anything because Offley so loved it and

worked so unceasingly to keep it up, that I might always have a bright and cheery outlook—with all the loveliest masses of colour.

I cannot write a very long letter today as I have just heard one of my servants wishes to have leave at once to go to his home for a time—and with company and a small lunch party tomorrow this always upsets me—though Stewart looks after it and usually settles it all—I still like to have a look at the one that replaces or acts for the departing one—and as in this case—it happens to be my House-bearer (sort of chambermaid's work) I look for a clean and agreeable one to replace 'Shafid'.

Will you ask Uncle Joe how it was that my income from Grand-father's trust estate in June last was only $98.00—always before in June it was $200.00. I know he will give me the right explanation—which does not however make me any the richer, no doubt!!!!

The rumour that the C. in C. was to go, or rather vacate his appointment to go home as a witness to the Mesopotamia Enquiry Commission is now <u>a fact</u>, and a new C. in C. has been appointed and arrives very shortly. I have also just heard that Sir Percy Lake has been relieved of his command and will go home on the same errand—as he was C. in C. here when the war broke out. I feel very anxious as to what will now become of Offley. I also feel deeply—hearing so much criticism of the Army Headquarters and poor old Indian Army matters generally. The truth <u>is</u> they have each and all done magnificently and even more magnificently when one knows, as I do, how hampered and tormented by the Finance peo-ple they have been—and how looked down upon generally by the parvenu civilian men one meets with here.

September 1st, 1916   **Mount Pleasant**

My dearest Aunt,

On Tuesday last, my birthday, I had six people to lunch—dear old Sir Valentine Chirol, among others, came over from Viceregal Lodge (he carried off some of the nice books Uncle Joe had sent me) and at tea time a number of people dropped in and were delighted with my little American hot cakes—'flannel cakes' I think their real name is at home—I gave them for tea. Stewart brought the receipt from Margaret the cook at Narragansett. I felt very proud when Mrs. Gamble came up to me yesterday and said, 'How beautiful your luncheon was, and how delicious, I've never had anything better or more delightfully served even at Viceregal Lodge or Snowdon or any of the big houses—if as good and as prettily done!'. She was full of praise of my cook, my linen, my lovely table things etc. etc., and when I told old Stewart—she simply turned up her nose and said, 'Of course, she was quite right, but we won't tell that extravagant old rascal our cook or he'll be more extravagant than ever'.

I have felt very sad and so sorry for the Lakes—as Sir Percy is returning having been relieved of his command—and does not quite know what his future is to be. I think he is sure to go home on the 'Mespot' Commission—but of course knows nothing about it. Criticism of Mesopotamia is very rife, very hot, and very scathing, but Offley has for the present been given the C. of S. to the new Commander, a General Maude, and one never knows when his turn might come to be 'fired out' as they say. Only I hope that they may yet see, value, and appreciate his devoted services—for several officers have spoken to me most kindly of him—and the other evening I stopped in to see dear Mrs. Hill and finding her not very well and on her couch in her room she made me come up stairs and sit and talk with her. It was as if I were sitting talking with you or dear Mother. She was so sympathetic and kind and interested and Mr. Hill came in (he is a member of the Viceroy's Council) and both assured me of Offley's being well thought of. While I was with Mrs. Hill, shrieks of delight came from the direction of the nursery where Rosamund and little Margaret Thesiger and two or three other little girls—after the dancing class—had got Sir Valentine Chirol up to the Nursery and down on all fours to play bear and were having a heavenly time—Sir V. just like Uncle Joe always in his element with the little people.

❧ ❧ ❧

September 22, 1916   **Mount Pleasant**

My dearest Aunt,

Yesterday those of us who considered ourselves his friends, and all the officers of the General Staff and Members of Council met on the lawn of 'Snowdon' to bid 'good-bye' and God's speed to Sir Beauchamp Duff who vacates his post as Commander in Chief, having been recalled to give evidence on the Mesopotamia Commission of Enquiry. It is a very sad ending for Sir B.D.—a man who has seen 43 years service in India and who has in the past done some most valuable service to the State, who was hailed as 'the' man for Chief here next to K. He has been a sad disappointment to his friends and to himself no doubt—a man who—to my mind—has missed his opportunity. He looked dreadfully saddened and old and one felt it deeply as he saluted his personal guard and bid farewell to all his Staff—all drawn up on the lawn—he shook hands with some 200 people.

Afterwards Sir Percy and Lady Lake came back here to tea with me—and I enjoyed it so much, but felt it was alas, for the last time in India as they too are sailing for home before very long. My news from Offley continues to be good. He is now the Chief of Staff, not Sub. Chief and one hopes he will get on and be well spoken of and appreciated for all his good work and Sir Percy Lake very kindly tells me he is doing very good work.

Again I have to come to a hurried close with my letter, as mail goes at 5:30 and I am also going to watch a tennis tournament at Viceregal Lodge.

October 6, 1916   **Mount Pleasant**

My dear, very dear Aunt Fanny and Uncle Joe,

How lovely it must be by the sea at Newport or Narragansett. Here the only water we get is the constant downpour of rain that the monsoon brings us. It creates numerous little waterfalls on the khud sides or hill sides and gives a certain pleasure to see the trickling water, fairy like, over the rocks or ferns—but oh—the rains! They are still with us and yet winter is nearly here! I have just sent my Christmas gift (and I think it must cover all my sins and omissions)—it's a small cheque for $500—to provide a good slice of plum cake for each and every British Tommy in Mesopotamia. I have also sent your birthday gift, the £100, to the Lady Hardinge College and Hospital for Women and it is to provide a students' library in the College. They wish to call it by my name—which is very nice of them but we shall see. I will send you the correspondence I have had with the President Sir Pardey Luhio—when it is all closed.

I feel very virtuous <u>at your expense</u> my dearest Aunt and Uncle—but it is a great pleasure to give and in such fat sums. I wish I could give more to our good soldiers in Mesopotamia—God knows how brave and true they have been and many have come out there from hard and long service in France and other fields of battle. <u>If only this war would come to an end!</u>

I feel very sad at the idea of selling dear old 230. I do so look forward to going home again—there—just as soon as this hateful war is over. I only long for Offley's safe return and ours together to some 'home'. The new Commander in Chief is expected the end of this month <u>here</u>, but it is <u>too good</u> to hope he might by some chance or other fetch Offley with him.

October 27, 1916   **Mount Pleasant**

My dearest Aunt,

We have been working fast and furiously all this week with our Xmas parcels for the front and my back and shoulders quite ache. In the ball-room at 'Snowdon' last Wednesday afternoon we packed and posted 1400 Xmas parcels! Magnificent! don't you think? My gift for the cakes (of money) enabled them to put in the order at once and some 20,000 Tommies will each receive a quarter of a pound. When Mrs. Phelps, the military tailor's wife (and one of our best workers) came to me and asked if I didn't want to see one of my cakes—I confess I felt very proud and pleased and even touched to see the great piles of cakes—beautiful cakes—ready in such a wonderfully short space of time and one hopes all the men will thoroughly enjoy them.

Offley has just been made Inspector General, Lines of Communication—with his headquarters still in Basrah. This is a <u>very important appointment</u> in this campaign, so Gen'l Maude told him, but I do so hope he gets his promotion to Major Gen'l. and with it a billet here until the end of the war.

November 9, 1916   **Mount Pleasant**

My dear Uncle Joe,

Your letter from '1704 Walnut' of October 6th—just after your return home—gave me a great shock for in it you say 'Betty's letter enclosing a notice from the office of the Censors in London, that Gen'l Shore was a prisoner of war, and telling her how to write to him', also that this information was mailed from Liverpool Sept. 23rd and addressed <u>to Betty</u>!!

It is a <u>horrible fake</u> thank God. Offley is not a prisoner, nor ever was—and please God he never may be. I only hope neither you, nor Betty nor any one has acted upon this information—as it can be but some German wickedness and 'ruse' to get things or letters from Betty, and I trust none of you have been caught in the trap. When our officers are made prisoners the government informs the wives or mothers—<u>no one else</u>—and it is the last thing likely that Betty would be notified or any of my people in America. And alas, the Turks have not shown themselves any more human in the treatment of our prisoners than the Germans. Some cases have been well cared for—such as Charles Townsend—but very few.

Please God that no such contingency happens— but if anything of the sort were to happen I feel very sure I should be the first to let you hear of it.

Yesterday Mrs. John Walter let me know of the election of Mr. Hughes as President of the United States. I hope now that the U.S.A. will under his Executive redeem her pitiful behavior toward

Mexico and struggling Europe. I was too shocked at the sinking of the Arabia with the Lakes on board to have any pleasure in hearing of the American Elections, but I am relieved today to hear all were saved. Still it will have been an awful experience and shock to the poor Lakes and many others—Lady Lake dreaded to go home so much.

Lina had been hoping for a change in the Presidency. On October 13 she had written to her Aunt:

I am sorry to see how President Wilson still talks over all this submarine and loss of life in American waters. Fancy any man of honour—and leader of a people—or head and President of a State—talking of German good faith. God grant he is not your President for a second term—and one wonders and marvels the American people put up with such a man.

November 15th, 1916   Mount Pleasant

My very dear Father,

Mother's birthday! and how well I remember the flowers and the little birthday remembrances we used to prepare for her. How sad she would be over such days and times. It is with a very, very heavy heart I sit down to write my letters tonight—for last night just as I got up from dinner I had a wire from Offley saying he had been in hospital with jaundice for ten days—that he was better and out again—still I feel very anxious, very, and hope and pray that the medical authorities will send him back here to me—but it looks doubtful—and now they have very good doctors and hospitals in Basra I am only afraid they will keep him there—and all this comes immediately on top of having seen the new C. in C., and Col. Tom Scott, the Military Secretary, and ever so many others just back from Mespot and all said how very well and how splendidly O. was looking.

Oh, I do hope—after having been out in that poisonous climate for now nearly a year that they will send him back here on a month's leave at least. They owe it to him for his services—I know—have been valuable.

You seem to have elected Wilson again in U.S.A. Where have people with hearts and minds of humanity gone to!! However as a very big man said to me here—it seems to be a choice between six of one and half a dozen of another. It is all so pitiable—not to speak more strongly.

Today is the last day of the great Exodus from Simla to Delhi and this evening I went up to the Mall and scarcely saw a soul I knew and could have had any shop I wanted to myself.

Of course my movements are very uncertain. Just now I have wired O. asking if he cannot come here and I am preparing to leave on Monday for Karachi. I shall await his answer to my wire here, but in any case should I go to Karachi, it takes me 2 days nearer to him, thank God.

Oh, this war, this war, and when will it ever end in spite of the glorious stand we and our allies are making.

The contradiction over the result of the Presidential election was a real one. With only the California votes outstanding, the results showed Charles Evans Hughes as having defeated Woodrow Wilson by a small margin. The votes from California reversed the decision.

Letter from Offley

| | **British Red Cross and Order of St. John,** |
| **November 21, 1916** | **No. 3 British General Hospital, Basra** |

My dear Aunt Fanny,

I have just come down in a hospital ship from Amarah en route for India—and have found a perfectly gorgeous box of Havannah cigars, beautifully packed and absolutely undamaged, waiting for me, in my mail! from you and addressed by Lady B. I do thank

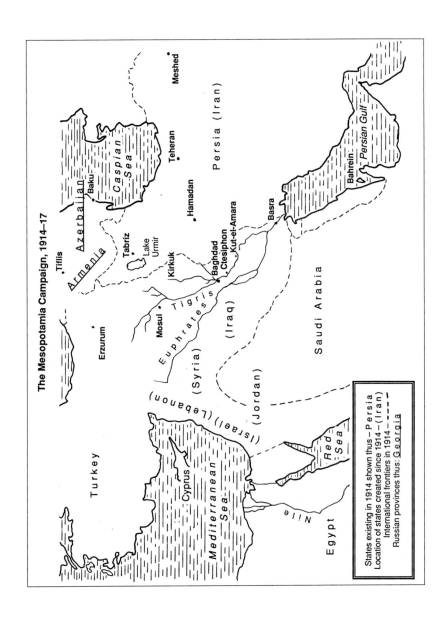

The Mesopotamia Campaign, 1914–17

States existing in 1914 shown thus — Persia
Location of states created since 1914 – (Iran)
International frontiers in 1914 – – –
Russian provinces thus: Georgia

you for your kind thought and I am feeling rich in the possession of real havannahs, which are almost unheard of, out here.

From what I have already said, you will see I have at last been laid by the heels and fallen into the medical net: lucky to have only contracted an attack of jaundice when so many other microbes are around: cholera, plague, small pox, typhoid, para A and B, etc. etc. It leaves one however rather weak and they are accordingly giving me 4 weeks in India (voyage to and fro not counting) to get well again.

I have wired Lina to keep the house open or get rooms at a hotel in Simla, as the doctors think the bright clear cold there will do one more good than the coast ports or the plains. But this contretemps is an unfortunate one from the point of view of one's work, delighted though I am to see Mistress Schtaz again, as you may well guess. I have always had the feeling that the only way out of this country was by the long white ships with the green band and red cross on their sides—but I never thought I should, personally, leave Mesopotamia by _that_ road.

I was on my way up river on a tour of inspection, when they discovered at Amarah that I was looking yellow, and promptly sent me to bed in the Officer's hospital there, where I stayed for 12 days and then was allowed out, at the end of a string, for a week. So you see, we all get caught, some time or other.

I have just heard that my Aunt Mrs. Stovin, has lost her butler, an old and valued servant of the type that is now becoming extinct, and I am sure she is feeling it very keenly. To 'Old Wheeler' I was always 'Master Offley', even as a Colonel and he could never get out of the way of calling me that. He began life as my Grandfather's groom. The family belongs to _him_—and it was always 'our house', 'our horse', '_we_ do this' etc. etc. A last link with feudal times!

I find it difficult to imagine that any progress in the West can make very much difference until the Russians are able to put in their full weight of men and guns. When they do—and may it at least come with the Spring—the German is likely to have _his_ Louvain and his Mons,[13] but it is a weary wait for those whose fate has detailed them to the unimportant theatres! but even they are more fortunate than those others, condemned to garrison duty in far off lands, who are dying to take an active part no matter where. I only hope succeeding generations will be grateful! (They won't be: they will very soon forget). However, I trust Lina and I may soon be excused further service and be able to rejoin you all, before many years are past. (I had almost said 'months', but it's no use deceiving ourselves—we will keep the months as a little surprise?)

November 25, 1916   **Mount Pleasant**

My very dear Uncle Joe,

Your letter of October 20th has <u>this moment</u> been received, and I hasten to answer it at once. I know and can imagine what your anxieties for O., on hearing this news that he is a prisoner of war, with the Turks, <u>must be</u>, and I appreciate your interest and your affection for him which adds to your trouble and anxiousness for both of us, but thank God it is <u>not true nor ever has been</u>. At that date, 23rd of Sept. last, O. was Chief of Staff to the Command in Mesopotamia and doing <u>exceedingly well</u>, so much so that he was mentioned specially in despatches by Sir Percy Lake who gave up his command just as O. became C. of S. and Gen'l Maude seems to have been equally pleased with O. who had the difficult task of C. of S. during the reorganizing and readjusting of all things when the new commander took over. The C. in C. (the new one, Sir C. Monro) and a large staff of officers from Army Headquarters India General Staff here, who went out to Mesopotamia all told me of seeing him and were particularly flattering in all they had to say of him, 'How well he was—how well he had done' and this was quite unnecessary, had it not been <u>perfectly</u> true. He, O., is now much to my joy on his way back here, a sudden and slight attack of jaundice having brought about the deeply longed-for 'leave' after a long year of trying climate and after tremendous zeal and activity to do his very best for the Service, his King and Country.

I hope you will be kind enough to <u>contradict it</u> publicly in the Ledger as you say this <u>erroneous</u> report was put into the papers upon <u>confirmation</u> by my brother Charlie!!!! How did <u>he</u> know so exactly? I would have telegraphed to you to contradict the report when I first heard it through your letters, but I realized that it was more than 40 days old, and by the date I could have cabled you, you would have received my letters telling you of O. as usual, and of his very important appointment as Acting C. of S. etc. etc. followed by the new appointment of Inspector General, Lines of Communication, which is one of the greatest importance in this campaign. No doubt the reason you hear little or nothing of Mesopotamia in your newspapers is because things have been developing with greater rapidity and importance elsewhere. All has been going on surely but slowly in Mesopotamia and perhaps policies have been taking shape there of another kind. India has done magnificently in Mesopotamia through the men of such splendid persistence and character that she has in her officers, O. not the least among these, and she has had in Mesopotamia a climate and country and campaign to fight through to which France was a joke! A mere joke!! The mistakes are not to be mentioned besides the difficulties overcome or met with and one cannot praise too highly what has been done on the Tigris and Euphrates by the soldiers, rank and file. Had the Govt. of India and the Home Govt. behaved as they should have many things would never have happened as there is no excuse in war time for an attitude that regards any obstacles to necessary action as insuperable. Alas the Govt. was often at fault here and treated the Mesopotamia Expedition as a 'side show' much too long or else a railway would have been made there at once, and there would have been no such thing in history as the fall of Kut-el-Amarah. But I could go on for pages and pages and no doubt bore you intensely with matters we soldiers' wives feel very, very deeply in India and a good many in England too, but God grant a great and vigorous success everywhere and soon, and very particularly all success and honour to those men who have done so gallantly in the mighty and most difficult task in Mesopotamia.

Love to you all and deepest gratitude for your affection and anxiety for me, for us. I am more thankful than I can tell you and I am sure you are all glad to know that O. is not, nor ever was, a prisoner of war. Could I but make him my prisoner here no task would be a happier one for I dread the parting with him when he has to go back again.

On his arrival in Simla Offley wrote to his father-in-law:

December 7, 1916   **Mount Pleasant**

My dear Mr. Sinnickson,

I have already told Uncle Joe that your kind pre-occupation over my alleged capture in the field is fortunately not a fact, circumstantial though the newspaper account was. Unless there is another General Officer of my name—it is difficult to account for the London Censor's Report. So far I have not had the fortune to be in the firing line and so far as I know have not been in danger of being raided while on my travels up and down the Euphrates and Tigris. We cabled you two days ago to put your minds at rest.

I have to go before a Medical Board about the 15th January to see whether they consider me fit to return to Mesopotamia. If they don't—my future employment will be entirely problematical. If they do—I suppose I shall rejoin in my present position of Deputy Inspector General, Line of Communications, and have to go through another summer. However, I never worry nowadays—and just take things as they come.

It is perfectly splendid being back with little Mistress Schatz again. The poor thing is delighted after all these months of solitude. Just eleven—since I left Delhi and unfortunately not much to show for it all. Still I have done my best and 'saved face' by getting a nominal mention in despatches and a recommendation for a Servian Order! which by the same token debars me from any other foreign decoration, and, of course one would have infinitely preferred a Russian one. They haven't promoted me and I personally don't think they will. Senior Cavalry Officers are not wanted and in this theatre of war they are not giving them Infantry commands as in France. In fact, if one hasn't been to France, one is not supposed to know anything of modern fighting. I knew in 1914 and 1915—when they refused to spare me to go to France, that I was pretty well 'done' and so it looks like shaping. However, as I said before—'Je m'en fiche' and I'm not envying any man his luck. Mine is good enough to get back and be with Lina again.

December 15, 1916   **Mount Pleasant**

My Very dear Father,

Offley has been back here with me now for ten days—and besides the very joy of being together, it has been exceptionally glorious weather and we have walks together and need I say, he finds lots of work in the garden so we virtually live out of doors, all day from breakfast to tea-time—when it grows dark and we come into the study—not to go out again that day—and have a cheery fire and a visit from the doctor—Sir James Roberts—a charming little man— late L'd Hardinge's private physician and now the Civil Surgeon for this end, the 'West end' of Simla. The newspaper comes in the evening and O. and Sir James discuss the news of the day, the situation etc. etc. and are now—from deep interest in each other's serious wish to see the Empire—especially in India—do more than she is at present—strain every nerve etc. etc.—concocting a long letter to L'd. Curzon—out of which I hope some great good may come. Things look very bad indeed with Bucharest in occupation by these Germans—and one now has to contemplate two if not three years of this cruel war. Offley—at present writing—has to leave me again for Mespot. the first of February—but need I tell you how I long, hope, and pray for some appointment in which his energy and brain are more useful to turn up <u>here</u> for him or somewhere where we can be <u>together</u>.

If he were to be ordered to France I should not so much mind as it is a white man's climate but Mesopotamia is poisonous—and a year is enough for a man of his age to put in there. However this is my point of view and doubtless is not necessarily that 'of the powers that be'. O. is sadly, sadly thin and looking very much older— but he seems wonderfully better even in these short ten days and I give him the best of food, and he finds his own room and his bed and bath and everything 'magnificent'—although it is all of the sim- plest and we have to do without many things since we have to meet an income tax of 5 shillings in the pound, constant appeals for the suffering ones, constant appeals for the local charities who suffer so much by the war—and living expenses have greatly increased.

Jams and preserves are <u>very expensive</u> and I have been won- dering if you would not order sent out to me from California directly via Japan a box of clear honey, preserved figs and asparagus—

perhaps some strawberries, peaches, and cherries too—say a dozen of all the above things.

Offley to his Father-in-law on 23 December wrote:

Schatz reminds me that today 10 years ago, I first turned up at Rittenhouse Square! Ten years: in some ways it seems 20 or more, in others, as it were only yesterday, and I remember how infernally cold it was, landing at New York, and how pleasant you all made that first Xmas for me.

> *Lina in her Christmas Day letter to her Aunt described Offley, 'much better but still shockingly thin', spending 'the whole day out of doors over his trees and flowers'; and 'devouring all the books you and Uncle Joe sent'. 'In fact we have never had such a holiday since we have been married.' She described the Christmas dinner with turkey and plum-pudding and the children's parties, and gave thanks for the 'delightful little black evening dress which came yesterday in perfect condition'. She hoped that 'our soldiers and officers in Mesopotamia may have a peaceful, restful day and enjoy our parcels'.*
> *She reported receiving letters from the Lakes on their experience in the torpedoed* Arabia.

92 babies were on that ship exposed in dripping wet clothes for 36 hours. The Lakes lost everything they possessed and as she said in her letter to me—what care we took to pack all our boxes and to get them on the ship with us. She said the experience was awful—and now in London she says it is dreadful—constant aeroplanes and Zeppelins coming over London and dropping bombs—even by day—but yet they fortunately do little damage.

She contrasted President Wilson and Prime Minister Lloyd George:

Mr. Wilson seems to be giving you all a very anxious time in America and I wonder what the end of it all will be—we feel very proud of

*HRH The Prince of
Wales arriving at the
Military Review on
the occasion of the
Quebec Tercentenary
Celebrations, 24 July
1908. Lieutenant-
Colonel Offley Shore
leading.*

Lina photographed by Lafayette immediately following her Presentation at Court on 26 February 1909.

*Honorary Major General Nawab Malik Sir Umar Hayat
Khan G.B.E., K.C.I.E., M.V.O., A.D.C., Tiwana.
Honorary Colonel of the 19th King George V's Own
Lancers, 1935–1944. (Head of the extended family whence
came so many members of the Regiment that the name
Tiwana was incorporated into the regiment's title.)*

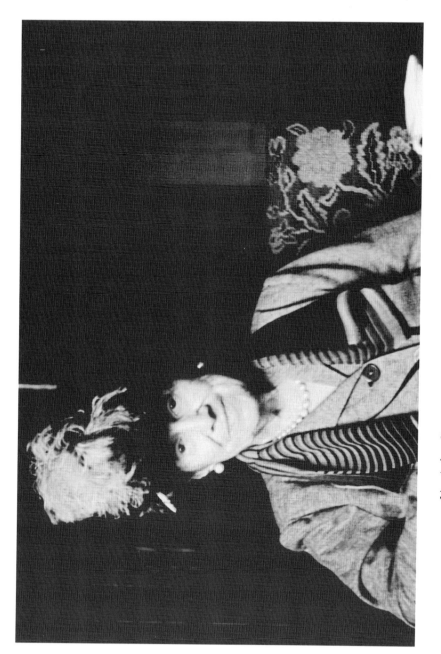

Lina in her Grace and Favour apartment at Hampton Court, 1955.

Mr. Lloyd George and his vigorous attitude and policy. One wishes there was another 'Lincoln' in U.S.A.

January 5, 1917   **Hotel Cecil, Delhi**

My dearest Aunt,

You see where we are by the heading of this letter. We left Simla on the 3rd and such glorious weather with many regrets, but as Offley had to meet his 'Medical Board' here we both felt it was better to come away while the weather was so fine than to run the risk of being caught in by bad weather for our journey down. Delhi is also very lovely just now and quiet.

I do hope so much they will keep O. in India or somewhere where I can be with him—Russia or France even—but not that poisonous Mesopotamia. However—wishes are of little avail—and no one realizes that better than I do at this moment. We are thoroughly enjoying being here quite 'on our own' and have stopped to leave cards or pay a 'pop' visit to friends and are deluged with invitations to tea, lunch and dinner quietly so that I don't think the Hotel Cecil will see much of us. Tonight we have been reading the 'Press Opinions' on Germany's impudent Peace suggestions.[14] I wonder much if Peace will really appear on the horizon within this year. Poor bruised and sorrow-stricken Europe. I do feel so deeply for her—but not one jot for Germany—the wickedest and most degenerate people the world has ever yet seen.

Thank you for the concert programmes and the newspaper cutting about the wonderful Opera—I looked for Betty's and Fanny's names and a description of their dresses.

Although we have the whole long days together—we do not find them long enough. We look over New Delhi as though we were its King-Emperor and Empress—and Offley looks at the trees and shrubs and new roads—with his eye of approval or otherwise but always with a keen interest, and we get up each morning and feel it is good to see the sun and be alive and thank God we are together. Offley looks at everything of mine—an old hat he may have liked, or notes the least change in my dress—admires some remade one and says delightful things to me—just the same lover as ever he was the day he married me and in another few days we shall have spent nine

wonderful years together—bar this last, lonely, long separation. If
Offley has to go back I shall go to Karachi or Bombay with him
and after that I can't say what my plans may be—but of course I
have the house 'Mount Pleasant' at Simla and would probably go
back there again.

I am so glad you get my letters regularly and yours are treasured
I do assure you, and looked for eagerly week by week.

January 25, 1917   **Hotel Cecil, Delhi**

My dear Uncle Joe,

We <u>do so very, very</u> much appreciate all your kind sympathy in
your letters and the kindness done in so many ways. The consideration and thought for us—believe me how very much it touches
me. Your constant solicitation and activity to help or cheer me—us.

We are very happy to be together again though, I confess, anxious
with regard to the uncertainty of our future. It does not seem to
have been very fortunate for Offley—being with Sir Percy Lake—a
man who though a kind friend was never definite or direct enough
and I fancy has been not only his own downfall but the end of many
an officer under him. People are now criticising Sir P.L. for <u>not</u>
doing a great many things Offley begged and pleaded with him to
do. Of course O. could not go further than that—or rather further
than a certain point. I am naturally <u>not</u> anxious O. should go back
to Mesopotamia but I am equally naturally desirous that O. should
go on into some good appointment here or in France or Europe, to
become a Major Gen'l. which (did the authorities not swindle to suit
themselves and place their friends) should, as a matter of course, happen
to a man of O's record and ability. However things look very black
ahead—just today!!! and one must just take it all as it comes.

Last Tuesday O. and I went out to tea with Dr. Kate Platt and
all over the Lady Hardinge College Hospital [Dr. Platt being the
first Principal—Ed.]. It is excellent in all its beginnings and should
prove a great factor and boon in the life of the Indian. They have
begun with about 30 students. I saw the library room and the

bookcases into which my books, bought with your birthday gift, are to go. I told Miss Platt of you and the Philadelphia College. She has been in America and knows the Philadelphia one and I have promised to give them a book plate—but my brain is not quick in these days of anxiety and uncertainty to plan what it should be.

Mr. Lutyens and I drew plans all over every available piece of paper or book for my house in New Delhi which I should so much enjoy to build—but here again comes an abrupt uncertainty—so one must continue only a 'Chateau en Espagne'.

January 31, 1917   **Hotel Cecil, Delhi**

My very dear Father,

This has been a week of anxiety more or less—as Offley's fate has been lying in the lap of the Gods (queer sorts of gods to be sure) and he had a medical board and an interview with the Commander in Chief—the result being that he is <u>not to return</u> to Mesopotamia and that India not having any appointment in which to place him lets him go on unemployed pay!!! Thus much! is all of thanks or gratitude there is on the part of so <u>unholy</u> a thing as a Government Service, and that—to a brilliant clever staff officer of an unusual record. He has asked to be allowed to go to England and Lord Montagu[15] has or will ask to take him with him to Russia on Special duty—so you may see us with you sooner than you expected—as if we are allowed to go to England we shall try to go via U.S.A.

I feel so glad to get O. safely back that I cannot feel the rest very deeply and he is <u>not</u> kicked out—my best Beloved—only unemployed because he has had no experience in France! and that because they would not let him go—though Douglas Haig asked for him.

In the midst of all this which is trying, comes your generous Christmas gift and kindest thought of us. Thank you so much and thank you too for your ever affectionate letters. Yesterday came the sweetest and smartest hat from Betty and Fanny and though the crate was shattered and battered the hat came out fairly all right and I put it on at once to go to an investiture of native officers and non-commissioned men in Viceregal Gardens and O. said it was most becoming and I looked very smart. It was a most interesting occasion when the brave officers and men marched past the Viceroy to be decorated. 4 V.C.s and all the other various orders of this War—besides our own orders some Russian ones and some French—'Croix de guerre' etc. It was sad to see those wounded men pass—some with only one leg—many on crutches and in several cases where the men were dead, the old Father or a sorrowing yet proud brother came to receive the posthumous order.

February 7, 1917

One heard the mail was not going out as usual so I kept this over and now great news of America at last breaking off diplomatic relations with Germany, also Austria; and every day brings an intense interest for 'what next?'. I wonder what you will think and feel about it at home, and if this will not really bring us more nearly to the end of the war.

I hope this reaches you safely but the 'mad dog' Germany, growing madder and madder, may catch this with one of her torpedos—only I hope not while the U.S.A. is about. How splendid it is our all being allies—Great Britain and U.S.A.

February 9, 1917

Offley went this morning to the Foreign Office and to the Adjutant General's and Quartermaster General's re our passports and hears an Admiralty order forbids all passports and passages to women under all and any conditions whatever unless ordered on duty or on doctor's certificate to proceed home for an urgent operation or some such thing, even to these cases exceptions will not in every case be made.

This hits me very badly—as I have always taken up a certain line about what is best and right and my duty toward Offley, than whom no more devoted husband and lover could be found, and I had planned to be near him or with him always. It is a long way off to have him in England or France and find myself here. But we shall find some solution. All that is magnificent in a man, that is Offley, and I cannot forsake him in ill-health and worried.

February 23, 1917   **Hotel Cecil, Delhi**

My dearest Aunt,

I cannot thank you enough or begin to tell you how much they
[your letters] mean to me—especially are they dear to me—so full
of calm interest and touches of real, very real home life—surrounded
by all the old friends and the family old and young—little and big,
while we are full of uncertainty—of the dread and fear of another
great and long separation—all the harder after the long strain of the
one just undergone. Should O. go to Russia I cannot go with him
now—and this is equally so to France or England.

It has been very, very warm here the last week—and one longs
to be out of the heat and worry of things and back in my sweet
garden in the beautiful Spring air in Simla, but not without Offley
for then is my whole world changed.

We had extremely interesting letters from Sir Percy Lake, Sir John
Nixon and General Kemball last mail re the Mesopotamia Commission.
All we do hope very sincerely is that the good names of many of these
honest gentlemen and officers may be cleared—if nothing else comes
of it at least we hope for that. I am most interested to hear what they
may say of the railway etc. and why it was never placed there at the
beginning of the campaign. It was Offley—very distinctly Offley—who
pleaded for it from the very beginning and who finally carried his
point and got it there when it did come, and whatever of success is
achieved in that desperate land of flats and floods and appalling
climate is due—most surely and assuredly to that railway.

I must not close without thanking Uncle Joe for his generous gift
which he wrote of depositing, and which Browns also sent me notice
of having put to my account.

I have enjoyed the motor—at his—my dear and ever excellent
and adored Uncle's expense and so has Offley and we both thank
him so much and so often and in these sad yet happy days we bless
you both thousands of times.

*On 2 March in the middle of a letter written in Delhi to
Aunt Fanny beginning: 'Here we have remained on and on,*

*not having had any final orders . . .', Lina started a new
paragraph:*

At last—orders have come—not yet however on paper and it would
be best to send all letters <u>from the date you receive this henceforward</u>
to me, Madame, seulement,[16]—c/o Thomas Cook and Sons, Shanghai—which we hope to reach by the end of April—first week in
May, our destination being in the direction of our great great grandparents. You and Uncle Joe will understand this. I am rubbing up
my languages and being taught a new one! Think of me sailing
through hot seas while dreaming of the days ahead when, God willing, I shall be warmed by sables (the <u>real</u> and beautiful thing—as
dear Aunt Mary would have said) and using the proper bath towels—again the real thing!! No more mystery tonight.

*This was followed five days later by a letter to her father in
which one paragraph read:*

You will have received our cable through Brown Bros. and perhaps
not be surprised at our new destination. In these days the high seas
are very uncertain, but I feel I must be with Offley as much as I
can and where'er I can and so I am off <u>with him</u> the end of March—
beginning of April. We leave here Thursday night for Simla to sell
up the whole house and sublet it and then, not for our first time,
do we take our steps Eastward—to Russia or possibly to you. It is
impossible to tell you of various plans and movements in these days
of strict censorship—but you may be sure we shall cable you from
place to place of our progress and our ship etc. etc.

*From the next letter it is apparent that there had been a complete
change of plans.*

Connaught House,
March 28, 1917   **Queen's Road, Bombay**

My dear Aunt Fanny and Uncle Joe,

Ever since the New Year began there has been for us nothing
but uncertainty and plans made only to be re-made or changed. We

packed up the sweet little house at Simla, sold most of the furniture and disposed of all the good servants—parting with my good Mrs. Stewart, who has been by my side and so closely devoted for the last seven years. I felt parting with her deeply and she felt it equally— but in these days one has so much responsibility that one could not beg her to leave her children and come with me—I know not where— or even when—and how! We felt the only way to get out of India (where they have treated O. so disgracefully) was to come here and jump into the best boat or train available, but nothing is more difficult than that. Just as we left Simla a charming letter came for O. from General Haig—and I know and feel the best thing to do would be to see him—but the great trouble and difficulty is to get me home now that I have no house or home to go to and the hotels in every hill station are packed to overflowing. I don't know where to turn. O. does not wish to leave me behind and we have made every arrangement possible to go via Russia or America, and cannot get a boat. Yesterday they sent a cable to the Secretary of State to see if I could not possibly go directly home from here—as a certain number of ladies have been permitted to on very slight excuses—and we must just wait and see.

Bombay, already a huge place when I first came to India, has grown enormously. It is the rich and magnificent gateway of India undoubtedly. Just now deep in war work or hospitals everywhere. We lunched yesterday with the Governor and Lady Willingdon. Both delightful—both full of exceptional charm and personality. It was a small party—just the staff—Lord Montagu, who is staying there, ourselves and Sir 'Something' [Ratan—Ed.] and Lady Tata—influential and interesting Parsees.

I know you will all wish to know all details of our plans, but I can tell you nothing, absolutely nothing for we know nothing ourselves nor should we be permitted to say the name of the ship or her destination or anything about her—in short you must realize we are at a military port and in war-time, and comfort you as we would, it may all be censored and we too might be hung up over such indiscretion. Only take it from me and for each and all of you who are interested and concerned for us, that all we can let you know we shall and as the moment admits.

Apart from a short letter written on 18 April at sea, approaching Aden, containing absolutely no information, the next letter to reach Lina's family was from London.

Hyde Park Hotel,
Knightsbridge, London, S.W.

May 6, 1917

My dearest Aunt,

That we have reached here safely thank God, you know from the cable O. sent the morning after our arrival.

We were packed and ready to go Eastward via Russia when permission was granted for me to come directly home with O. Two days notice was all we had in which to make all our arrangements for the change in the journey, but after 3 weeks of the great heat in Bombay one was glad to be going to sea and there was no time to be nervous or anticipate any trouble. It was very, very hot up to Aden. The Red Sea felt quite cool by comparison and we were fortunate to have a good breeze all along. At night however one felt the stuffiness of the cabins and saloons with every window, door and porthole shut and not allowed on deck and no lights anywhere outside etc. etc. It was a curious sensation. At Aden the Gen'l Officer Commanding sent for us to come on shore to sleep and dine and we were just starting off with Lord Sidmouth when the Captain's orders came to say we could not be made an exception and no one was allowed to land.

At Suez there was a good deal of excitement when the military authorities waylaid some 30 officers and took them off then and there for service in Africa or Egypt somewhere. I feared for O. for a few moments but fortunately he was not recognized as he was traveling simply as Mr. Shore. We landed at Port Said and though it was very hot, it gave one an outing and a change for which we felt all the better. There is now a very fine hotel 'Casino Palace' right on the sea with the statue of de Lesseps directly in front and there we lunched O. and I and Mr. Lutyens.

That night we went into the Mediterranean and the 'danger zone'. I confess I felt very nervous, and was very seasick in consequence. However, nothing happened, nor did we hear or know what was going on or which way we were taking our course, until we found ourselves early one morning in harbour at Messina and were told we had been chased by 3 submarines, one of which we had only missed by about ten minutes. From there onward to Marseilles we had a beautifully calm sea and often saw the Italian coasts, passed Elba and got safely into the haven at Marseilles with a very grateful sense of God's Mercy.

The journey by day across France up the Rhone Valley was a never to be forgotten sight. The young fruit trees all white and pink with exquisite blossoms. The fresh green of willows and poplars and the full rushing beautiful river. Avignon, Arles, Nimes, Vienne and up to Lyons, one continual glow of Spring. But one noticed the dearth of men everywhere. Only old men, women and wee children were working in the fields. At all the big stations pretty looking French girls in the Red Cross dress came to the carriage windows to collect money and presented us with lilies-of-the-valley. A wonderful sunset, a restless night and awake at dawn to find ourselves in one continuous camp from Paris to Boulogne. At 6 in the morning someone saw a Tank just back from active service and we saw every kind of preparations and training and so many English soldiers one felt it must be England. At Boulogne one felt this even more. We found we had just missed the morning boat and must wait there. This greatly to the annoyance of most of our fellow travelers, but for us we were rather pleased. We had wired to Florence but we did not see her as she is now in charge of a hospital train based in Rouen. However we lunched, took a taxi and went out to see the hospital at Vimereau where Flo had worked so long and saw all the hospitals and the town, so rich in my mind with Thackeray's many delightful characters and memories. It is a charming place, most certainly a bit of England in France and I hear the French are more than ever afraid now that the English have come there to stay! Nurses of every age and kind and in all the varied costumes adopted by this war, hospitals and ambulances and motors everywhere and men and women flying around in equal independence. Many of the nurses with military rank and in khaki and it gives one a very strange feeling and a certain shock at first, and coming from the land of so much ceremonial and salaaming as I have so lately.

At seven o'clock we caught the boat going to England with 'officers on leave' and we simply flew over! It was packed with gallant looking men and we found a number of friends among the

fellow passengers, [here follows a long list—Ed.] and last but not
least the Prince of Wales. We were escorted by 3 destroyers one
way at least and many the other way and went with quite a flotilla,
hospital ships etc. and <u>flew</u> along the crest of the waves, reaching
our beloved England at sunset. It was all wonderful, and I felt so
thankful. It was midnight however before we got to London, and
then it was <u>extraordinary</u> seeing the women carrying boxes and doing
porters' work. Here the old servants gave us a great welcome and
for the present we shall remain <u>here</u> although it is <u>very expensive</u>
and we long for our own house or flat, but it is better to do nothing
until I see what O. is to do. W.O. wants him still to go to Russia
while <u>he wants</u> France. No more now but great love to you each
and the joy of feeling so much nearer to you and please God I shall
soon go to see you.

England: May 1917 to January 1919

Immediately on their arrival in England Offley began searching for some form of employment. The United States had declared war on Germany on 6 April and Colonel Theodore Roosevelt— President from 1901 to 1909—was trying to raise a volunteer force. Offley wrote to Uncle Joe to find out whether this might offer him an opening.

May 8, 1917

**Hyde Park Hotel,
Knightsbridge, London**

My dear Uncle Joe,

Would you ask Col. Roosevelt whether he would take me on with his force in any capacity, and any rank?

I want to get to France before the show is over.

There are 2 close Rings here—one in France and one at home—and I fear an 'Indian officer' hasn't much chance. I have had a varied experience during my service and think I could be useful.

Medical people in India passed me fit for service in the field in Europe from 1 May '17 but refused to let me return to Mesopotamia. Am now fit again.

Lina quite well—and looking up friends in town. She's better here than left in India, all alone.

Meanwhile they had to find somewhere to live.

Hyde Park Hotel,
Knightsbridge, London, S.W.

My dearest Aunt and my dear Uncle Joe,

Your letters so constant and so much appreciated and I fear I am becoming worse and worse as a correspondent, however I have so much to do, and so much strain and anxiety. It is often difficult to sit down and write and put all the thoughts one would into words.

We are seriously thinking of taking a small, wee house here, to bring our own things about us and have some pied-a-terre we can call 'home', where quiet may reign and our friends come and go and especially if O. goes abroad again that he may have a house of his own to come back to or to keep me in!

I am very comfortable here, but it is never-the-less a hotel and expensive and difficult with the present rationing. You would not understand unless you were on the spot and I am old-fashioned enough to love a house and home of my own. The trouble is that we have practically no furniture. In India the furnishings of my house, suitable only to that country, were sold and did not fetch much in the way of payment. I have in that country some few boxes stored, of necessity until we are allowed by Government to bring them to England. At present we are not allowed to do so. There I have glass, china and plate, linen and some treasures accumulated during the 8–9 years I lived there. In USA I have linen and silver and all the contents of my sweet room, my bed-room, at '230' and much as I would like to have these things at hand here, there again I believe there are restrictions against bringing them across the Atlantic just now. I still have a small part of the $5000 (about $1500–$2000) given me by you and Uncle Harry from my Grandfather's estate but it will not go very far. O. proposes to buy the lease of the house for me, in my name, and I will have to furnish it.

We have also had rather a shock on our return to London to find some of our securities have been 'requisitioned' by the Govt., and others it is unwise to sell at this time as they would have to be sold at a great sacrifice. We would gladly have lent our things to Gov't. but were not told of this in India, nor was O. sent any word to Mesopotamia. Now O. proposes to invest this money in the house lease and I am writing Betty and Father to sell such furniture of

mine as I have at home in USA and I will then replace it here with
such suitable pieces as we require. (I remember Grandfather Rosengarten telling Mother 'An investment in a house could not run away'.)
Betty knew and saw my house in Simla and must therefore know
I am not <u>unnecessarily</u> extravagant, but practical in the arrangement
and adjustment of such things, and as I have lived for 10 years, or
nearly, with the very simplest make-shifts, I do think I deserve my
own little house and home in Europe after all the long years in
India, and with only such arrangements as one has, Indian fashion.
<u>Not that I am</u> complaining for I have spent such happy years there
and loved so much my own house and home and the interest of it
that I want to settle down <u>here</u>.

The house we are thinking of is about the size of Aunt Mary's
little 15th Street house, not quite so quaint in its arrangements but
with small stairs which make for happiness with the servants. The
rooms are an <u>agreeable</u> size, though small and the situation is very
charming. I <u>do not</u> ask you to give it me out of Grandfather's Estate
and I only write in full thinking you will all be much interested.
O. may be off any day and I hope it can be fairly settled, if possible,
before he goes. He, O., has asked Burrell Baggallay as solicitor in
drawing up the lease and I am looking forward to something of real
interest to throw myself into should there be long, lonely days while
O. is away. The joy of preparing the house for his return. God grant
that all will go well.

*Offley received a prompt reply from Uncle Joe to his inquiry
concerning Col. Roosevelt's volunteer force.*

June 1, 1917   **Hyde Park Hotel, London**

My dear Uncle Joe,

So many thanks for your prompt action re approaching
Mr. Roosevelt for his reply: tho' I don't think the latter encouraging,
and by cable of course we know that <u>his</u> Divisions have not been
accepted. Maybe he may be commissioned as a General Officer and

come to Europe—tho' I doubt it, so long as your Gen. Staff has Regulars to put up for such work.

I am very much afraid the Russian situation is bad [the Czar had abdicated on 15 March—Ed.]: and that the combined action of the European Socialists is going to make for trouble. However matters must take their own course and we must accept it so long as the nations do not agree to a Compromise instead of a Conclusive Peace.

My own movements are still uncertain. I have appealed again to Sir Douglas Haig to take me on—and failing that, I know I must accept War Office orders and go where I am told. In the interval I am glad enough of a few quiet weeks in my own country. I have been making notes of where to go to get a new war kit—either for a European or Eastern Theatre—but I am hoping I may not be sent back to India, any way.

Glad to hear of your war preparations and hope I shall see some of your War Divisions shortly. Equipment will no doubt be your difficulty at the outset—as it was ours, in the early days.

In a letter dated 24 June Lina wrote to Uncle Joe:

Here we are almost at the end of June and just enjoying our first summer in England together when orders come that mean taking Offley off to the uttermost ends of the globe and separating us again indefinitely. I fear by the time this reaches you he will be on his way to S.E. Russia via Petrograd. Many of his friends seem to think it a matter for congratulations—but to me you can imagine what it spells.

Offley had hoped to take me with him but the Foreign Office and 'the powers that be' will not permit it—and we hear it is so expensive in Russia now.

These few days appear to have been a period of order, counter-order and inaccurate dating of letters.

At some unclear date Lina told Aunt Fanny: 'Offley's orders for Russia have come and he leaves on Tuesday next, July 3rd'.
On 27 June she reported that his departure had been delayed.
On 28 June Offley wrote to Uncle Joe: 'Nothing fresh to report as regards myself. I am still awaiting orders, but I do know they

consider me too old for France'. Perhaps he was more concerned
about censorship than was Lina.
On 8 July the situation was clarified.

Sunday 8 July, 1917   **Hyde Park Hotel**

My dear Uncle Joe,

A line to tell you they have ordered me off at short notice to a
Russian force operating in N.W. Persia, somewhere S. of Lake
Urmia—as liaison officer—and I leave in a day or two—travelling
to Petrograd—thence to Tiflis and onwards by rail, steamer or road—
a pretty lengthy and troublesome journey. I do not know what address
to give except in care of our Embassy in Petrograd, for the present.
Of course I do not know the duration of this detail, but it is probably
until the end of the War. The appointment is under the W.O. and
nothing very grand, but one must do one's best for the country in
any capacity in which they think one can be useful.

Getting together a fresh outfit—for extremes of heat and cold, in
a country where nothing is procurable, or if procurable at all, is out
of all reason expensive—has been a serious business. They give me
the temporary rank again of Brigadier General but only pay me as
a Gen. Staff officer 1st grade (which rank I held in 1909!). However
I agreed that if I could not manage to get to France I would take
any orders the W.O. should have for me and so I could not go back
on that: much as Lina would have wished me to get something to
keep me in England.

I am much exercised about her, poor little thing—but think she
had better remain on here in this hotel, where the management and
servants know her—where the situation is central and air from the
park good, despite the perfectly hideous rates they are charging. I
calculate she cannot live here, with a small sitting room, bath and
bedroom under £1500 a year! and that without a maid. I know it
will cost me a great deal more than my pay in Russia, and so the
outlook is very unsatisfactory. However I see nothing else for it.

Lina would, I know, come over to you at the very first opportunity
for a lengthened stay—as soon as women are allowed to leave
England—which they are not at present, and perhaps, when released
from service, I might come overland Eastwards and join you all.

Whilst here, she will be in touch with all the influential people at home and though they will have little leisure to attend to <u>her</u>, still I am in hopes they may give her early information both as to myself as also of the general situation. Staying on here, Lina will have Juliet Baggallay, Lottie Bellairs, Mary Noel-Hill and other old friends—close by—my aunts, Mrs. Stovin, and the Baroness Farina are also not far away, and know where L. lives.

I am very much obliged to you for Mr. Roosevelt's letters and am more than sorry that his scheme did not mature—although I quite see the point raised by your Gen. Staff. Still it is a great disappointment—because I should have much liked to be associated with your forces. Anyway, I suppose it was not to be—but it was worth trying for.

Lina will have told Aunt Fanny about the little house close by—which I proposed buying for L., how our offer, based on Mr. Rawlin's surveyor friend's report on the house, has not been replied to by the owner—who was 'opening his mouth' to an absurd extent. He evidently thinks he can get his price. So we are still without a definite home, or stable pied-a-terre, which we both are anxious to have: particularly since my Aunt Caroline is a very old lady and if anything happens to her, Lina will have to take over all my old family pictures, furniture and other effects etc. Her house reverts to the Clerical Commissioners[1] on her death—and is not large enough or sufficiently up to date to take on.

Yesterday we were at Fortnum and Mason's in Piccadilly when a large German airfleet swept over us—at a very low altitude—and we could easily count them, whilst the shells were bursting in and around them. For a few minutes everyone was out gazing up at the swarm of bees or flight of great birds as they swung away to the S.E.—despite the efforts of the management to get all the women down to the basement! (L. sensibly went down and encouraged the women employees to do ditto.) My taxi driver was out of his seat and among the crowd looking up at the Germans, and I couldn't get hold of him to pay him! I have never seen so many planes in fighting formation before—nor so clearly. They did not drop any bombs in Piccadilly. The raiders seemed to suddenly drop through a dense bank of cloud in the N. and N.W. and come down on the city very rapidly. They were really moving very fast but did not appear to be doing so, from below.

They still seem to censor all your letters here—probably with the object of acquiring financial and other information and this must delay delivery: but it does not appear to me that they reach us very regularly. My sister Florence is over on a few days leave from her hospital train and I have been glad to see her before leaving England again. Fancy we have only been here 2 months! and it seems years already. But the fact of having been 'under orders' all the time has detracted from the restfulness and calm which would otherwise have prevailed.

You will understand that any cards or letters from me from Russia will have to be in guarded language: and will not, I fear, convey much more than news of weather, and so on.

July 12, 1917   **Hyde Park Hotel**

My very dear Father,

I parted again with Offley a few days ago. He has gone on a long, long journey and in a very difficult, tho' a good appointment to Russia. I cannot tell you how crushed and lonely I feel. His sister, Florence, who came home for a short leave from France is still here with me—and she is in a way a comfort—but poor girl she does not make herself very congenial—and I am utterly <u>lost</u> without O. I tried to come out to see you all for the summer but I was not allowed to do so and then I also tried to go <u>with</u> O. but again I could not get my passport visaed for such a journey—the War Office say 'when I can go out to join him they will let me know and help me in the matter'.

The offer we made for the little house was not accepted and so I am staying on <u>here</u> and making <u>this</u> my headquarters as O. wished me to do, though I feel it is <u>very</u> expensive—but then <u>everything</u> in England is horribly expensive now. O. considered this one of the healthiest positions in London and wishes to think of me here—so here I shall stay unless I should find it too excessive.

I wish I could tell you more about O.'s new appointment—but I <u>cannot</u> just yet—in a few weeks time I will do so with details. All my letters from you are censored and I daresay yours from me are also treated to the same.

You would love to read the magnificent things they say in the newspapers about Mr. Wilson and I tell everyone how confident you were of him all along—from the very beginning—I was not!

I am very lonely and very anxious without my Best Beloved and God grant he keeps safe and well and returns to me soon.

Offley would be away for nine months. During his absence Lina would busy herself with a wide variety of activities.

She became a member of Queen Mary's Needlework Guild, a group of ladies working in St. James' Palace sewing requirements such as quilts for hospitals and comforts for the soldiers. Through her relations in Philadelphia a Queen Mary's Guild was established there.

She became a 'hospital visitor' making regular visits to talk to, comfort, and entertain the wounded, buying gramophone records for them and arranging supplies of much needed sweets from the United States.

She was active in fund-raising efforts on behalf of the large number of refugees from German-occupied Belgium, helping to sell the lace they were producing in an effort to make some sort of a living; and later, on behalf of the Russians who were stranded in Britain or managed to make their way there after the Revolution.

She sent weekly food parcels to Offley, trying to vary them each week and including some champagne by hand of a King's Messenger in time for Christmas.

Air raids became frequent, as she reported in a letter dated 11 November 1917.

Alas we have had more air raids, but that is to be expected and fortunately I am not nervous, nor do I intend to allow them to unnerve me, but one does not like them—and if the Germans but knew how they—the air raids—enraged everyone and are but adding up to what they someday will have to pay for, they would not consider them worth the candle.

The wounded were a common sight in the streets:

Mind you this cruel war is close, close to us—for every day we are brushing up against the halt, the maimed and the blind—otherwise the glorious youth and manhood of this Empire and the sights one sees are enough to make one cry aloud—to sob in a bus—or <u>to</u> <u>choke</u>, as one passes—as I did today—a handsome young officer being lifted from a motor into a chair on the pavement and in that to be carried into one of the great houses (now a hospital) in Belgrave Square. You will—in America—be spared many of these heart-rending sights—thank God.

The following extract from a birthday letter to Uncle Joe describes a meeting with a taxi-driver whom, when in London with her mother back in 1900, Lina had known as a coachman.

Yesterday the most wonderful thing happened. I was walking in Berkeley Sq. with Florence and finding we were late for an engagement for tea we tried to pick up a taxi. It seemed hopeless and I saw one standing at the entrance to a flat house, so I thought he might be waiting to be paid and thus be free and I asked him if he was 'engaged'. Something very familiar made me look back at the man for I felt I knew him and so I went back and said, 'Is your name Sewell?' (Sewell was our coachman when we lived at Walsingham House and dear Mother had a 'voiture de remise') and he said, 'Yes, Miss Sinnickson, it is and I have been looking for you folk many a day'. He said no one had ever been so kind to him as Mother and two great tears came into his eyes. He asked after Betty and Fanny and spoke of the day when Mother sent him to Henley with us and I gave him my card and my name and address and engaged him to come on Monday and take us, Florence and myself, to Ealing, when we are going to see her Father's old friend, the nurse who nursed him in his last illness. I feel so pleased to have found this good servant. O. and I hunted him again and again when we first married and came here so much, but we never could find him. Do tell Betty and Fanny for they will be <u>so</u> interested.

July 25, 1917   **Hyde Park Hotel**

My dearest Aunt,

Last Sunday we had another air raid—I was just getting up—and
the guns began booming all round. I dressed as hurriedly as I
could to go down stairs and get out of the way of bombs, but it
was all over before I was ready to leave my room. I felt no fear
at the time but a little upset after it was all over. I am on such
a strain and feel so anxious all the time for O. There is much to
do here—O.'s affairs to settle and his boxes of food to send off
every week. (He has to feed himself entirely and everything goes
from here in the F.O. bag once a week.) I make slight changes
from time to time or rather I am to do so. My living and his
expenses are enormous. One is horrified at the cost of everything
and the demands made on O.'s private purse—over and beyond
his pay—are very heavy.

Last Saturday Juliet Baggallay and I took out seven men—3 of
whom could not walk. I took Sewell with his taxi and Juliet hired
a big Red Cross motor driven by a young lady, and we had little
Virginia Baggallay and the nurse with us. Sewell was our pilot and
the drive was chosen by him more or less and we went through
every park and common in or near London until we came to Richmond Park and from there we went to a tea house on the river
and gave all tea—soldiers, Sewell, Lady Chauffeur, Nannie and
Virginia and the men were so pleased and so grateful and I never
enjoyed anything more in my life. Of course it was an expensive
kindness but Juliet and I shared and we felt so glad we had done
this. One man said when he returned to the hospital, 'Sister, just
put me to bed and let me dream I'm drivin' about England with
a General's lady!' and so many of the men were so exceptional.
One had been a newspaper correspondent and Sewell told them
all about Mother and Betty and Fanny and 'her folks', (so the
nurse told us) and said, 'Just what Mrs. Sinnickson would have
done, just wot she'd have liked!' and I believe she would have—dear
Mother.

I have plenty of things to do to keep me busy—and having no
maid I have all my own mending to do and my washing to sort and
so on—a little reading and lots of letters to write.

I am afraid O.'s Aunt Caroline is not very long for this world as

she seems very, very much older each time I see her—I even notice
a change in each few days interval between the times I have last
been there. I am so glad to have had his other Aunt here and we
are very sympathetic.

August 16, 1917   **Hyde Park Hotel**

My very dear Uncle Joe,

How I wish you could have seen our American Troops march
through London yesterday. It was a very heartening and historic
sight that made one proud of the deep significance of it all. Very
earnest looking men they were and they created a most stirring impression. Everywhere there were Stars and Stripes waving and when
going to St. James Palace in the morning I took the omnibus at this
hotel to go to Piccadilly and the top of St. James' St., but instead
of going up Piccadilly straight and as usual, the street was being
cleared by the police and we made a detour up Park Lane to Oxford
St. and along Regent St. to Piccadilly Circus. There I descended
and found as I turned into Piccadilly everyone running hard through
St. James' St. and the crowds getting greater and greater so I went
into a tea shop at the corner of Bond Street and upstairs from a
deep bay window in the luncheon room I saw splendidly, and two
ladies were so pleased to find an American in me and bade me look
out the windows and up the street where I could see the long line
of the evenly marching men all the way to Hyde Park corner. The
cheers seemed very loud and deep and gay and all I met with were
so pleased, so impressed with all it means.

I felt too much to cheer. I took out my handkerchief to wave,
but found myself weeping. It is indeed a great thing to be fighting
and waging war together in so great a cause and against so much
evil, and everyone made the same remark 'We are one kin, we are
one and the same race'. With the same ideals, yes, and the same
aims and I could but feel the depth of personal interest in it all,
that they are working and fighting with O. to the same end, to the
same goal. It is such a long, long time since I have heard from him

and I am indeed so lonely and so often so depressed I scarcely know how I shall go on. I enjoy my visits to the hospital and last time Lady Ripon sent a beautiful gramophone to the ward where the bad 'face' cases are and I brought them some few records of the <u>lively</u> kind the men like, so that tomorrow when I go I know what happy men I shall see, and that gives me great joy.

August 19, 1917   **Hyde Park Hotel**

My dearest Aunt,

Things seem to be progressing well but slowly in France—here we have great anxiety over labour questions and a contemplated strike in the railways—while Russia has shown the world the fallacy of so many socialistic ideas—why will people not look and learn the lesson!! I go on Tuesday into the country with Juliet for ten days—and returning take over my new quarters—where O. and I were in 1912—and the little maid is coming to me. I hope the change will make things brighter for me. O. so insistently desires that I should be comfortable and in the very brightest and best of quarters etc. etc. I feel so <u>very, very</u> lonely and equally anxious—somehow I feel so <u>very, very</u> much further off from Offley here, though I know it is a good place for me to be and O. so wanted me to be safely in England—feeling India was so very far away from every-one—from all of you for instance. Perhaps it is because I lived for years—as though I pursued an enchanted journey—<u>with Offley, near</u> him—always with the feeling that he was coming or going within reach of me—and so somehow I felt none of the aches and pains or little discomforts—or personal irritations or money troubles to the extent I do now. I seemed to have confidence—certainly more confidence in myself than I have felt lately. However I must not complain—nor do I complain—it is not complaining I would have you think I am—only one must give vent to this anxiety. Yet I know I must pull myself together and be plucky and then too when I get at some real work again—and I hope I may soon—I shall not have so much time to think about things.

Later

Just as I was dressing this morning the telephone rang and Sir Percy
Lake asked me to go with them to Hurlingham. I accepted with delight
and at 4 o'clk they came for me and we drove down in a taxi and it
was so lovely! We had what the boys and girls would call a 'ripping'
tea—or perhaps they say 'whacking'—anyhow you can imagine it was
something delicious and the trees and grass smelt so good—people
were playing tennis and croquet or just sitting about as we were or
wandering over the velvety grass as we did.

*In a letter of 24 August to her Aunt, Lina wrote of a visit to her
Bank:*

for the re-adjustment of my affairs—with no good Uncle Joe or
Father to advise and assist one and Offley so far off—not to say
the difficulty as equally, the wisdom—in these days of censors—of
not writing and discussing details—but I feel very much happier
since I have been there and after talking things over with Herbert,
who is anxious to be of any assistance he can—and I hope with
care and perseverance to bring matters to such a successful conclusion that they will come to the same annual payments as before—but
that of course takes time and patience.

*In a letter dated 10 September to her Aunt and Uncle, Lina com-
mented on the marriage of her sister Betty:*

To my great surprise I received a telegram from Betty telling me
she is to be married today to Mr. Saportas. I have sent her a wire
to 230 Rittenhouse Square, Philadelphia, not having or knowing any
other address, to wish her every happiness. I hope so much she may
find as great and congenial and devoted a lover in her man as I
have found in mine, but I am a little troubled over such sudden
news as I knew of no engagement nor had I heard anything even
hinting of such a thing from anyone but Clifford, and knowing how
dearly he loves Betty I thought he might be only feeling some little
pang of jealousy and scarcely thought of it again. In any case, I

wish her everything of the Best. She is such an unusual character and has been such an inspiring and wonderful person through all her sorrows, for I feel she has felt dear Mother's absence so deeply and I wish I had been able to be with her just now, just at this time.

Offley's first letter to Philadelphia after his departure reached its destination on 12 November.

c/o Colonel Marsh, British Agent,
Staff Headquarters
Russian Armies in the Caucasus,
Tiflis

September 13, 1917

My dear Aunt Fanny,

This is to tell you that I am, at last, on the particular heath which I have been trying to reach for the last 2 months!

I have made the acquaintance of several charming people—visited one or two obscure places, such as Urmia and Tabriz—come in contact with French and American missions, and generally had 'the devil of a time' travelling by rail under war conditions, and during a Revolution. The latter experience knocks anything I have ever gone through into the proverbial 'cocked hat'.—Simply concentrated hell—.

Of course it is highly inconvenient of these people to have chosen this particular time to put their furniture outside on the lawn and do a bit of Spring cleaning! It is also more or less of a nuisance not to be able to get little luxuries such as sugar, milk, eggs, butter—and to find the shops absolutely sold out of everything—or to have to pay 80–100 roubles for a pair of boots and 300–350 for a knock-about suit of clothes!

It riles one to discover that no man is out to do his job—and that wild impossible ideas as to the equality of all men are floating around: and that there is a general notion that the Lord, or the Americans or the English will somehow arrange to re-establish order—but the only thing to do is to look on calmly and wait until the people find things so confoundedly uncomfortable and impossible that they will find a way out of it for themselves. Self-help is an idea that

will have to be let into their headpieces with a hatchet: possibly
that of hunger: for it really does look as if they will be starving
before long if they don't watch it. And in the meantime Wilhelm
and Hindenburg are having the time of their lives.

Persia I found to be uncommonly like dear old Asia—same old
dust, same old heat, same environment—possibly less smells but
quite as many flies as in India. Hills and plains absolutely bare
except where water has been delivered to the land—and there you
have an oasis of green.

I have at last received 4 letters from Lina, in rapid succession—
after 6 weeks of silence—and am glad to say I think she is comfortably installed at last in the Hyde Park Hotel. I have telegraphed
her once or twice—but am not all certain that she gets them—as
the Russian land lines are doubtful and I must use the more circuitous
and infinitely more expensive route via Persia and India I think.
The Americans here are getting stores sent out to their Embassy in
bulk, for distribution to all their Consulates—so as to tide over the
winter—and this I think a very wise provision.

I have received the greatest kindness already from many of your
people, and especially at Urmia—where as you doubtless know there
is an 80 year old Mission under Drs. Packhard and Shedd. Wonderful
people.

There is no doubt about it, everybody down here is heartily sick
of the War: and I think they would welcome peace in any form—no
matter at what cost: however, whether it be peace or internecine
war, they have a mighty task in front of them before things can be
smoothed out and put into running order again. All eyes are turned
in your direction and everyone is asking how soon will that American
army be in France! Can they really put a million men in the field
in Europe? Do they really mean business!? and I tell them once the
Anglo Saxons put their hand to a thing, there's no drawing back:
they are out for a fight to a finish—but I don't think they are convinced! We want a big smart body of British and American troops
here—to show them what smartness, energy, and determination—
coupled with sane administration—can do.

Lina tells me she has heard from Clifford—by now he must have
got into his stride, and have much of interest to relate. I do hope
he is well—also all the other officers of that hospital. We just hear
now and again that things are progressing favorably on the Western

front—and the Germans being pushed steadily back: but it doesn't seem to prevent them paying more attention to the Eastern and S.E. fronts than we care about. Really their conduct of the war is a triumph of organisation and energy! I certainly am ready to take my hat off to them, on that score.

Give my love to Uncle Joe, Mr. Sinnickson, Lady Betty and Fanny, and tell them how long it has taken this letter to reach you, in case they think of writing to me! You will forgive the featurelessness of this note but remember we have a Censor in London, who is particular!

October 7, 1917   **Hyde Park Hotel**

My dearest Aunt and Uncle,

We have been through such days and nights of excitement and apprehension that they have run into weeks without one's realizing it. The raids were indeed trying and required all one's pluck and nerve—if not at the time—afterwards—for they certainly leave an uncomfortable effect on one—added to this I had all the surprise of my dearest B's marriage—as I had known nothing of the seriousness of her feelings and so on—and I awaited all your letters and even Clifford's—to hear more of it. Then there was the dear old Aunt C.'s household—so upset by the raids that I had to go there and see her safely off to her nephew, Harrington Offley Shore, in Oxfordshire—as her servants behaved in the most undutiful manner—and left town—having given her—an old lady of 89—an ultimatum—as it were—to get out of her house. Not a relation was in London at the time! and I did what I did as tactfully as possible—but I am very vexed with those servants—and would like to feel that they never entered her house again. Her maid fortunately was very respectful and calm—and left town for Oxfordshire with her—with Aunt Caroline.

All this time I am worried and very greatly so, over the state of our exchequer. The position is this—after very heavy expenses for our return journey from India we reached London—O. on half pay— or unemployed pay—which does not go very far—to discover all and the best of our Colonial and American securities were requisitioned. That was, not borrowed by Govt. but bought outright at the market price of the day—and of these—the greater part have not been paid over to me—to us—yet!!! O. was ordered away again in less than two months after our return here and he had in consequence—very heavy unanticipated expenditures to get ready his kit for such a journey and such a climate and conditions as he was going to meet. The state of the country to which he was going etc.—obliged him to be well equipped in purse and person. His pay was to be adjusted and paid partly by one country, partly by another. To avoid any difficulties by being hung up for money etc. we bought in London—to be put at his disposal on arrival in Russia £1200 worth of roubles—but, on arrival—even in Finland they—the Finns—would not touch roubles if they could extract English cheques or notes and, added to this, cabs and meals etc. were charged for in pounds rather than in roubles or kopeks and even to change a 100 rouble note they asked 25% during the chaotic days of his journey. Upon going into Persia no Russian money is thought of—hence a cable to London—to put £700 in sovereigns to his credit in S. Russia and in Persia—as he had to move between the two. I did this at once—but you can imagine I am utterly depleted in pocket. We are, I should say; and on a visit to the Bankers—I discover that only a part of his pay has been paid in to his agents as they have to wait for O.'s signature or authority to pay this!!!! Thus much for Govt. Red tape and meanness—O. having made every arrangement with the various pay offices (and I have the copies—though unsigned—of his letters and notes to this effect)—to pay in monthly to his bankers his pay for my use and comfort. The consequence now is that it will be the first of the year before this can be done and we have already spent almost every spare farthing that we have and I dislike intensely to go on increasing the advance made me by the bankers. O.'s pay is—or rather should be—about £1000 a year—and his railway expenses are or should be paid—all else he must meet himself—and as I have already said—'all else' in that country is now at the most unheard of and monstrous prices—people ask what they want—and you may take it or leave it—as the case may be.

I am hoping to send this letter to you so it may not meet the censor's eye—and I have been advised by my bankers here—not to write anything more than necessary on the subject of affairs with

my bankers; and in fact to do that, in every possible case through
them—not my own.

I am going tomorrow, Monday—at the suggestion of the Manager
of O.'s bank to certain gentlemen at the various Govt. offices under
which O. comes—with his notes—to see what can be done—but, it
was much the same in India, I waited 5 months before the disbursing
office met my case and then only on getting a letter from me—O.'s
letters having been mislaid or overlooked or, some such wretched
excuse. He will be furious when he knows of all this—as a kinder,
more considerate, more generous man does not exist, and I have
never in all my married life had a moment's disagreement or un-
generousness on his part or unthoughtfulness in the matter of money.
In fact, I so often tell him he would do without things himself rather
than that I should miss even the slightest desire in the matter of
expenditure. And now no more. Kindly keep this to your good selves
with the exception of my Father, and I will let you know results of
my visits to offices.

*In another letter at this time, Lina wrote further on Betty's mar-
riage:*

I hope so sincerely that Betty's marriage will turn out very, very
happily. I hope you and Uncle Joe and Father and Fanny will keep
ever in closest touch with her. Her letter—Betty's—was so sad to
me—that I feel grieved and worried and anxious for every detail.
It seems so distressing that she had no woman to use a tactful,
sympathising though restraining part with her. I am so glad Charlie
has taken such a big brother's stand—and one can only hope and
pray for the best and happiest results. My own marriage has been
so exceptionally happy and my Beloved such an exceptional man
of honour, of gallantry and integrity.

On 19 October Lina reported to her Aunt:

Two letters from O. with whom the conditions are very black—and
appallingly uncomfortable. I received a wire from him also—saying

I must go to the War Office to hear from a certain Gen'l various things. I cannot see him (this Gen'l) for some days and the suspense is trying. Could some cigars or food—a little sweet corn and figs and sugar plums not be sent out to him from U.S.A. through the American Embassy?

I feel very anxious about his food. I send from here every week— but at present things seem to be very difficult, or perhaps the American Red Cross in that country would take him something—a little claret or a little whiskey—California claret preferably. I do wonder if Col. Landis could help me to get some things to him from U.S.A. through the Embassy or the Red Cross.

I have tried to get things to him from India—but it is impossible.

Lina ended this letter with:

It has been a glorious October day. A little misty tonight and one hopes there may be no raid. They say Tuesday—Wednesday night— being the clearest moon of the year, we must be prepared.

On 1 November, Lina started a letter written 'at King George's Hospital' to Uncle Joe with:

I have finished my hospital visits—10 men of the K.R.R.'s (King's Royal Rifles) or known familiarly as 'the 60th'—finished also making up my book—tally for the end of the month that is copied and sent in as my Report—and I am waiting for Juliet Baggallay to finish her 'Rifle Brigade'.

The King's Royal Rifle Corps was raised in the North American colonies as the 60th Royal American Regiment during the Seven Years War—1755/63, known in the United States as the French and Indian Wars. Battle honours were won at Louisberg (1758) when a French fortress on Cape Breton Island was destroyed by a land force under Gen. Jeffrey Amherst, in conjunction with a Royal Naval force under Admiral Boscawen, and at Quebec (1759) when the French forces under Gen. Montcalm were defeated by General Wolfe on the Plains of Abraham. Some American volunteers served with the K.R.R.C. prior to the United States' entry into World War I.

Lina was not at first aware of this but later came to refer to 'my regiment'.

In the same letter she thanked Uncle Joe for his prompt response to her statement in the previous letter of her—and Offley's—financial position and asked whether it was a loan or a gift. She ended: 'You must feel proud and pleased to have seen Americans are now in the fighting lines.'

November 23, 1917   **Hyde Park Hotel, London**

My dearest Aunt,

So busy am I now—that I have to snatch my evenings at home and the time between dinner and bed-time to read, sew or write—as I go to work to Queen Mary's Needlework Guild at St. James' Palace—every day but Saturdays and Sundays.

I received a note from Lady Lawley giving an appointment time for me to come, so off I went and had I been Royalty or a former Vice-reine I could not have been more happily and kindly received. I was shown everything and introduced to everyone. Both Lady Lawley and Lady Dawson asking after Offley and very interested in him whom they and their husbands have long known. I told them I could do almost any of the work—needlework or clerical—and so they asked me what I would prefer to do. My reply was 'anything where you can make me most useful' so as there is a large order for quilts which Her Majesty is very anxious to have quickly done—I was put on to those.

But I must tell you about the high praise the Philadelphia work and Bessie Hays got. I told Lady Lawley of it having been started in my old home—our town house in Philadelphia and so she showed me all the Philadelphia parcels and all the records in her big Ledger book. I told her of all your generosity and of the real interest in our English troops, that had been, had existed, from the very beginning of the war.

As for the old Palace rooms themselves—they are the very rooms Offley has gone so often through—when attending the King's Levées—and going to my work room I pass through a wonderful little ante-room with beautiful old tapestries and then through one great State-room after another until one comes to the throne room. The number of doors I open and shut on this journey—and such splendid doors! and I walk by portraits of the Queen and Prince Consort by Winterhalter and of George IV, of the magnificent Stuarts—and then to reach my sunny corner that looks out into the Garden and across the Park—St. James'—and beyond are the towers of the Houses of Parliament and all the offices I know so well—the Foreign Office, the India, and the Horse Guards' Parade.

In the next letter Lina makes reference to the early disasters of the Mesopotamia campaign.

December 8, 1917   **Hyde Park Hotel**

My dearest Aunt and Uncle,

Your two dear letters to acknowledge—Nov. 21st and Nov. 22nd and many thanks for the enclosure about Gen'l. Maude. He is a great, great loss and was such a good man and in so many ways—and a particularly dear and devoted husband too. I am so glad it speaks as it does of Sir Percy Lake for it is all too true. He did a great deal—and so did my good man, my General Sahib—to clear away and clean up that wicked chaos they went there to meet. I only wish it had mentioned O. by name too.

You will be interested to hear I had news, a few days ago, from the War Office that Offley was shortly returning to England, by what date he leaves and by what route I don't yet know and the next month or so will be a most anxious one for me. I have not heard from him lately by letter or by wire and the wires come in such a mutilated fashion. Father wired me you had had a wire from O. and I have been feeling very upset and anxious since I heard of this from Father—for it does not seem to be very clear. I find it very difficult to see or talk by telephone to any of the W.O. people just now—they are so excessively busy with Italy and many other matters. The F.O. are much kinder, but alas, they have not so much to tell me of my good man.

The cables referred to in the above letter and Lina's response were the following:

Offley to Uncle Joe *(Received 4 December)*
Tiflis First December must ask you telegraph ten thousand pounds to Lina financial difficulties here reply General Offley Shore Cammilage via Indo.

Father to Lina *(Dated 5 December)*
Uncle Joe has cable from Offley asking sum of money be sent you fail to understand is Offley in trouble answer.

Lina to Father *(Undated)*
Offley not in trouble to my knowledge just heard returning England will wire you any information received.

December 15, 1917   **Hyde Park Hotel**

My dearest Aunt and my dear Uncle Joe,

Sir Percy and Lady Lake came in to late tea with me straight from the Commemoration Services of the First seven divisions. It must have been very impressive. He was in uniform and looked so well. I was busy in my room and heard the shouts and cheering and I had to drop everything and run down to see those left (only about 700) pass by. They looked so wonderfully gay and smiling—and when one thinks what those men and officers have been through! A gallant lot are our men—and another long roll of honour we have had but lately after Cambrai. [Surprise British attack, first use of tanks, 380 of them—Ed.]

Sir Percy—like you was just telling me that the 60th was first recruited in America and that I had a strong tie there in my work for them. They were—he said—at Louisburg and Quebec he thought too—but I shall get the History and talk to my good men with real and definite knowledge.

I will give my men some little Christmas crackers and try and have an American and English emblem combined. I see they have heaps of these things in the shops and I overheard a good Yankee voice say to some children 'they must buy American flags in London shops!' I have had four new men since Cambrai, hit there—2 with gun shot wounds in spine—these are sad cases and they rarely recover—and such nice men. I love my morning's work—and Lady Keppel has initiated me into the private ways and stairs of the Palace—so I can run out through the Ambassador's Court and get away quickly. The Queen came in unexpectedly last Friday. H.M. calls my Lady Keppel by her first name which is Bridget and speaks of me as the wife of the King's Staff Officer—what memories these Royals have! I had a message on the 4th or 5th that Offley was returning and ten days later I got a message that he will not leave Tiflis for at least a month and may very likely come via Baghdad and which will take another 2 months. I felt very disappointed but the Lakes and Lord Southborough both think it augurs good things to come for him. Please God this is so. So now more pluck and more patience. One's anxieties don't bear thinking of too much—or one's loneliness without him.

Thank you so much for all your kindness—for the kindest way in which you put things and encourage me. I am so glad to know Aunt Fanny has got on so well and please God she continues to go on so. How I wish I had been there to be of use to her or read to her.

You mention Mr. Atterbury [A new cousin by marriage—Ed.] having tried to see me. Entre nous, he did not try very hard. Asked at the War Office for me! and was told this was my address. I wrote to him care of his Bankers in Paris—never have received any reply whatever. I should very much have liked to have seen him at the time—coming so directly from Philadelphia as he did—but no doubt he was exceedingly rushed. If he ever does come through London I hope he will come and see me. I am not unknown in London, nor are my where-abouts. The War Office, the Foreign and the India all know where I am to say nothing of several Bankers, used by Americans.

I had a very nice visit from the Mr. Ellis—evidently an exceedingly busy man, whom Offley had met and he came almost directly from having seen Offley. Let me know at once he reached here and I fixed upon a half hour between a visit to Lord Bryce and an interview with Lloyd George. He spoke so nicely of Offley and what was best to hear was that in spite of the difficult and appalling conditions he was fairly well.

P.S. I hope the dear eyes are better.

There is a further reference to 'Mr. Ellis' in Lina's letter to her father dated 28 February 1918. He had been to the United States and while there had seen and talked with her father and with Aunt Fanny and Uncle Joe. Nowhere does Lina give any indication as to who he was or what was the purpose of his journeyings between Tiflis, London and the United States.

December 30, 1917   **The Foleys, Aldershot**

My dear Uncle Joe,

This morning I have received your letter of Dec. 4th telling me of O.'s wire asking you to lend him £10,000 (I feel sure he must have meant $10,000). I will give you such explanation as I can but it is difficult to do by letter and still more so as I have to guess to a great extent why he did it.

I feel sure it has occurred in this way, that the local financial conditions and the behavior of the W.O. and I.O. are responsible for his trouble about money, as for example they sent for him, a fairly big sum of money that was paying certain sums for the past 4–5 months, to the Consul General at Meshed! Only some 1000 miles away from any place where O. had ever been. I found this out quite by chance and have now had it adjusted and received an apology from the I.O.

Getting no money paid him and the chaotic state of affairs at that moment when they would not even take cheques, (for which they had been so keen only a short time before), he wired me to keep everything I had in London and wire him such sums as he asked for.

From time to time and just after he had done this he received my letters full of my anxieties at that time and of which I wrote you, and he tells me in one of my last letters that he 'feels considerably upset', all this came at this same moment! and I feel sure he acted upon the impulse of the moment in wiring you as he did. In any case I regret so much his having done so and only wish he had wired me, as I have felt so exceedingly troubled and anxious ever since I received Father's wire regarding the cable you had from O. Here I am now financing him from London, from his own pay and his own monies, the securities that were requisitioned now turned into War Loan and if he requires any particular sum, should he get into difficulties, I should like to be the first to know of it. I feel sure it has been some anxiety for me on his part, as well it might have been and not for himself, but had it been a ransom or any such thing, naturally I should have wished to meet it and act with the greatest promptness and in these days in which we live, and out in Russia, these things are quite possible.

I have not had any letter or even a wire from O. since November, over a month now and I am told I cannot expect this as the couriers and messengers have not been getting through from Russia lately, with Revolutions and counter Revolutions everywhere, but on writing to the War Office I hear he has not yet left Tiflis, and with what one sees in the papers etc., my mind and heart is very troubled and anxious.

January 4, 1918   **Hyde Park Hotel**

My very dear Father,

Upon my return from Aldershot on Wednesday . . . I found a letter, a very old one of November 14th from O. . . . and in it some reference to former letters, and which I have never received, regarding certain things I am to try to arrange with his securities in Phila. and which he is unable to get at.

I shall not guess at things, but evidently an explanation clear and reasonable will one day be forthcoming re his cable to Uncle Joe for a loan, which according to his letter he wished, and this evening the wife of the American Consul General [at Tiflis—Ed.] came in to see me and she said her husband had spoken several times of O. in letters which she had got all together (for two months she had none!) and she says O. was working at a big scheme with her husband, but that it had been O. undoubtedly who has saved that part

of Russia from the hands of the Germans. This was a great thing
to hear and Mary Noel-Hill was here with me when she said it and
it gave us both a start of delight to hear this calm, quiet woman
say such a thing. You might tell this to Uncle Joe, as it opens up
a great many possibilities and suggestions, but do not mention it
otherwise. Now please insist upon it not being even spoken of or
hinted of as no one but this lady has told me of this. W.O. only
said he was doing valuable work. You and Uncle Joe and Aunt
Fanny, but no one else not even little Fanny please.

God bless you all, how much I wish we might go out together
to see you all when O. gets safely back, and please God he does
get back safely and soon, for I am sometimes nearly mad with depression and anxiety and loneliness.

January 18, 1918   **Hyde Park Hotel**

My dearest Aunt,

My letters from Offley come so few and far between—I know
he writes me most regularly—but our messengers are held up and
the journey becomes double and treble the time and length. I had
a note from an officer just returned from Tiflis and they—he and
his wife—were 42 days in coming to London!—a journey that in
normal times—or even just before the chaotic disturbances in Russia—only took some ten days to two weeks.

I hear from the W.O. that Offley has not yet left Tiflis—and this
afternoon I got a wire from him saying 'leaving tonight' and dated
January 16th. The young officer who is supposed to let me know
these things from the W.O. has been very remiss and unmindful of
'poor me'. However it must still be a long weary waiting before I
can hear again or more—even by wire—and I must write now to
Baghdad to meet him and please God he reaches there safely—and
comes also safely from there on, and that we may be able to keep
together, for these long and impossible separations are not easy
to go on with, very especially quite out of one's own home or I
should say house and home and accustomed environment. In trouble

sometimes one needs so much the place and things one is more or less familiar with—not that I do not find great pleasure and comfort in my charming quarters here—and in the few kind servants who knew my sisters and darling Mother and who all know Offley and ask after him constantly. I also find the greatest happiness in having O's beautiful old things about me—the portraits—I have seven in this room and they are much admired—so are my chairs—sweet white painted things—supposed to have actually been done by Angelica Kaufmann. Silhouettes of O.'s Aunts as children—a little water colour of 'Norton Hall' made in 1778—and with cattle grazing and two gentlemen in three-cornered or cocked hats walking with dogs and horses also—all looking very 18th century and quaint! Satin wood tables and I rub them and treasure them and wonder much of their former possessors—my Offley's people. You could easily imagine you were in some country-house.

It is fortunate I am interested in these things that can live with me inside four walls—as one cannot have the pleasures of motors or country drives—or of extending any hospitality beyond a 'rationed' tea or lunch. I take a brisk walk in the park sometimes or I walk back from my work on fine days. This afternoon I am going to tea with Mrs. Stephen. I must remember to take my own sugar when I go there this afternoon. So many take tea without sugar. I don't enjoy it thus—and now everyone has a sugar card of coupons for the months etc.—½ pound of sugar per week is one's allowance for everything to include that used in cooking too—and of butter 4 ounces per head per week I think. At any rate it is amazingly little. And when I think of the beautiful butter I always had in Simla—it was made in my own butter pantry—Stewart and Shaffrullah teaching the servants to set it and heat it, and Offley and all my friends so enjoyed it. Coal, too—we are of course rationed with—but here I am fortunate in having central heating in my little hall—and by having my bed-room and sitting room doors open when I am in—one can save coal and warm the rooms. My friends in houses have much to 'work out' and to try them, and so has one here—but of course to a very much less extent—and then all have a great pride in keeping within the requirements and none more abstemious than their Majesties—so Lady Keppel was telling me. They've never any pudding and most simple things and much cheese to make up for other deficiencies.

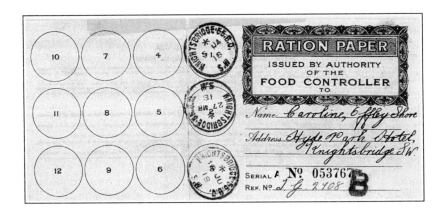

Lina's ration card in London, early 1918.

It is still some two months since O.'s had any pay—and the agent who collects it—his Banker—is as shocked as I am. Words fail one for the disgraceful behaviour of W.O. or I.O. in this particular, but I am very, very careful—and doing my best for my Beloved Offley whom I am afraid has been very anxious on my behalf, to say nothing of the anxiety that has been on his own account. He has had to advance to his young officers etc.—always confident the delay was somewhere in Russia!—but this is not the case.

Still no explanation of his telegram to Uncle Joe—but no doubt great stress of circumstances and anxiety for me as well as himself—and some 'mutilation' of the amount. I have wired him £500 and please God he gets safely back.

January 25, 1918   **Hyde Park Hotel**

My very dear Father,

We began our 'meatless day' today and everyone had fish. I lunched at the Baggallays, coming on from St. James' Palace and going on to King George's Hospital. A long afternoon with my men—and the new interest being two of their 'repatriated prisoners of war'. Just back from Germany—both my men had an arm or a

leg amputated, one his right arm and Juliet said it was the same
with hers. No endeavor was made to save a limb for a moment. I
fear they have been through most awful experiences and I dread
what our poor Americans will have to suffer in their turn. I see lots
of American soldiers in the streets now—and I am struck by the
fact of how many wear glasses!

The death of Sir Beauchamp Duff was—it seems to me—a very
graceful thing and surely a great relief. He had his chance and failed,
failed so distinctly and everywhere that one cannot but feel he is
better in another world. More I will not say—in his day he had
done very brilliantly—made an excellent Chief of Staff to Lord K.
in India and had a long and good record to his credit up to the time
of this war, and then he failed right and left and in everyway. It is
colder tonight but we have had a week of mild weather after intense
cold and I seem to have caught cold! and my throat aches though
I think it is nothing but being lonely and anxious and tired out.

I cannot now hear from Offley for some time—perhaps a month—
even by wire and the days are hard to wait through. I expect Florence
tomorrow or Sunday for a few days leave. She means to go to Scotland to some cousins for part of it, but I hope she will spend a few
days with me or in town at any rate. I am so glad that Aunt Fanny
has got through so well and I hope she continues to be strong and
well and all the better for it. Tell Fanny her box of sweets has saved
my life—indeed they have—and what I shall do when they are gone,
I don't know. I think I wrote to Uncle Joe or Aunt Fanny, that we
now have American airmen going up in London at nights. Lady
Keppel told me this.

February 5, 1918   **Hyde Park Hotel**

Dear Uncle Joe,

Last night I had a grateful surprise. I was sitting sewing, waiting
for Florence to come in—when the telephone rang and it was Mrs.
Willoughby-Smith to ask me to dine with them that evening to meet
Mrs. Marsh. Mrs. W.S. is wife of the American Consul General at

Tiflis and Mrs. M. is the wife of Col. Marsh who has just returned from there—where she was with her husband up to December 1st and saw Offley. She was very full of politics and her own experiences and importance—but I had my head right enough to ask her various questions I particularly wanted to know, and though she could not tell me much about his journey she told me the route she thought he would take and that he would, of course, have an escort—this has much relieved my mind.

In one of your recent letters you said you would be so glad to send something to any hospital through Mr. Clement Newbold's British Relief work. My hospital is the King George Hospital, Stamford Street, London, S.E., Waterloo is the district. If gifts, do send them to the above hospital but address to Mrs. Algernon Hay, Lady Ripon's Gift Stores, and much to be wished for are gifts of 'sweets' these days and also gramophone records. No doubt shoes will be much appreciated too.

I have just seen Mrs. Hay this evening after my visits to my men. The last new men in have been repatriated prisoners of war—and such nice brave fellows. The older men were not inclined to speak of their experiences but I sat for half an hour with a young fellow with his right leg only a stump and a friend—an armless one of the Middlesex Rgt.—these two had been together and they talked very calmly but very freely of the treatment—the starvation and the sneers they were subjected to—not bitterly, however they said they had been shown maps of England with the place marked where London had been, as it was now utterly destroyed—by German aeroplanes etc. etc. 'But we knew better than that', said these two lads—'though we got to thinking about it sometimes and wondering'. How nice they are, how grateful and pleased to see me—in their own way. I had a long talk with a man from Leicestershire—we talked of hunting and the 'old days'—as though I knew of every water jump or 'Bull-finch' in Melton—but this Great War vanished and we—(I along with him)—were carried back into almost fairyland—to those blessed pre-war days in his beloved Shire. Sometimes I'm told all about the laundry business—just as if I was going into it—sometimes it's Staffordshire and pottery. There I am on more familiar ground and another of my men was a 'seaman' and he can draw and sew and talks to me of pictures and history. You would be amazed at the things I am learning.

We have been put on very careful rationing with the first of this month and yet the prices of what little we may have have been put up enormously. When I came in yesterday I found a notice in my room that a scuttle of coal would be henceforth 4 shillings and six pence! It has been 2 shillings and so it is with everything. One slice of war-bread and one wee bit of butter or margarine is 6 pence.

I gave up my maid to retrench and now I fear I shall next have to give up my sitting room. Telephone calls are 4 pence each.

Their Majesties have come back to town again from York Cottage so we shall no doubt have some 'Crowned head' 'poppin' ' in any day. You know the swagger way of talking. The fashionables leave all their 'g's' off at the end of the past [sic] participle!—comin', goin', huntin', and yachtin' etc. quite catchin' (!!) I assure you! while the lower classes haven't an H. among 'em! My regiment is the King's Woyal Wifles etc. and then the Wifle Brigade and so it goes. When one's heart is heaviest there's ever something to see the funny side to.

From the first sentence of the above letter it is apparent that Florence was again in London. On this occasion Lina commented to her father:

Poor old Florence—she is so shy and difficult, though I know she adores O. and takes me into her big, kind heart with the same adoring affection—but she is entirely wrapped up in her work—a great blessing of course—but I find her so hard to understand. I go on chattering like a magpie and she says nothing but 'Yes' and 'No'. I find she knows several people—I might have had to meet her—but she only tells me all too late.

February 28, 1918   **Hyde Park Hotel**

My very dear Father,

Somehow I have been finding it really difficult to sit down and write letters lately. Not that I have not much to tell you, but it is just that spirit of restlessness and expectant anxiety that I cannot throw off while I know Offley is making his long and difficult journey.

Well—on Thursday I saw the Queen and yesterday I saw Mr. W. T. Ellis who had so lately seen you and my Beloved Aunt Fanny and Uncle Joe. It was such a happy thing to have heard of actually seeing and talking to you all so very recently. Just before Mr. Ellis came I had a telephone message from a friend to meet her in the Park for a walk as she had something wonderful to tell me of O. Naturally I flew out and she told me of a magnificent thing my Best and dearest has done and which she heard from Lord Southborough. So I hope one day we shall all hear of it and more of it. Please God he comes home safely. It is all very well for people to talk and say he could come home any way—etc. etc. He is under orders and must come as his Chiefs will it. It is already 6 weeks since he left his appt. and it is likely to be all that time and more again before he can return here—and this—if he is not kept anywhere in another job.

Well—dear Father—now to tell you about my wonderful Queen. Owing to Lady Keppel's nice, kind, charming self I was particularly picked out to be distinguished by H.M. who came right up to me in my corner of our work room in that delightful old Palace and she asked me all sorts of things about the work in Philadelphia, about Betty—my sister—and so on—so I said my little part as graceful as I could and of Betty and Bessie Hays and how the whole thing began in my old house and home. She said the things were so nice—and she hoped much had not been lost—etc. and then she asked me all about myself and Offley and if I was quite comfortable here—in this hotel where I live—and of India and of my dear Lady Bradford—Her Woman of the Bed-Chamber for so many, many years—and in fact I felt I was talking to the kindest and most interested of old friends. She looked extremely handsome. Her gold, gold hair is now streaked with white—like silver—and it is most becoming. She wore a green cloth dress and brown furs and wonderful emerald earrings. Five gentlemen in waiting came with her and as there are but six of us in Lady K's working party we had a most happy visit and laughed and chatted with greatest pride over our work and our 'machines'.

Today one of my fellow workers and I came through the State

dining room and looked at the portraits as we passed—all the Kings and Queens from Edward VI down to Victoria. But there was one bare space and someone was missing—the portrait that hung next to an exquisite Lawrence of George IV. 'It is George the III who's gone!' said my companion, so I replied, 'Of course it is and out of consideration for <u>my</u> feelings!'

March 2, 1918   **Hyde Park Hotel**

My very dear Uncle

You speak of the many good friends I have—<u>indeed</u> I have— many and so many who are well worth the knowing and having. I was just off this afternoon to see an old friend [when] in came Sir Percy Lake—free—a Saturday afternoon and going to Chelsea Hospital to see the Commandant, so going in the same direction he accompanied me. Some day I <u>do</u> wish <u>you</u> would write him a little letter to say how deeply I appreciate and value the friendship he has ever displayed toward me—he and Lady Lake. He is a wonderful man—of sterling worth and puritanical character— perhaps not quite forceful enough as a soldier—but for so much that goes to make up a high principle and true friendship, I value all that he and Lady Lake have been in their affectionate attachment to Offley and myself.

What a calamity this Russian debacle is—will the elements in one way or another conspire to defeat the wicked Hun in attaining his infamous ends—Je m'en doute! It is too late for the snow and ice that Napoleon met with and one scarcely credits the present day Russian with the pluck or character to set his land on fire. O.'s reports of conditions are appalling. I am so thankful he is out of that country, where I hear he has done <u>magnificently</u> as far as he could deal with them.

The 'calamity' Lina referred to in this letter was the opening by Russia of negotiations with Germany in December 1917 leading to the Peace Treaty of Brest Litovsk signed on 3 March.

On 6 March Lina reported to Uncle Joe:

A message from the W.O. that my precious Best—had reached Baghdad in safety and the A.C. had ordered him to proceed to England. <u>Thank God</u>, and please the same good Heavenly Father—he comes safely and with all speed. He comes via Paris and to see General Foch en route—I am thinking if there is permission to meet him there possible—that to Paris I'll go—but one must still wait some weeks yet to think of this and maybe it will be wiser to receive him here and that <u>here</u>—in his <u>own</u> surroundings with his own old pictures and furniture and with all the pleasures of such a little bit of home-like atmosphere as does exist—and will increase—once he is in these rooms—it would be a far happier welcome, for from here he would not have to move again—and I should be fresher than after the exigencies of the journey with all of its attendant requirements.

March 14, 1918   **Hyde Park Hotel**

My dearest Aunt,

No further news from my Dearest precious Offley since the wire letting me know of his safe arrival in Baghdad and I find it <u>very</u> hard to be patient. I count and re-count the days that must elapse ere he could possibly get here—and I try to interest myself in everything round me.

Today I heard that some property Lord Crewe had sold, and also Lord Shaftesbury, had been bought by the great London chemists Boots. He has shops all over London—rather like 'Evans' of Philadelphia, Lady Hindlip told us with much amusement—and Lady Keppel in her bright and charming way said 'Ah, Master and Miss Boots may one day come to the "dancing class" and prove a "parti" for my Anne or Victoria!'. We all laughed but these things are often only too true. But wasn't it all <u>so Philadelphian</u>! I find London—the families and friends one is thrown with just a counterpart of my beloved old home—just the same family pride, just the same interest in cooks and accounts and what we have to eat, drink, or avoid—just the same snobbishness. [It will be remembered that Lina's beloved grandfather founded a very successful pharmaceutical business in Philadelphia—Ed.]

On Friday I went to spend a long afternoon with Lady Keppel—in her sweetly pretty house—I may have written you of it before—it opens out of the Ambassador's Court and is part of St. James' palace.

Lady Keppel made so much of me in her very simple, unaffected way, both with the Princess Victoria and with the Queen—and said— 'I hope you really felt you had a nice talk with H.M. She told me she (the Queen, bless her) was so glad to have talked with you about your husband and India and Philadelphia.' As for Princess Victoria, I find her immensely agreable.

You will think my letter so full of great names and the Royalties—but I am lucky to be so happily thrown into the good company of these particularly pleasant members of this London World and they make me feel my very best self—I do assure you—and I talk of you and Uncle Joe to them just as I talk to you of them!

On 31 March, Lina wrote to Aunt Fanny of the great 'Spring Offensive' when the Germans, after a surprise attack beginning with a bombardment of 6,000 guns and a dense gas attack, broke the British line and in two weeks advanced 40 miles.

The week has run on and I have never written to you—as is my usual custom to do—but we have been going through grave and anxious days for the past week and more—with our kith and kin all in the thick of this desperate struggle—and I—with my most precious one probably on the high seas again. You can in no ways imagine what the strain is here—although perhaps you, my dearest Aunt, can better than others having had to go through those dark days of the Civil War.

April 28, 1918   **Hyde Park Hotel**

My dearest Aunt and Uncle Joe,

Have I missed writing you before another week is out? I am afraid I have, but if I do so sadly depart from writing regularly my excuse is that I am so busy, so deeply engrossing myself in my work to keep me from the anxious, restless thoughts that torment me in my impatient waiting for O. People say to me, 'But you are so patient, Mrs. Offley' and cheer me on. I hope I am, but I am ever hoping and praying please God He brings him safely and soon. This is Sunday and I have had a very pleasant day with the Baggallays from luncheon to tea and then on to Lady Sprot's to see Sara Mann and her baby girl who parted with Husband and Father this morning at 7 a.m. after long leave and a job in Norfolk near his old home, as Major Mann is a young Gunner and has been 3 times wounded, but he bravely went off and was eager to get back to his guns, while Sara and even baby Anne, not yet 3 years old, could not hear his name mentioned without bursting into floods of tears. I looked at this sweet black-eyed, brown-haired little person and then said to Sara, 'Well, there may be something of her sweet Mother in her that I should see, if I knew her better, but she is the absolute image of her Daddy!' and as I said, 'Daddy', up went Grandmamma's hand and Aunt's and visitor's and Mamma's, and floods of tears from this sympathetic little morsel until she was calmed and diverted by a little shawl and baskets and other things. Such a great consolation she is to her Mother! But I must struggle on alone and try to understand 'it is best for me thus'. Oh, the weariness of it all and the wondering and longing but, please God he comes soon and safely and well.

!!!!!!!

May 6, 1918

And now O. is here and the whole world is changed. On Tuesday the 30th, about 7 or 7:30 in the morning my telephone rang and it was O.! Telephoning me from Southampton to let me know he was once more safely back in England.

Needless to say I made hot haste to get up and dress and have everything in readiness for O.'s arrival here. I got lovely Spring flowers and a young lilac tree and the rooms looked delightful with the tulips and daffodils and wild hyacinths and primroses and some wonderful carnations and a few lilies-of-the-valley and after arranging these and his dressing things I thought I would help the maid to make my bed, as I could neither sew, nor read, nor write, I was so agitated, and chatting away with my house-maid, spreading the bed, and putting on one of our own pretty counterpanes, when in walked my magnificent General Sahib Bahadur.

He looked older, and <u>very thin</u> and greyer, but he looked well and I felt both our hearts beating and throbbing as he put his arms around me. We have been so very happy every day and all day talking and talking and telling each other so much! so many things! He had a very anxious journey all the way from Alexandria, spent a day with the Embassy in Paris and came back quite quickly the latter part of his way, but it has been long and hard, taking in all nearly four months. Through heat, and ice and snow.

When I telephoned to my work room that 'I would not be there today' nor could I lunch at the Palace, as I was to have done, <u>everyone</u> sent me a note, a wire, or a telephone message of congratulations.

The following Tuesday I took O. to King George's Hospital to see my K.R.R.s and he saw and talked to Mrs. Hay.

We lunch and dine and fly round together as one does on a honeymoon. Of course there are days when he spends hours away from me at the W.O. and the F.O., but I know this must be and I am picking up my work again two or three days a week instead of every day. We have both got appalling colds, and O. seems to have a good deal of fever and today we have had to change over rooms from the beloved little flat where we lived when we were here before when we were first married and in which I have spent my lonely, weary days without him, but as we have each other now perhaps it does not so much matter. I wish so much Lord Reading [British Ambassador at Washington] would ask for O. to come to U.S. and to Washington.

May 14, 1918

Have I ever thanked you dear Aunt Fanny <u>enough</u> for your kindness and sympathy and generosity, yours and Uncle Joe's to me and to O., your lively and untiring interest and your wonderful sympathy and understanding. I <u>do so always</u> from my heart and in my prayers and so does O. He is now in bed with all sorts of coats and covers on top of him to try and break this horrid fever. His cousin has come in to talk to him and I am at <u>last</u> finishing my letter to <u>dearest</u> you and Uncle Joe.

The four letters following were written by Offley during the weeks after his return, the first being to his sister-in-law Betty.

May 3, 1918 **Hyde Park Hotel**

My dearest Lady B,

Me voilà—enfin de retour! I left Tiflis on 16th January and have been 3½ months on the continuous journey—down through the Persian passes blocked with snow to Baghdad—thence down river to Basra—Bombay—Suez—Alexandria—Cairo—Luxor—Marseilles —Paris—Havre—etc.: stayed with a number of interesting 'personages', and escaped your friend's submarine attentions—thundering lucky to get back. I found little Mistress Schatz looking very sweet and so thin, that I fear the poor little thing has been denying herself and worrying to an extent that has made me quite anxious. Her rooms here were too dainty and delightful for words—after the life I have been living, I can hardly believe my surroundings are real!

I cannot tell you yet what is going to happen to me—but hardly expect any further employment. Shall probably hear in the course of 10 days. At present we are wandering round shops, having luncheon and tea out—and I am just trying to get into perspective again— and preparing for a good old fight with the sleepy authorities on the subject of finance. That's another story, which I may recount to you someday, when we meet again.

I tell you, it is good to be back again and to be feeling well—just splendid—and it would have all been so much more interesting if I could only have had that little creature with me—despite all the frantic difficulties.

I am dying to hear all your news, and have often and often thought of you during the last 9 months. A 'compagnon de voyage' from Alexandria was Sir Richard Ewart from Dar-Es-Salaam who enquired in the kindest way after you. One of your Indian conquests, if you remember! Only had the inside of the day in Paris which was looking gloomy and cold. France as a whole was green but damp! and we haven't had much sun since I landed in this beautiful country.

They 'insulted' me by bestowing the 4th class of the Vladimir with swords on me as I was leaving Tiflis—(and I dodged the C. in C.'s farewell kiss, catching it on my neck below my left ear, instead of my cheek!). However, they had nothing else left to give, poor things, and as you know all honors and decorations are abolished in Russia—except the Cross of St. George for bravery and this Vladimir—the Anne and Stanislaus are only worn in the ribbon. I have come back with the minimum amount of kit—the Bolsheviks got all my beautiful plain clothes! and I suppose some 'howlers' are masquerading about even now in some of Mr. Pulford's best tweeds! Confound them. To Lina's astonishment I have landed my tea-basket, which over and over has saved my life!

Frisky times, my dear, and we are not through yet—but with the assistance of your people, we shall be, soon, I hope.

All my love to you—and write <u>at once.</u>

May 19, 1918   **Hyde Park Hotel**

My dear People:

I fear we shall have to leave it to a future meeting on your side of the water, to tell you several interesting facts re which I know you are dying to hear about. In the interval I can only beg of you to believe that worried almost beyond belief I never went actually 'off my head'. Things certainly developed in the most sudden and unexpected way, and I got badly 'left' as we say, by people on whom one was naturally leaning—and so on. And eventually got more or less swept out, 'with the dust' at the back door! The only comfort perhaps, was that the other fellow who came smirking up the garden to take my place, <u>never got in!</u>

At present I am enjoying a pestiferous go of malarial fever combined with an appalling cold on the chest, and therefore hardly looking my best. I am worrying myself about finding a job to carry me on after the war (as I don't want to go East again or leave Lina any more) and am ready to camouflage myself and take on a light outdoor job, or failing that even go into an office or a factory. I don't feel like loafing or sitting still. I feel if I have been able to see my recent circular tour through, I'm not quite so old or rusty as they make out—per contra: I think I've had my share of poisonous climates, and blankety blank

Exile and fortune's fickle side. So if you know of anything, let me know quickly. You all know how adaptable I am!

The view from our windows here looking over the Park to Hornsey Rise in the North is <u>too beautiful</u>, with the Serpentine and the Row just below and the gorgeous trees all coming out with the lilacs and flags and azaleas and stocks and the glorious maytrees and laburnums. The green of the grass is too wonderful, in the sunlight, and air positively delicious. I am so grateful to think this is where Lina was able to pass the long months of separation.

May 22

We have had a few days of unusual heat, but are still hesitating about discarding our underclothes—they seem however to have done <u>me</u> good and I think my cold and fever are breaking. I am now diving into boxes left behind, to try to find some plain clothes, in which I shall hope to take refuge and hide myself from the salutes. Also, for the third time during this war, I have reverted to the rank of Colonel and must get all my badges changed. I think you may bet on 'Mr.' being good enough for <u>me</u>, when we are all dismissed and I am finished with this nonsense!

We had an air raid a night or two ago. L. and I went down to some of her friends on the 2nd floor (we are on the 6th), but I didn't hear the buzz of the Hun machines on account of the barking of our own guns—and I didn't see anything exciting going on in the sky, because Lina would pull me away from the windows! It's extraordinary how naturally everybody takes these things now-a-days—and 4 years ago they would have stood for hours in the streets gazing up at them, (until there came a blinding flash close by - - - -).

May 29, 1918   **Hyde Park Hotel**

My dear Uncle Joe,

I am interested to see by your letter of the 6 May that you good people are evidently under some impression that I have been detailed to France—but unfortunately that is not the case. A colleague of mine in Tiflis asked me, when passing through Paris, to go and see Gen. Foch, and personally report to him on the activities of the French in S. Russia—this, owing to that General's subsequent (to my departure) elevation to Generalissimo, I was naturally unable to do. Voilà tout.

Whatever plus or minus results may have been—of one thing I am at least convinced and satisfied and that is, that I established the most friendly relations with all the foreigners with whom I was brought in contact, and knew privately the terms in which they referred to their own Governments on my being recalled. I do not think they were lying out of mere politeness! Events over which I had no control, swept me 'out of the back door with the dust'! and I take it, my so called mission failed, and like so many other good intentions, all one's efforts 'were sent down below'. Pure matter of luck and concomitant circumstances. The stars in their courses were against me. I often think of an eloquent cartoon in 'Puck' or 'Life', depicting a long road leading to eventual success and glory, away on the horizon: the road was thickly strewn with the graves of thousands who had fallen by the way,—in their endeavor to attain success: the motto was 'These also win who have struggled yet fallen in their great endeavor' or something to that effect.

My various efforts appear to have gone to swell those who 'also ran'. The only thing that counts, here below, is to reach that horizon, or to stand up there, once you've reached it!!?

I am not much of a believer in Democracies—anyway we haven't arrived at the right kind of democracy yet. You remember Kipling's 'As Easy as A.B.C.' and 'Macdonogh's Song' in his 'A Diversity of Creatures'? and our system of party politics bids fair to be our own undoing. Self interest and blank unscrupulousness seem to be the only principle of life. Perfectly appalling?

When I think of intelligent Russians asking me whether they had not, at least, been successful in pointing the way to the Democracies of the Future—I simply gasp and wonder what purpose the Gods can have in turning the whole world mad! hopelessly, idiotically, mad. We haven't begun to understand the fundamental laws of existence. Who is to teach them?

June 11, 1918   **Hyde Park Hotel**

My dear Uncle Joe,

I am reading with great interest your copy of Mr. Davis' Handbook
of N. France—though I put it a bit above the powers of assimilation
of the average American private soldier! It makes me think a bit
and hold my head, every now and again. Enclosed may interest
you as the latest 'chit' or 'Servants character' that I have received
—but it must be acknowledged that the Russians know how to be
polite—even if they do 'lay it on with a soup ladle' in the matter
of praise. As a matter of fact I was opposing them to such an extent
that I must have been a positive thorn in their side: yet this is their
'godspeed you'. Per contra, my own people have not even had the
good grace to say 'thank you for what you have done', or even—'we
are distinctly displeased with you'. Not one d—ned word. Talk about
psychology! no wonder the Hun finds us an almighty puzzle.

The march of events in France is, of course, a daily absorbing topic
for us all. There is a great deal of public criticism of our own people—
but I fancy, in the main, wonderful results are being achieved and
while we bite our own people's tails, we forget to allow for the enemy's
failures and desperate straits. Whilst I deprecate our continual paeans
of joy over his 'appalling losses' which he is incurring knowingly and
carelessly, his breaking point may not be far off, if we only knew it!
The ordinary man in the street is only surprised that we have not been
able to assume the offensive with a 5 to 1 superiority at the moment
of a standstill being called to the enemy's massed attack. 'Le retour
offensiv'. But of course we don't know enough—although we appreciate—i.e. some of us do—the colossal nature of such a movement.
Certainly the Hun offensive is an amazing triumph of staff work and
discipline—and their intelligence systems must be marvellous. The
great thing is the armies are confident of holding him, tho' they are
giving more ground than we care about.

I personally would like to be employed in some way over on
your side—or, in conjunction with your people and the Japs in
Siberia—Vladivostock side, but don't know how to work it as one
can't ask personally here—with much chance of success.

Mr. Laughlin of your Embassy in London has forwarded a copy
of a letter I wrote him on the subject of my pleasant relations with
Mr. Willoughby Smith, American Consul at Tiflis—to your State

Dept. Washington, which I hope may do W. Smith some good—his wife who has been v. ill, is close by here, and we saw her last night. She has had no direct news from her husband for months—only communications from Moscow in April to the belief that he was alive and well. Tiflis is pretty well cut off.

General Count de la Panouse, Mil. Attaché of the French Embassy has also forwarded my letter about my relationships with my French colleagues in the S. Caucasus to Gen. Foch—who, if he ever has the time to read it, may do something for them. It was the least I could do, in return for all their courtesy and kindness, and at all events proves that I 'got on' all right with both Americans and French. I also know, privately, what they said about me to Washington and Paris and so on.

Lina and I have been busy fixing ourselves up at the dentist, cleaning, replacing and renovating my attenuated field kit—and I am ready for further activities if they come my way.

Florence says deuced little, but I conclude came in for some of the recent Hun bombing of the hospitals tho' she seems terrified of mentioning the occurrence! I have told her we read all about it in our newspapers! Gov. casualties: what the hades is there to keep from the public? The same everlasting foolery.

The Financial Dept. of our Sanctified W.O. and I are having a special campaign of our own on the subject of the very heavy amount I am out of pocket, as a result of my recent deputation! and I can't give an idea yet as to what my chances are of getting it all back. They really are antediluvian in their methods, and past description, mean.

The 'chit' referred to in the above letter reads as follows:

Order
by the GOC in C. Caucasus Front

Tiflis
19 Dec. 17
2 Jan. 18

The principal British military agent (General Shore) attached to the staff of the Cauc. Front is vacating his appointment and leaving the Caucasus.

During the relatively short time that Gen. S. has occupied this position he has known how to evoke the liveliest sympathy from and command the respect of, all those with whom he has been brought in contact.

Devoted to his work he has rendered inestimable services in the matter of liaison between the British and Russian Armies.

Taking leave of Gen. Shore I consider it my duty to express to him both on my own part and that of the Staff at the Front our genuine gratitude for his useful activities and to wish him strength and health in the new Sphere to which the English High Command has called him.

General of Infantry—Prjevalsky

Over the period that Offley was writing these letters Lina gave a much more detailed account of the state of his health.

May 18, 1918   **Hyde Park Hotel, London**

My dear Uncle Joe,

Offley has had a bad attack of his old tropical malaria fever complicated by a very bad cold so that I have had him in the house for ten days—and <u>very</u> anxious I have been about him. He has treated himself as he did when he last had it—in Simla—just four years ago—but though better, it still hangs on, so tomorrow I am determined to send for a doctor whom Lady Lawley has told me of and who understands these tropical fevers. His temperature goes to an appalling height as is the case in India with such things. No doubt it is the re-action—after all his hard and weary work and travelling through storm and snow, through heat and dust. The excitement of it all kept him going and now in the luxury of his own surroundings—a good bed to lie in (alas he goes and puts himself in it and does not feel equal to moving further from it than a few feet!!!!). This is very unusual for Offley unless he is really ill! and looking so thin as he does—and so much older—it gives me a great heart ache. I <u>do</u> very sincerely wish he would be <u>asked for by and from</u> <u>the U.S.A.</u> on some mission. Does not anyone of the family—my brother George—or Adolph, who you say goes to Washington—come in touch with the British Mission or Lord Reading and could put in a nudge and O.'s name, to be asked for <u>there</u>? You see one cannot go oneself <u>here</u> and say 'Please send me to Washington to co-operate with the Americans—in Forestry—or over the Russian question etc. etc.' Can one? but, as I understand, that for his happy cooperation and assistance with the American and French Missions in Tiflis—he—Offley—has been spoken of to General Foch and to Washington as well as Paris so that he and his work must be somehow known at your headquarters.

June 30, 1918   **Hyde Park Hotel**

My dearest Aunt,

So behind hand do I feel these days and so rushed from the time I get up until the time I go to bed again that everything has a sense of being badly done or not done at all—altogether unsatisfactory—and it is ever thus with one's letters—and you my dearest and best of Aunts—so <u>unfailing</u> in your regular letter, I feel most deeply and unhappily about—if I do not get off my weekly one to you.

[Everyone is saying to Offley] 'Government ought to avail themselves of such a man as you are.'—while to me they put it more strongly and say, 'a man of such brilliance as your husband etc. etc.' and yet <u>they</u>—the Government officers under whom he has served have treated him so casually. It is shocking and all one can see—or say—is that they are jealous of him—and only satisfied 'to pick his brains'. However I am most thankful to have him safely back and only hope some 'turn in the lane' is at hand that may take Offley into different spheres of activity and where he comes into more of <u>his</u> own—as it were.

We dined at Nanny Burr's and are taking her two merry young daughters to the big baseball game July 4th of which I shall write you before closing my letter.

July 4th: Independence Day

And such a July 4th! How many moments today have I felt choking with emotion. Offley and I went down to luncheon where we found American flags at the head of the menus and charming little silk ones stuck in the flowerpots that decorated our table. When we went out to find Sewell with his taxi we saw Knightsbridge <u>brilliant</u> with splendid American flags and our hotel doorway draped with a magnificent and huge one. Char-a-bancs filled with American soldiers and sailors, old four-in-hands and motors or taxis filled the streets as we drove through Park Lane and into Hill Street to pick up Nannie and her girls and the whole way out to Chelsea there was shouting and cheering such as one never before heard in one's life in London. It was like Philadelphia on a great Football game day—<u>only more so</u>—and when we got to our seats, which were excellent—I think I never heard such pandemonium. Everyone who came in was treated to loud yells and cheers. Just in front of us sat Lady Randolph Churchill, the Duchess of Marlborough and Lady Herbert and her husband. Lady Dawson and Sir Douglas— who is the King's Comptroller of the Household, and she the Secretary and my fellow worker at St. James's Palace. Clive Wigram the King's Military Secretary and of O.'s old regiment, the 18th Bengal Lancers and his wife—then in the royal party came Queen Alexandra looking so wonderfully young and handsome—the Princess Royal and her two daughters—and my friend, the Princess Victoria, the King and Queen and Princess Mary and several American Army and Naval officers— and the roars and shouts and cheers—made even O's eyes fill and all it meant and means to us—this splendid—this magnificent Race Federation and in such a cause. Everyone seemed delighted with the hearty pleasure and fine spirit displayed everywhere—and I assure you I <u>do</u> think our King is marvellous—God bless him. There he sat, first beside the Queen and then between his lovely mother and sisters, chatting and delighting in it all. I said to Nannie 'It's very Philadelphian here again—for everywhere there is a family party!'. Everybody talked to their neighbors and it was as hot as hot could be, as it should be for a 'Glorious Fourth!'. Offley decorated little Pamela Burr's hat with an American flag and in fact all London was more American in appearance today than anything one could ever have imagined.

July 27, 1918   **Hyde Park Hotel**

My dearest Aunt,

I am putting into my letter various enclosures about the successful time we had at 'The Shower' of gifts at Queen Mary's Nursing Guild. I also wish to put into my letter my best birthday greetings to you dear Aunt Fanny for August 13th. Many happy returns of the day. We are all feeling so pleased and proud of the splendid fighting men the Americans have proved themselves and that things are going more happily in France. It is most comforting to hear on all sides the liveliest admiration of the Americans and 9 times out of 10 I am not suspected of or known to be one and thus I have the pleasure of getting a very sincere appreciation. We are still busily house-hunting and have seen about 2 to our taste but there is always some drawback. At the same time I feel I am more practical and shrewd at taking over a house—than most people, as I have lived in so many and benefitted, I think, by being by your side and dear Mother's when you were arranging your houses. Of course one wants a small house—but after being in India in the big rooms it does give one a very cramped feeling to be in too small rooms and then too one has one's furniture to consider—if one went into a very wee house—the lovely old things of Offley's would all have to be sold as they are too large—however no doubt something will turn up. I want a good open out-look, nice neighborhood—and altogether a good investment—a house that I can rent easily etc.

We have closed down our work for a little rest and I feel the need of it. My hospital work continues and we now have a lot of Americans in the hospital—the very first one I met with coming from Philadelphia—from 61st and Woodbine Ave. and belonging to the National Guard before he joined up—such a nice man—and this brings me to some new work which I am just taking up and which I do plead for your assistance and Mrs. Scull's—to whom I shall write at once. It is to help the loyal Russians and those who continue to be our allies—to help themselves and to give them all the help we can. Here in England are many Russian men and women of the very best class—penniless and how are they to go on?! I met at Lady Egerton's, who is the Russian wife of a British diplomat (he is now dead) the most delightful men and women stranded here because the Russian Govt. is no longer able to pay them—and the present Govt. in Russia is not one they credit. Charlotte Bellairs—with her great heart—is helping all she can and the proposal is to open a shop to which these ladies can send their handiwork and their things of artistic value, but to start it we want some subscriptions. Uncle Joe will tell me who in Philadelphia is in touch with Russia and to whom to apply for subscriptions. Are there any of the Harrison family who made their great fortunes in Russian railways—to whom one could write for a donation? If I should do well in engaging the interest and sympathy in America in this good cause it might take me there—to the U.S.A.—to see the scheme increase and develop. I cannot tell you more of the plans just yet—but the scheme is a great deal bigger than just the shop and Russians here. We hope to see it become an Anglo-American Relief that will take the good Russians back to Russia at an early opportunity etc. etc.

August 17, 1918   **Hyde Park Hotel**

My very dear Uncle Joe,

You may remember how many wonderful schemes O. had for the salvation of Russia and that part of that great country in which he worked so desperately and so earnestly for the Allies when Chief of the British Military Mission there. The F.O. here seemed very pleased with him, but the W.O. under whom he actually was, received his ideas with derision. However here is some real gratification, a small thing in its way but to me it gives the very greatest pleasure and I do so much wish the 'Gaulois', who has published it, did but know and give the name of the man whose 'daring conception' they so rightly admire. It is a little bit of history making that Monsieur Jusserand [French Ambassador at Washington 1902–15—Ed.] might be proud to publish, i.e. the name of the man whose scheme it was and that has been carried out with an entirely unjust secrecy to that man.

It was O., and O. utterly and entirely alone against the most tremendous odds, that risking his life in making the journey from Baku down to Baghdad, through dust and heat, through ice and snow, without even a personal body servant and with an escort he had to teach and to assist through every conceivable hardship is now in London unacknowledged for one of the biggest and most brilliant plans of the present demands of this appalling war. His idea was that at one and the same moment the Japanese and Americans should move into Vladivostok and the British up from Mespot and Persia to the Caspian etc. etc. This he advocated from Tiflis in Oct. Nov. Dec. Jan. and always and constantly by telegram, and it was scouted and laughed at. He now thinks that commercial pressure must have been brought about to make them try. This he also had a hand in as well, so strongly did he feel. I think I wrote you how happily he got on with his French confrères in the Caucasus and if his return journey had not made him just too late to see Gen'l Foch in Paris, his, O.'s, name might have been sent in for some recognition by France which even yet would be graceful, as he did much for the Frenchmen he worked with and for all, as Mr. Ellis must have told you.

Lina in the above letter was referring to this press cutting from the Evening Standard *of 17 August:*

BAKU EXPEDITION

"SIGNAL FOR LIBERATION OF ARMENIA."

The "Gaulois," describing the arrival of the British in the Caucasus as a tour de force, says:

"It is not a commonplace achievement to send an important expedition from its base at Bagdad to the shores of the Caspian Sea, about a thousand kilometres, without railways or roads. What must be admired in this tour de force is less, perhaps, the skill employed in the execution of this plan than its daring conception. We may congratulate ourselves upon the task already accomplished by our British friends and the consequences which it may have.

"The march to Baku not only gives the signal for the liberation of Armenia, but it may also have great influence upon the regeneration of Southern Russia. In any case, it must constitute a barrier which will arrest not only the appetites of the Turks dreaming of pan-Turanian expansion, but German plans for a march to India."—Reuter.

The operation described was known as Dunsterforce after its Commander, Major Gen. L. C. Dunsterville. The primary purpose was to secure the oil supplies in the Caspian area. In early February it advanced from Baghdad to Hamadan where as Gen. Dunsterville wrote in his The Adventures of Dunsterforce *(Edward Arnold, London, 1920) several important people were awaiting him: 'firstly Gen. Offley Shore, recently returned from Tiflis, who was to post me in all the latest information concerning the South Caucasus.' The force reached Baku on 4 August, but had to re- linquish it to the advancing Turks on 14 September.*

Life was quiet for the next two months. The following are extracts from Lina's letters which during this period run on from date to date.

August 25, 1918

In London the 'bus' and now the 'tube' strikes have been very serious and we feel it is so disgraceful when transportation is so important a factor in the war. At the same time one sympathises with those women who are doing exactly the same work as men did and yet have been getting less pay for it.

August 30, 1918

Here we are spending ten days with Juliet Baggallay and her children in a quaint old Hampshire cottage just across the field from another mutual friend and her boys—a Mrs. Bowker—a former school friend of Julie's, and we do have such good times together, Offley hay making or gardening or walking to his heart's content.

Nothing seems to come in the way of an appointment or work of some sort for my Beloved O—which is more than trying and irritating and yet he is kept on 'at disposition' by the W.O. on half pay and <u>worst</u> of all and unhappily—virtually idle in <u>these days</u>! Fortunately he is not embittered by this disgusting treatment—but is actively keeping up his Russian and in touch with all that goes on so far as he can from London.

September 2, 1918

In church on Sundays <u>everywhere</u> they now give praise and thanksgiving for the great assistance the Americans are giving us—this seems the most near and personal tribute one can imagine and is very gratifying to me who owes allegiance and love to both countries.

September 7, 1918

So quietly do the days fly by and weeks run into months with so much ever to be done and a holiday in the country all too soon finished and over.

Yes, the Americans are doing splendidly as <u>we</u> had every belief they would do—O. and I—and the nicest, pleasantest intercourse and friendship seems to be coming about between the two countries of all classes.

Clara wrote to me of Sarah's expectations—I can scarcely realize it is the same little Sarah we remember at our wedding. As for the ten years that have flown by since then I often wonder how it can be <u>so</u> long or why it is not really 20 or more. Offley often makes just the same fuss over me today as he did when we came here on our Honeymoon and there are no little land marks as the children would be to date us. I only wish there were.

September 21, 1918

Sir Douglas Haig finds time to write himself to O. which I value— from that very strained, very busy gentleman. I have felt very much worried over my Beloved O's position of affairs—<u>very worried</u> as I fear he has—(by having been too direct and straightforward in the letter to his chief on his return from Russia) created an enemy. As O. said— he thought he was working with a 'big man' and finds he was not—and I fear from various things one has heard etc. etc. that he, i.e. the W.O. man, under whom he <u>last</u> served—is <u>now</u> blocking him! This is

extremely serious—and I feel very deeply and strongly on the subject
and that this should not be the end to such a career. I am ambitious—but
I am more—I am anxious that O's services should not be lost to the
nation at such a time—and I also know that it is a very painful punishment to him with his active brain and body—with his broad experience
and brilliance—to be idle—utterly idle all this time.

Two young Americans came in about tea-time. They had just
reached here from Russia and Tiflis where O. had known them.
They have had a most difficult and exciting journey and are lucky
to have escaped with their lives—one of them said, 'When Gen'l.
O.S. was withdrawn from the Caucasus we lost the Caucasus for
the allies—his personality and his efforts and schemes had they been
looked to by Great Britain etc. we should have been in possession
there today!' This is of course very gratifying, but I am afraid it
does no good to say such things to me!

October 3, 1918

Isn't the war news splendid, but Oh! such ghastly fighting as
must be going on.

October 25, 1918

Lady Keppel, who had spent the afternoon yesterday at Marlborough
House, found Queen Alexandra and Sir Dighton Probyn working out a
scientific scheme of lighting the fire from the top—one O. had recommended to me and put a newspaper cutting about it away so carefully
that it cannot be found.

November 2, 1918

War news is very good and the Americans are doing magnificently
and one sees, actually sees, the end of the fighting clearly in view,
but oh, there is so much, so much else then to be done and as I have
just been writing to one of my good riflemen, 'Please God England
meets her re-action as manfully as she met her enemies.' Questions
political and social are very serious here. Truth is, I fear, the nation
is going today—as she has often before in history—strides ahead of

the Government—Labour looks us appallingly in the face—as one of our most difficult problems.

November 5, 1918

Offley in bed with a chill—and numbers of sad people who have struggled back from Russia coming to see him. I hope Uncle Joe's cold has disappeared. Colds these days make one anxious. I so hope to 'knock' Offley's as it is really good for him to stop in bed—fires are so short and a scuttle of coal so dear—4shs/6d!! that he is safest in bed with a hot water bottle.

And then ten days later:

My dearest Aunt,

Such wonderful things have taken place since last I wrote to you. The signing of the Armistice on Monday, the 11th and thus the end and Victory for the Allies and USA of this Great War. The announcement, made by the guns we knew so well here last winter, when warning us for an air raid, gave one a great thrill. Should one laugh or cry? I rushed in to O. who was sitting up in the drawing room and threw my arms round him and said, 'Now we shall go to America first thing!'. There was a great calm and quiet, as of some expectancy in the streets and suddenly people flew out and flags fluttered and there were screams and cries of joy and gaiety and weeping and shouting, and this seems to have gone on ever since.

I think the most wonderful and splendid thing of all is that all unconsciously and naturally the great crowds hurried directly to Buckingham Palace and there acclaimed their joy and happiness and amid all their sorrow (for many were crying) to our most wonderful King and Queen, and indeed they have been wonderful. Yesterday the Americans made a demonstration there and a great band and merry-making at the Horse Guards Parade, and last night there were beautiful fireworks in Hyde Park, which we could see and enjoy, as though they were in O.'s honour (!) from our windows. I wish I could write more happily of O. He has been very ill and looks so thin and worn. The temperature goes up at nights and his nights have been very restless and disturbed. Last night a little better he thinks, and I hope he is right.

I have not been to my work for nearly a fortnight, but I wrote to Lady Keppel and told her the reason and I feel sure she will understand. I was on my way to the Palace, St. James', on Monday to tell them and to express my good wishes and happiness at the news, but I found everyone had run off with the rest of the populace to Buckingham Palace, except the sentries, but even they had something to say! and saluted me in their great pleasure and in their turn showed their delight in the news.

Sunday, November 17, 1918

I should have liked to go to St. Paul's for the great Thanksgiving Service, but O. was not well enough for me to leave and so one must wait for some other great occasion and there is sure to be one. How wonderful will be the entry into Brussels of King Albert and Queen Elizabeth, she riding in white at his side, as she seems to have done all through the terrible war, to comfort and cheer their people.

It must be indeed a changed world even though we cannot realize it yet. Wilson has made a great name for himself, but I prefer to think and to say it is the great people—the Americans—who let him dictate and talk, rather than have the very slightest little word or thought of difference or discussion which has been what the Germans would like so much to bring about.

I enclose some very fine writing paper, initials with coronets. I remember when we were young people we used to collect these and perhaps my little cousins or nieces may do the same. When I was tearing up letters today I found them and enclose them.

The doctor came again today to see O. and wants me to take him out of town for a little change and we are planning to go to Eastbourne for a few days, if we can get rooms: failing that perhaps Bath. Of course we shall have to keep on our rooms here, or else we shall find ourselves homeless, as London is so full and rooms in such demand. We are most comfortable here, though we find our coal rations very meager in this cold weather.

So President Wilson is coming to France![3] Things do not look all they ought to in the carrying out of the Armistice demands, do they? and these devilish Germans appear to be as untrustworthy as ever. The Kaiser should not have one moment's respite in Holland and it is indeed a most unfriendly act in that country allowing him to be harboured there.

Well, my darling Aunt, if we cannot reach you for Christmas we shall make a great, great effort to go as soon after to America as it is possible. With dear, deep love and thanks.

Five days later Lina added to this account:

the wonder of it all here—has been the splendid way in which <u>all</u> classes have acclaimed the King and Queen. It is more like the adoration one sees in India to the persons of Their Majesties—and long may it last—and God bless them.

This was written on note paper of the King's Royal Rifle Corps and alongside the Regimental crest Lina wrote 'My Regiment and my sons!'

December 18, 1918   **Hyde Park Hotel**

My dearest Aunt,

I am much afraid we have missed the Christmas post to have our letters reach you in time. But rushed and busy is not the name for what I've been and my beloved Offley still so very wretched. The doctor says 'feeding up and sunshine and quiet' are what he requires. He suffers excruciating pain in his arm and back from the neuritis and he looks so thin and ill that I sometimes feel and <u>do</u> cry when I look at him—however we are otherwise making the most of the happiness of being together. I am so glad you liked the little 'Sou-bols'. They are very wonderful and beautiful to me—they are the work of the poor suffering lace makers of Belgium—made in Belgium of English thread sent to them. The lace is point-de-Venise. I have sent you six of the Arms of the Allied Nations and I hope some day to give you the rest of the set—14 in all. These are historical as actually having been made during the war. Tomorrow our own Generals return from France—or at least F.M. Sir Douglas Haig and his generals commanding armies etc. and I hope to go with Offley to his Club to see their State arrival and escort on their way to the palace to lunch with the King. The weather has been so bad—but I am hoping for a fine day and brilliant sun to greet our conquerors. What an ovation Mr. Wilson had in Paris—and I hope we shall see him here soon after Christmas. The sooner the better it would seem to me.

January 1, 1919   **Hyde Park Hotel**

My dearest Aunt,

Last night we drank your good health and that of all those who are dear to us but far away. We dined here quietly in our own rooms, only having Mr. Charles Burr as guest.

The President of the United States and Mrs. Wilson's visit went off beautifully and every one seems very pleased with it and I feel sure it makes for safer and sounder relations between the two countries. I was decidedly attracted to him and his agreeable appearance. Mrs. W. was pretty and attractive in face—otherwise she did not interest me. I hear from one of the Queen's ladies in waiting that the negro maid interested them all so much. I wish we had been at one of the great parties!

Our elections have surpassed everyone's most sanguine expectations—but oh—the problems for this dear old Empire to work out.

I had a charming little letter—by command—from the Queen this morning. She has, through the Needlework Guild given our King's Royal Rifles and the Rifle Brigade a most generous and prompt contribution and O. says it is all because I asked so nicely. Isn't it nice of him to flatter me thus?

London has been so full this winter and it has now grown very cold—and my Beloved O. feels the dampness—in general he is better, but the neuritis is so very painful. This morning came Uncle Joe's dear letter and its enclosure telling me of the splendid gift from both of you through the British Relief Society—for toffey for

King George's Hospital. Thank you both dear, dear generous aunt and Uncle. I hope it may be the same 'Ackers Toffey' as it gave great ease to the poor, parched throats of starving men.

Oh, dear, oh dear, how much and how often I wish you good people could come on a tour of inspection with me to my two beloved interests in my war work—my Queen's Guild and my King's hospital—it seems a curious thing that mere accident and good fortune put me in the way of these compensating interests.

The election referred to by Lina took place on 14 December and was known as the Khaki Election. A coalition Government, with Lloyd George again as Prime Minister, was formed with a programme of full reparations for the costs of the war; punishment of war criminals; restrictions on dumping of foreign goods in Great Britain. Women over 30 were enfranchised.

This is the last letter written from England. The next was written in Philadelphia early in March. None has been found covering what must have been a fairly sudden departure.

United States and Britain: 1919–22

There is no record of their journey from England to the United States. The following is the first extant letter after their crossing written from the Sinnickson home in Philadelphia. Salem, which Lina mentions, was the Sinnickson ancestral home in New Jersey, where her mother had been buried. The date 'full of memories' to which she refers is that of the death in 1890 of her maternal grandfather, George David Rosengarten.

March 18, 1919
230 W. Rittenhouse Sq.,
Philadelphia

My dearest Aunt,

Many thanks for the box with the pieces of my wedding dress—so beautifully kept. I intend taking it with me to Salem to see if it could be made up and useful for some of the vestments or a lecturn cover—as I think I told you.

Offley and I will use the tickets for the opera with pleasure tonight. And as I write I remember how full of memories this date must be to you—and to Uncle Joe—and I understand. To me too it brings such a host of recollections of <u>him</u> whom I adored and remember as the gayest, kindest and most delightful person who spoilt me exceedingly—as you dear Aunt Fanny and Uncle Joe and Offley have ever continued to do.

After three months stay in Philadelphia they began to travel to visit relations and friends and Lina wrote to Aunt Fanny on 16 June:

Thank you both so much for all the pleasures you were ever giving us during our long visit to Father and Fanny. It was very wonderful after those 4½ years of War to have actually achieved the accomplishment of a journey 'home' to Philadelphia to see you all again. We used to talk about it in India and again on the way home in 1917—and again Offley used to write of it in his letters from Russia—planning to take me—if he got back safely—and how I do thank God he came back to me and that we all have been together all these past few months and that we are soon to be with you again.

Lina was by now forty-nine: her relationship with her aunt was still as close as ever. While staying with Uncle Frank and Clifford in Jamestown, Rhode Island, she wrote on 4 September:

I cannot tell you how much I miss you and how you are always on my mind. I have a sense of something left out because I have not you, to run into your room and have a good talk or just sit silently by and knit and sew while you, dear Aunt Fanny, are writing—or at your accounts.

In the letters of this period there is no reference to their departure from England or any discussion of permanent plans or any indication of what they were proposing to do next. Then on 25 September they were en route via Montreal and Chicago to Santa Barbara, California, expecting either to return to the East Coast or to England in the spring. Offley had been suffering from a prolonged cough during the summer and it would seem that the doctors had advised that he spend the winter in a dry climate.

	San Ysidro Ranch
October 12, 1919	**Santa Barbara, California**

My dearest Aunt,

Your 2 letters, one from Lenox and the second yesterday from Beechwood Inn, with Uncle Joe's booklet describing the place, reached us here. We arrived last Tuesday evening and our delight and admiration are continually increasing. It is a wonderful and glorious climate and an amazingly lovely combination of sea and mountains, of trees and flowers and <u>this</u> particular spot. This Ranch and our wee cottage are perfect. Just the sort of little wee house and home we want for the moment. Set upon a hillside, in the midst of an orange grove, with palms and olives, eucalyptus, pines and pepper trees. We are looked after by a sweet and charming Englishwoman, whose place it is and who receives only such people as her friends send out to her or who are in some way introduced to her. She is the daughter of a clergyman who had a living in Warwickshire near Kenilworth and her mother and sister now live in Leamington. Mr. Johnstone was a Bostonian coming here first for his health and ending, as so many people have, by making it his home. He is now dead and Mrs. Johnstone, until her 3 children, 2 boys and a girl, aged 22, 20 and 18, are fixed in life, is running the place in this way, renting her cottages and providing the service etc. etc. The breakfast is brought to us by a Chinese boy, English or Irish-American maids do the housework or act as table maids in the dining room. Spanish Americans are the chauffeurs and gardeners, etc. and a Philipino is a sort of Jack of all work. Everything is simple, in excellent taste, as refined and nice as one could possibly wish and we could not have hit upon anything pleasanter.

Monday

We went to the Free Library to put our name down and get some books, a delightful building in the Spanish style and so simple and pleasant inside. Yesterday afternoon we took a wonderful drive, the Mountain drive, passed the old Spanish Mission and up, up into the very tops of the hills. It is very Italian to me, bigger and broader is the stretch of the basin below you, but it reminds me so much of the Riviera.

Mr. Wilson seems to be very ill according to the papers, but I feel and can't help wondering if it isn't his best political position just now?![1] With dear Love to you both and so glad you had such a beautiful and successful motor trip.

October 29, 1919

**San Ysidro Ranch
Santa Barbara, California**

My dear Uncle Joe,

We have been here only 3 weeks today, but we are quite in love with the place—and particularly with this side of it and view of life—from San Ysidro Ranch. We live in an orange grove with little garden plots of violets and lilies and roses and hedge-rows in between—pleasant people in the dining room—about a hundred yards off from this cottage—and we meet them at lunch or dinner as we have breakfast and tea in our own house! and charming those little breakfasts are too—with a glass of fresh orange juice to begin with and a well heaped plate of fresh figs and other fruits or wonderful honey to wind up! At present we have a dear old Mr. Stowe—son of Harriet Beecher Stowe—at the table next to us. He is full of stories of great people from Washington to Wilson and has a memory for verse which he not only quotes but can parody.

We have now got our motor—a little Sedan 'Ford'—Mr. Stowe also has his and runs it himself—having learnt in 3 lessons—and he tells me his age is '69—not less'. He and Offley compare notes upon their machines—and they both have a young Mr. Grey—a former Vice-president of the great Ford Company, to advise.

We hear the Colin Campbells are here. She was Miss Nannie Leiter and Offley is going today to hunt him up for they are very old friends of O's. Yesterday we went into Santa Barbara for the first time, running our car by ourselves. I confess I felt a little nervous—but Offley did it remarkably well.

A great batch of letters came from home yesterday and the 'strike rations' were even less than at the most difficult war ration—but everyone writes how cheerfully and how magnificently people fell into line to help, Lords and Ladies driving any sort of motor—and even engines. A cousin of Offley writes from Scotland that he and Lord Elgin ran a train. The King and Queen motored all the way to town from Balmoral—and Prince Henry and the household came from Aberdeen by steamer. Hyde Park was turned into a depot and parking place and almost everyone worked hard and seemed to enjoy it and can prove to the devils the utter wickedness of such behavior.

San Ysidro Ranch,
Montecito, Santa Barbara,
California

November 2, 1919

My dearest Aunt,

I can't let the day go without at least starting a letter to you and this day has been such a pleasant one. Offley and I started off in our own car—Offley driving and all by ourselves—to lunch with the Colin Campbells in Santa Barbara at 'El Mirasol' where they are stopping until he goes into a home he's rented and she goes home to her children—later to fetch them out here too. She is so very nice and particularly agreeable and of course we have so many friends and interests in common. Offley was delighted to see Colin Campbell again and he wants to encourage Offley to settle out here!—to become an American citizen and all sorts of things!! and indeed the place is very beautiful and if one has a few congenial friends—and good ones—one could not be in a better place. Goodnight for just now and more tomorrow.

November 3rd

We lunched in Santa Barbara again today as we had a motor lesson in all the 'ins and outs' and insides of our car—and various errands in the afternoon. Insurances etc. arranged and a beautiful drive home—but to find sad news waiting for us—a little letter to me from the old servant left in charge at Connaught Square London—to tell us that Aunt Caroline had passed away very peacefully October 14th. It has naturally made us feel very deeply that it means the final break-up of the house and home in London where we always found a welcome and which Offley has known since he was such a little boy that his rooms are still spoken of as 'the nursery'—'Master Offley's room and day nursery' is the way the old butler has often spoken of them to me—and the distinguished Uncle Frederick was also his Godfather and Aunt C. ever his adoring Aunt and such a sweet and charming little old lady. How much you would have liked her.

November 7th

These glorious days just spin by—so full—now that there is the little car to work at—and the trips into Santa Barbara take up a greater part of the day and when on the Ranch we go up the hill sides and the Canyon and Offley collects all sorts of flowers and leaves and bushes and is studying the trees and flora of this lovely place. He is much better, but there is a <u>great deal</u> to wish for yet and he continues to be <u>so</u> thin it quite frightens me.

Today comes your letter of the 30th. I am so glad you had such a delightful meeting with the King and Queen of the Belgians—and I can just see <u>you</u> dear Aunt Fanny—<u>quite</u> naturally making the prettiest of bows. I hope you had some conversation with them.

We have already <u>started</u> finding out if we can get our things from India <u>here</u> and <u>you</u> must plan to pay us a visit here this coming summer. Why not?

Florence is still at work in France—in command of a train again.

We hope we shall not have to return to England in the meantime. Offley has heard that his resignation will now be accepted and he has sent in the formal and usual letter saying he 'has the honour to present' it etc. etc.

November 12, 1919   San Ysidro Ranch

My dearest Aunt,

The more we see of this lovely coast country round Santa Barbara the more we love it and we have been going all over the place and seeing houses or bits of land on which we might put a house. The climate is so excellent and the doctor here whom Offley has seen tells him it is most necessary that he should have a dry, high climate to live in. He is better but I am more than anxious over the state of his general health.

I think I wrote you that dear Aunt Caroline had died, passing away very quietly at her nephew's in Oxfordshire. We have as yet heard nothing of her will and the disposition of her things or of <u>ours</u> that were in her London house. We hope shortly to hear from

Harrington Offley-Shore or the solicitor and we hope it may not necessitate a return to England. Offley has heard from an officer in the India Office that they would now accept his resignation and that he would be retired as Brigadier General—which rank he held in all his appointments through the war—so he has sent in his papers and looks forward to the acceptance of the same coming any day.

I am so sorry you are still so bothered with your dear eyes—but so glad to hear of Dr. Pokey's re-assurances. How I wish we could be together and it gives me a very real heart-ache that in Offley's interest we must for a time, at least, keep in a dry climate, but if fine weather comes in May or June we might go East again—that is if you really felt you could not come here. Servants are one of the most serious difficulties here and a reason against going into a house of one's own, but surely there must be some in the world who would be delighted to come to such a place as this, but wages are very high here—still, if one only could get a house and home under my grand-father's trust in such a lovely spot as this, I feel sure I could work out the other problems—and only am I too ambitious to have a home of my own—but if it is not possible to get one's house out of the estate then of course another arrangement must be considered and that would deplete one's income so much that added to the deductions for English and American income taxes—not much would be left to work on.

Offley is looking into the question of lemon or walnut ranching too but with lemons the problem seems a little difficult and in all California water is a very serious matter—to have it as a certainty and to have your own—as well as a company's—if one exists in the neighborhood. However all these things are of interest and let one into many other interests and tell-tale matters relative to this lovely country.

November 20, 1919   **San Ysidro Ranch**

My dearest Aunt,

Thank you so much for your dear letter to me and Offley with your sympathy in Aunt Caroline's death. It is the fading of an era.

She was the last of her generation of a family that boasted men and women of distinction—a very real and live personality—and I used to enjoy so much hearing her talk of courts and balls, of reviews and pageants of Queen Victoria's day—of travels to Germany and Italy and Australia and America—at her house one always found 'pleasant people droppin' in'—to whom she used to introduce me with so much pride. Offley was her 'beau ideal' and they were so very charming together.

I can see her now and hear her laugh—at Offley when she came to bid him good-bye on his departure for Russia. That was the last time O. ever saw her and I feel glad that it was so—as it left a most happy impression.

The Doctor here—after a thorough examination of my Beloved Offley says much as our London physician said—that his general constitution has had such a severe strain—lungs etc.—not so young and strong as they once were etc. and says he should remain in this climate at least two years—if possible also to live out of doors. His coughing though nothing like so bad as it was still makes me very anxious—but his spirits and general interest in all the beauty of the world around us quite revives me too. At any rate I know from all I have seen since his return from Russia and his attack of influenza with that burning fever in London last winter—that one should bend every effort to meet this most simple treatment of an open air life in a good climate—and not treat him or think of him as an ill man and please God he will recover himself and we can have years together yet and for many a long day.

The little 'Ford Sedan' we find a charming thing—though I am much more nervous with it than you would have believed! perhaps that is as well—only I want to understand driving it and get more confidence in myself—for in this age it is of such utmost importance.

We hope things are all right with the arrangements and provisions in Aunt C.'s will—but we fear that Harry Offley-Shore has made his Aunt change her will in his favour almost entirely. He was the great beneficiary as he has little children etc. etc. and Offley was looked upon as having good pay and various reasons why he should not require further monies—however times have changed and particularly the financial situation of most of us—and very seriously affected the soldiering man whose income is a fixed one—but just

*Voice from underneath—Now. Hurry up—do—, with those windows! We've got her
brake-shoes to tighten up yet—and we're late!*
*Lady perspiring at the back of the Car—Well, Offley! You know I wasn't brought
up to do this sort of thing—and I'm quite unwell—and very nervous! and you'll say
I scratched her! and oh! dear, I'm so tired I can hardly stand up!!! &c. &c.*

as liable to the inroads of income tax. However I am inclined to
look on the happier side of things and be thankful for what does
remain to one—and if we get a place here I <u>know</u> Offley will love
working at lemons or fruit on his own place.

*In her letter to her Aunt dated 30 November Lina commented on
her sister Fanny's engagement, of which she and Offley clearly
had an earlier knowledge:*

I am so glad to hear that Fanny has told you her <u>great news</u> and
she seems very happy in it all—doesn't she? When she told us, we
were not so sure she was so sure of herself, or so <u>we</u> thought, but
now she seems quite happy and fixed in her decision and he seems
to be a very nice young man.

Entre nous, my dear Aunt, I always felt rather more ambitious
for her. She is so lovely, but she is <u>difficult</u>—and it is always best
that one finds one's own happiness—particularly in these days.

December 19, 1919   **San Ysidro Ranch**

My dearest Aunt and Uncle Joe,

I cannot be thankful enough that we are here—and must have no regrets—for this climate has, I know, been the saving grace in Offley's health. He still coughs—but I fear he always will—but he is looking much better and is in very much better spirits, and he is so interested in all the plant life here—this little cottage looks just like a 'forcing house' with its numberless little pots with things started in them which we hope may be the trees on our place here some day, for we are considering very seriously an extremely beautiful little property here—with a magnificent view and good soil for Offley to work at fruits etc. Not just a lemon ranch, but a place where one can have a 'nest' to live in and a garden to work and play in—and not too far from the delights that go to make up the comfort and pleasures of a domestic!!!!! Mrs. Langdon Irving told me when next she chose a house and home its first requirement must be that it was 'on 2 bus routes'! We, of course, want everything. A heavenly view of sea and mountains—(difficult to get)—good soil, some trees, in short 'another Eden, earthly Paradise'. Wildflowers such as we had at Wildflower Hall—and what not!—and I think, however, it is very 'hot-butter-blue-beans' as we used to say as children when we played at 'hide and seek' and nearly found the treasure. Only—we are very badly hit over the fall in British securities and in the exchange—and also at 'settling' down in life at such a very expensive moment. We have already sent for our things in India and the joy it will be to see those again—even if they all have to live in one room until we can work out how to build the house—on next-to-nothing-a-year! But it will be great fun and do us both infinite good and you two must surely come out and criticise and lend the benefit of your experience and advice.

Not a word has come from Harrington Offley-Shore about the dear old Aunt—nor from the solicitor as yet. Florence wrote to Offley of having been at the house and seen the servants, but no details and Offley feels very sad when he thinks of it all.

Sunday, December 21st

The beautiful little piece of property is ours! One telegram was sent, one received and a cheque was written. Offley gave me the pleasure of

writing the fattest one of my experience drawn on his 'nest egg' and
the telephone rang late last evening to tell us of our possessing it. But
there is no house on the place. It is just a fallow field with an exquisite
view of sea and mountains with some lovely oaks and a rich and
excellent soil. We had the place surveyed for soil by an experienced
man in fruit-growing through the kindness of Mrs. Johnston. The view
is very beautiful and enchanting and it is the very last little bit left in
the valley so near to the town—being about 3 or 4 miles from the Santa
Barbara limit. The polo field and little polo club are the nearest neighbors marching with our small piece—so there will be open space all
round us—and we stand so high that it is impossible that any building
near or in the foreground could ever interfere with the view. Many are
the schemes dancing today in both our heads—but though it may be years
before one can build—one can plant and plan and play in one of the
prettiest of spots. A little Spanish-Italian country house with a pinkish
plaster finish and bright jalousies or shutters and the terra-cotta tiles of the
old adobe houses in this California country—which keep one cool and
over which glorious vines from natural wood trellises love to climb—is
what we aspire to and would cost between $10,000 and $15,000, but we
must wait for a better British exchange before we start off on such
things—and we neither of us wish to deplete our already small income
so that one may not meet 'the rainy day' or comfortably pay our way
East or to England—to see you when we liked—that would never do.

*Early in January Offley received details of Aunt Caroline's will
and Lina wrote about this to Uncle Joe on 4 January, 1920:*

The bulk of her fortune goes to Scholarships and Exhibitions at
Rugby. Her youngest nephew—the clergyman—who has 3 little children gets what remains after servants' legacies and others are paid,
and her 5 nieces—her wardrobe and personal property. Offley was
left the town house, but I think the dear old lady did not realize
that the long lease had come to an end. By this Offley gets nothing—but fortunately he said he never expected anything and had
never either thought about it or counted upon it. I do admire his
fine spirit, but I can't help feeling how nicely it would have come

in just now to build the house. Of course I am glad that Harry gets a comfortable sum—but we both feel sure she was influenced by him when her mind and memory were failing; it will mean more for the little people in these days of such straitened circumstances for all of us whose source of income comes from England.

The problem of building a house on their property was to prove ever more difficult, as the following extracts from Lina's letters to her Aunt and Uncle show.

January 11th, 1920

We are asked to join the Country Club, but we feel we must go slowly as dues are high and we want to build our house some day.

January 20th, 1920

Many thanks for your letter and letters. That of Jan. 14th is the last date, and with yours and Aunt Fanny's ever kind interest, you write in this of your interest in our house. We amuse ourselves with plans and schemes and sketches and a few days ago made the acquaintance of a Mr. Reginald Johnston—a young architect who has built a number of very charming houses that seem so appropriate and suitable to this place—and when we took him over our field and told him of the simple little house we wished—3 or 4 master bedrooms and 3 or 4 small airy servants' rooms, dining room, living room and small library we were so horrified at the cost of building that we don't quite know what we shall do about it.

Mr. Johnston wants to submit some plans to us and of course we are most happy to look at them. We don't want to spend more than twenty-thousand dollars on any house for ourselves, but as carpenters are $9.00 a day here and all material from 5 to 6 times the price it was 3 years ago—I think we may have to wait or give it up altogether unless we use a portable house—and these can be very pretty and very comfortable. Then if one has visitors one just orders another section.

March 19, 1920

Two architects have now told us that the <u>small</u> house we wish will cost at least $40,000 to $50,000 to build now—and even have shown

us plans for a more expensive one! Three years ago the same house
could have been built for $15, 20, or 25,000—but a gate house now
costs $10,000 at least. However we shall wait. Meantime we have
started a 'House Fund' and mean to deposit in a special account with
Browns for this particular object—and also to inform ourselves in every
particular and detail as to the requirements etc. etc. Our land cannot
run away, nor can anyone build out our view. Betty's suggestion is not
a bad one—that we build the house ourselves! But I am afraid that
would only end in costing us a good deal more! as it does when you
think you will be so economical and put in a window pane—such a
simple little thing you say to yourself—and to do it you smash about
ten! Obviously with the fluctuating prices of labour and material and
the high and increasing cost of living we must wait and try to collect
sufficient to put up a gate house or gardener-handyman about the
place's cottage and live in it to begin with—hoping for better days and
times to come—when the exchange admits of bringing English money
here etc. etc.

*The other subject which occupied Lina's letters at this period
was Florence's death as recorded in the following press report
from the* New York Times:

'London, Jan. 14—Miss Florence Nightingale Shore, a second generation cousin of England's 'Lady of the Lamp' and
a sister of Brig. Gen. Offley B. Shore, who is now in California lies at death's door from wounds inflicted by an unknown person while she was travelling by train from London
to Bexhill.

Miss Shore, who followed the profession of her great
namesake and did distinguished nursing service during the
war, is about 50 years old. She was seen off at the station
by a woman friend, who said that the compartment in which
Miss Shore sat was entered just before the train started by
a young man. When the train arrived at Lewes Miss Shore
was found in an unconscious condition, with a wound in
her head. Her money and railway tickets had been taken.

A great sensation has been created by the outrage, both

because of the personality of the victim and the fact that the English system of compartment carriages is in present times peculiarly dangerous.

Miss Shore has not regained consciousness since the attack, and so far no clue has been found to the supposed assailant, the description of whom issued by the police is vague.'

Florence was taken from Lewes to the East Sussex hospital at Hastings. She never recovered consciousness.

January 20th, 1920

Then came the shock and distress of my sister-in-law, Florence's tragic death and one can scarcely think of anything else. We hope that Scotland Yard will discover and punish the villain, but poor consolation if any—yet perhaps all England may wake up to the fact of these stupid and dangerous kind of old fashioned carriages and do something to make for greater safety in traveling.

We have as yet no details from home other than those given us in cables. We had hoped so much that Florence would soon follow us out here and how she would have enjoyed it for like Offley, she was a great lover of flowers and of beauty in nature and there are so many pleasant people from England here. She too might have liked to have a cottage of her own here. However God in Heaven has ordered it otherwise.

February 8th, 1920

We have an enormous number of letters from home of kind sympathy at Florence's tragic death and from all sorts and kinds of people. The mighty and the poor and lonely to whom she gave herself so entirely. Aunt Mellie I feel will feel it the most deeply and miss her and so will her great friend who wrote a most piteous letter to Offley—and alas, Offley feels as did Urith and Aunt Caroline—that Miss Rogers—Flo's friend—alienated her from her family. I suppose she did, but I begged Offley not to try—in seeing more of his sister—to separate the two friends at their age—Florence was 56—and of a most determined and pugnacious disposition—in fact these traits made her great character and worth—and I think I brought about a very much happier relationship between her and Aunt C. and also Offley—who never let go of her or lost sight of her—in spite of all her determination to lose herself among the people she worked for and cared for—and at least I flatter myself this was so.

March 8th, 1920

We are very gratified by an announcement in the 'Times' that 'the safety of women in trains has been brought up in Parliament with reference to the case of Miss Florence Nightingale Shore'.

These letters reminded this editor that as a small boy he had heard this very murder discussed at the family breakfast table. The conversation had passed over his head and been completely forgotten.

March 30, 1920   San Ysidro Ranch

My dear Uncle Joe,

Many thanks for sending us Strachey's book, 'Eminent Victorians'. We read it about a year ago and Offley who knew his cousin Florence Nightingale so well—feels it is indeed a very excellent portrayal of the lady, who was most imperious and a demon at work. I see a great deal in this pen picture of her that I find strongly characteristic of the Shore family. They—none that I knew or have known—were merely 'clever' people, they were <u>very great</u>, and great factors in action and with most earnest, honest purposes, full of unsparing energy and an amazing enthusiasm and interest.

There is, of course, a tender side which the author, not being of the family, has missed.

Flo used to have much to tell of her—and she paid her regular visits.

The Lakes come here on Thursday to this Ranch and we shall no doubt hear much of the conditions at home as Sir Percy has only just returned having been back to London to settle an Aunt's estate. I am thankful Offley does not have to go on account of Florence's estate—but that his cousin who is co-trustee with him is in London and can do it all and begs Offley to remain here. Though in another year's time we will undoubtedly have to return home—to see to many things. In the meantime I wish we could put a house, during this summer, on our land.

My boxes have been dispatched from India on the 20th of February and I fear it will take nearly six months before they can reach here—and I don't want to spend a penny in rent that one could put toward building.

I shall sort out my things when they do arrive and sell any that are unsuitable for a house here. Offley wants me to sell all we can, of which there is a small amount of very valuable old silver. My tiara is now sold, but the lovely earrings and pendants are entailed. Offley thinks that might be broken these days—but I remind him I have promised myself, and them, to take Priscilla and Louise [daughters of brothers Charles and George, both eleven years old at this date—Ed.] to Court one day! and I think we shall have to do as little Louise said 'not wait until she's 18!'.

I told Offley, I felt as if I was reading of a party in my own old house when I saw in my London paper that the King had held a Levée, the first since the War, in St. James' Palace. I am not only so familiar with those beautiful old rooms—the Throne Room, Queen Anne's Room, the ante-rooms and private stairs and passages, but I can see the old servants bristling with pride at 'the good old days' (or the outward appearance of them) coming back. Ah, but they never will—and somehow one equally just doesn't want them to. Let them pass out with as much dignity as they may.

In a later letter Lina reported: 'My Father-in-law wrote us of the Levée at St. James' and said that the old "full dress" was worn as before the war—and many old fellows were very tightly tucked into their finery too.' [Nothing is known of a second father-in-law—Ed.]

April 3, 1920   **San Ysidro Ranch**

My dearest Aunt,

Your letter of the 22nd, and the embroidery which came two days ago have not been acknowledged and now comes your kind letter of the twenty-eighth telling us how welcome we should be if we came for Fanny's wedding. I am indeed sorry and quite disappointed that we have no chance of being present. I knew nothing of her plans beyond what she told me when we parted last autumn and was quite taken by surprise by her wire of the 26th saying she would be married on the 7th of April. Only ten days notice and the journey takes five days at post haste! so that barely 4 days notice for reservations in the train is not by any means time enough to get anything short of a 'private car'!! We had already been making enquiries about going East and found reservations were impossible to get over two lines in less than a month's notice. We enquired again before wiring Fanny on the 27th and could get nothing as this time of year the travelling is very heavy—and now we shall not come until Autumn or Spring—as the final payment upon our property here is to be made in May or June and we also expect our things sent from India and despatched in February will be reaching here in the summer and must be looked after. It is a biggish thing to gather one's household together after a great and a long war as we have had it—and, of course, neither here nor in England is there anyone to do these things but ourselves—and I sadly miss my good and excellent Stewart.

I hope I do not dilate too much upon the chances of having my house. I fear I do however. I should so love to see it simply and prettily and comfortably arranged and you and Uncle Joe paying us a visit! The Lakes—Sir Percy and Lady Lake are here now—having arrived on the evening of the 1st. and Offley teases me—saying we've scarcely had our noses outside of a church since!!! We went to the 3 hours Service on Good Friday at our little Montecito Church and then into Santa Barbara to hear the Passion music at Holy Trinity. The 3 hours Service was conducted by Dr. Drury who has been spending the winter here and has preached a number of times at our little church and he is much liked. He is the Headmaster of St. Paul's School where so many Rosengarten boys have gone. I have not met him, but if I do I shall speak to him of my young cousins.

This is a glorious day, warm and beautiful, but with a little galling wind. Offley has gone off for the day to motor to a mountain pass and there take horses and ride over into a wonderful and glowing country. I did not go out today but am taking things a little quietly as I have had much headache lately and—I am sorry to say—I do not think I shall be able to work at the embroidery as the canvas is so fine and my eyes ache a good deal when my head aches.

I have no doubt my headaches will pass away with a little resting up. The doctor says it is quite a usual thing to feel as I do after the strain and shocks of the past five years and the changes of life and climate from India to England and to America etc.—so do not feel anxious on my account, I simply put it in my letters as I tell and talk to you of everything.

Write me every detail of Fanny and tell Betty and Uncle Joe to do the same. I am interested in every one's account and every detail.

Some months after wishing she had her 'good and excellent Stewart' with her Lina reported: 'A long letter from my dear old Stewart—she would very much like to come to America as India, like every other place, is very changed.'

In her next weekly letter (10 April 1920) Lina expressed her reaction on listening to Sir Oliver Lodge:

Sir Oliver Lodge and Lady Lodge have been here and people seemed vastly interested—and as they say 'almost convinced'—by what he has to tell. I confess it sounds clear enough—but to one's ears—not one's eyes or mind for my part. I, who believe in the old orthodoxy, 'the Communion of Saints', feel it would be taking away a great deal of the dignity of things as they are—as the Almighty has still allowed them to exist—unexplained, magnificently mysterious still—to us His children. In fact after having been so long in India, where many curious things happened under my very eyes—as we say—I think it is too tricky—too much like the juggler's art and we cannot begin to know or understand these things from 'the vasty deep'. And now good-night my beloved Aunt and Uncle.

April 17, 1920   **San Ysidro Ranch**

My dearest Aunt,

It must be nearly a fortnight since I wrote to you last! I have however written joint letters to you and Uncle Joe and also to Father.

The Lakes leave today and it has been such a pleasure, such a privilege to have had them and to have realized again our intimate and sincere friendship, and they too intend to make their future home in Victoria. So we shall not be far apart and so charmed have they been with this place that they hope to come back next winter.

It makes one a little homesick to bid adieu to so many friends going to the East Coast or to England for the summer—but I realize we just can't go, and content myself by knowing we are in a charming place at any season—by next Spring things will be better let us hope. I have had no letter from any of you at Philadelphia since Uncle Joe's of the 8th saying how pleased he was with Fanny's quiet wedding—no details and those we await from you and Betty with interest. We received two dainty boxes of the wedding cake from Father and these I am acknowledging today. I had a nice letter from my brother George—I wish he wrote oftener—telling me of his resignation from the Pennsylvania Railroad and their plan to go to England and France this summer. I have sent him a few letters to friends that may be of interest to him to meet.

I suppose the railway strike has held up my letters. It does seem such a pity always to resort to strikes. We had tea yesterday with an English lady—just from home—and she says things are beginning to look a little better—but for a time they were rationed again and still are for sugar. So many Americans are going to England this year and so many have already gone there that they call it 'The American Invasion'.

With the coming of spring Lina began to be dissatisfied with their little Ford car.

On 5 May in a letter to her Aunt she wrote:

You will be spending your Sundays again in the country now and taking long motor drives. I shall be thinking of you speeding along in your comfortable Cadillac. Mrs. Gray takes us sometimes in hers when they go in the same direction as we do and the other day brought me home from a lady's luncheon party and I told Offley I felt something of 'myself' as we rolled smoothly along. It all seems like a dream to think of those days in India when I had my pretty little Viceregal Victoria with coachman and footman in scarlet and gold and the gentle spoken Shaffrullah would ask in English 'and to what place next is it the Lady Sahib's pleasure?' or my own landaulette motor would be put at a friend's disposal—or wait all night at a dinner dance and enjoy the privilege!!! Times have changed. However I thoroughly enjoyed all that while I had it—and was anything smarter than dear Mother's beautiful Victoria and her pretty matched pair? But I show my age reminiscing like this! 50 next birthday!!!

Two weeks later she wrote again.

I would much like to have a little better class motor than our 'Ford', happy as we are to have that, but I have not felt very well at times and the Ford car is rough on these roads out to the Ranch and such places. We are very envious of a little Coupé Cadillac or Buick a lady has here—but I fear they must be very expensive. Do you know what the cost of the 'Buick' car was that Uncle Joe gave Betty? He wrote me of giving her one and I should very much like to know the kind of car—its capacity and class. Your Charles would be able to give me some advice. I don't remember exactly what Fanny's car was—that Uncle Joe gave her, but I think that was a Cadillac and it seemed a small and useful size. My sisters have been so pre-occupied with new husband and new house etc. that they don't answer my questions always. So I go to the gentleman at the top! Uncle Joe! and he, with Charles, will tell me something of their cost and relative value for the price paid.

Lina at this time was feeling homesick—for England. On 9 May to her Aunt she wrote:

Letters lately from England have made me very homesick and one to Offley asking if he wishes the Ambassador to this country to decorate him or if he will be home soon—fills me with a desire to

have him receive his final decoration from the King himself—as I
feel we must go back early next Spring to see to our things and our
affairs—all so hurriedly left in order to get off to America and see
all you dear people when the chance presented itself. If we could
go in October I would go but early spring is a safer season for
Offley than autumn when one runs the risk of cold and storms.

Then again on 22 June:

Then there are always nice English people coming and going and
staying and this helps to make Offley feel 'at home' in this place
though he is happy at any time with his trees and books and walks
and motor drives. I get little fits of homesickness for you all and
for my English life—but someday we shall go back no doubt and
enjoy it all the more for all this country has done for us.

June 25, 1920   **San Ysidro Ranch**

My dear Uncle Joe,

Your letter of June 20th—a date that looms <u>so big</u> in its place
in my life—being an anniversary I always remember as my particularly dear and admired Grandfather's birthday and the death of my
beloved Mother. It was also Lord Hardinge's birthday—and after
the foul attack upon his life in Delhi in 1912—we always celebrated
his birthday during his Viceroyalty, when children's fêtes were given,
and gifts to hospitals and to the poor in his name and as a 'thank
offering' for his life.

We have had workmen clearing underbrush and dead wood etc.
on the place—also saving—as they cut out the rubbish—saving the
lovely wild gooseberry and the native white and blue lilac or
ceanothus—and opening and picking up the earth around the oaks—
some of which are very fine, and cleaning up our magnificent
eucalyptus and we have 3 very splendid and very large old ones—
with a few young trees of this delightful character coming on. An
Italian—one Francheschi Fenzi—who calls himself a landscape gardener took on the job for us. He is an Italian gentleman and a very
gentlemanly fellow of the Corsini family. Offley too went over every
day and worked as well as gave orders. Mrs. Whitehead tells me

Mr. Fenzi is one of the very best of men—and she knew his distinguished old Father and Mother who lived here too. They have been out here many years, but the two sons went into the Italian Army during the war—and particularly distinguished themselves.

It has been an expensive thing to do—but oh—how it shows up our beautiful place.

I will tell you what we are doing about our house. Mr. George Washington Smith—the architect here—and a Philadelphian by birth (his sister was a school friend of Betty's) is making some plans for a house which he hopes to find he can build for between 30 and 40 thousand dollars. At this price and in these days it means a very small, very simple house—but with 3 master bed-rooms and 3 servants' rooms and only the necessary living or reception rooms—as they call the dining room and drawing room. In the meantime Offley and I are putting aside in a Building Loan deposit in our Santa Barbara Bank—the National County Bank, given us by Brown Brothers. We have begun with $2,000 and shall add as we can—and this is at 6% per annum—and when plans are ready and the probabilities of labour and building look better and our purse has filled to nearly the required sum, we shall begin—but not until then—and people think here that things must come down—and very likely will after the general elections. Offley hopes shortly too to have Florence's and Aunt Caroline's small estates settled and the monies put in to securities payable in New York or London. Florence left £1000 to the Nursing Home and to her friend Miss Rogers and very generous sums to a Godchild and to a Scotch cousin who is badly off—and what remains— very little—to Offley—and some small sums Offley gave his sisters now reverts to him. Aunt Caroline left so much to Rugby that very little comes to Offley from her—and that in Consols which are now so depreciated—and it has been lucky for us that Harry—Offley's cousin, Harrington Offley-Shore, was left as 'Residuary' as he has to settle up everything and pay all 'house dilapidations' poor fellow—but he is on the spot and Offley hopes he will make use of many things and anything we don't want—from the town house. Offley is also giving the furniture for the Florence Nightingale Shore Memorial. Dear Flo—what pride and pleasure she would have taken in this house.

Of course I am anxious to make a start as, since the physician here said Offley's health must be our first consideration—and this climate and plenty of it—was his prescription—everything has been toward that end. My things have reached this country from India, but not yet got here to Santa Barbara. I am hoping to see them in another fortnight or more. My English saddle I intend sending to Betty and several friends here wish to see our Chinese things—so I shall hope to dispose of some of those beautiful things. I do wish so much you could see them. Come out here for September and October and I will engage you rooms at El Mirasol. Lots of older people than dear you and dear Aunt Fanny take long and less comfortable trips. Look at the Empress Eugenie going out to Spain at 92. She told me she was going after the war—and she did and to see her niece's and nephew's new house. So there you are. Now don't be outdone by an Empress—or such an old one at that. Just come along.

A few days later Lina's 'things' were cleared through customs.

Everyone was as nice as could be and so interested and about four o'clock all was finished—every box had been opened, and though I could not thoroughly inspect all the contents, things looked so well, and my linens so smooth and beautiful and the silver actually glowing! It had been hermetically sealed and came out ready to set forth on any table. The customs inspector remarked upon this with equal surprise to ours. My dear, old faithful butler, Shaffrullah, whom Betty will remember and who now writes to me as 'Your Majesty' was rubbing as he packed. Mr. Stevens—the customs inspector and his wife and two children were so appreciative of the old glass and the beauty of the old plate—a huge quartering of Arms on an old tray that was taken out among other things—gave a joy to their pride too—they told me they were of English and Scotch descent— we ended up taking them all to tea in the garden of this Club. [Lina's Club—The Little Town Club—Ed.]

> *In a letter to Uncle Joe dated 4 July Lina wrote both of her sister-in-law, Florence Nightingale Shore and of the latter's great-aunt, Florence Nightingale.*
>
> *She thanked Uncle Joe and others in Philadelphia for their interest in the establishment of a memorial to Florence.*

I only hope it will arouse some sympathy. Perhaps some Philadelphia nursing orders or Women's colleges might be inclined to subscribe—which would prove a very proud and friendly example in these days of Anglo-American rapprochement. Queen Mary's Needlework Guild (Philadelphia)? British Relief?

How well I remember my first visit to 'Aunt Flo' as they called the great Florence Nightingale, among my people-in-law. Offley looking so distinguished in frock-coat and top hat—I in my best of trousseau afternoon dresses—drove to South Street—to No. 10 to see the old lady—face to face—as one of the family—the great personage I had heard of from Mother and Miss Irwin [the Principal of the school from which Lina graduated—Ed.] and even dear Grosmutter. Yes, I quite remember her telling me of her and with what a thrill 'they' heard of a woman going to the scene of war in the splendid spirit in which she did. My people-in-law and Offley always were impressed with her forcefulness. Aunt Carry was quite afraid of her, but not so Offley who spoke of her as 'that Demon'—but our own gentle Florence thought a great deal of her and loved and admired her—then there was a longstanding and very deep affection between the two cousins—F.N. and Offley's Father—and they were constantly exchanging notes and letters and cuttings from papers and illustrations, suggestions and what not.

She left most of her money to the State for institutions in the interests of nursing and nursing sisters—and for a nursing home for officers' wives and families of which I am a patron (having almost forgot all about it).

Having completed the unpacking of her boxes from India Lina wrote to her Aunt on 18 July:

It makes me so keen to have a house of my own to put the things into but of that I despair. Offley has given me some of dear Flo's monies for the house but with good, old fashioned securities in England standing at their very lowest just now—and the exchange a dollar below normal—one would be mad to bring it here for on every thousand pounds one loses one thousand dollars at present rate of exchange and so one must just go on very, very carefully and try to save up a small though sufficient sum in this country.

We had an offer of nearly 3 times what we paid for our land the other day and a great lump came into my throat—it seemed as if we ought to have taken it. I referred to Offley when the Real Estate man came to make it and Offley's reply was, 'The property is yours, Schatz, you must do what you will', and I refused—but I am afraid the next time we have an offer we may be taken quite off our feet.

July 25, 1920   **San Ysidro Ranch**

My dearest Aunt,

Offley's dear Aunt Mellie has been going through papers and boxes of Florence's and Urith's and with this labour of love for Offley—she has written him her reminiscences of their childhood— of the lovely, gay little people they were—of the proud Mother and Grandmothers, how well Flo rode, how eager and alert Offley was, and with her recollections of him and his people I have told him of mine and the big part you and my beloved Grosmutter took in those days—and Grosvater too.

How kind of you and Uncle Joe to have sent £10.00 to the F. Nightingale Shore Memorial. I sent a donation asking that flowers might always be kept in the visiting sister's room as Florence and Aunt Florence were always so fond of them—just as Offley is.

We 'staked out' our house a few days ago with the architect and builders and are now considering the site and the details of the plans. Even the builders said they'd never seen a more glorious view—but oh—I do find it difficult to plan out.

July 28, 1920   **San Ysidro Ranch**

My dear Uncle Joe,

I am working hard over my plans for the house, and here again, it is a problem to keep things down to a possible price. I want many things I have learnt to understand the value of by experience, or that one has a taste for, and the architect wishes to use his artistic flare and (unfortunately!) so many people remind him that I am cousin to so many Rosengartens who have beautiful houses and lots of money. Fortunately Mr. Washington Smith realizes that I am not on the business side of the house—and like most people who have what dear Mother called 'a taste for champagne' have but a pocket for beer! Offley is working hard himself at his trees, I almost fear over-tiring himself, but he very thoroughly enjoys it.

On 27 August Lina reached her fiftieth birthday. In letters to her Aunt and Uncle she wrote:

Your letter of July 26th from Narragansett with its splendid gift to me toward my home and shall I say—as my semi-century birthday gift! has just come in—and thank you again and again for it—indeed it is magnificent of you and dear Uncle Joe. Your loving interest in us all along—inspires and ever has inspired the closest intimacy and when I write, as I do so often, long tirades of all I feel and think—and whether I am 'down' or 'up'—I always know of your sympathy and interest and I may forget and say too much or speak too strongly—but I also know of your loving correction or gentleness with me in such a case.

Offley will be writing himself directly to Uncle Joe and to you. He has such a lot of correspondence to meet the last few weeks with regard to his sister's affairs—and it has left him—I know, with an aching heart—so I have tried to divert him with garden plans—or a game of cards in the evenings.

50 years! Good-bye youth! but I don't feel nearly as old as I am and the time has flown by so fast.

I look back to the past with the greatest gratitude to the Almighty for the immeasurable blessings and pray our life may continue so blest. With Offley beside me—with all the clear concise memories of such wonderful things in which I have taken part—with the pleasures of travel and music and pictures and people and places seen side by side with you and Uncle Joe—with the tender care and affection of my beloved and wonderful Mother—with Papa's companionship like that of a 'big' brother—with devoted servants and warm and distinguished friends and a remarkable family and family-in-law. The only thing in the world to wish for would be children of my own—and failing those I hope my nieces may one day fill that longing. I would too that the years had flown as well spent as they have flown fast.

On 31 August Lina reported to Uncle Joe:

Offley has had his pension increased: only a £100 a year, but for 'good service', and instead of a Knighthood, and much as I should enjoy that, I am quite content to share his good name, these days it is better—though I own it might amuse me to have signed my name in the good old fashioned way as Caroline, Lady Offley Shore.

On 4 November in a letter to Uncle Joe Lina wrote:

I am glad to hear you are feeling better as I was indeed distressed when Aunt Fanny wrote you were not well.

Her subsequent letters continued to make reference to his health.

November 14, 1920   **San Ysidro Ranch**

My dearest Aunt,

We were so very sorry to hear Uncle Joe was so unwell but glad to have had a nice letter from him making little or nothing of it—and we hope and trust he is quite recovered. I am better—but still have had bad days with headache. The doctor and my friends all say 'take it quietly' and with rest etc. it will disappear—it is a sort of nervous reaction.

Our place is looking very, very pretty and as prices are falling I am in hopes we can really soon see a house upon it. We or I have decided to give it a Spanish name instead of Nonsuch as a Spanish one fits into the address and surroundings so much better—and so I call it 'The Gift'—or Souvenir—Remembrance—which in Spanish is 'El Regalo'—Offley having given me the lovely, lovely property and the house when it comes will be of many other gifts and Remembrances—yours, and Grandfather's and Uncle Joe's.

December 3, 1920   **San Ysidro Ranch**

My dearest Aunt,

Over the Thanksgiving everyone was holiday making until the following Monday and I was left <u>suffering</u> intensely with my head and teeth. I went out to lunch and to dine to share 2 different turkeys—if I didn't eat much, I was at least diverted and yesterday after much suffering from pain in my head and shoulder I had my second big back tooth out! It was surrounded by small pus pouches and I hope <u>now</u> this is to be the end of all my trouble and depression, for I have <u>been</u> very depressed. No doubt reaction and a combination of various things may have come together aided and abetted by this trouble and I hope equally all may culminate and disappear with it now.

We are no nearer building than we were last year—in fact this time last year we had just bought the property and we felt full of hope and readiness to build, but now—the architect and his builder say it will cost <u>so</u> much—at least $50,000 to put a house and roadway etc. etc. on our site, and I feel we simply live beyond our time! However everyone says 'things' are going down by Spring—perhaps—but incomes don't go up! and income taxes don't seem to come down!

Both Aunt Mellie and my Father-in-law write of the impressive services for the Unknown Soldier in London—and of Mrs. Asquith's scandalous book. Aunt M. tells us of Mrs. Asquith having said to Mr. Balfour 'I hope I've not annoyed you with anything I may have said of you in my book' and Balfour's reply, while star gazing was 'Ah—really, what book!'.

December 5, 1920   **San Ysidro Ranch**

My dear Uncle Joe,

Many thanks for your nice letter of the 28th but it doesn't do—to
have a charmingly young old gentleman like your good self feeling
badly—that is for an old lady—a really old lady like me! but now
that my poisonous back teeth have been taken out and cast from
me I hope I shall begin to feel quite young and gay again. I wish
I could run Eastward and have a look at you and dear Aunt Fanny—
but I should not feel satisfied to do so without Offley and he must
not risk the severe weather at this season of the year. I too have
been feeling so unlike my usual self with all this pain in my head.
Of course I am impatient and expect it to leave me like a flash—
directly my tooth has been taken out—but the doctor says that is
too much to look for and that it will be all right in time.

*The next extant letter is dated 21 January. Uncle Joe had died
on 14 January.*

January 21, 1921   **San Ysidro Ranch**

My very dearest Aunt,

The days slip by and are so full, and while I am busy sewing or
mending or even reading my thoughts fly to you, dear Aunt Fanny.
Knowing so well that you are thinking only of that best and most
wonderful brother, my beloved Uncle Joe who has now gone on
that journey we all must take. But that he is safe in God's care and
the memories we have of him in a thousand things, of gentleness,
of patience and kindness, of sound advice, of numberless things,
and of care and interest in us, and so many generous and unselfish
things done, console me immensely as they must you, dear Aunt.
And in these things he lives forever, to you and to me, to his family
and to his country.

I am sending you some of the letters I've had that you can see
how my friends know you and Uncle Joe too.

Much dear, dear love from both of us. These are sad days for O.
too. Just a year ago his sister's shocking tragedy.

January 27, 1921

My dearest Aunt,

Here is such a kind, kind spontaneous little letter from Mrs. Fayweather, my sister-in-law Florence's young friend whom you and Uncle Joe went to see last autumn. Wasn't it very nice of her to write and as she sends you a kind message in her letter I send it on to you to read and you will return it I know, and when you feel you can do so, dear, dearest Aunt Fanny, do sit down and tell me all you can and care to about dear Uncle Joe. I know you are brave and calm and meeting God's will. Thankful too that dear Uncle Joe was not allowed to suffer and lie ill for long, and always strengthened by the precious possession to you that he was and is and will be all your life as it will be all my life.

Rebecca [a sister-in-law—Ed.] has written to me so kindly and so sympathetically, but I do <u>so</u> much want a letter from you, my own most, dear, dear Aunt. I am wearing mourning as I did for dear Mother and as I feel I like to do and you all will be wearing and I have met with such a kind and nice dressmaking establishment here, who take the kindest interest in arranging for me simple yet pretty things, and are so much interested in hearing of you and Uncle Joe. Do you remember he once bought me a dress, and such a pretty fateful dress it was too, the dress I had on when I met Offley.

Good-night, my dear dear Aunt, all my love and may the days fly until we are with you.

January 29, 1921   **San Ysidro Ranch**

My dearest Aunt Fanny,

My very dearest Aunt, it grieves me so deeply not to be at your side just now—however I hope the days will fly along until we are speeding toward you and then, oh then, in the soft Spring weather I hope we shall be with you, and you and I must have good talks over and over those good days—our most sacred and precious possession when Uncle Joe and darling Mother were beside us to tease or tell some amusing or interesting experience. Oh, what good times we had—what wonderful and vital affections our lives have been blessed with—and so much of it added to and enhanced by you—dear you and Uncle Joe.

I enclose you some little notes from my friends—many telephoned me kind messages—as is the way of today. I also send you a letter from Mrs. Rawlins—to whom I will write of Uncle Joe, as well as to the Rochambeaus; and is there anyone else you would like me to tell what has happened to dearest Aunt Fanny?

This is our wedding day. Offley has brought me white roses—and snowdrops and violets. I enclose you a violet and the drawing Offley has made to give you an idea of the great size of these lovely things. Do write me just a few lines. I think of you the live-long day and know you feel much as I did when Offley was taken off to the war—it is God's will I used to say to myself, and try and order my heart to be the stouter and stronger, but there was indeed a lump in my throat more often than I intended—and days when I felt the burden intolerable. Yet how much all my loneliness and work brought me—blessings in disguise. Good-night, and God bless you and keep you dearest, dear Aunt.

On 5 February Lina wrote to Aunt Fanny telling her of all the people who had called to condole with her on Uncle Joe's death and listing the letters she had received from various parts of the United States, from Britain and from India and, as she had done in the two preceding letters, she begged Aunt Fanny to write to her: 'Do write me a little letter, my dearest Aunt. I miss yours so much and I want you to tell me just what you feel and think and like to speak of about dear Uncle Joe. You are both together and so often in my mind.' No further letters to Aunt Fanny, who died in 1925, have been found.

Only one more letter from Santa Barbara has been found, and that from Offley to his sister-in-law Betty.

March 13, 1921

Dearest Lady B.

Among your numerous friends are probably individuals who have personal experience of Mexico—Mexico City, and of various towns in the 'tierra templada' at a lesser elevation than M.C. and little diurnal variation and we should be very interested in hearing which is the best place to go for a pleasant <u>dry</u> climate and some sustaining interest! where and how to live, relative cost of living as compared with the U.S.A. generally, and how one sets about financing oneself down there—because I hear they have cancelled their paper currency and only use silver and gold.

I am also informed that one has to go through no end of fuss at Washington about passports.

When you have discovered by how much your annual income will be increased by Uncle Joe's legacy (or under his will) do tell us, because it will help us to work out our 'prospects'. We hope that Uncle Harry remembered you to some purpose in <u>his</u> will or left you a fat little interest in the concern as a memento of your work in the War. If he didn't, no doubt the cousins will combine to present you with a 'memorial'! (Greenbacks <u>not</u> vellum).

I am past expecting any kind of windfall: I used to nurse such hopes once and it was so very unsettling.

We were often promised candy and ponies on a holiday, when children, and then told at the psychological moment that it wasn't forthcoming and the promise was only an exercise in fortitude! so we soon ceased to cry at disappointments! That's the way <u>my</u> Spartan Mother brought <u>us</u> up.

Lina can't understand for the life of her—how one can merely say 'Cut it out'—'no use in crying'—'that's gone or done with' when your best and most cherished plans melt into the air.

Everything just now is savour-less. Montecito has come into line with other wicked places and now has her motor bandits who relieve buxom females of anything that glitters when en route to dine at some great house—that's an advance on stealing coats and hats and robes, or even the entire machine when left standing alone. Of course Lina can't be called 'buxom' yet—nor does she glitter—(she doesn't wash much or paint) but I can see she is getting apprehensive. Please advise us what to do. As chauffeur I am particularly interested.

Nothing new is known to have happened to produce the wide-ranging deep despair in which Offley wrote this letter, other than, presumably, the final realisation that they never would be able to build the home on their property for which they had so excitedly planned and worked.

Nothing either is known of what they did or where they lived for the next eighteen months. By September 1922, however, they were visiting in Britain, in particular in what Lina described as the 'Shore country' including Norton Hall near Sheffield, the home of Offley's ancestors, and Snitterton Hall, the home of the ancestors of Sir John Shore, first Baron Teignmouth, Governor-General of India from 1793 to 1798. See Appendix A for more detail on these families and these houses.

September 22, 1922
                                                Prince of Wales Hotel,
                                                  Harrogate, England

My very dear Father,

So many thanks for your letter of September 7th and with its enclosure, the financial page of The Ledger. It keeps me 'au fait' with the trend of things in U.S.A. and during these exceedingly uncertain days and times. Watching seems very necessary and what days we live in! What big blunders our rulers keep on making. No Statesmen and no policy, it is very pitiable.

We have just come here from a most delightful and romantic journey in Derbyshire, where we went to see the Shore country, to Snitterton Hall where Charles I was hidden by a Sir John Shore, to Tissington Hall the palace of the Fitz-Herberts, incidentally to Haddon Hall, looking so beautiful in its decaying glory, to Chatsworth and to Hardwick Hall and then to Norton Hall, Offley's

Grandfather's and Father's[2] beautiful old Adam house and home. It still stands in its 'home' park and is a stately and lovely place, shut away by its fine site and remaining trees sufficiently to be away from the din and bustle of Sheffield and its teeming busy factories. How I should love to live there! and to rearrange the house with such of its old furnishings as we still possess, and the church is full of charm and interest and the little village that lies at the park gate nearest the house is all that is pleasant and dignified.

We were treated as only Lords of the Manor could be. Curtseyed to and blessed for our coming and there are still one or two of the keepers at the Lodges who remember O.'s grandfather. We have been going over and over the possibility of going back to live there.

The place was requisitioned during the war as Officers' Headquarters of an area for camps and aeroplane building, hence the house is empty and much is in a bad state of repair, from ill-usage only however, as it is a most substantially built place of mellow stone, and the interior is Adam, and of a livable and lovely style. There would be room for all of you. The nurseries are there and ready for Sheila,[3] and rooms for you, dear Father, and for Betty, and Clifford could come and fish in the Derbyshire rivers with Offley. Betty and George could hunt and race with the best, while you and I ran the household and amused ourselves as we liked best.

Snitterton Hall is a smaller place and though it once was a great Squire's house counting a 100 rooms it has had more vicissitudes than Norton, for Norton,[4] though of great antiquity has been built and rebuilt many times. The house there now still embodies part of the old Hall of early Stuart days but it is an Adam house rebuilt from the time of the marriage of the heiress, Urith Offley to Samuel Shore and kept up to this very day. The great steel magnates who took the place upon Offley's grandfather's misfortunes are now ready to hand the place back. Their children are all married and away and the steel factories are much closed down with all these Labour troubles.

What a romance would it then be if O. and I could go and live in the place for a few years and bring our nieces and nephews round us there. (O.'s young cousins call us Uncle Offley and Aunt Lina or Aunt C. here.) Sheffield is an interesting and busy place. O. took me to the Cutlers Company's Hall, a fine old room or rooms of magnificent proportions and they had some rare plate and fine cutlery used on their great occasions.

You would like this. You could wander about to the baths and drink the waters and visit all sorts of shops and drive to see historical sites and live forever! So there, and if we do settle at Norton you shall do this, but it is all a question and a calculation of L.S.D. [Symbols for pounds, shillings and pence, prior to the metrification of the British currency—Ed.]

I invested in some U.S.A. bonds as you suggest and also took some U.K. of G.B., may they prove a success and minister to my welfare and my wishes.

I have not been well enough to take some mud baths here this time but I should have liked to do so, and may return another year to have a course. We leave here for Edinburgh and the Campbells at Pitlochry. Their place is called Tordarrach, and we may go to Offley's Moncrieff cousins, the Moncrieff-Wrights.

It will much depend on how I am, for I have had so much pain in my head. It is however wearing away somewhat, and I am in hopes it will disappear as mysteriously as it came.

I am sending you a book called 'Chantrey Land', if dear Aunt Fanny is ever read to, please lend to her nurses to read to her.

I was most interested in the list of plates of old Philadelphia, and much wish I had some, especially of Rittenhouse Sqr. if it should show our house, old or new. What do they cost? No more now. Very dear love to you all.

Never have I seen O. so excited as when visiting Snitterton and Norton.

October 10, 1922

**Tordarrach, Pitlochry,
Scotland**

My very dear Father,

Here we are in the heart of the Highlands—round the corner, as it were, from Killiecrankie and next door to a wee house known as 'Queen Mary's Harper's House'. The countryside is glorious with its moors and rivers and the trees are grand, just now resplendent in all the gold and glory of autumn. Rich coppers and browns and brilliant golds, set off by dark pines and yews of an age. We are with Sir Frederick and Lady Campbell and are made <u>most thoroughly</u> at home—fed and warmed and toasted with a most generous hospitality. Every afternoon we motor out through some park-like country, stopping to tea with a nearby Laird or coming back to our own cozy fireside. We spent ten days in Edinburgh and found it hard to come away. O. saw his Agent—a charming man—a Mr. Pence(!) who is a Lawyer and a W.S. (Writer to the Signet) an old Scotch term. Saw O.'s Scotch Grandfather's big house in Drummond Place, and his Aunt's old house in Great King Street, ate scones and Scotch cakes and porridge and nearly ruined ourselves at Romanes and Paterson, with a new rug and some woolies, and came here by way of Falkirk, Stirling and Kinross and Perth, stopping to see some more cousins en route.

I must not forget to wish you many happy returns of the day for the 18th of October, and also a good wish that you may spend a summer with us in Scotland and England before another year is out, for I'm sure you would love it. Fred Campbell wears a kilt all day long and his black coat and silver buttons at dinner give things a festive air and he is always 'at home' in his tartan stockings and little cap, and being a large and handsome man it is quite a distinction going about with him.

Long before this reaches you we shall probably be back in town, making arrangements for some winter sojourn to warmer climes as I am feeling rather anxious about Offley who for the last few days has felt the cold and does not seem to get really warm. I am very much afraid he left off putting on warmer clothes as soon as he should have, and we have had so much rain this summer it quite gets into one's bones.

O. will write himself, as soon as he feels up to it, and gets well warmed through and over this horrid chillyness. We both send much love and best of birthday greetings.

c/ **Sir Frederick Campbell, K.C.B.,**
Tordarrach, Pitlochry,

October 21, 1922   Scotland

My very dear Father,

Where to begin and how to write you of my beloved Offley I scarcely know. From my last letter and from my wires you will now know that he was struck down with chill or heart or both suddenly, somewhere between the 9th when he wrote in his diary, 'I cannot shake off this feeling of nausea' and again 'Still feeling poisonous, everything is an effort, have to force myself to put one foot before another'. I did not know or realize this but thought he looked rather cold and counselled warmer clothes for Scotland, and by the 18th when he was in bed with the local doctor, (a very good man by the way) he appeared very very ill but we hoped to get him away South at once. The 19th, the 2nd doctor, also an Edinburgh graduate was called in and he told me things were <u>very grave</u>, very grave indeed and as they are still. Yesterday I asked the doctor to get a specialist if he felt it would give him confidence and I took a few minutes to decide if I would have up our London man, or one from Edinburgh. I decided upon an Edinburgh physician. He should be of the best, also that it was nearer and therefore we could act with greater promptness, and by 4:40 Dr. Branewell was here and a nursing sister with him, and another nurse comes from Edinburgh tomorrow—Monday morning. The doctors held their consultation here. Sir Frederick came back from Glasgow where he had gone to a conference and by dinner time, 8 o'clock with us, this house was turned into a hospital and the household all at my disposal to do everything and anything for Offley. The doctors' verdict was '<u>very very very</u> ill indeed', matters <u>very grave</u> but he was to be given a fighting chance with the best of nursing and no stone unturned.

You know how much at home I am in Edinburgh and how confident one can feel of Edinburgh physicians. The personality of the doctors, 'big' man and others, are all pleasing and the Nursing Sister, a 'dear'—business like and self reliant. Our chauffeur (George may remember him) proves to be a treasure, and helps me on every hand, and I was despairing at my circumstances two or three days ago, at not being in my own house, at having no personal servant, and lo! such kindness, such tenderness and such sincerity and helpfulness meets me on every hand. Lady Seton in Edinburgh kindly sent down a bed table and other things <u>at once</u> and an affectionate letter followed. Sir Bruce Seton is a cousin to Offley, still more a devoted friend.

Monday (October 23)

Yesterday they had prayers in Church for Offley, and <u>all</u> are most kind and tender and solicitous. The chemists and the whole little community of Pitlochry seem like old friends and <u>nothing</u> is left unturned to be done for my broken Lover—<u>my</u> Offley. Thank you for your cables. I keep sane by much to do and the great kindness of all round me, best of all in the companionship of my warm and attached friends—otherwise I am grieved beyond expression.

Three days later Offley died, of pneumonia and heart failure.

The following month Sir Frederick Campbell wrote to Lina's sister, Betty.

November 27, 1922
                                        Tordarrach, Pitlochry,
                                              Perthshire

Dear Mrs. Saportas

Thank you very much for your letter of the ninth.

You will have heard from Mrs. Offley by now how she left us soon after the sad funeral in Edinburgh and we hear from her in London where she is in her old rooms again I think. She has a splendid young Sister (nurse) with her—who was one of those who attended Offley. So it is doubly soothing to your sister to have her just at this juncture. The Sister is cheerful and bright and sensible and I don't think your sister could have had a more fortunate companion at the moment.

When these partings come—it is a knock down blow—but the realisation for a time thereafter must necessarily be the more terrible time—until a further period has elapsed—knowing them as we did we feel very sad at heart for her. But I do think she is bearing up bravely and looking at it not as a parting but a going before—and he is just as present in the spiritual sense as ever.

One can hardly put him out of mind—not that one wants to do so—but he was an exceptionally lovable man and friend and we often feel as though we hear his musical pleasing voice—dear fellow—I am afraid I am not giving you any news—but am writing just what comes to mind.

It really is sad you should all have been separated from him and your sister at this time, and it makes it all the harder for you all to bear, because somehow letters seem so cold and hard.

Dear Offley—I never heard him utter one word about himself or his illness. I am inclined to think he did not realise its real seriousness—and as he got weaker his mind did not work on that line. When he pulled himself together he collected his thoughts wonderfully and there was the old fire in his speech and the old brightness of eye—and with all the old dash of humour in it.

I am enclosing a p.c. picture of the house (but there was no snow, only sunny weather during his illness) showing Offley's bed-room window—from his bed he could see out across the valley into the hills opposite—and he loved to see the trees and hills all bathed in sunshine.

You will grasp from rough diagram how easily and well he could see out—which was a pleasure to him as he often said.

By now you will have heard of the burial in his grandmother's vault in Dean Cemetery, Edinburgh. All the arrangements worked smoothly and we motored back here some 90 odd miles the same night—stopping for tea in Perth.

My wife sends her love. We hope we may have you here with us when you next come to Scotia.

Epilogue

No more letters of any consequence have been found. To whom should Lina write the weekly letters she had been writing for the previous fifteen years? Her mother had died in 1911. Uncle Joe had died in 1921 and shortly thereafter Aunt Fanny had become incapable of either reading or writing letters. Her father died in 1925.

From here on her Visitors Book is the main source of information. The first page is inscribed:

> Caroline Offley Shore
> Her Visitors Book
> 9, Berkeley Square
> London W.
> 1924

Dated 14 May 1928, is the entry:

After some very happy seasons spent in Berkeley Square and abroad and a journey to America I came into my own 'Country Hall in Town'— the drawing-room floor flat, 49, Grosvenor Square, W. London.

To this flat Lina removed an Adam fireplace from Norton Hall.

In 1938 she recorded:

In 1935 His Majesty George the V gave me the apartment in the Clock Tower, Hampton Court Palace and after nearly 3 years of restoration (finding 'dry rot', crumbling stone and other effects of age) and also during the procedure discovering many interesting features of Tudor

The Astronomical Clock Tower in Hampton Court Palace. The Clock made by
Nicholas Oursian in 1540.

days, of Wolsey's and Henry VIII's, I came here May 10, 1938, to live in this most lovely part of this loveliest of old Palaces.

The Visitors Book records visits by many of those friends and relations from both sides of the Atlantic whose names have appeared in the letters, and her absences when travelling: a visit to Betty and Fanny, a cruise to the West Indies and South America

in 1935, and a long visit to the United States in 1946–7, during which she sold the land Offley had given her in Santa Barbara.

Occasional letters and press cuttings record her presentation at Court of her niece Eleanor Offley-Shore on 26 June 1925; a visit to the Maharaja of Jodhpur in 1934; in 1941 a cheque sent to her husband's Regiment for 'comforts for the troops', as she herself had made and sent during the first World War. This was returned to her with thanks as the Regiment was still in peace time quarters in Lahore.

In 1942 she wrote, 'went up to London for the Winter, but became ill and could not get back here as soon as I had hoped.' She made no reference to the air-raids of the second World War.

The entries dwindle after 1946 and the last is in 1951.

In 1948 there was formed a Reunion Association of ex-Officers of her husband's Regiment which, in 1921, in the sort of re-organisation which always follows a war, had been amalgamated with the 19th Lancers (Fane's Horse) to form the 19th King George V's Own Lancers. In 1947, at Independence and Partition, this Regiment was then transferred to Pakistan as the 19th Lancers.

Lina attended the annual reunions of this Association from 1949 to 1954 at Gunters, or the Naval and Military Club, as did I. Had I but known then how involved I would become, some thirty years later, with this gallant lady's life, what questions I might have asked her!

In 1955 Lina sent 'apologies for absence'. In 1956 nothing was heard. In the following year the Association's News Letter recorded:

Mrs. C. Offley Shore, widow of Brig. General O. B. S. F. Shore, C.B., C.I.E., D.S.O., who was in the 18th Lancers from 1885–1911, died on March 11th, 1957, at her home in the Clock Tower, at Hampton Court Palace.

A Note on the Two Shore Families

Lina made many references to a connection between her husband's family and that of Commander Henry Noel Shore, R.N. (5th Baron Teignmouth, 1916) and his three sons: Hugh Aglionby, Indian Public Works Dept.; Lionel, drowned at the Battle of Jutland, 1917; and Noel, Indian Police, transferred to the Indian Army, 1917. See in particular Lina's letters of 3 and 10 August 1912.

For the purposes of differentiation in this note the two families are identified by the names of their ancestral homes: 'Meersbrook' and 'Norton Hall'—both near Sheffield—in the case of Offley Shore's family, and 'Snitterton'—near Matlock in Derbyshire—in the case of Henry Noel Shore's family.

The Sir John Shore—the 'staunch Royalist' knighted in 1662 for service to the Stuart Kings—was not an ancestor of Offley's. He was of the Snitterton family, and was the great-grandfather of the first Lord Teignmouth, Governor-General of India, 1793–98, and great-great-great-grandfather of Henry Noel Shore.

The first Shore occupier of Norton Hall was Samuel Shore, of the Meersbrook family, who married Urith Offley of Norton Hall in 1759. A present-day descendant of this Shore's brother John states that 'It is said that [the two families] were of one stock originally, but no one as yet has been able to say when the family divided'.

Furthermore there exists a manuscript note written some time in the latter part of the nineteenth century by Harrington Offley Shore, an uncle of Lina's husband, which reads:

In 1839, Mr. Offley Shore of Norton Hall, having applied to the Heralds at Arms for a confirmation of the Arms always borne by his family, it appeared there was no record on the register of any previous grant having been made to his branch of the family—altho they have been borne by them since the XVth century—further, that the grant of the Shore Arms to Sir John Shore was limited to the male descendants of Sir J.'s father only.

Thereupon it became necessary—in consequence of no such grant being found to have been registered, and in consequence of Sir John Shore's Arms having been allowed to him in 1662—to prove by documentary (Parish registers) evidence the missing links of connection which undoubtedly exist between the Norton and Snitterton branches. Although search was accordingly made, it proved fruitless and finally a Grant of Arms was made to Mr. Offley Shore of Norton Hall and the descendants of his Grandfather—similar to the Ancient Arms borne by the Shores with slight alteration in the figure.

The Mesopotamia Campaign

(See Map on page 300)

Prior to the opening of World War I the waning power of the Ottoman (Turkish) Empire still extended southward from the Black Sea, through the whole area between the eastern shore of the Mediterranean and the valleys of the Tigris and Euphrates, to both shores of the Arabian peninsula.

In the first days of the war, German warships in the Mediterranean took refuge in Turkish waters off Constantinople; Indian Army troops moved into Bahrein to protect oil refineries; Turkey declared war on Britain and her allies on 29 October 1914; and the Indian troops in Bahrein moved up the Persian Gulf and captured Basra (23 November 1914).

Here the Tigris River Expedition, largely Indian Army, was established under the command of Sir John Nixon, under orders from the Indian Government—the Viceroy and the C. in C., India—which, in policy matters, was responsible to the Secretary of State for India in London.

In June 1915, Nixon sent a force under General Charles Townsend, consisting of one strengthened division and a small naval flotilla, up the Tigris to reconnoitre an advance to Baghdad. In September this reached and took Kut el Amara, some one hundred miles down river from Baghdad as the crow flies, but many hundreds as the Tigris winds.

In November, Townsend was ordered to advance to Baghdad and though he reported that his force was inadequate for such an operation he was not reinforced. He successfully advanced as far as Ctesiphon, four-fifths of the distance from Kut to Baghdad, but at this point he was held by the Turkish forces, suffered some 4,600 casualties and retreated to Kut. Here he was besieged from 3 December to 29 April 1916 when, his troops being near starvation, he surrendered; 6,000 Indian and 2,700 British soldiers were taken prisoners. Unsuccessful relief attempts had suffered over 21,000 casualties.

In January 1916, General Sir John Nixon had been withdrawn on grounds of ill health and replaced by General Sir Percy Lake. Brigadier-General Offley Shore accompanied the latter as his Chief of Staff and later was appointed Inspector-General, Lines of Communication, a pivotal appointment since the operation was greatly handicapped by appalling terrain and inadequacy of transportation.

The Kut el Amara disaster raised a great public outcry in Britain and in August 1916 a Commission of Inquiry was appointed which reported in May 1917. (Mesopotamia Commission Report, Cd 8610.) Both Sir John Nixon and Sir Percy Lake gave evidence, the latter having been withdrawn from Mesopotamia for this purpose. He was replaced by General Sir Stanley Maude.

The Report of the Commission of Inquiry spread blame for the disaster widely over Civil and Military authorities, but particularly on Sir John Nixon. The Government proposed to establish a special court to inquire further, but objections to this were raised in Parliament. The Army Council called for written explanations from military personnel involved and an announcement was subsequently made in the House of Commons that Sir John Nixon's explanation had been accepted. In 1919 he was created G.C.M.G.

Sir Percy Lake on his withdrawal from Mesopotamia was created K.C.B. and in 1917 appointed to the Ministry of Munitions.

Offley Shore had developed jaundice late in 1916 and had been invalided back to Simla.

Sir Stanley Maude in December 1916 began a fresh advance up the Tigris, re-took Kut el Amara in February 1917 and secured Baghdad in March.

The British Mission to the Russian Army of the Caucasus 1917–18

Czar Nicholas II abdicated the Russian throne on 15 March 1917. Lenin and other Bolshevik leaders returned from abroad in April and Trotsky in May. A provisional government with changing leadership held office until the October revolution established the Bolshevik regime. An armistice with Germany and the Central powers was concluded on 15 December.

These Government changes led to a reduction in the effectiveness of the Russian armies, one of which was the Russian Army in the Caucasus with headquarters at Tiflis (now Tbilisi), the capital of the province of Georgia. The soldiery were not being paid and many were deserting, being more interested in protecting their own interests at home in a time of revolution than in prosecuting a war on the periphery of an empire which was showing signs of disintegrating. The provinces of Georgia, Armenia and Azerbaijan, incorporated into the Russian Empire early in the nineteenth century, established the Transcaucasian Republic in September 1917 and would proclaim their independence of Russia in the spring of 1918.

Britain, the United States and France had an interest in maintaining the Russian Army in the Caucasus as a block to a German/Turkish advance to the Caspian oil-fields and beyond. British missions were therefore established at Tiflis to provide military advice and to channel financial aid. It was to the latter that Offley was assigned. He left London in the guise of a King's Messenger sometime between 8 and 12 July 1917, travelled via Oslo, Finland and Petrograd, and by 13 August had arrived in Tiflis, where he gave his address as c/o Colonel Marsh, British Agent, Staff Headquarters, Russian Armies in the Caucasus, Tiflis. An unpublished private diary records that Offley found there a Russian Army Commander considering the demobilisation of his whole force.

Two references to his activities have been found in published sources. Ranald MacDonell,[1] British Vice-Consul at Baku, in his autobiography *And Nothing Long* records that, finding himself isolated and virtually unemployed, he applied for a posting elsewhere and was directed to the British Mission at Tiflis. 'General Offley Shore, Head of the British Mission', he wrote, 'decided that I was the right and proper person to act as courier between Tiflis and Baku to fetch and carry the mounds of paper roubles which were to be sent out from Persia. My first journey was uneventful; the General, who was proceeding to another post, came with me.' They had a guard of four French soldiers.

Secondly, General Dunsterville,[2] commanding the British force to which Lina refers in her letter of 17 August, 1918, recorded a meeting in Hamadan on 7 February, with 'General Offley Shore, recently returned from Tiflis, who was to post me in all the latest information concerning the South Caucasus.' Offley's assignment had been terminated, he had departed Tiflis on 16 January 1918, and begun his journey via Teheran, Hamadan, Baghdad, Basra, Bombay, Alexandria and Paris to arrive in London on 30 April.

Lina's letters give no information on what Offley was doing; she probably had none. In her letter of 19 October 1917, she tells of a wire from Offley telling her to go to the War Office 'to hear from a certain General various things'. On 28 February she tells of walking in the Park to hear from a friend of 'a magnificent thing my Best and dearest has done' about which the friend had been told by Lord Southborough, then Secretary of the Grand Committee on World Trade. And in her letter of 4 January she believes that the sum of ten thousand English pounds which Offley had cabled Uncle Joe to send to Lina in London was somehow related to some 'big scheme' in which Offley was involved with the American Consul-General in Tiflis, 'which was not to be even spoken of or hinted at'.

No later references have been found in the letters of this request of Offley's and no reason is known for his need for what was, at this time, a very large sum. Lina's first explanation, in her letter of 30 December, that his pay and allowances were not coming through, seems inadequate. The diarist referred to earlier in this Appendix believes that Offley was connected with a small group in London who were raising a large loan for some purpose not now known.

Offley in his letters of 19 May, 29 May and 11 June described and commented on the termination of his assignment and the appointment of a replacement, who never arrived. In her letter of 17 August Lina wrote, 'The Foreign Office here seemed very pleased with him, but the War Office, under whom he actually was, received his ideas with derision.' This may have been the basic cause of Offley's difficulties and his recall. The then British Agent in Moscow, Bruce Lockhart,[3] complained that there was a lack of coordination between the different British Missions in Russia, of which there were seven, and that the Foreign Office and the War Office were pursuing different policies.

In the outcome however Offley's withdrawal was fortunate for him. Following the cessation of hostilities between Russia and Germany with the signing of the Treaty of Brest Litovsk on 3 March a German force occupied Tiflis on 12 June. The British Mission escaped and started to trek northwards but had only made about a hundred miles when they were captured by a local Bolshevik force. The officer then commanding the Mission, Colonel Pike, was shot. The remainder were taken as prisoners to Moscow and eventually repatriated after diplomatic negotiations.

Viceroys and Commanders-in-Chief

Viceroys

Baron (Marquess) Curzon of Kedleston	1899–1905
The Earl of Minto	1905–10
Baron Hardinge of Penshurst	1910–16
Baron (Viscount) Chelmsford	1916–21

Commanders-in-Chief, India

Viscount (Earl) Kitchener of Khartoum	1902–09
Sir O'Moore Creagh, V.C.	1909–14
Sir Beauchamp Duff	1914–16
Sir Charles Munro	1916–20

Biographical Notes

Adam, James (1730–94), Architect to King George III.

Adam, Robert, F.R.S. (1728–92), Architect.
Scottish architects responsible for many buildings in London, including the Adelphi, and country houses.

Baker, Sir Herbert, K.C.I.E. (1862–1946)
Architect. Examples of his buildings are to be found in South Africa; Kenya; Zimbabwe; New Delhi: the Secretariat and Legislative buildings; London: the Bank of England, India House, and South Africa House.

Bell, Gertrude Margaret Lowthian (1868–1926)
Traveller, explorer, archaeologist, administrator and mountaineer. First class honours in Modern History at Lady Margaret Hall, Oxford, 1888. Travelled extensively in what are now Iran, Iraq, Syria, Jordan, Lebanon, Israel and Saudi Arabia, 1892–1914. Spoke Persian and Arabic. Joined the Arab intelligence Bureau in Cairo, staffed by persons with pre-war experience in the Middle East, 1915. When Lina met her in Delhi as described in her letter of 25 February 1916, she had been sent by the Bureau to assist the Indian Government in the preparation of a gazetteer covering the area of the Mesopotamia Campaign, and from there went on to Basra, the Headquarters of the Mesopotamia Expeditionary Force. Oriental Secretary of the British High Commissioner in Iraq, Sir Percy Cox, 1917. Appointed honorary Director of Archaeology, Iraq, 1922. On her death in 1926 a plaque was placed in the Baghdad Museum, reading in part:

Gertrude Bell
Whose memory the Arabs will ever hold in
reverence and affection

Created this Museum in 1923.

. . . . . .

King Faisal and the Government of Iraq
In gratitude for her great deeds in this country
Have ordered that the Principal Wing shall bear her name.

(See *Gertrude Bell*, by H. V. F. Winstone; Cape, London, 1978.)

Bernstorff, John Heinrich, Graf von (1862–1939)
German Ambassador to Washington, 1908–17. Following the torpedoing of the liners *Lusitania* and *Arabic* in May and August 1915, with the loss of American lives in both cases, Bernstorff warned the German Government that unrestricted submarine warfare would bring the United States into the war. The German Government gave assurances acceptable to the U.S. Government. In January 1917, however, they gave notice of resuming the unrestricted policy on 1 February. The United States severed relations with Germany two days later.

Bethmann-Hollwegg, Dr. Theobald von (1856–1921)
German Chancellor, 1909–17. Attempted to bargain a German undertaking not to occupy French or Belgian territory in return for British neutrality in the approaching war, 29 July 1914. Retired July 1917.

Bigge, Lieut. Col., The Rt. Hon. Arthur John, 1st Baron Stamford-ham, P.C., G.C.B., G.C.I.E., G.C.S.I. (1849–1931)
Assistant Private Secretary to Queen Victoria, 1880; Secretary to Queen Victoria, 1895–1901; Secretary to Prince of Wales, 1901–10; Secretary to King George V, 1910–31.

Bryan, William Jennings (1860–1925)
Appointed Secretary of State by U.S. President Woodrow Wilson, 1912. Did not agree with Wilson's increasingly belligerent policy towards Germany and, on 9 June 1915, resigned rather than sign a second, stronger note of protest on the sinking of the *Lusitania*.

Bryce, James, 1st Viscount of Dechmont, P.C., O.M., G.C.V.O. (1838–1922)
Barrister. International Jurist; British Representative at the Hague Court; Ambassador at Washington, 1907–13.

Cambridge, George William Frederick Charles, 2nd Duke of, P.C.,

K.G., etc. (1819–1904)
Son of Adolphus Frederick, 1st Duke, 10th child of George III
and Princess Augusta Wilhelmina Louisa, daughter of Frederick,
Land-grave of Hesse-Cassel. Commander-in-Chief, British Army,
1856–95.

Carmichael, Sir George, K.C.S.I. (1866–1936)
Member of Executive Council, Bombay, 1915–20.

Chelmsford, Frederick John Napier Thesiger, 1st Viscount, P.C.,
G.C.S.I., G.C.M.G., G.C.I.E. (1868–1933)
Governor of Queensland, 1905–9; Governor of New South Wales,
1909–13; Viceroy of India, 1916–21; First Lord of the Admiralty,
1924. Viscount Chelmsford's name is associated with that of Edwin
Montagu, Secretary of State for India, in the Montagu Chelmsford
Report, which led to the Government of India Act of 1919, following an announcement by the Secretary of State in the House
of Commons that 'the policy of His Majesty's Government with
which the Government of India are in complete accord, is that
of the increasing association of Indians in every branch of the
administration and the gradual development of self-governing institutions with a view to the progressive realisation of responsible
government in India as an integral part of the British Empire'.
Included was a provision for the increased Indianisation of the
officers of the Indian Army.

Chirol, Sir Valentine, Kt. (1852–1929)
Clerk in the Foreign Office; traveller and writer; Director, Foreign
Department, *The Times*; Royal Commission on India Public Serv-
ices, 1912.

Choate, Joseph Hodges (1832–1917)
U.S. Ambassador to the Court of St. James, 1899–1905.

Cornwallis, Charles, 1st Marquess (1738–1805)
Governor-general of India, 1786–94; reappointed in 1805, died
the same year.

Cornwallis-West, Mrs. George (died 1921)
Née Jennie Jerome, daughter of Leonard Jerome of New York.
Married in 1874 the Rt. Hon. Lord Randolph Spencer Churchill
who died 1895. Mother of Sir Winston Churchill.

Creagh, General Sir O'Moore, V.C., G.C.B., G.C.S.I. (1848–1923)
Afghan war, 1879–80; China Expedition, 1900; Secretary, Military
Department, India Office, 1907–9; Commander-in-Chief, India,
1909–14.

Crewe, Robert Offley Ashburton Crewe-Milnes, 1st Marquess of,
K.G. (1858–1945)
Secretary of State for the Colonies, 1908–10; Secretary of State
for India, 1910–15; Ambassador to France, 1922–8. The Marquess
of Crewe and Offley Shore had an ancestor in common in William
Offley, mercer, Bailiff of Stafford in 1510.

Cromer, Evelyn Baring, 1st Earl of, P.C., G.C.B., O.M., G.C.M.G.,
K.C.S.I. (1841–1917)
Finance Member of Viceroy's Council, India, 1880; Agent and
Consul-General in Egypt, 1883–1907.

Curzon of Kedleston, George Nathaniel, 1st Marquess, K.G.,
G.C.S.I., G.C.I.E. (1859–1925)
Under-Secretary of State for India, 1891–2; Under-Secretary of
State for Foreign Affairs, 1895–8; Viceroy of India, 1899–1905;
Leader of House of Lords, 1916–24; Secretary of State for Foreign
Affairs, 1919–24.

Dane, Sir Louis William, G.C.I.E. (1856–1956)
Secretary to the Government of India in the Foreign Department,
1902–8; Lieut. Governor of the Punjab, 1908–13.

Dudley, William Humble Ward, 2nd Earl of, G.C.B., G.C.M.G.,
G.C.V.O. (1867–1932)
Governor-General of Australia, 1908–11; represented Australia
at the Quebec Tercentenary Celebrations, 1908.

Duff, General Sir Beauchamp, G.C.B., G.C.S.I. (1855–1918)
Adjutant-General in India, 1903–6: Chief of Staff in India, 1906–
9; Secretary, Military Department, India Office, 1910; Commander-in-Chief, India, 1913–16.

Duveen of Millbank, Joseph, 1st Baron (1869–1939)
Trustee and benefactor of several London art galleries and trustee
of the Museum of Modern Art, New York. Endowed a Chair in
the History of Art at London University.

Eugénie, Empress of the French, 1853–70 (1826–1920)
  Married Napoleon III, 1853. Fled to England after the surrender
  of Napoleon to the King of Prussia at the battle of Sedan, 1870.

Ewart, Major-General Sir Richard, K.C.M.G., C.B., C.I.E., D.S.O.
  (1864–1928)
  A.D.C. to King George V, 1911–16; Deputy Director Supply and
  Transport, Indian Corps, France, 1914–15; D.A. and Q.M.G., East
  African Expeditionary Force, 1915–18; Red Cross Commissioner
  to Berlin to repatriate British prisoners of war, 1918–19.

Fitzgeorge, Col. Sir Augustus Charles Frederick, C.B., K.C.V.O.,
  (1847–1933)
  Son of 2nd Duke of Cambridge and Mrs. Fitzgeorge.

Foch, Field Marshal Ferdinand, G.C.B., O.M. (1851–1929)
  Marshal of France, 1918; Field Marshal (British), 1919; Generalissimo of the Allied Forces, France, 1918.

Godfrey-Faussett, Capt. Sir Bryan Godfrey, G.C.V.O., R.N. (1863–
  1945)
  Equerry to King George V, King Edward VIII and King
  George VI.

Goltz, General Colmar von der (1846–1916)
  German Governor of occupied Belgium, 1914.

Grey, Rt. Hon. Albert Henry George, 4th Earl, P.C., G.C.B.,
  G.C.M.G., G.C.V.O. (1851–1917)
  Administrator of Rhodesia, 1896–7; Director of British South Africa
  Company, 1898–1904; Governor-General and Commander-in-
  Chief, Canada, 1904–11.

Grover, General Sir Malcolm Henry Stanley, K.C.B., K.C.I.E. (1858–
  1945)
  Inspector-General of Cavalry, India, 1908–11; Secretary to Government of India, Army Department, 1911–12; Commander 4th
  (Quetta) Division, India, 1912–16. Retired 1919.

Gwatkin, Major-General Sir Willoughby Garnous, K.C.M.G., C.B.
  (1859–1925)
  Manchester Regiment, 1882; Major-General and Honorary Lieut.
  General, Canadian Militia.

Haig, Field Marshal Douglas, 1st Earl, K.T., G.C.B., O.M., K.C.I.E., G.C.V.O. (1861–1928)
Inspector-General of Cavalry, India, 1903–6; Director of Military Training, 1906–7; Director of Staff Duties at Army H.Q., 1907–9; Chief of Staff, India, 1909–12; Commander-in-Chief Expeditionary Forces, France and Flanders, 1915–19; Commander-in-Chief Forces in Great Britain, 1919–20.

Hanbury-Williams, Major-General Sir John, G.C.V.O., K.C.B. (1859–1946)
Secretary and Military Secretary to Governor-General of Canada, 1904–9; Chief of Military Mission with H.Q. Russian Army in the Field, 1914–17.

Hardie, James Keir (1856–1915)
Elected to Parliament in 1892. First leader of the Labour Party, 1906; Chairman of the British section of the International Socialist Bureau. His speeches on India during a visit there in 1907–8 and thereafter aroused widespread anger in Britain.

Hardinge of Penshurst, Charles, 1st Baron, P.C., K.G., G.C.B., G.C.S.I., G.C.M.G., G.C.I.E., G.C.V.O. (1858–1944)
Permanent Under-Secretary of State for Foreign Affairs, 1906–10; Ambassador at Petrograd, 1904–6; Viceroy of India, 1910–16; Permanent Under-Secretary of State for Foreign Affairs, 1916–20; Ambassador at Paris, 1920–3.

Hastings, Warren (1732–1818)
First Governor-General of India, 1744—84. On return to Britain he was impeached on various charges, prosecuted by Edmund Burke, and acquitted in 1795. A century and a half later individual Indians still remembered this prosecution in Britain's favour.

Hewett, Sir John, G.C.S.I., K.B.E. (1854–1941)
Lieut. Governor, United Provinces, India, 1907–12. President, Coronation Durbar Committee, 1911.

Hindenburg, General Paul von (1847–1934)
Commander-in-Chief, German Armies in the East, September 1916; Chief of Staff, German Field Armies, August 1916. Elected President of Germany, 26 April 1925; died while in office, August 1934; Hitler assumed sole executive power.

Hopwood, Sir Francis John Stevens, 1st Baron Southborough, G.C.B., G.C.M.G., G.C.V.O. (1860—1941)
Secretary, Board of Trade, 1901–7; Under-Secretary of State for the Colonies, 1907–11; Civil Lord of the Admiralty and Secretary, grand committee on War Trade, 1914–17; President, Commission to India on Reform, 1918–19.

Hughes, Charles Evans (1862–1948)
Republican candidate for American Presidency, 1916. Defeated by incumbent President Woodrow Wilson: Electoral vote 277–254; Popular vote 9,129,000–8,538,000. Served on the World Court at the Hague, 1926–30. Chief Justice of the Supreme Court, U.S.A., 1930–41.

Impey, Lieut. Colonel Lawrence, C.S.I., C.I.E. (1873–1942)
Indian Army, 1885–7; transferred to Political Service, 1887; Political Agent: Alwar, Bhopal, Eastern States, Rajputana, Bundelkhand; Resident at Baroda; retired 1917. Fourth generation to serve in India, beginning with Sir Elijah Impey, 1732–1809; First Chief Justice of Bengal on the establishment of the Supreme Court at Calcutta under the Regulating Act of 1773.

Joffre, Joseph Jacques Césaire, Maréchal de France, Hon. G.C.B., O.M. (1852–1931)
Chief of French General Staff, 1914; Commander-in-Chief French Armies, 1915–17.

Jusserand, Jean Adrien Antoine Jules (1855–1932)
Entered French Foreign Office, 1876; Counsellor of Embassy at London, 1887–90; French Ambassador at Washington, 1902–25. Publications: *English Wayfaring Life in the Middle Ages* and many other works relating to the U.K. and U.S.A.

Kauffman, Angelica (1741–1807)
Portrait painter and decorator, particularly of ceilings, of Swiss nationality. In England 1766–81. Often employed by the Adam brothers. One of the original 36 members of the Royal Academy, founded in 1769, at which she frequently exhibited.

Keighley, Lieut. Colonel Vernon Aubrey Scott, D.S.O., M.V.O. (1874—1939)
26th Regiment, The Cameronians, 1895; transferred to 18th Bengal Lancers, 1899; A.D.C. to Lord Curzon; commanded Viceroy's

Bodyguard at Coronation Durbar, 1911; Commandant 18th King George's Own Lancers, France, Palestine, Egypt, India, 1917–21; retired 1922.

Kirkpatrick, General Sir George, K.C.B., K.C.S.I. (1866–1950)
Director Military Operations, India, 1914–16; Chief of General Staff, India, 1916–20.

Kitchener of Khartoum, Field Marshal Horatio Herbert, 1st Earl, P.C., K.G., O.M., G.C.S.I., K.C.I.E. (1850–1916)
Commanded Khartoum Expedition, 1898; Chief of Staff, South Africa, 1899–1900; Commander-in-Chief, South Africa, 1900–2; Commander-in-Chief, India, 1902–9; Committee of Imperial Defence, 1910; Secretary of State for War, 1914–16. Drowned *en route* to Russia in H.M.S. *Hampshire*, sunk by torpedoes, 1916.

Lake, Lieut. General Sir Percy Henry Noel, K.C.M.G., K.C.B. (1855–1940)
Gazetted 59th Foot, 1873; Chief of General Staff, Canadian Military, 1905–8; Inspector-General, Canadian Militia, 1908–10; Division Commander, India, 1911–12; Chief of General Staff, India, 1912–15; commanded Mesopotamia Force, 1916. Retired to Victoria, B.C., Canada.

Leiter, Levi Zeigler (1834–1904)
Prominent American businessman. In partnership with Marshall Field established the Chicago store of that name, sometimes referred to as the American Harrods, 1867. His three daughters married Englishmen: Mary Victoria (1870–1906) married, 1895, Lord Curzon of Keddlestone, Viceroy of India, 1899–1905. Queen Victoria is said to have enquired of her Prime Minister, Lord Salisbury, as to whether an American could properly perform the functions of a Vice-Reine, and was reassured; Marguerite Hyde (Daisy) (1879–1968), married the 19th Earl of Suffolk, one of Lord Curzon's A.D.C.s during his Viceroyalty, killed in action as a Territorial Officer in France, 1917. Nancy, born 1872, married Colin Powys Campbell, one of Lord Curzon's A.D.C.s during his Viceroyalty. Settled in Canada after the war.

Lesseps, Ferdinand Marie de (1805–94)
French engineer and diplomat. Planned the Suez Canal while serving in the Consular Service in Egypt. Completed its construction

in 1869. Began the Panama Canal in 1881, but failed through unforeseen difficulties and lack of funds.

Lloyd George, David, 1st Earl of Dwyfor (1863–1945)
Elected to Parliament as a Liberal, 1890; President of the Board of Trade, 1906; Chancellor of the Exchequer, 1908; Minister of Munitions, 1915; Prime Minster of a coalition government, 1916–22.

Lutyens, Sir Edwin L., O.M., K.C.I.E. (1855–1945)
Planner of New Delhi and designer, with Sir Herbert Baker, *q.v.*, of that city's major buildings. Other well known examples of his work are the Cenotaph in Whitehall, London and the British Embassy in Washington.

McMahon, Colonel Sir Henry, G.C.M.G., G.C.V.O., K.C.I.E. (1862–1949)
Transferred from Indian Army to Indian Political Service, 1890; Durand Mission to Kabul, 1893; responsible for delineation of the frontier (McMahon Line) between Baluchistan and Afghanistan, 1894–6; Foreign Secretary to Government of India, 1911–14; thereafter service in Egypt and Middle East.

Maude, Lieut. General Sir Frederick Stanley, K.C.B., D.S.O. (1864–1917)
Military Secretary to Governor-General of Canada, 1901–4; Private Secretary to Secretary of State for War, 1905; Commander-in-Chief Mesopotamia, August 1916.

Minto, Gilbert John Murray Kynynmond Elliott, 4th Earl of, K.G., G.C.S.I., G.C.M.G., G.C.I.E. (1847–1914)
Various military appointments, 1867–82; Military Secretary to Governor-General of Canada, 1883–5; Governor-General of Canada, 1898–1904; Viceroy of India, 1905–10. Lord Minto's name is associated with that of the then Secretary of State for India, Lord Morley, in the Government of India Act of 1909, known as the Morley–Minto Reforms. The provisions and results of this Act included the admission of an Indian member to the Viceroy's Legislative Council, the increase in the number of Provincial Executive Councils, the increase in their size and the proportion of elected, including Indian, members, and the widening of their functions. The Indian historian Dr. Kalikinkar Datta wrote, 'Though [these] Reforms marked an important step in the

introduction of representative government, they did not give Parliamentary Government to India'. (*An Advanced History of India* by R. C. Majamdar, H. C. Raychandri, and K. Datta (MacMillan, London, 3rd edition, 1967, p. 911.) Lord Morley said, 'If it could be said that this chapter of reforms led directly or necessarily to the establishment of a Parliamentary system in India, I, for one would have nothing at all to do with it'. (*House of Lords*, 17 December 1908).

Montagu of Beaulieu, John Walter Edward Douglas-Scott-Montagu, 2nd Baron, K.C.I.E., C.S.I. (1866–1929)
Adviser on Mechanical Transport Services to Government of India, 1915–19. Interested in aviation, railway and all transport matters.

Morley, John, 1st Viscount Morley of Blackburn, P.C., O.M. (1838–1923)
Secretary of State for India, 1905–10; Lord President of the Council, 1910–14.

Nicholson, Brigadier-General John (1821–57)
Killed September 1857, leading the storming of the Kashmir Gate, ending the siege of Delhi.

Nightingale, Florence, O.M. (1820–1910)
Trained as a nurse in Germany and established nursing as a respectable profession in Britain. Shortly after she had completed her training, war between Britain, France and Turkey against Russia broke out in the Crimea Peninsula (1854). Organised care for the wounded in war was almost non-existent. When news of the appalling conditions in the Crimea reached Britain, Florence Nightingale was sent, with 38 nurses, to establish and develop a hospital system. The results of her work were apparent in the reduction in the death-rate among the wounded and in the amenities available to them. After the war, with a fund of £50,000 raised by public subscription in her honour, she established the Nightingale Training School for Nurses at St. Thomas' Hospital in London. Thereafter she continued to work for improvements in public health and in nursing services.

The Shore family shared a common ancestor with Florence Nightingale: Samuel Shore of Meersbrook (1716–85).

Nixon, General Sir John, G.C.M.G., K.C.B. (1857–1921)

Served in The 25th The King's Own, Borderers and 18th Bengal
Lancers. Inspector-General of Cavalry, India, 1906–8. thereafter
held the following Commands: 7th (Meerut) Division, 1910–12;
Southern Army in India, 1912–15; Northern Army in India, 1915;
Expeditionary Force in Mesopotamia, April 1915–January 1916.

O'Dwyer, Sir Michael Francis, G.C.I.E. (1864–1940)
Lieut. Governor of the Punjab, 1913–19. Assassinated in London
in 1940 at a meeting of the Royal Central Asian Society by an
Indian, in revenge for the deaths of a large number of bystanders
in the Jalianwala Bagh at Amritsar during a period of rioting in
April 1919.

Otter, General Sir William Dillon, K.C.B., C.V.O. (1843–1929)
South African War with the Royal Canadian Regiment, 1899–
1900; Chief of General Staff, Canada, 1908–10; Inspector-General,
1910–12; Director of Internment Operations, 1914–19.

Probyn, Rt. Hon. Sir Dighton Macnaghten, V.C., P.C., G.C.B.,
G.C.S.I., G.C.V.O. (1833–1924)
Colonel, 11th King Edward's Own Lancers (Probyn's Horse). Private appointments in the Royal Household, 1872–1910; Comptroller to Queen Alexandra, 1910.

P'u I
Last Emperor of the Manchu Dynasty. Succeeded to the throne
at the age of two years in 1908 on the death, within two days,
of the previous Emperor and the powerful Dowager Empress.
Abdicated on 12 February 1912, following the election on 30
December 1911 of Sun Yat-sen as President of the United Provinces of China. Known popularly at the 'Boy Emperor'.

Ranfurly, Uchter John Mark Knox, 5th Earl of, G.C.M.B. (1875–
1933)
Governor and Commander-in-Chief of New Zealand, 1897–1904;
represented New Zealand at Ottawa Tercentenary Celebrations, 1908.

Reading, Rufus Daniel Isaacs, 1st Marquess of, P.C., G.C.B.,
G.C.S.I., G.C.I.E., G.C.V.O. (1860–1935)
Solicitor-General, 1910; Attorney-General, 1910–13; Lord Chief
Justice of England, 1913–21; Special Envoy to U.S.A., 1917; High
Commissioner and Special Ambassador to U.S.A., 1918; Viceroy
of India, 1921–6; Secretary of State for Foreign Affairs, 1931.

Richardson, Colonel James Jardine, D.S.O. (1873–1942)
Nephew of Rachel Jardine of Dryfeholme, Lockerbie, Scotland. North-West Frontier of India, 1897–8; European War, 1914–18; Colonel 13th/18th Royal Hussars, 1938–42.

Roberts of Kandahar, Field Marshal, 1st Earl, P.C., G.C.B., G.C.S.I., G.C.I.E. (1832–1914)
Siege of Delhi, 1857; Afghan War, 1878–9 (whence title); Commander-in-Chief, India, 1885–93; Commander-in-Chief, British Army, 1901–4; Colonel-in-Chief, Overseas and Indian Forces in Europe, 1914.

Robertson, Field Marshal Sir William, 1st Baronet, G.C.B., G.C.M.G., G.C.V.O., D.S.O. (1860–1933)
Quartermaster-General, British Expeditionary Force, 1914; Chief of General Staff, B.E.F., 1915; Chief of the Imperial General Staff, 1915–18; Commander-in-Chief, British Army on the Rhine, 1919–20.

Roosevelt, Theodore (1858–1919)
Twenty-sixth President of United States. Vice-President, 1901. President on assassination of President William McKinley, 1901; President, 1905–9. Organised 1st U.S. Cavalry Volunteers (Roosevelt's Rough Riders) and commanded it in Cuba in 1898. Offered to raise an Army Division, after declaration of war, and take it to France, 1917; offer declined by President Wilson.

Roos-Keppel, Sir George, G.C.I.E., K.C.S.I. (1866–1921)
Indian Staff Corps, 1897; Chief Commissioner and Agent to Governor-General, North-West Frontier Province, 1908–19; Member of the Council of the Secretary of State for India, 1920.

Southborough, Baron
See Hopwood, Sir Francis John Stevens.

Stamfordham, Baron
See Bigge, Lieut. Colonel The Rt. Hon. Arthur John.

Sun Yat-sen (1866–1925)
In 1894 began forming secret revolutionary societies, with support from overseas Chinese, which in 1911 achieved the Chinese Revolution, the election of Sun Yat-sen as President of

the United Provinces of China at the end of the year and the abdication of the 'Boy Emperor' early in the following year.

Tata, Sir Ratan (1871–1918)
Partner, Tata Sons & Co., Bombay; Director, Tata Ltd., London, and numerous family and other industrial concerns in India; son of Jamsetjee Nasarwanji Tata, who founded the mercantile firm of Tata & Co. at Bombay, with branches in Japan, Hong Kong, Shanghai, London, Paris and New York.

Tirpitz, Admiral Alfred Peter Friedrich von (1849–1930)
German Minister of Marine, 1897–1916. Responsible for the expansion of the German Navy beginning in 1898, resulting in development of friction with Britain. At variance with the Kaiser over the retention in port of the German High Seas Fleet, he resigned early in 1916.

Waddington, Charles Willoughby, C.I.E., M.V.O. (1865—1946)
Principal, Gujarat College, Ahmedabad, 1889–92; Principal, Rajkumar College, Rajkot, 1892–1903; Principal, Mayo College, Ajmer, 1903–16; Indian Army Remount Depot, 1916–18; Secretary, Food Control Board, Simla, 1918–19; Guardian to the Maharaja of Jodhpur, 1919–23.

Wigram, Clive, 1st Baron of Clewer, P.C., G.C.B., G.C.V.O., C.S.I. (1873–1960)
18th Bengal Lancers, 1897; Military Secretary to General-Officer-Commanding-in-Chief, Aldershot, 1908–10; Private appointments in the Royal Household, 1910–60; Colonel, 19th King George V's Own Lancers, 1932–45.

Willingdon, Freeman, Freeman-Thomas, 1st Marquis of, P.C., G.C.S.I., G.C.M.G. (1866–1941)
Governor of Bombay, 1913–19; Governor of Madras, 1919–22; Delegate for India, Assembly of League of Nations, 1924; Governor-General of Canada, 1926–31; Viceroy of India, 1931–6.

Wilson, Thomas Woodrow, (1856–1924)
Twenty-seventh President of the United States, 1913–17, 1917–21. President Wilson's 'Fourteen Points' formed the basis of the Peace Conference which opened in Paris in January 1919. He was the leading protagonist for the forming of the League of Nations. The inclusion of the Covenant of the League of Nations in the Treaty

of Versailles caused the United States to reject ratification of this Treaty.

Wolseley, Lady
Wife of field Marshal Lord Garnet Wolseley, Commander-in-Chief, British Army, 1895–1900.

Glossary

The Western spelling of Indian words varied over time and often at the whim of the user. The servant who waited at table might be spelt *khidmatgar*, *khidmutgar*, *khitmatgar* or *khitmutgar*. Lina and Offley used different spellings and Lina was not consistent. One form only is used in this Glossary.

Ayah	a nurse-maid or lady's maid.
Badshah	a King; here King-Emperor.
Bahadur	originally a title of honour conferred by the Mogul Emperors. Later an honorific signifying 'brave'.
Bandobast	arrangements; as in *bandobast-wallah*—he who makes the arrangements.
Bhisti	a carrier of water, as Kipling's Gunga Din, originally a goat-skin allowing evaporation to keep the water cool.
Calèche	(French) a two-wheeled horse-drawn vehicle with a folding top: especially in Quebec.
Charpoy	a bed consisting of a wooden frame strung with strips of cloth or light rope.
Chicks	screens of bamboo or reed hung over windows or other openings which, when kept wet, lower the temperature within by evaporation.
Chit or chitty	a short written message; especially a reference given to a departing servant.
Chota Hazri	the early morning cup of tea; lit. 'small breakfast'.
Crore	ten million; or one hundred *lakhs*. q.v.
Degchie	a cooking pot; anglicised to 'dixie'.

Dhobie	the man-servant who does the laundry.
Dhursi	a tailor
Dhurrie	a thin cotton carpet.
Diwan-i-Am	Hall of Public Audience.
Diwan-i-Khas	Hall of Private Audience.
Durbar	a formal reception of his people by their ruler or of his troops by their Commander.
Jhampanies	privately employed rickshaw men whom Lina contrasts with 'ragged rickshaw men of the hired sort'.
Kadir	The Kadir Cup; the pig-sticking trophy.
Khedive	title of the rulers of Egypt under the Turkish Empire.
Khidmatgar	a servant who waits at table.
Khud	a precipitous hillside.
Kukri	the Gurkhas' traditional weapon; a broad bladed curved knife.
Kurta	a loose blouse or tunic reaching to the knees, opening down the front to the waist: see photograph of Offley Shore on p.11.
Lakh	one hundred thousand.
-log	a category of people: as in *Sikh-log*, the Sikh people; *Bandar-log*, Kipling's Monkey-people; the *Sahib-log*, the Sahibs in general.
Lungi	a length of cloth used variously: wrapped around the body and tied at the waist to form a skirt, or, as here, to form a head-dress.
Mali	a gardener.
Muharram	a religious festival held in the first month of the Mohammedan year.
Octroi	town or other local import duties.
Parti	a partner, a match.
Pugree	a form of head-dress consisting of a length of cloth wound several times round the head; a turban.

Pushtu	language spoken in Afghanistan and Northern Pakistan.
Sari	the dress of Hindu women: a long length of cloth wound round the body in such a manner as to provide cover from head or shoulder to feet.
Shamiana	a flat-roofed cloth marquee, sometimes without sides, often richly decorated.
Soubol	(French) doily; lit. 'under the finger bowl'.
Sowar	a mounted soldier.
Syce	a groom.
Tonga	a light two-wheeled one-horsed carriage for hire.
Voiture à remise	a carriage for hire.
Vuitton	Louis Vuitton: the Parisian luggage manufacturer with branches world-wide, including Philadelphia.

Section Notes

Section One

1. Colonel Sir Augustus Charles Frederick FitzGeorge (1847–1933): son of the 2nd Duke of Cambridge and Mrs. FitzGeorge: see note 2 following.
2. The 2nd Duke of Cambridge (1819–1904), here referred to, was a grandson of George III. His mother was of the family of the Landgrafs of Hesse-Cassel, to whom Lina's maternal ancestors had been bankers. From 1856–1895 he had been Commander-in-Chief of the British Army.
3. Khedive: The title of the rulers of Egypt under the Turkish Empire.
4. English Officers: British troops had been stationed in Egypt since the occupation of Cairo in 1882 and the appointment in the following year of Sir Evelyn Baring (who became Lord Cromer in 1892) as Resident and Consul-General, with British advisers supervising the major Government departments.

Section Three

1. Marlborough House: The residence of the Prince and Princess of Wales.
2. Major Richardson: Rachel Jardine's nephew, James Jardine Richardson, D.S.O. (1873–1942).

Section Four

1. 'The Siege': 1857. The recovery of Delhi by British and loyal Indian forces based on 'The Ridge', from mutineering Indian forces. During the taking of the Kashmir Gate, Brigadier John Nicholson, first Chief Commissioner of the Punjab, was fatally wounded.
2. 'The Peacock Throne': The throne of the Mogul Emperor Shah Jahan (1628–1658), carried off as booty by Persian invaders in 1739.
3. The intention to transfer the seat of the Central Government from Calcutta to Delhi was announced by King George V at his Coronation Durbar, held at Delhi in December 1911. The development of New Delhi, under the architects Sir Edwin Lutyens and Sir Herbert Baker, and the transfer of the Administration, proceeded during the following years.
4. Lina would find that the 'burden of leaving and returning cards' had been greatly eased by the establishment in 1904 of the Postal Calling League. Ladies

joining this League agreed to pay and return formal calls by sending their
cards through the mail. 'In consideration of the little leisure that Gentlemen
on duty in Simla have to devote to paying calls' the Ladies agreed to admit
such Gentlemen to their League.

5. Patiala and Dholpur: The Simla residences of the Princes of these two States.
6. Lina was referring to the 'Boston Tea Party' when, in 1773, American colonists,
   with cries of 'No Taxation without Representation', dumped three hundred and
   forty chests of tea being imported by the East India Company, into Boston
   Harbour.
7. Peary's sometime disputed claim to have reached the North Pole.
8. The Greek influence in this area dates from the invasion by Alexander the
   Great of Macedonia late in the 4th century B.C.
9. Rudyard Kipling's poem *As the Bell Clinks*.
10. Watergate: The official residence of the Commander-in-Chief-in-India.
11. 'The historic Ridge': The British and loyal Indian base at the siege of Delhi,
    1887.

Section Five

1. See Appendix A.
2. In 1911 there had been the political crisis arising out of the rejection by the
   House of Lords of the Parliament Bill designed to reduce the powers of that
   House. The Trade Unions were active; the transport workers and railwaymen
   had struck in 1911, and in 1912, a million-and-a-half coal miners struck.
3. On 18 October, Bulgaria, Servia, Greece and Montenegro attacked Turkey and
   made rapid advances towards Constantinople (First Balkan War).
4. Delegates to the London Peace Conference which opened on 17 December and
   culminated in the treaty of London on 30 May, by which Turkey lost much
   territory in Europe. The conflicting interests of the European powers in the
   results of war in the Balkans created the possibility that the conflict might
   spread throughout Europe, as it eventually did in 1914.

Section Six

1. Civilians: The Indian Civil Service.
2. Tiffany diamonds: Father's wedding gift.
3. July 25th: The anniversary of the death of George David Rosengarten, Father
   to Aunt Fanny and Uncle Joe and Lina's Grandfather.
4. Kutab: The Qutb Minar, the twelfth century tower begun in the reign of the
   first Muslim ruler at Delhi. A favourite place for picnics.
5. On 28 June 1914, at Sarajevo, then within the Austro-Hungarian Empire, a
   Serbian nationalist assassinated the Archduke Francis Ferdinand and his wife,
   heir to the Austro-Hungarian Emperor, Francis Joseph. Lina in her letter of 4
   August summarised the ultimatums, the mobilisations, the declarations of war,
   which opened World War I.
6. Wanamakers: John Wanamaker in 1861 established what was to become

Philadelphia's leading Department Store, renowned for its imaginative merchandising, with, at one time, a branch in London.

7. Charlie, one of Lina's brothers; Clara, a cousin.

Section Seven

1. The force available to the Indian Government, under the Commander-in-Chief in India, consisted of the Indian Army proper, with, varying with the needs of the time, a number of British units attached.

2. New Poland.: During the last quarter of the eighteenth century the Kingdom of Poland ceased to exist as a sovereign state, having been absorbed by Russia, Prussia and Austria in the course of three separate partitions. Lina was presumably referring to the Polish legions raised by Josef Pilsudski on the outbreak of World War I to fight with Germany and Austria against Russia, with the intention of re-establishing their Kingdom.

3. German troops entered Brussels on 20 August and within a few months almost the whole of Belgium had been occupied and a German Governor, General von der Goltz, had been appointed.

4. Mons: Town ten miles east of the Franco-Belgian frontier. Scene of first battle between British and German forces. British retreat.

5. 'Put in our papers': To submit one's resignation.

6. The *Lusitania* was torpedoed off the coast of Ireland on 7 May with the loss of 1,198 passengers including 139 Americans.

7. Germantown: The north-western section of Philadelphia originally established by German immigrants.

8. 'Shell Scandal': Lina was referring to a disastrous shortage of ammunition which led to the setting up of a Ministry of Munitions on 2 July.

9. Montenegro: Recognised as independent of the Turkish Empire in 1878. Surrendered to Austro-German troops in 1915. Incorporated into Yugoslavia after 1918.

10. 'Entente Powers': Britain, France and their allies.

11. Erzerum: Town south of the Black Sea captured by Russian forces advancing westward against Turkey.

12. 'Mr. Baggy Breeches': The British soldier's name for the Turkish soldier.

13. 'His Louvain and his Mons': Two allied defeats in August 1914 in the course of stemming the German attempt to reach the English Channel through Belgium.

14. 'Peace suggestions': On 12 December, Germany had appealed to the United States to mediate peace, but had mentioned no specific terms. Three-cornered discussions involving the opposing powers and the United States continued until Germany decided to open unrestricted submarine warfare and on 31 January 1917 so notified the United States. Three days later the United States severed relations with Germany and on 6 April declared war.

15. Lord Montagu of Beaulieu was between 1915 and 1919 Adviser on Mechanical Transport Services to the Government of India.

16. 'Madame, seulement . . .': In order to avoid any reference to Offley either by name or rank. When they did finally travel he went simply as Mr. Shore.

Section Eight

1. The Clerical Commissioners: The Ecclesiastical Commissioners for England, established by Parliament in 1836, initially to report on the business affairs of the Church of England and subsequently retained as the body responsible for the administration of those affairs, including the functions of a landlord.
2. In May, Czech troops who had deserted from the Austrian to the Russian armies revolted against the Communist regime and gained control of the Trans-Siberian railway. In August, British, Japanese, American and French forces landed at Vladivostok, the eastern end of the railway; contact was made with the Czechs at Irkutsk.
3. President Wilson arrived in Europe in mid-December heading the U.S. delegation to the Peace Conference. His prime concern was the incorporation in any treaty of a plan for the establishment of a League of Nations. This was approved by a unanimous resolution within a week of the opening of the Conference and incorporated in the Treaty of Versailles signed ca 28 June, 1919.

Section Nine

1. On the President's return to the United States he was immediately met by intense vituperative opposition to the League of Nations clauses of the Treaty of Versailles which would involve the signatories in military support of any member nation finding itself the subject of aggression. It soon became clear that the Senate would not ratify the Treaty. On 3 September, Wilson started touring the country in the hope of generating public support. In many areas he was successful, but isolationist sentiment was well organised against him. On 26 September he suffered a break-down from which he never fully recovered. The United States never ratified the Treaty.
2. Offley's father was aged five when the family left Norton Hall.
3. Sheila: mentioned in the Author's Preface when she invited him to examine the box which held these letters.
4. In fact Norton Hall had changed hands again at the turn of the century.

Appendix C

1. Ranald MacDonnell, *And Nothing Long* (Constable, London, 1938), pp. 178–202.
2. Maj. Gen. L. C. Dunsterville, *The Adventures of Dunsterforce* (Edward Arnold, London, 1920), chapters 1 and 2.
3. R. H. Bruce Lockhart, *British Agent* (Putnam, London and New York), pp. 260 and 271.

Family Trees

Caroline Sinnickson's family was critically important to her. Her letters are sprinkled with enquiries, concerns and judgments relating to so many people that a selective Rosengarten/Sinnickson family tree seemed required to guide the reader. Likewise, when she married into an ancient British family, her concern widened to include members of that new family and her curiosity in the Shore family lineage was intense if not always firmly rooted in fact. The Offley/Shore family tree gives selected members.

Notes to the Rosengarten/Sinnickson family tree:
1. Arrived in Philadelphia in 1819 from the Electorate of Hesse Cassel.
2. Arrived in Philadelphia in 1819 from Hamburg.
3. Forebears from Scandinavia settled in Salem Co., New Jersey in 1638.

Notes to the Offley/Shore family tree.
1. Robert Offley, 1640–1714, succeeded to Norton Hall following the death, without issue, of his maternal uncle Cornelius Clarke, of Norton, in 1696.
2. Urith Smythe, 1681–1711, daughter of Samuel Smythe, of Colkirk, Norfolk (d. 1699) and Catherine Elizabeth (d. 1686), daughter of Sir James Harington, Bart. (d. 1680).
3. Mary Bohun, d. 1740, daughter and sole heiress of Humphrey Bohun, of Westhall, Suffolk (d. 1703) and Hannah, daughter of Francis Warren, of Beccles, Suffolk.
4. William Shore, d. 1822, grandfather of Florence Nightingale, O.M., after whom Offley B. S. F. Shore's sister was named.
5. Took the surname Offley-Shore in 1924.

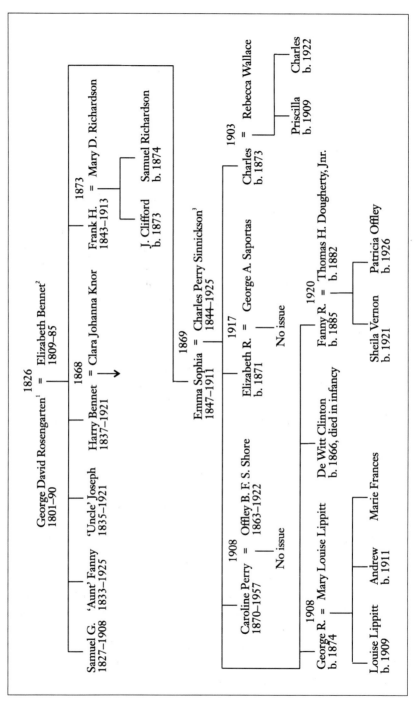

Extracts from the Rosengarten/Sinnickson family tree.

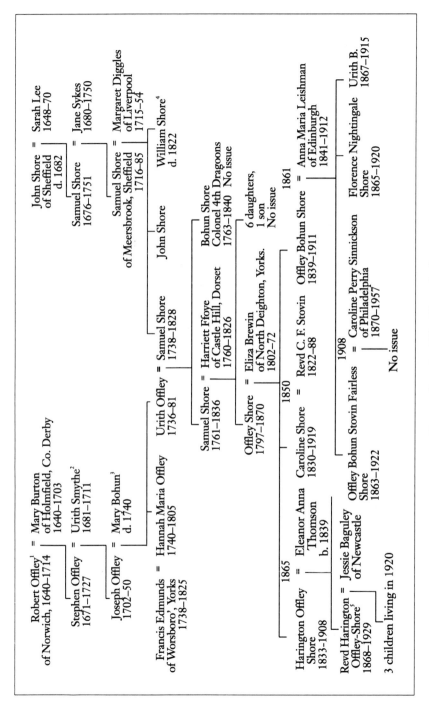

Extracts from the Offley/Shore family tree